MEDICAL INFORMATICS 20/20

Quality and Electronic Health Records through Collaboration, Open Solutions, and Innovation

DOUGLAS GOLDSTEIN
eFuturist, Medical Alliances, Alexandria, VA

PETER J. GROEN, MPA
Undergraduate Research Coordinator
Department of Computer & Information Systems
Shepherd University, Shepherdstown, WV

SUNITI PONKSHE, MS
Healthcare Information Technology Expert Healthlink, a Division of IBM
McLean, VA

MARC WINE, MHA
Adjunct Faculty Member
The George Washington University, Washington, DC

JONES AND BARTLETT PUBLISHERS
Sudbury, Massachusetts
BOSTON   TORONTO   LONDON   SINGAPORE

World Headquarters
Jones and Bartlett Publishers
40 Tall Pine Drive
Sudbury, MA 01776
978-443-5000
info@jbpub.com
www.jbpub.com

Jones and Bartlett Publishers
Canada
6339 Ormindale Way
Mississauga, Ontario L5V 1J2
CANADA

Jones and Bartlett Publishers
International
Barb House, Barb Mews
London W6 7PA
UK

Jones and Bartlett's books and products are available through most bookstores and online booksellers. To contact Jones and Bartlett Publishers directly, call 800-832-0034, fax 978-443-8000, or visit our website, www.jbpub.com.

Substantial discounts on bulk quantities of Jones and Bartlett's publications are available to corporations, professional associations, and other qualified organizations. For details and specific discount information, contact the special sales department at Jones and Bartlett via the above contact information or send an email to specialsales@jbpub.com.

Production Credits
Publisher: Michael Brown
Production Director: Amy Rose
Associate Production Editor: Daniel Stone
Marketing Manager: Sophie Fleck
Manufacturing Buyer: Therese Connell
Composition: Auburn Associates, Inc.
Cover Design: Kristin E. Ohlin
Printing and binding: Malloy, Inc.
Cover printing: Malloy, Inc.

Cover Credits
The binary code is © Andreas Nilsson/
     ShutterStock, Inc.
The hand is © Mark Aplet/ShutterStock, Inc.
The DNA strand is © Scott Bowlin/
     ShutterStock, Inc.

Library of Congress Cataloging-in-Publication Data

Medical informatics 20/20 : quality and electronic health records through collaboration, open solutions, and innovation / Douglas Goldstein . . . [et al.].
     p. ; cm.
     Includes bibliographical references and index.
     ISBN-13: 978-0-7637-3925-6
     ISBN-10: 0-7637-3925-1
     1. Medical informatics.   I. Goldstein, Douglas E.
     [DNLM: 1. Medical Informatics—organization & administration.   2. Medical Records Systems, Computerized. W 26.5 M48972 2007]
     R858.M43 2007
     610.285--dc22

                                                                2006019228
6048

Printed in the United States of America
10 09 08 07 06 10 9 8 7 6 5 4 3 2 1

Contents

Acknowledgments

This has been a group effort over several years by the authors to synthesize the people, process, and technology elements necessary for the development of the Medical Informatics 20/20 concept and strategies captured in this book. This group effort reflects one of the main points made in the book, the need to encourage more '*Collaboration*' amongst those working in health care. So acknowledging the contributions of each of the authors and the patience and support of their spouses, family members, and colleagues during this journey seems like the right place to start. We believe that collaboration is in our DNA.

'*Open Solutions*' is a key topic addressed throughout the book. Much of the material and solutions contained in the book reflect the amazing work being done by thousands of medical informaticists, clinicians, executives, and managers around the world who are committed to improving the health status of all people through the open source software, open architecture, open standards, open innovation, open healthcare, and the overall 'openness' movement. This book is a tribute to all of these people and we are proud to be associated with the movement and contribute to it in some small way.

More specifically, in many of the chapters we reference the VistA clinical information and electronic health record (EHR) system repeatedly. We would like to acknowledge the tremendous work of the clinicians, technology staff, and the thousands of other U.S. Department of Veterans Affairs (VA) employees who helped develop and implement the tremendously successful VistA system in VA medical centers and clinics across the country.

We would also like to acknowledge the VistA Software Alliance (VSA), WorldVistA, and the Pacific Telehealth & Technology Hui. These organizations have played a key role in moving the VistA system into the private sector throughout the world. VistA and other open source EHR solutions will play an increasingly important role over the next several decades in improving healthcare services around the world affordability.

The third major theme or strategy covered in the book is 'Innovation.' There are tens of thousands of clinicians, managers, and medical informaticists around the world working collaborating on interoperable, open health information standards, electronic health records (EHR) systems, personal health records (PHR) systems, heath information exchange (HIE) solutions, and other innovative bioinformatics advances (e.g. genome biorepositories, nanotechnology, wearable intelligent information technology health systems). We would like to acknowledge their often unsung efforts to improve health care for all of us.

There are a number of specific individuals who without their leadership, support and contributions this book would not be possible. Robert Kolodner, MD, the Chief Health Information Officer (CHIO) for the Veterans Health Administration and interim National Coordinator for Health Information Technology, has been a visionary leader in health IT who has inspired all of us over the years as he has quietly and effectively advocated consumer centric, inter-connected healthcare for all Americans. Kenneth Kizer, MD, former Undersecretary for Health at the VA, has also been an inspiration as he has taken a very public stance supporting the open source movement in health care. There is Stanley M. Saiki, Jr., M.D., Director of the Pacific Telehealth & Technology Hui who has been instrumental in directing the development and release of an open source version of VistA running on a Linux platform. We also would like to recognize Scott Shreeve, MD and Steve Shreeve, the founders of Medsphere Systems Corporation that have been a powerful force in bringing VistA into the private sector to support patients and clinicians in quality care.

We would like to recognize the contributions of a number of leaders who have shared vital knowledge and experience in the innovation and collaboration case studies and other sections of this book. Special thanks to David Pryor, MD, Senior Vice President, Ascension Health for his leadership and extreme focus on making healthcare safe and high quality. The Ascension Health Exchange is a recognized leader in innovation and collaboration for better healthcare services and this is a direct result of the leadership of John Doyle, Chief Strategy Officer, Eric Engler, Vice President, Strategy Development and Jeff Stolte, Manager of Knowledge Strategy and Sherry

Brown, CIO. In addition, John Garbo, Director Clinical Excellence and Pamala Jones, Knowledge Transfer Specialist have developed a connected online Community of Performance within the Ascension Health Exchange that is an outstanding example on how to accelerate proven practices spread for quality care within large health systems.

Thank you to Bon Secours Health System. BSHSI is a leader in innovative, holistic, quality focused healthcare and is a result of the leadership of Richard Statuto, CEO, Ed Boyer, Senior Vice President, William Varani, MD, JD, Vice President, Quality, H. Douglas Sears, Director of Performance Improvement and Knowledge Transfer and other key executives such as Barb Oot-Giromini, Kathy Connerton, Ken Turner, Maria Gatto and the entire BSHSI team.

The insights on the Air Force Medical Service's Knowledge Exchange and its ability to support rapid cycle knowledge transfer would not have been possible with the contributions of Lieutenant Colonel J.D. Whitlock, MPH, MBA, chief, knowledge and content management, United States Air Force Medical Services.

The Thomson Micromedex's case study on clinical decision support technology was made possible through the support of Jerome Osheroff, MD and Michael Soars. Jonathan Schaffer, MD offered invaluable insights on the role of business intelligence tools and techniques on quality care. Additional thanks to Kevin Fickenscher, M.D., Executive Vice President, healthcare transformation for Perot Systems for his insights and perspectives on the future of health care.

There are many other leaders truly making collaboration, innovation and open solutions work in health care that we would like to recognize. This includes Donald Berwick, M.D. founder and CEO for the Institute for Healthcare Improvement, Molly Coye, MD, President of Health Technology Center, Larry Grandia CTO and Joe Pleasant, CIO of Premier Inc., Peter Basch, MD, Director of eHealth for MedStar Health, Dale Schumacher, MD president of Rockburn Institute, George Conklin, CIO, CHRISTUS Health and many others. We also want to recognize the innovation acceleration contributions that Richard Singerman, PhD has made in the private and public healthcare sectors.

Also a special thanks to Roger Maduro, CEO of LxIS and editor of the "VistA & Open Health Care" newsletter, who contributed key material on open source software including some of the open definitions and other insights that has been woven into different parts of the book. Cheryl Toth and Maggie Fisher, key Medical Alliances team members, provided invaluable support and assistance to the content, flow, and effectiveness of the manuscript.

However, as we have said, the 'Open Solutions' movement includes thousands and thousands of people all collaborating and contributing to the goal of improving health care for all of us through the latest Internet based multi-media technologies. Putting this book together and writing about the collaborative, open solutions, and other major innovations that are occurring in the field of Medical Informatics to support optimum health for all has been exciting and truly rewarding.

Douglas Goldstein
Peter J. Groen
Suniti Ponkshe
Marc Wine

Author Biographies

Douglas Goldstein is a globally recognized healthcare strategist, entrepreneur and "eFuturist" focused on how electronic and emerging technologies can improve the quality of life and healthcare today and tomorrow. He is a thought provoking author and keynote speaker. His recent publications have included *e-Healthcare: Harness the Power of Internet e-Commerce & e-Care* (Jones and Bartlett 2000) and *Quality, Patient Safety and Cost Effectiveness through Leadership and Technology.*

As President of Medical Alliances, he guides the world's leading organizations in performance excellence through alliances, knowledge management, and "Distinctive Innovation." He has been the strategist and developer of cutting edge projects including: *Ascension Health Exchange*—the knowledge transfer strategic initiative of Ascension Health (a $9B health system); *QualityFirst*—Bon Secours Health System's quality effort that leverages knowledge transfer for performance excellence quality, outcomes and pay for performance success; *Premier Inc. Web Services Strategy* to support next generation service to their alliance members; *e-Strategy and Health Information Technology Sharing*—Veterans Health Administration (a $25B health system); *Medformation.com* for Allina Hospitals and Clinics (Best of the Best Hospital Web Sites—Modern Healthcare Magazine 2000) and *Health Adventure* (1998 Smithsonian-Computerworld award). He also has led the development of DreamDog Media, a multimedia children's edu-tainment company that has developed the brands *Jazz the DreamDog*™ & 'Adventures of *CiCi & Ace*'. In addition to the recent publications, he is the lead author of five Internet Best of the Net Online Guide books (McGraw Hill) and three respected healthcare management books:

- *Best of the Net Series* including: *Best of the Net—Online Consumer Guide to Health and Wellness, Best of the Net—Online Guide to Personal Finance and Investing, Best of the Net—Online Guide to Healthcare Management and Medicine, 1997, Best of the Net—Online Guide to Business Guide to Financial Services, Best of the Net—The Online Business Atlas, 1997*
- *Building and Managing Effective Physician Organizations,* Aspen Publishers, Inc. 1996
- *Alliances: Strategies for Building Integrated Delivery Systems,* Aspen Publishers, Inc. 1995
- *Medical Staff Alliances: Building Successful Alliances with Your Physicians,* Hospital Publishing

Goldstein has served as the Internet columnist for Managed Care Interface Magazine, where he penned the "Medical Internet" column. He has served as founder, Chairman and CEO of Health Online, Inc., a rapid growth Web services company, and he was a co-founder and vice president of 1-800-DOCTORS, a doctor information and appointment service that has served 11 million people. He is a graduate of the University of Michigan, School of Natural Resources where he studied environmental communications/advocacy and business. He is currently working on his Six Sigma Black Belt certification from the Juran Institute.

Peter J. Groen, MPA, is a faculty member of the Computer & Information Science Department at Shepherd University. He is also currently serving as their Undergraduate Research Coordinator and has helped found the Shepherd University Research Corporation (SURC). Mr. Groen is the former Director of the Health Information and Technology Sharing Program within the Veterans Health Administration (VHA) of the Department of Veterans Affairs (VA). He has over 32 years of federal service and has occupied a number of senior Information Technology (IT) management positions within VA Headquarters and in the field. Mr. Groen has served as the Director of the Medical Information Security Service, the Director of VHA Telecommunications Services, the Deputy Associate CIO for Enterprise Strategies, as well as the CIO at the VA Medical Centers in Atlanta, GA and Columbia, SC. He served as the national project manager for the VA Computerized Patient Record System (CPRS) as well as the VA Internet and VHA

Intranet Redesign projects. Prior to joining the VA, Mr. Groen served in the U.S. Navy for six years. He was a supervisor of the Combat Information Center aboard the guided missile destroyer, U.S.S. Sellers DDG-11.

Mr. Groen obtained his Bachelor of Arts degree from Clemson University and a Masters of Public Administration from The Pennsylvania State University. During his long federal career, Mr. Groen has received numerous awards for outstanding performance and special contributions. Over the years, he has also been published in a number of journals, magazines, and books focused on information technology in health care and is regularly invited to speak at various professional conferences.

Suniti Ponkshe, MS, is an experienced CIO and well recognized healthcare and information technology consultant in the industry. She has worked with a variety of clients and employers. She has supported many industries including health care, computer software, higher education, banking, warehousing, and retail.

Her experience encompasses executive leadership to IT function, strategic technology planning, strategic sourcing, contract negotiations and operational leadership. She is known for her executive leadership in information technology and ability to work with all levels within the organization. She is a highly effective communicator and excels as a change agent to impact operational efficiency.

Ms. Ponkshe's career has centered on management of information systems and professional consulting. She has established governance for a large healthcare system; provided oversight to an outsourcing venture; led major contract negotiations; led healthcare product companies through productization of their systems; participated in mergers, acquisitions, and divestitures; and managed large budgets. She has also worked on projects involving web-content development, development of framework to measure benefits of IT investments, and executive assistance in setting up board structure.

Today, Ms. Ponkshe works for Healthlink, a division of IBM and leads their Advisory Services which include strategy, clinical transformation, business process optimization, advanced analytics, and IT services. Prior to joining IBM, Ms. Ponkshe owned and operated her own consulting company, worked in several strategic partnerships with various companies, she served as CIO at Adventist Healthcare and DocuSys, Inc. She held the position of Senior Vice President for Superior Consulting

Company and served Georgetown University and Medical Center as AVP of Information Services and CIO. Ms. Ponkshe was VP of IS for Allegheny Health, Education and Research Foundation, began her executive career as a senior manager with Price Waterhouse and Accenture.

Ms. Ponkshe holds an MS degree in Management Information Systems. She participates in many professional organizations including Healthcare Information Management Systems Society, Indian CEO High Tech Council, and Healthcare technology of Greater Washington, to name a few. Ms. Ponkshe served on several community boards and Advisory Boards for companies. She has been a reviewer for HIMSS national meeting presentations for the past few years and speaks professionally on current IT topics.

Marc Wine, MHA, served as a Program Manager for the U.S. Dept. of Veterans Affairs, Health IT Sharing (HITS) Program. His role included facilitating collaboration projects involving sharing the VA computer systems and health IT knowledge with other federal health care providers, including the Department of Health and Human Services (DHHS), the Centers for Medicare & Medicaid, Public Health Service, as well as other federal agencies regarding the role of health IT in developing consumer-centric health care services. During his 24 years with the VA, Mr. Wine also held positions as an Implementation Manager for health IT systems and Project Leader in healthcare facilities planning and development. Mr. Wine held positions in the Dept. of Health and Human Services managing the implementation of the National Health Planning program, served as Management Consultant to National Council for Health Planning of DHHS and the Boston University Center for Health Planning. Also, Mr. Wine served as the Health Systems Planner for Acute Care with the Health Planning Council for Greater Boston. He earned his Master' Degree in Hospital Administration at The George Washington University in Washington, D.C. and graduated from Brandeis University in Waltham, MA. Mr. Wine also is an adjunct faculty member on health information technology at The George Washington University. Mr. Wine currently serves as Program Manager for the U.S. General Services Administration, Intergovernmental Solutions Division.

Expert Forewords

Kevin Fickenscher, MD—Gary A. Christopherson—Adam Smith—
Jeffrey C. Bauer, Ph.D.

Realizing Transformation through a Focus on People and Process with Technology as the Enabler

Today, we are at the forefront of a paradigm shift in how health care will be delivered, who will deliver it, and where it will be delivered. The already amazing health and medical care capabilities available throughout the United States and in countries across the world will be supplanted by new, emerging technologies and innovations over the next decade. Medical capabilities and knowledge are reaching new heights as clinicians and managers seek to harness the power of technology and process changes derived from *standardization, digitalization, nanotization, de-tethered mobile networks, peripheral intelligence, biogenomics, non-invasive modalities and robotics*—just to name a few of the extraordinary technologies that will dramatically improve medical care for all. Unfortunately, the distribution of these advances is inconsistent at best or more often than not, nonexistent. In fact, far too many people throughout the world will not benefit from these advances in science, informatics and process improvement.

We can do better!

Health care is at a crossroads. *Medical Informatics 20/20* identifies both the problems faced in realizing healthcare transformation and, proscribes vital solutions that can guide us in creating better systems to save lives, improve quality and reduce costs. The three strategies profiled in the book—Collaboration, Open Solutions and Innovation—are prescriptions for correcting what ails medical care.

Collaboration is the essential foundation to dramatically improve the sharing of our knowledge, methodologies, and wisdom in ways that raises our collective level of performance. In my work with healthcare organizations of all sizes and clinicians throughout healthcare, it has become increasingly obvious that the knowledge of how to do better is present at the bedside. But, the knowledge is in pieces and held by individuals as small kernels of information. Through collaboration—health care can begin to tap the vast reservoir of knowledge among healthcare workers and greatly accelerate our ability to solve problems.

Open Solutions is the next major wave in healthcare information systems. The use of open solutions will provide us the ability to interconnect clinical data and support the delivery of knowledge when and where it's needed most—at the point of care. The book explores how the world's largest health information system—VistA developed by the Veterans Health Administration—is now being used worldwide as an open solution without a license fee to support better, more cost-effective health care. It also appropriately recognizes that technology alone is not the answer. With an equivalent focus on changing and transforming people and processes, implementing the next generation of clinical information technology will finally give us the ultimate result we are seeking with these systems—the improvement of health care for people.

Innovation is a driving forcing and source of the problem solving that is a fundamental requirement for the future if health care is to overcome the challenges we face. Over the last half century, innovation has been the hallmark of the pharmaceutical and medical device segments of the health care industry. Innovation must now be rooted firmly in the delivery side of health care to realize the full benefit of the new, evolving communication technologies. The book's vision, practicality and approach make it a must read for today's healthcare leaders and clinicians seeking to transform the clinical and business process of their healthcare organizations.

Achieving healthcare transformation is an essential requirement for society. It can only be realized through the appropriate focus on people and process with technology serving as the enabler. Not only can we do better—we must do better!! *Medical Informatics 20/20* proposes a path for all of us who are committed to achieving a smarter, better, more productive health care system through collaboration, open solutions and innovation

Kevin Fickenscher, MD
Executive Vice President
Healthcare Transformation
Perot Systems

Building a Healthy America and Beyond Depends on Medical Informatics Vision and Foresight

Building a healthy America is a challenge that requires a collaborative, synergistic strategy, a strategy we call "HealthePeople". HealthePeople proceeds under the belief that America can reach this vision via an endgame strategy of a high performance, American health and long term care system for all Americans that is self-perpetuating, affordable, accessible, "e" enabled, and producing high health quality, outcomes and status.

Medical Informatics 20/20 provides critical insights into, support for and solutions to, "e" enabling a healthy American system. For policy makers and policy implementers, this book builds on the lessons learned from, and the value of, the highly successful VistA health information system and the design of the next generation HealtheVet-VistA, a key enabler of the high performance Veterans Health System successfully serving millions of veterans. The book then makes a second major contribution to the future by calling for the use of open source systems created collaboratively by and for the key stakeholders, people, and the clinicians and organizations that care for them here in America and throughout the world. Collaboratively developed and sustained open source health information systems can play an extremely important role in developing the common core for every system, and for providing systems for those who, for one of many reasons, find currently available systems unaffordable.

With the sage advice and forward thinking advanced in *Medical Informatics 20/20,* we are all better prepared to build the "e" enabled health systems envisioned in "HealthePeople" and essential to building a healthy America and beyond.

Gary A. Christopherson
Chief Information Officer (CIO) for
the Veterans Health Administration (former)
Principal Deputy Assistant Secretary and Acting Assistant Secretary of
Defense for Health Affairs (former)

Required Reading for Leaders and Policy Makers

"Medical Informatics 20/20 should be required reading for industry leaders, policy makers, and others working to lower costs and update our health system. Goldstein, Groen, Wine and Ponkshe show us the way to modernize the health industry and increase the use of electronic health records through collaboration, open solutions, and innovation."

Adam Smith, U.S. Representative (D-WA)

Delivering Realistic Advice and Appropriate Vision on Consumer-Focused Services, Technology and Collaboration to Support a Better Healthcare System

As a medical economist and health futurist focused on information technology as *the* critical success factor for solving health care's problems, I am delighted with the publication of this book. It is an excellent start-to-finish resource for anyone involved in preparing a healthcare organization, from a small medical group to a large health system, for the future. *Medical Informatics 20/20* is a compendium of background information, realistic advice, and appropriate vision for survival in the new world of healthcare delivery. It fills a big void. It is easy to read and very well-organized, with key concepts summarized in attractive and instructive diagrams.

The authors are experts who have been with health care information technology (HIT) since the beginning. Their contributions to this book are founded on many decades of collective experience in virtually every aspect of the digital transformation of health care. All four writers have been on the leading edge throughout their careers, sharpening medical informatics as a tool to take health care where it needed to go. This book is built on a solid foundation and headed in a necessary direction.

One of the book's greatest strengths is the fundamental focus on open solutions. Its COSI model (for Collaboration, Open Solutions and Innovation) reflects a clear consensus in the HIT industry and the policy community. Providers will continue to rely on a mix of software and hardware solutions for a variety of reasons, but the systems must be fully interoperable if health care is to reap the full benefits of information technologies that have successfully transformed other industries (e.g., banking, retail, transportation, engineering, biotechnology). If *Medical Informatics 20/20* accomplishes no other task than getting providers, vendors, and payers to focus their efforts on collaboration to achieve interoperability, it will be one of the most important books of this decade.

Happily, this book provides excellent information and advice in other areas that are equally valuable for the successful evolution of health care. The authors' pervasive emphasis on consumer-focused services is fully consistent with powerful industry trends in disease management, high-deductible health plans, and informed choice. The book also includes a rich collection of links between management tools that have been used over the past decade, such as process improvement and decision support, and their position in the COSI environment of the future. *Medical Informatics 20/20* will help to bridge gaps between operations managers, clinicians, and financial officers.

As strongly as I appreciate and endorse this book, I do have one concern about it. The title might give the impression that its content is "something to start thinking about thinking about," not something requiring action now. After all, 2020 is more than a dozen years away, and any health care leader today is consumed by problems that need to be solved right away. I am consequently concerned that the long-term implication of the title—in spite of its useful allusions to 20/20 vision and 2020 as a major milepost—is potentially misleading. The ideas and the actions presented in *Medical Informatics 20/20* are powerfully relevant today. I hope that the clever title will draw initial attention as the authors and publisher no doubt hope it will, but the book should be read now. Most healthcare organizations will have trouble keeping their doors open until 2020 if they do not follow the wise directions in this book by 2010.

Jeffrey C. Bauer, Ph.D.
Partner, Management Consulting, Futures Practice
ACS Healthcare Solutions

Authors' Foreword

Transforming health care by the year 2020 requires intelligent, innovative and insightful approaches to health information technology.

If we are to successfully move from a closed, provider-based medical delivery system to a consumer-driven, patient centered one, we must use 20/20 vision and harness the power of a Medical Informatics 20/20 model. In this new healthcare delivery system, quality and electronic health records will be essential components to improving patient safety and quality of care.

Traditional, closed, proprietary processes and software strategies are alone insufficient to address the challenges we face. Leaders must embrace performance excellence through a culture of 'collaboration' and 'innovation' enabled by appropriate 'open' solutions.

Medical Informatics 20/20 delivers vital knowledge, resources, and case studies that provide a roadmap for realizing a quality healthcare system supported by Electronic Health Records (EHRs) and interoperable health information technology. The Medical Informatics 20/20 Model illuminates the role of three critical strategies—Collaboration, Open Solutions, and Innovation (COSI)—critical to achieving the transformation.

This book's sections and chapters provide the insight and information necessary to help private and public entities create enlightened strategies in their organizations and leverage their existing fundamentals—such as the ability to serve community and provide services and treatments that heal. It also delivers new courses of action for organizations seeking to become high quality, patient centered, health care organizations through the use of EHRs and advanced clinical information systems.

The five figures that follow the Author's Foreword illustrate the core elements of the Medical Informatics 20/20 Model. The first figure, on

Health@Anywhere, establishes a person center focus that must guide our actions in transforming healthcare based on new processes enabled by technology being implemented by empowered team members. The second figure is a view of the entire Medical Informatics 20/20 Model. The three figures thereafter illustrate each of the three strategies—Collaboration, Open Solutions and Innovation—in the model. Each figure shows the major tactical areas and the specific tactics within each of those areas. Chapter 1 delivers an overview of these strategies. Chapter 11 provides a deeper review and analysis of 6 of the key tactics within the Collaboration and Innovation strategies. Sections II, III and IV address in detail knowledge and resources on the Open Solutions strategy within the Medical Informatics 20/20 model. These figures are also periodically referenced throughout the book.

Medical Informatics 20/20 delivers new courses of action for organizations seeking to become high quality, patient centered health care organizations through the use of EHRs and advanced clinical information systems. Although one focus this book is the transformation of the American health care system, the vast majority of the information within it can be applied to achieving similar goals in healthcare systems throughout the world. Case studies throughout the chapters highlight collaborative initiatives and innovative solutions that are already being used around the world.

We thank you for taking the time to explore the Medical Informatics 20/20 model and the resources in this book. Your contributions to the worldwide effort of improving care and patient safety are critical. We look forward to you sharing your results.

For more information and to share your thoughts Medical Informatics 20/20, visit: www.COSI2020.com.

Douglas Goldstein, Peter J. Groen,
Suniti Ponkshe, and Marc Wine

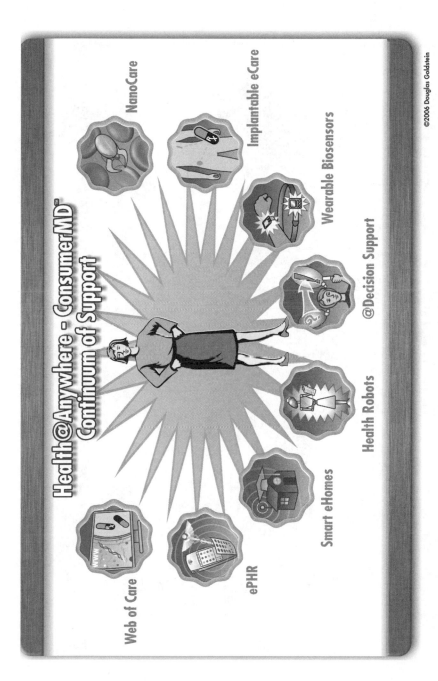

Health@Anywhere—ConsumerMD™ Continuum of Support

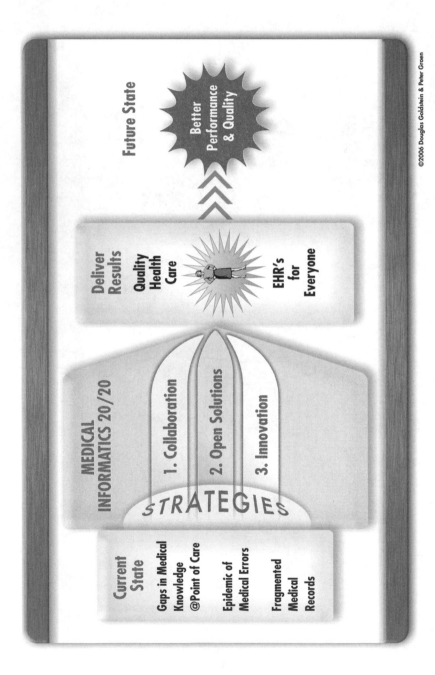

Medical Informatics 20/20 Model

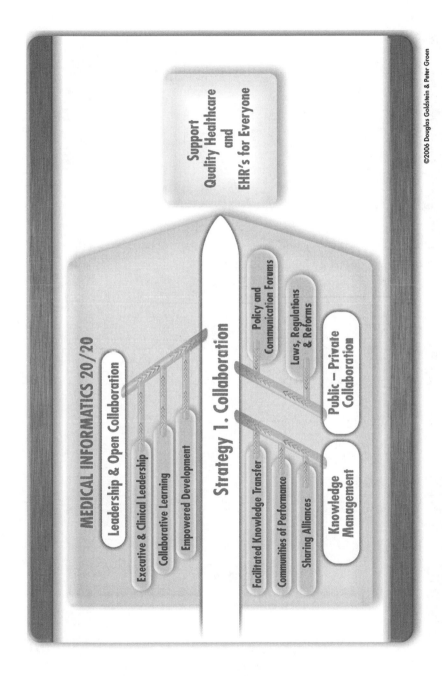

Tactics Supporting the Collaboration Strategy

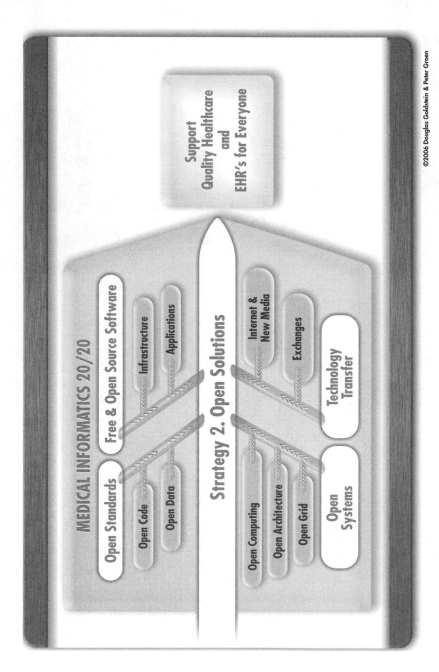

Tactics Supporting the Open Solutions Strategy

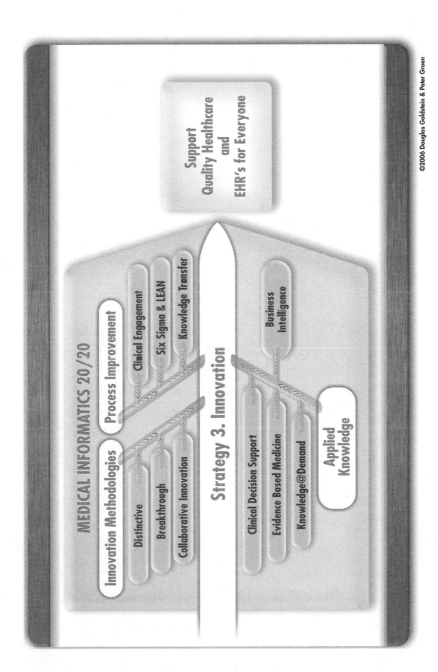

©2006 Douglas Goldstein & Peter Groen

Tactics Supporting the Innovation Strategy

Introduction

> "New economies don't just happen. They are built by visionaries."
>
> *2020 Vision by Stan Davis & Bill Davidson*

> "By computerizing health records, we can avoid dangerous medical mistakes, reduce costs, and improve care."
>
> *President George W. Bush, State of the Union Address*

> "Patients come first, second and third in a transformed, truly patient centered healthcare system. Healthcare professionals must partner with patients to end the epidemic of medical errors and deliver quality in every health interaction. Success depends on a doctor's black bag being enabled with advanced Medical Informatics"
>
> *Anonymous, MD*

Code Red!—Outdated and non-existent health information technology systems lead to high costs, poor quality, non-patient centric care, an epidemic of medical errors, and insufficient disaster preparedness.

At least 44,000 people, and perhaps as many as 200,000 people, die in hospitals each year as a result of medical errors that could have been prevented, according to estimates from three major studies. In addition to the cost in terms of human lives, medical errors have been estimated to result in total costs between $17 billion and $29 billion per year in hospitals nationwide.[1,2,3]

---

[1]National Patient Safety Foundation at the AMA: Public Opinion of Patient Safety Issues Research Findings, Louis Harris & Associates, September 1977.

[2]The estimate on the number of Americans that are harmed as a result of medical errors was based on two studies of large samples of hospital admissions, one in New York using 1984 data and another in Colorado and Utah using 1992 data, found that the pro-

Medical errors and poor patient safety are in large part a result of decentralized, disconnected and incompatible health information technology systems. This was confirmed in the key findings and recommendations from the Institute of Medicine (IOM) report *"Patient Safety: Achieving a New Standard for Care,"* which indicated that *improved information and data systems, and a national health information infrastructure, are needed to support efforts that make patient safety a standard of care in hospitals, in doctors' offices, in nursing homes, and in every other healthcare setting.*

Medical Informatics 20/20 is a solution to reduce errors, save lives and reduce costs—A series of Institute of Medicine (IOM) reports over the last five years have resulted in nationwide awareness about the chronic lack of health information technology in the United States health care system and systems across the world. In 2004, President Bush called for widespread adoption of interoperable electronic health records (EHRs) within the next 10 years, believing that EHRs will reduce medical errors, cut healthcare costs through increased efficiency, and ultimately result in improved patient care. The federal government's Office of the National Health Information Technology Coordinator (ONCHIT) has tasked our country's health information technology czars and various federal agencies with accelerating the effective use of information technology to improve the quality, efficiency, and safety of health care for all Americans. EHRs and information technology are essential to solving the problem, but only if they are intelligently applied, which requires the active participation of leadership, clinicians, patients and all those involved in healthcare.

Significant barriers to health information technology exist. Implementation costs are astronomical—between $27 and $50 billion—and there is a lack of clinical data standards for sharing information. Incompatible health information technology systems and proprietary software and technologies hinder the ability to delivery quality care. The President's goal to provide every citizen with an electronic medical record lacks the

---

portion of hospital admissions experiencing an adverse event, defined as injuries caused by medical management, were 2.9 and 3.7 percent, respectively. The proportion of adverse events attributable to errors (i.e., preventable adverse events) was 58 percent in New York, and 53 percent in Colorado and Utah. These estimates were multiplied against the total number of hospital admissions in a year in the United States to obtain the estimated total number of hospital medical errors.

[3]To Err is Human: Building a Safer Health System, Institute of Medicine Committee on Quality of Healthcare in America, National Academy Press, Washington, DC, 1999.

funding commitment to make it happen (PricewaterhouseCoopers Health Research Institute, Washington, DC). The President proposed $100 million in the fiscal 2005 budget for health information technology funding and demonstration programs, but that level of spending is a mere drop in the bucket if we are to digitize a $1.6 trillion industry.

Medical Informatics 20/20, based on Collaboration, Open Solutions and Innovation (COSI), is critical to improving healthcare quality— health care is one of the most under computerized industries on the planet. There is near universal agreement that applying information technology to health care is vital. Yet too often information technology projects fail because of the lack of participation and involvement of care providers. A more comprehensive and intelligent approach to Medical Informatics is needed—one that builds on the core values of community and sharing inherent in medical care yesterday and today.

The *Medical Informatics 20/20* vision and model articulated in this book provide a significant step toward the solutions required for an intelligent, empowered and participatory approach to health information technology. *Medical Informatics 20/20* has three core strategies—Collaboration, Open Solutions, and Innovation (COSI). In each of the three COSI strategies is a series of tactics, technologies, and techniques that deliver the keys to achieving higher quality, patient-centered health care, lower implementation costs, fewer medical errors, and better disaster preparedness. These strategies are evidenced by the actions of today's leaders:

- Healthcare organizations such as Veterans Health Administration, Ascension Health, Premier Inc., Bon Secours Health System and others are leading the effort to transform their organizations through innovation and collaboration with alliance partners.
- The Institute for Healthcare Improvement is at the center of an international collaborative network of clinicians, managers and healthcare organizations that are substantially reducing medical errors while improving quality through innovation and best practices.
- Federal Government agencies are actively deploying Free and Open Source Software (FOSS) solutions and leading FOSS development initiatives. The world's largest Health Information Technology system with the best outcomes data—VistA from the Veterans Health Administration—is available without any license fees in the public domain as Free and Open Source Software.

America's Veterans were Prepared for Hurricane Katrina

It was a sticky August in New Orleans, Louisiana. To escape the thick air and relentless sun, residents of the Big Easy sat inside air-conditioned homes while tourists lounged in cool, dark bars, sipping bourbon and listening to the blues. Late in the month, residents and partygoers began tuning in to television storm watchers describing a hurricane in the Gulf of Mexico. At first, no one paid notice. After all, this was just the beginning of the 2005 hurricane season and storm news in August was as much a part of New Orleans lore as jambalaya and beignets. But as the storm brewed in the Gulf, it became apparent that this was not a typical hurricane. It was quite possibly the 'big one' that scientists and engineers had warned city planners about for years.

And, as it turned out, it was. On August 29, Hurricane Katrina hit New Orleans with a fury. Wind and storm surges blew houses and families apart, but that was only the beginning. A day later, levees gave way, and water filled the Big Easy, where nearly 80% of homes, neighborhoods and businesses lie below sea level.

As water filled the city, the paper medical charts in New Orleans—in physician offices, hospitals, and nursing homes—were dunked under murky, putrid water overnight. The result: hundreds of thousands of medical records were lost and tens of thousands of seniors and the chronically ill stranded without their medications or any records of their prescription information. Many families had no knowledge of their loved ones' medical histories. Medical records were destroyed beyond repair, with no way to recover the information—ever.

The Center for Medicare and Medicaid Services (CMS) quickly began evaluating its claims data, but that would only indicate a small part of the story. What of the thousands of pages of patient histories, MRIs, CT scans, operative reports, physical therapy progress notes, and psychiatric evaluations? What of the paper-based prescriptions and medical information that was destroyed along with thousands of homes?

VistAverting Disaster

At the New Orleans VA Medical Center, something all together different was happening. Physicians there had recorded all patients' clinical information into VistA—the Department of Veterans Affairs (VA) health information system that includes a robust clinical informatics component and a comprehensive electronic health record (EHR) system that stores all available medical information on veterans. The Veterans Health Administration within the VA is one of the few healthcare provider organizations that is 100% electronic and can provide access to veterans' medical records almost anywhere. And because this data was regularly backed up and stored on servers located outside of New Orleans or the Gulf Coast—these patients' medical records were 100% intact. A displaced veterans from the Gulf Coast could walk into any VA facility anywhere in the country and get immediate access to their complete medical history and record.

It took the VA an estimated 100 hours to transfer all patient data from the destroyed New Orleans VA Medical Center to other VA healthcare facilities where evacuees began showing up. Just days after the disaster, a veteran displaced by Katrina could walk into a VA hospital anywhere in the U.S. and the attending physician could access his or her medical record. Conversely, paper medical records for tens of thousands of New Orleans residents—with decades of information about their health and well-being—will never be recovered.

- Open Solutions, including FOSS, are growing rapidly across all industry sectors and domains of information technology—in both the public and private sectors. Open Solutions was identified as one of nine key health care information technology trends for 2004 by Healthcare Informatics magazine.

The following story delivers a compelling example of the principles of *Medical Informatics 20/20* and its core COSI strategies.

The VistA information system supported patient care anywhere in the midst of this huge disaster, while other paper and electronic health record systems were lost and inaccessible.

Free and Open Source Software

For the purposes of this book, the term Free and Open Source Software (FOSS) will be used as a blanket term to cover all public domain software (which does not have a license agreement associated with it) and Open Source Software (which has a license agreement, has no charges for software use, and has its source code available under the terms of the license agreement).

The Katrina response illustrates how *Medical Informatics 20/20* principles and COSI strategies at worked when disaster struck. The Veterans Health Administration's long standing information technology strategy emphasized a patient centric focus, EHRs, interoperability, clinical data standards and clinical decision support for care providers. In fact, VistA has the benefit of being designed with a focus on clinical informatics. As a result, VHA's patient electronic records were transportable and interoperable so vital patient medical information was not lost. As the world's largest health information technology, VistA demonstrates the principle of 'Open,' in that it is available as FOSS through the Freedom of Information Act (FOIA). VistA has been adopted by public and private health care organizations worldwide—from Midland Health System in Texas and the Bureau of Indian Affairs (BIA) to NASA and international deployments in Egypt, Mexico, and Jordan.

Unfortunately, the adoption of health information technology (IT) has been slower in most healthcare institutions in the United States and elsewhere throughout the world because of its high cost and the limited availability of capital resources. Application of information technology in physician offices has been even slower, due to its cost and perceived lack of value. Open Solutions offers a series of strategies, tactics and technologies that are affordable, reliable, and viable.

- Boeing, Amazon, Google, E-Trade, and millions of organizations use Open Source Software, such as the Linux operating system, extensively in their enterprises. Two other Open Source Software applications, Apache for hosting Web sites and Sendmail for routing e-mail, are nearly ubiquitous, with dominant market shares.
- IBM, HP, Sun Microsystems, and other leading information technology companies are investing billions of dollars and designing significant aspects of their corporate strategies and new business models around 'Open Solutions.'
- According to Barry West, Chief Information Officer, DHS—FEMA, "Open Source Software is a huge piece of our country's disaster preparedness infrastructure within the Department of Homeland Security and National Weather Services."
- "Experts believe that virtually every organization uses Open Source Software in some form or another, and the use—regulated or not—will continue to grow as it becomes more accepted and less

feared."—Wick Keating, Senior Vice President and Chief Technology Officer, American Management Systems

The healthcare industry is embracing Collaboration, Open Solutions and Innovation to meet patient needs for health care anywhere, and radically improve the quality and safety within an affordable capital investment framework. Continued success requires receptiveness to enlightened strategic options that expand on shared needs, a common mission to heal the sick and a renewed spirit of collaboration among all players. This is exemplified by the rising interest and diffusion of VistA based health information technology systems. Hui OpenVistA is a FOSS version of the VistA HIT and EHR system. Hui OpenVistA was developed by the Pacific Telehealth & Technology Hui, a DoD/VA joint venture, to address the need for a cost-effective health information technology (IT) in remote hospitals and care facilities in the Pacific Ocean region. More recently HHS has collaborated with VA to release VistA Office EHR, an EHR system designed to support medical practices, under a free, no license cost arrangement.

But this is only the tip of the 'Open' iceberg. Join us on our journey in discovery as the Sections and Chapters of *Medical Informatics 20/20* share insight, know how and case studies on leaders who are transforming healthcare organizations for the better through Collaboration, Open Solutions, and Innovation.

Definitions and Acronyms

Types of Open

- **Open Standards**—The set of specifications developed to define interoperability between diverse systems.
- **Open Source Software**—A software program in which the source code is available to anyone for use and/or can be modified by anyone from its original design free of up-front license fees or charges. Open Source Software has licenses associated with it, but the licenses do not include fees for use of the software.
- **Open Systems**—Hardware and/or software systems that use/adhere to Open Standards.
- **Open Architecture**—An Information Technology (IT) architecture with public specifications that also provides a platform for interoperability.
- **Open Code**—Commercial proprietary software whose source code can be obtained, viewed, and changed within the guidelines of the specific license arrangement.
- **Open Data**—A standard way for describing data formats, as in "Open Data Format Initiative (ODFI) description." Also, a program to validate that a data file is "ODFI compliant."
- **Open Computing**—A general term used to describe an 'open' philosophy in building information technology systems.

- **Open Grid**—The Open Grid Services Architecture (OGSA) developed by the leading government research labs with Globus Alliance protocols to support supercomputing "Grid" development and management.
- **Open Knowledge**—A system of knowledge transfer using Internet technology to share best practices, emerging practices, knowledge and innovations within a Community (or Communities) of Practice.
- **Open Collaboration**—Using open communication circles among diverse stakeholders for solving problems, accelerating commitments and maturation of open standards, and (or thus) facilitating a collaborative incubator for innovation and enhanced processes.
- **Open Innovation**—An open minded and integrated approach to innovation that harnesses-both internal and external sources of new and improved ideas, processes and technology to synthesize products and services that meet customer needs.
- **Open Health**—A formal or informal digitally enabled network of professionals, people and patients who are collaborating to support and improve patient health and wellness.
- **Open Medical**—Open Solutions on the business and clinical side of healthcare in which multiple formal and informal networks are collaborating throughout the healthcare industry to research, develop, promote and facilitate open solutions application in the healthcare industry. Much of the efforts of these networks are focused on interoperability, on open standards for clinical data exchange in the support of Regional Health Information Organization development and on the overall National Health Information Network.

Additional Definitions

- **Collaboration, Open Solutions, and Innovation (COSI)**—The three core strategies that comprise the Medical Informatics 20/20 Model.
- **Closed Source Software**—traditional software where the source code is kept closed or secret from the users of the software. The source code of the software is critical to evolution and tailoring of software to the needs of users.

- **Shared Source Software**—This is an initiative of Microsoft, in which the source code of designated products is shared with a select group of partners.
- **Capability Transfer**—An application of subject matter expert time and energy to assist another team member (or other team members) in deploying a best practice. Also, knowledge shared through a knowledge management program.

Acronyms

- **CHI**—Consumer Health Informatics
- **CHIF**—Consolidated Health Informatics project of the Federal government
- **CI**—Collaborative Innovation
- **COSI**—Collaboration, Open Solutions, and Innovation
- **CoP**—Community of Practice
- **EHR**—Electronic Health Record
- **EMR**—Electronic Medical Record
- **FOSS**—Free and Open Source Software
- **HIT**—Health Information Technology
- **HIE**—Health Information Exchange
- **HITS**—Health Information Technology Sharing initiative of the Veterans Health Administration
- **I²T**—Intelligent Information Technology
- **KM**—Knowledge Management
- **KT**—Knowledge Transfer
- **LMS**—Learning Management System
- **MI 20/20**—Medical Informatics 20/20 Model
- **NHIN**—National Health Information Network
- **NHII**—National Health Information Infrastructure
- **OSS**—Open Source Software
- **OS**—Open Solutions
- **PHR**—Personal Health Record
- **RHIO**—Regional Health Information Organizations
- **VA**—Veterans Administration
- **VHA**—Veterans Health Administration
- **VHA Inc.**—Voluntary Hospitals of America

Medical Informatics with 20/20 Vision

Section Overview: Section I establishes the foundation for the book by defining and describing the key strategies of Collaboration, Open Solutions, and Innovation (COSI). This section will also explore the tactical areas and the specific tactics within each of the COSI strategies. It shares examples of leading organizations using Collaboration, Open Solutions, and Innovation strategies to achieve vital organizational goals. The emphasis throughout the book is around people working smarter with improved processes enabled by advanced or appropriate information technology.

Chapter 1, Medical Informatics 20/20—Vision, Model, and Strategies for Today and Tomorrow, starts with a vision of the consumer-centric Health@Anywhere where a new generation of anywhere services are available to support better health and medical care. Then the Medical Informatics 20/20 Model and the three key strategies of Collaboration, Open Solutions, and Innovation (COSI) and each of their associated tactics are defined and briefly described. The chapter frames how these strategies and associated tactics support improvements in quality of care, especially through the implementation of electronic health records (EHRs) and process improvement systems to reduce errors and improve quality.

Chapter 2, Open Solutions in Business—Definitions and Market Expansion, discusses in depth the rapid growth of Open Solutions in government and all private sector industries worldwide. It also highlights the growing acceptance and use of collaboratively developed Open Source Software by public and private sector organizations. Chapter 2 highlights and profiles selected Open Solutions from U.S. government agencies and leading business organizations in the private sector.

Chapter 3, Growth of Open Solutions in Health Care, describes the status and application of innovative Open Solutions in health care. The Open Solutions topics that are explored include collaboratively developed EHR, PHR, HIE, Public Health, and other specialized health and medical informatics. Included in the chapter are highlights of selected Free and Open Source Software (FOSS) applications.

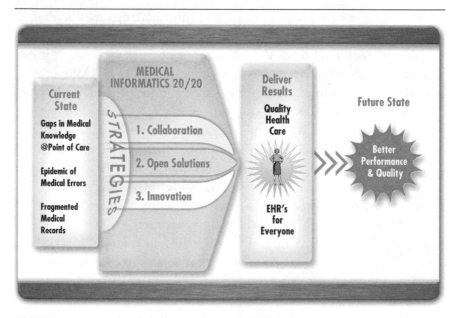

FIGURE I-1 Medical Informatics 20/20 Model

CHAPTER 1

Medical Informatics 20/20: Vision, Model, and Strategies for Today and Tomorrow

"The future belongs to the unreasonable ones, the ones who look forward not backward, who are certain only of uncertainty, and who have the ability and the confidence to think completely differently."

Bernard Shaw

"As managers, we need to shift our thinking from command and control to coordinate and cultivate—the best way to gain power is sometimes to give it away."

Thomas W. Malone, The Future of Work, HBS Press

A 20/20 Vision for the Future

Imagine a future healthcare system that is customer-focused and patient-centered, one in which every American has health insurance and a secure, private Electronic Health Record (EHR) that is available whenever and wherever needed, enabling the highest degree of coordinated medical care based on the latest medical knowledge and evidence.

Imagine a healthcare system in which digital and mobile technologies, medical knowledge at the point of need, and collaboration among providers deliver safe, high-quality care for everyone—a healthcare system that does not require the patient to complete the same forms at every access point. Instead, imagine a healthcare system where primary care physicians have access to your specialty medical information and specialists have access to your primary care information via inter-connected "smart" EHRs that are integrated with personalized eHealth service providers and delivered directly to a multi-purpose, intelligent, mobile digital device that can be carried in one's pocket.

This consumer-centered system will use a variety of technologies and innovations to generate the "smart" EHRs of the future that:

- *Deliver information, services, and data via Mobile, Multi-purpose Devices (MMD) anywhere, anytime.* Imagine a small mobile multipurpose communication and coaching device that has a phone, embedded health-coach software, GPS, instant messaging, camera, music player, and e-money dispenser, all of which are interconnected to deliver health care to active, busy citizens.

- *Remind you when it is time for your annual checkup and anticipate your need with an intelligent digital coach.* Imagine embedded, health-coach "mindware" programmed right in to that MMD. This mindware allows the device to "learn" each time additional medical data is added, and automated programs scan the Internet or licensed medical service databases for the latest medical research and knowledge relevant to your medical conditions and genomic type.

- *Integrate physician records, hospital services, medication histories, and other clinical information into a unified digital record that is available to patients at home or at the point of care.* Imagine that accessing your health records or paying medical bills is as easy and convenient as checking your banking records or paying bills online.

- *Monitor vital signs and clinical indicator continuously and communicate wirelessly and seamlessly.* Imagine an easier way for diabetics to monitor their glucose levels using a glucose watch or implantable "nano-tear," a contact lens–like device that uses nanotechnology to monitor the glucose level in a person's tears and then transmit the results to an MMD, which would then dispense insulin automatically via an implanted nano-device, as needed. Such a subscription-based monitoring service could be sponsored by a doctor, hospital, health plan, or even your credit card company.

Medical informatics has the power to deliver these services and many more. And in the year 2020 we will see a practical application of the creativity and genius of today's clinicians, researchers, patients, and technologists who are working together to help and heal. Figure 1-1 illustrates the concept of Health@Anywhere and shows how patients will evolve into medically empowered ConsumerMDs™, surrounded and supported by a variety of interactive devices that deliver health and medical services at the point of need.

Medical informatics in 2020, through its strategies, tactics, processes, and technologies, will surround and support patients wherever they are. It will engage patients to be active partners in their medical care. And as patients become partners in their own care, they will actively support efforts to continuously improve the quality of care, reduce deadly medical errors, and cut unnecessary costs. As Figure 1-1 illustrates, they will do this in a variety of ways:

- **Web of Care** Consumers will have "always-on" access to public Internet and subscription-based medical/health knowledge databases

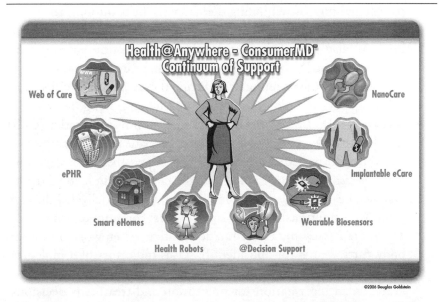

FIGURE 1-1 Health@Anywhere—ConsumerMD™ Continuum of Support

that deliver a vital connection to rapidly obtain medical knowledge based on interest, diagnosis, treatment protocol, or topic of interest.

- **ePHR** The next generation ePersonal Health Record (ePHR) will be electronically connected to the Internet, *e*volving with *e*merging technology, and *e*ntelligent™—electronically connected with the latest "health–coach" mindware that anticipates health needs and enables the storage, management, and intelligent use of a patient's personal medical record to improve health and medical care. The ePHR will be available through multiple options supported by a health partner such as a doctor, hospital, health plan, patient advocacy group for those with chronic disease, or financial services company.

- **Smart eHomes** Homes of the future will be embedded with all types of Internet-connected monitors, including biomonitors tailored to the individual needs of the residents. Biomonitors could measure a patient's gait or vital signs. A pillow-embedded monitor could track respiration. These technologies will involve simple, low-cost sensor technology affordable to even the lowest income earners. A data-mining element will yield additional health information for the linked ePHR, and the entire system will be customized to individual and cultural needs.

- **Health Robots** "Healthbots" will assist elderly and special needs patients at home by reminding them to visit the bathroom, take medicine, or schedule an appointment with their doctor. These healthbots will also function as a conduit for connecting patients with caregivers through the Internet. Professional caregivers will directly interact with patients remotely, reducing the frequency of visits while collecting data and monitoring patient well-being along the way.

- **Anywhere@Decision Support** Consumer health informatics (CHI) will deliver tools, resources, and support for patients and healthy people who need to better manage prevention and treatment decisions. These decision-support modules will be tailored to individual demographics, health profiles, and conditions and will be delivered through print, Web, multimedia, video, and any other communication vehicle.

- **Wearable Biosensors** Detection devices that, when worn on certain body parts, search for and identify status indicators of a biological function such as heart rate and glucose levels—will painlessly provide needed information for prevention and treatment decisions. Today, the GlucoWatch provides diabetics with automatic, noninvasive glucose readings as frequently as every 10 minutes. Bio-sensors will monitor everything from glucose levels and heart rhythms to cancer indicator molecules and brain function.

- *Implantable eCare* The insertion and management of artificial devices within the human body will become increasingly common for maintaining and improving health. "Implantables" have already evolved from artificial hips and knees to assistive devices that have built-in electronics such as pace-makers and cochlear implants. Implantable eCare is the next wave: integrated, internal implants that communicate with external monitoring devices outside the body and through the Internet to an ePHR.

- *NanoCare* Next-generation implantable eCare, "NanoCare," is the creation of tiny components that will be constructed, inserted, and applied within the human body. The National Institute of Health's Nanomedicine Roadmap Initiative anticipates that in the next 20 to 30 years, nano-sized implants will search out and destroy cancer cells that would otherwise cause a tumor to develop in the body, and be used to create miniature, biological devices to replace a broken part of a cell. An insulin-dependent diabetic could use such devices to continuously monitor and adjust insulin levels autonomously and automatically.

The Health@Anywhere examples above are based on technologies that exist today and those that will evolve in the not-so-distant future. Our health and medical system is transforming, and segments of our customer-focused and patient-centered future are already in place. Now the challenge that exists for healthcare leaders, clinicians, and managers is to plan for and deploy the knowledge and information technology tools that empower patients and enable care providers. Complex systems require comprehensive processes and tools to transform care processes. And the transformation of processes must be guided by empowered and educated managers and clinicians within the framework of an advanced medical informatics paradigm.

Overview of the Medical Informatics 20/20 Model

Life is change. In the recent past, health care has evolved rapidly from an inpatient to outpatient focused business. Now the transition is to an "any-

What Is Medical Informatics?

In this book, we broadly define "medical informatics" as *the applied science at the nexus of the disciplines of medicine, business, consumer centered care, and information technology, which is instrumental for significant and measurable improvements in both healthcare quality and cost-effectiveness.* It is this integrative discipline that defines tactics and technologies along with the tools, resources, and methods required to optimize the intelligent use of the latest evidence and knowledge in health and medicine.

Medical informatics tools, technology, and tactics include not only computers and information systems, but also clinical guidelines, formal medical languages, standards, interoperability, and communication systems. The various tools, technologies, and tactics are designed to support the progressive realization of the optimal delivery of health and medical care.

According to our definition, medical informatics includes the subdomains of clinical informatics, bioinformatics, nursing informatics, consumer health informatics, public health informatics, dental informatics, and what has recently been coined as "bio-info-nano" informatics by a NASA–Google collaboration.

where service" where patient customers are monitored and supported at home, at work, or anywhere. Just as the information technology infrastructure of the past evolved to support outpatient care, now it must transform even more radically by becoming clinically driven inside of care facilities while also extending itself to go mobile and virtual with customer patients.

The Medical Informatics 20/20 framework and strategies presented throughout this book offer an approach and a set of tools to accelerate the transformation and address the challenges we face including:

- *Epidemic of medical errors* due to system complexity, lack of information technology, communication gaps, etc.
- *Not diagnosing and treating with the latest medical knowledge* and evidence base at the point of care.
- *Poor vital health statistic performance* relative to other developed countries despite spending more money on health care.
- *High failure rates in the implementation of health information technology solutions.*

- *Partial, fragmented patient medical records* due to paper records at numerous sites of care.

There is near-universal agreement that solving these problems will require a new and improved wave of health information technology (HIT) that supports transformed care delivery processes. Consequently, there is a dire need for a new, comprehensive model for medical informatics that is integrated with knowledge in technology, business, and medicine and that delivers strategies, tactics, tools, and techniques that address the human and system issues in overcoming the above challenges.

The sidebar "What Is Medical Informatics?" defines medical informatics and outlines its sub-domains and relationships. The Medical Informatics 20/20 nexus is the intelligent use of technology with the active engagement of clinicians, managers, and patients/consumers to transform health care within the intersection of technology, medicine, and business.

Figure 1-2 illustrates the current state of poor outcomes and nonintegrated care that can be transformed by the three strategies of Collaboration, Open Solutions, and Innovation (COSI). Later in the chapter is a series of three figures, one for each strategy, that outline tactical areas that have one or more specific tactics associated with each strategy. The COSI strategies and tactics enable the realization of intelligent and practical deployment that supports a future state of connected health care with electronic transportable patient records and higher quality care.

The multi-faceted elements of the Medical Informatics 20/20 Model are the connective tissue that will allow scientific breakthroughs to be integrated with policy, business, and information technology and effectively translated from the research bench to patient bedside or to anywhere a patient receives care.

Quality Healthcare and Electronic Health Record Implementation Through Collaboration, Open Solutions, and Innovation (COSI)

Industries and businesses throughout the world are being revolutionized through the application of three unique and powerful strategies. When combined, these strategies create a robust model for accelerating change, reducing medical errors, and improving quality in the U.S. and other countries' healthcare systems.

- **Collaboration** shares and disseminates knowledge, know-how, and resources to healthcare leaders, patients, and consumers, allowing them to save time and money across the many health and medical industry tiers and markets.
- **Open Solutions** facilitate the ability to communicate and share information in a way that is completely interoperable and transportable across large scale, macroeconomic, and information technology systems.
- **Innovation** unleashes the knowledge and applied creativity power of team members in healthcare organizations to improve processes and transform culture to better serve customers, professionals, partners, and patients.

The COSI strategies of Collaboration, Open Solutions, and Innovation are absolutely essential for transforming the health and medical culture, the processes, the leadership, and the technology necessary to support better, safer, and higher quality care in the American healthcare system and other healthcare systems across the globe. In the early 21st century, the application of these strategies is already evident throughout other major industries.

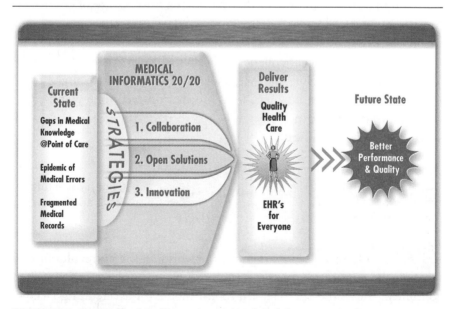

FIGURE 1-2 Medical Informatics 20/20 Model

One example of a company that that has transformed itself using COSI strategies is IBM. In 1999, it began investing billions in the Linux operating system and in 2005 made 500 of its patents freely available to anyone developing and designing software standards for the health and education industries. The result is the company's "openness" strategy, which allows IBM employees to collaboratively innovate by connecting with international networks and communities active in development of open-source software and open standards.

Implementation of the COSI strategies will accelerate the adoption of the standards necessary for the seamless interoperability of Electronic Health Records (EHRs) for all Americans and will support EHR adoption in developed and developing countries worldwide. The comprehensive, progressive, and empowered implementation of these strategies is vital for public health, healthcare quality, and national defense relative to natural or man-made disasters, such as biological threats or nuclear terrorism. Additional information on these and other examples of COSI

Being "Open" for Quality

The development, deployment, and use of the VistA health informatics system by the Veterans Health Administration exemplify the principles within the COSI strategies. VistA, the world's largest health information technology system, is based on open standards and has an open architecture, and the source code is available in the public domain without license fees. The collaboration and innovation have resulted in higher quality and a wealth of data greater than any other healthcare information system.

The adoption of VistA in various forms outside of the VA is accelerating. The Indian Health Service and Military Health Service use a form of VistA, as do many other health systems around the world. Now, private health systems such as Midland Health System, private doctors, and many others are adopting forms of VistA because of its many benefits. For more information on VA quality reviews and Awards, see Chapter 12 and review information and data in the VA VistA profile.

For access to VistA software visit:
  www.vistasoftware.org
  www.worldvista.org
  www.va.gov/cprsdemo

strategies and their associated tactics, tools, and technologies within health care are detailed in subsequent sections of this book.

The authors are patient advocates and technology agnostics. Our purpose is to accelerate the improvement of quality, the reduction of medical errors, and the enhancement of cost-effectiveness through the intelligent use of Medical Informatics 20/20 strategies and tactics. We are active in the strategy, development, deployment, and support of "open" and "closed" health information systems and applications, and view "Free and Open-Source Solutions" (FOSS) and open solutions as viable options for any healthcare provider seeking to implement clinical informatics, decrease the cost of clinical informatics, and realize better patient care by transforming care delivery using information technology.

The COSI Strategies Support the Medical Informatics 20/20 Model

The Medical Informatics 20/20 Model, with its three strategies of Collaboration, Open Solutions, and Innovation, is focused on supporting improvements in performance and quality of care by implementing comprehensive EHRs and clinical informatics systems that will be used by providers and patients everywhere. When fully deployed in 2020 and beyond, the end result will be improved health status for everyone and a lower rate of annual increase in healthcare costs.

As shown in Figures 1-3, 1-4, and 1-5 in this chapter, there are a series of tactics that support the intelligent application of the Medical Informatics 20/20 infrastructure needed for quality and EHRs. Within each tactic there are tools, technologies, and techniques that enable intelligent and integrated execution of the tactics supporting the strategies. First, let us examine the problems faced by healthcare managers and clinicians.

THE PROBLEMS TO SOLVE

Rich Country, Poor Health

The richest country in the world, the United States, ranks at or near the bottom of all industrialized countries in terms of vital health statistics. Of 13 developed countries, the United States ranked:

- 13th for low birth weight.
- 13th for neonatal mortality and infant mortality overall.

- 11th for postneonatal mortality.
- 13th for years of potential life lost.
- 11th for female life expectancy at 1 year, 12th for males.
- 10th for female life expectancy at 15 years, 12th for males.
- 10th for female life expectancy at 40 years, 9th for males.
- 7th for female life expectancy at 65 years, 7th for males.
- 3rd for female life expectancy at 80 years, 3rd for males.
- 10th for age-adjusted mortality.

(Source: Barbara Starfield, MD, MPH, JAMA July 26, 2000–Vol 284, No. 4, http://silver.neep.wisc.edu/~lakes/iatrogenic.pdf)

In 2005, the United States spent 16.3% of the country's Gross National Product (GNP) on healthcare services. This is the highest percentage of any developed nation, yet the resulting outcomes are some of the lowest among developed nations.

An Epidemic of Medical Errors

In addition to this poor performance in vital health statistics, there is a human-spawned epidemic of deadly, costly medical errors. Depending on which of three major studies you read, at least 44,000 people, and perhaps as many as 200,000 people, die in hospitals each year as a result of medical errors that could have been prevented. In addition to the cost in terms of human lives, medical errors have been estimated to result in total costs between $17 billion and $29 billion per year in hospitals nationwide.[1,2]

But annual deaths from medical errors in hospitals are only one area of danger. There many areas of "near misses" in the chain of treatment that cause harm to patients. According to the *Journal of the American Medical Association* (JAMA), these are estimated to involve:

- 106,000 adverse reactions to improperly prescribed prescription drugs.

---

[1]National Patient Safety Foundation at the AMA: Public Opinion of Patient Safety Issues Research Findings, Louis Harris & Associates, September 1977.

[2]The estimate on the number of Americans that are harmed as a result of medical errors was based on two studies of large samples of hospital admissions, one in New York using 1984 data and another in Colorado and Utah using 1992 data. They found that the proportion of hospital admissions experiencing an adverse event, defined as injuries caused by medical management, were 2.9% and 3.7%, respectively. The proportion of adverse events attributable to errors (i.e., preventable adverse events) was 58% in New York and 53% in Colorado and Utah. These estimates were multiplied against the total number of hospital admissions in a year in the United States to obtain the estimated total number of hospital medical errors.

A Deadly Medical Error Results in
Leadership Collaboration for Quality

In January 2001, Josie King climbed into a hot bath and burned herself. This accident was a tragedy, but it's not what killed her. Josie made a marvelous recovery at the prestigious Johns Hopkins Children's Center in Baltimore, Maryland, and after 10 days in the pediatric intensive care unit, she was well enough to move to the intermediate-care floor. But it was in the ICU that a series of catastrophic medical mistakes—what her mother would later call "a combination of many errors, all of which were avoidable"—ended her life.

The first sign of trouble was Josie's desperate thirst (dehydration, it was discovered later, from a preventable catheter infection). Her mother was told not to let her drink anything. When she sucked at washcloths, the staff in charge of her care did not recognize the dehydration. Then her eyes rolled back in her head, and staff members assured her mother that Josie's vital signs were fine and children just sometimes do that. And then there was the dose of methadone, which Josie's mother questioned as there had been a previous order for no narcotics. It was administered by a veteran nurse who said the no-narcotics order had been changed. The methadone caused Josie to have a cardiac arrest while her mother was at her bedside. Josie King returned to the intensive care unit, where she died of dehydration and misused narcotics.[3]

Josie King's death fueled Johns Hopkins Medical Center's decision to create dedicated patient-transport teams, place pharmacists in ICUs, initiate medication reconciliation at the moment of nursing discharge, develop daily short-term goal sheets for patient rounds, and re-label buretrol and epidural catheters.

The important legacy of Josie King is one of collaboration of healthcare professionals with parents and patients. Josie's parents, Sorrell and Tony King, are committed to making sure that Josie's death was not in vain. The overarching message is that there is a need for an ongoing and balanced communication between parents and caregivers and that it is critical to know why medical errors happen so they can be prevented. Along with

---

[3]*To Err Is Human: Building a Safer Health System*, Institute of Medicine Committee on Quality of Healthcare in America, National Academy Press, Washington, DC, 1999.

their Johns Hopkins partners, the Kings want all caregivers, parents, and patients to realize that in today's complex health system there is a higher likelihood of error and that, more often than not, errors are a result of system failures, not necessarily the error of an individual.

The collaboration has taken several important forms. Sorrell King and the Josie King Foundation have been active supporters of the Institute for Healthcare Improvement (IHI) and its campaign to end the 100,000 lives lost each year to medical errors. The Patient Safety Group was established by an alliance of Johns Hopkins, the Josie King Foundation, and other nonprofit entities, and led to the development of the Comprehensive Unit-Based Safety Program (CUSP) to support improvements in safety based on the rigorous collection of empirical data. In addition, the program is an advocate for safety and creates a channel for open communication for *all* staff, from clerks to executives.

For more information visit www.josieking.org and www.patientsafetygroup.org.

- 80,000 infections in hospitals.
- 20,000 other errors in hospitals.
- 12,000 unnecessary surgeries.
- 7,000 medication errors in hospitals.[4]

In addition, there are medical errors and mishaps that cause harm or death in long-term care facilities and everywhere else along the continuum of care. For instance, it was also estimated in the JAMA article that there were 199,000 deaths from medical errors in outpatient care. By totaling these estimates there could be upwards of *424,000 annual deaths per year in the American medical system, which would make the system itself one of the leading causes of death in the United States.*

Even worse, the National Council for Patient Information and Education reported that an additional 125,000 deaths occur annually due to adverse reactions to drugs that physicians never should have prescribed. The annual death toll from synthetic prescription drugs, both from the correctly prescribed and the incorrectly prescribed, amounts to about

---

[4]Dr. Barbara Starfield of the Johns Hopkins School of Hygiene and Public Health (*Journal of the American Medical Association,* vol. 284, July 26, 2000).

231,000 deaths every year. To put this into perspective, this is the equivalent of a World Trade Center disaster every week for over a year and a half, or the crash of two fully loaded Boeing 747 airliners every day of the year.

Medical errors and lack of patient safety are largely due to decentralized, disconnected, and incompatible health-information technology systems. This fact is confirmed in the Institute of Medicine (IOM) report "Patient Safety: Achieving a New Standard for Care." The report found that improved information and data systems and a national health-information infrastructure are needed to support efforts to make patient safety a standard of care in hospitals, doctors' offices, nursing homes, and every other healthcare setting. A Markle Foundation survey indicates that 72% of Americans support such a nationwide health-information exchange or network for doctors and patients.[5]

Medical informatics, intelligently and appropriately applied to the healthcare delivery process, is integral to radically improving the quality of care and reducing near-miss and fatal medical errors. The use of the VistA electronic health record system by the Veterans Health Administration is just one example that substantiates this claim. More detail about this is provided in subsequent chapters of this book.

Medical Knowledge Gap@Point of Care

The next major factor that supports the need for serious transformation using medical informatics technologies and techniques is the gap in the delivery of clinical knowledge at the point of care. Yes, what doctors don't know (but could know with the appropriate information systems) can hurt or kill you. When you see a doctor or go to the hospital, you've got a 50-50 chance you'll be assessed using the most current medical evidence.[6] That's right: 50% of the time, you're *not* getting the latest treatment information available. And the quality of treatment differs markedly by disease. For example, 76% of people with breast cancer received the recommended treatment. Only 23% of those with hip fractures did.[7]

---

[5]"Attitudes of Americans Regarding Personal Health Record and Nationwide Electronic Health Information Exchange," Markle Foundation, October 2005.

[6]RAND Health Study: Landmark Study Finds American Adults Often Fail to Get Recommended Care, Posing "Serious Threats" to Health. June 25, 2003.

[7]RAND Health Study: Landmark Study Finds American Adults Often Fail to Get Recommended Care, Posing "Serious Threats" to Health. June 25, 2003.

Why aren't physicians using the most current clinical data available? It's not that they aren't good doctors; they simply don't have a way to easily access a vast array of clinical knowledge repositories at the point of care. The vast majority of Americans who visit physicians do not have an EHR. Their medical records are on paper, so receiving the most current medical evidence electronically at the point of care is impossible. Although fragmented databases do exist, they are not connected. Even more important, they are not easy to access at the point physicians need them: in the exam room with their patients. This lack of access not only impedes a physician's ability to recommend the latest treatments, but it also creates expensive duplicate tests and consultations. In fact, a new Dartmouth study indicates that one-third of the $1.6 trillion spent on health care each year is wasted on duplicative or ineffective care.

Medical informatics provides the technical support to implement and distribute knowledge at the point of care, and most Americans support this connectivity. But we have a long way to go before we can truly integrate clinical, pharmaceutical, and administrative knowledge electronically at the point of care where it is needed; however, major inroads are being made.

The bottom line is this: achieving the vision of a safe, high-quality healthcare system that puts patients first depends on our ability to build a better mousetrap—one that combines connectivity, openness, and collaboration as a central theme. One of the biggest challenges facing health care is the implementation of interoperable health information technology that supports delivering the current evidence base at the point of need and providing an EHR for everyone.

Again, let's ask ourselves—Why, in the richest country in the world, aren't all medical records electronically maintained? Why can nearly every American access his personal bank account at an ATM anywhere in the world, but can't access his full set of medical records electronically from anywhere?

Why don't physicians have a "medical knowledge button" that links them directly to the latest clinical research and treatment guidelines, whether they are treating a patient in their office, in the hospital, at home, or at work? Yet people can find almost anything they want on the Internet with a quick search on Yahoo or Google or a next-generation search engine such as Grokker.com, Clusty.com or Live.com.

The modern medical industry has evolved piecemeal over the last 100 years across clinical, technological, business, and managerial dimensions.

At an ever-accelerating rate, we are seeing breakthrough medical treatments and cures, the birth of new clinical specialties, the addition of government health and access programs, significant changes to healthcare reimbursement mechanisms, new pharmaceuticals, a burgeoning uninsured population, and significant changes to medical facilities and equipment. The fact that each of these changes has evolved independently into its own small cottage industry has resulted in a complex web of processes, layers, and bureaucracies. Each of these systems has its own culture, its own set of norms, its own set of processes, and its own small piece of the financial payment maze.

Adding new clinical informatics and information technologies to this fragile mix of systems will require significant job-altering changes to how physicians, nurses, physical therapists, billing staff, hospital administrators, and managers perform their daily work. This is a scary proposition for most people. Generally speaking, we are asking people to modify the job they have been doing the same way for many years and begin using EHRs and other systems intelligently to improve the quality and cost-effectiveness of health care. That said, we cannot let resistance to change be the hurdle that keeps us from digitizing and humanizing health care. If we do, we will continue to put human lives at risk.

The man-made epidemic of medical errors created as a result of system complexity needs immediate attention so that Americans like one-and-a-half-year-old Josie King no longer die from preventable mistakes.

Do not underestimate the time and pain involved in making this happen. Change like this is *hard*. It may take decades to do it right, but hopefully it will only take a few years to apply Medical Informatics 20/20 strategies and tactics with passion, vigor, and leadership.

Now that we have defined the problem, Chapter 1 will highlight the major tactics within each of the three main Medical Informatics 20/20 strategies. In *Section IV, Toolkit for Medical Informatics Excellence and Quality Improvement,* expanded information on each of the three COSI strategies provides detail on tactics such as process improvement tools, including Six Sigma, knowledge transfer, collaborative innovation, sharing alliances, clinical decision support, and open standards.

Failures in Implementing Information Technology

The last major factor that we have identified that supports the need for a new age of medical informatics are the past failures in deploying clinically based information technology in health care. For various reasons, throughout many industries there is a high failure rate for the deployment of enabling information technology. One factor that stands out is the lack of understanding of the human factors involved in planning, deployment, and use of information technology. This is particularly acute in medical informatics, where success depends on integral involvement of clinicians who understand information technology, medicine, and transformation of business/clinical processes for better care.

In its list of "Barriers to Adoption" of health information technology, the Office of the National Coordinator for Health Information Technology (ONCHIT) cited the "high failure rate for electronic health implementation" as one of the major barriers hindering adoption across the country (www.os.dhhs.gov/healthit/barrierAdpt.html). Also noted is a high failure rate for business reengineering and the lack of experienced information technology (IT) professionals with both clinical and IT experience.

Scot Silverstein, MD, a leading clinician and medical informatics expert, has assembled a Web site at http://home.aol.com/medinformaticsmd/failurecases.htm that maintains a running list of failed health-information technology projects. In summarizing his findings over the years, he stated:

> IT personnel in hospitals often believe that success in implementing management information systems applications ("business computing") supersedes or actually renders unnecessary the mastery of medicine in leading and controlling implementation of clinical computing tools. Experts in clinical computing must provide effective solutions via seasoned application of the concepts, techniques, knowledge, and processes of medicine, and display an expert level of critical thinking in applying principles, theories, and concepts on a wide range of issues that are unique to clinical settings. Business IT experience alone does not provide a sufficient background for such responsibilities to be carried out effectively. Leaders in clinical IT must be experienced in medical sciences and in the complex social and organizational issues of health care, such as the need for multiple, contextual levels of confidentiality, the politics and psychology of medical practice and referral, the complex medical workflow and the need to rapidly improvise due to the unexpected ("there are no committees in cardiac arrest situations"), and societal and personal sensitivities towards the physician–patient interaction.

The Office of the National Coordinator for Health Information Technology (ONCHIT) also noted that another of the key problems faced is that "limited capacity for interoperability" standards are lacking in most information technology products and that the standards are not rigorous and lag behind commercialization.

Implementing information technology in any setting is hard. But implementing clinical health information is very hard due to the complexity of medicine, the fragmented nature of the current health-information ecosystem that exists in healthcare organizations, and the variability of the human body. Failure is frequently a factor due to "human" issues, which range from a lack of participation in planning and selection, to poor training and resistance to changing how work is done.

Health care is very complex. The paper-based and manual processes that have evolved over the last 100 years will not change easily. The need to involve clinicians in transforming processes from paper to electronic media is the reason that often 50% of the expenditures for implementation are not related to the technology but to involving clinicians, educating them, obtaining their input, and supporting them in learning by doing. Any technology tool will require humans to run that tool, so involvement, training, careful process mapping, and redesign are critical. In the end, medical informatics deployment is more likely to fail due to human factors rather than a failure of the technology itself. This reality demands the application of collaboration and innovation tactics related to a rigorous process-improvement methodology, an empowered knowledge-transfer effort to rapidly spread better ways of delivering care, and other tactics that are part of the Medical Informatics 20/20 Model.

In the first half of this Chapter the major problems contributing to the poor current state and need for health care transformation were outlined. Next we provide an overview of the three critical strategies–Collaboration, Open Solutions, and Innovation–and their associated tactics that enable the successful execution of the strategies.

THE MEDICAL INFORMATICS 20/20 STRATEGIES

Collaboration as a Key Strategy

Our market-based healthcare system has demonstrated over the past 25 years an inability to solve the electronic health and medical record challenge. But it has identified and developed valuable pieces needed to complete the puzzle. The federal sector has not solved the problem either, but important steps have been taken, and industry-wide collaborations are gaining traction. Out of the Josie King tragedy, dedicated professionals and patients learned from medical mistakes and created a collaboration to support change. The Institute for Healthcare Improvement (IHI) was established more than 19 years ago by Donald Berwick, MD, and now has a worldwide collaboration in place to support improving quality and patient safety in health systems around the world. (See Chapter 5 for the case study on the collaborative efforts of IHI to transform healthcare systems into high-quality organizations.)

Within the COSI strategy of Collaboration are three major tactical areas:

- Leadership and Open Collaboration.
- Public–Private Collaboration.
- Knowledge Management.

Within each of these areas are a series of tactics used to support the successful execution of the Collaboration strategy. What follows is a brief highlight of each of the tactical areas within Collaboration, as illustrated in Figure 1-3. Details on the three COSI strategies and their associated tactics are described in depth in Chapter 11, Section IV.

- **Tactical Area: Leadership and Open Collaboration Leadership** is absolutely needed to transform healthcare organizations into places

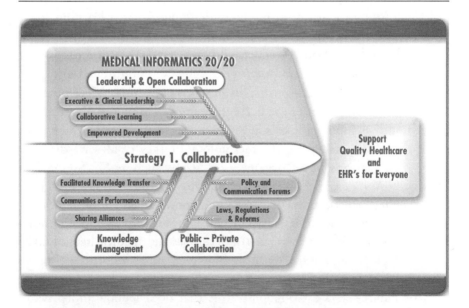

FIGURE 1-3 Tactics Supporting the Collaboration Strategy

where quality comes first. Leadership must become self-educated and engage by actively supporting the team members who will have to transform business and clinical care processes. Executive boards need to put quality performance criteria first, and compensation systems must change to reward quality before financial performance. Open Collaboration involves the use of open communication, learning, and applying problem-solving circles among diverse stakeholders. Open Collaboration is an extension of the mission-driven hospitals and health systems across the country, many of which are faith-based or nonprofit. Key tactics of Open Collaboration include:

○ *Executive and clinical leadership* must solve the challenges of error reduction and quality care with knowledge and passion. The first question CEOs must ask when monitoring the drive for performance excellence is "How are we measuring up on quality indicators?" Clinical leaders must be empowered by an executive leadership who understands, participates, and supports rapid-cycle improvement in quality.

○ *Collaborative learning* is an umbrella term for a variety of approaches that involve cooperative efforts by managers and clinical professionals to reduce errors and improve quality. This cooperative approach uses the conferences, virtual networks, adult learning theory, and online and computer-based learning management systems to increase medical informatics knowledge and know-how of care providers and managers in health care.

○ *Empowered development* represents an enlightened and proactive clinical involvement in all stages of planning, development, and deployment of medical informatics technologies. Institutions such as Johns Hopkins have also engaged the patient voice. This involves increasing the technology literacy of all care-delivery associations in an organization. Tools such as Six Sigma and LEAN, described later, offer a step-by-step methodology to guide transformation, thus creating an empowered and educated development process. If clinicians are not empowered and appropriately involved in all phases of development, then the likelihood of deployment failure of information technology will rise.

• *Tactical Area: Public–Private Collaboration* The key underpinning of Public–Private Collaboration is that both federal and private-sector leadership must step forward to expand the forums and foundations already in place. Within the federal government, the Consolidated Health Informatics efforts of all federal agencies help to establish standards for clinical data exchange. One of the most important federal efforts has been the establishment of the Office of the National Coordinator for Health Information Technology and the appointment of the first health-information technology and medical informatics czar. Key tactics are:

- ○ *Policy and Communication Forums* Meetings, conferences, and events that are policy or educational based to spread the diffusion of information and provide a forum for dialogue and participation.
- ○ *Laws, Certifications, and Reforms* Federal, state, and local laws that are passed or reformed in an effort to improve public health, healthcare quality, and safety. This would include ensuring patient privacy and security through regulations, certifications, and laws.

- *Tactical Area: Knowledge Management* Is your healthcare organization wasting resources and reinventing the wheel? Knowledge Management (KM) integrates human processes supported by technology to create, organize, and share knowledge and the intellectual capital of an enterprise. Traditional mentorship is a form of KM, but today, KM is a discipline focused on liberating the power of human capital within an organization while also capturing, archiving, and diffusing the knowledge rapidly throughout an organization. A KM program addresses all four of these fundamentals: leadership, processes, technology, and people. These elements support the achievement of organizational goals. KM involves the processes, people, and technologies for knowledge database development, organizing, searching, and application. KM is a vital component in the rapid spread of demonstrated best practices, transference of explicit and tacit knowledge, and the framework for sharing and working better and smarter. Key tactics include:

  - ○ *Communities of Performance™ (CoP)* Associates with common problems collaborate over an extended period to share ideas, exchange resources, invent improved processes, and find solutions. Today, CoPs are usually supported with Internet and communication technologies that accelerate the diffusion of information, resources, and materials. CoPs connect people and leverage human capital to achieve set goals. Communities of Performance focus on achieving measureable goals inside an organization or across inter-organizational boundaries.

o *Facilitated Knowledge Transfer (FKT)* The use of dedicated people who specialize in identifying, profiling, and archiving evidence based best practices and community based proven practices using multimedia communication and information technologies to educate and empower people to improve. FKT experts are storytellers, producers, and trainers of the organizational knowledge universe. Their mission is to identify and package, in a compelling, complete, and interesting way, a best practice so that it can be rapidly diffused to support rapid-cycle change. FKT recognizes that sharing to support goal achievement in geographically distributed and complex organizations does not often happen naturally. FKT in health care works to train and support all clinicians and managers in an organization in how to share effectively to improve performance.

o *Sharing Alliances* Formal or informal relationships to support the transfer of tacit and explicit knowledge within or across organizational boundaries. A formal knowledge-sharing arrangement between two large separate multi-location healthcare organizations would represent a Sharing Alliance. A good example of a sharing alliance are the participants in the CMS/Premier, Inc. Pay-for-Performance demonstration project who agreed to share their data with each other and publicly entered into a sharing arrangement to improve quality.

Open Solutions as a Key Strategy

Open Solutions are vital to realize a better healthcare system. Generally speaking, Open Solutions are software application source code, communications, standards, knowledge, or other assets that are available on a no-cost license basis and/or their innerworkings are exposed to the public. The Open Solutions strategy has a range of tactics to lower the implementation costs of health-information technology deployment in healthcare delivery systems, today and tomorrow. Consider this:

• *Open Solutions in the form of open standards* will be essential to support interoperability and clinical data exchange. This is critical to the successful deployment of EHRs for all Americans and will ensure that medical records are accessible and readable across the healthcare system and wherever patients need access to care.

- *Open Solutions in the form of open-source software* will play a critical role in reducing the cost of health information technology in the near term by delivering competitive pressures to closed-software solution vendors and offering a viable, no-fee license option to organizations who otherwise could not afford closed-source software solutions.

- *Open Solutions in the form of open architecture* will be vital to connecting open and closed information technology systems for integrated and lower-cost operations that can support better health.

The benefits of Open Solutions include lower costs, better quality products (because they are constantly being improved by those using them), accelerated innovation and problem-solving, and reduced cycle time. Often overlooked, yet integral to solving the problems that face today's healthcare industry, Open Solutions are the key to achieving higher-quality health care, lower implementation costs, and better disaster preparedness with affordable solutions and greater scalability.

Frequently, Open Solutions are seen as a "commons," much like a public park where many—but not all—members of a community contribute and there are a set of norms that govern the maintenance and evolution of the commons. Commons, communities, and common actions for the common good have long and deep roots in the human psychological composition. Companies that pursue an Open Solutions business model in the open-source software field generate revenue from implementation and ongoing service and support but not from upfront license fees for the software.

Open Solutions Tactical Areas

Within the COSI strategy of Open Solutions are four major tactical areas: Open Standards, Free and Open-Source Software (FOSS), Technology Transfer, and Open Systems. This is illustrated in Figure 1-4. Each tactical area contains specific tactics, initiatives, tools, and technologies that support the Open Solutions strategy. Following are brief overviews of these. Section II and III of this book focus on the assessment, deployment, and management of Open Solutions with a specific focus on Free and Open-Source Software (FOSS) in the various forms of VistA and other EHRs being implemented in healthcare organizations around the world.

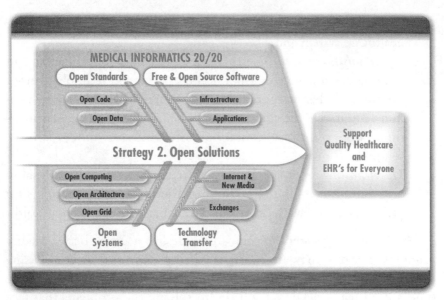

FIGURE 1-4 Tactics Supporting the Open Solutions Strategy

- *Tactical Area: Open Standards* Open Standards are the set of specifications developed to define interoperability among diverse systems. Other related concepts and tactics that support diverse health-information technology system interoperability are:
  - *Open Code* Commercial proprietary software whose source code can be obtained, viewed, and changed within the guidelines of the specific license arrangement.
  - *Open Data* Describes data formats (e.g., "Open Data Format Initiative description") and programs to validate that a data file is "ODFI compliant".

An important example is the federal government's Consolidated Health Informatics (CHI) initiative. The U.S. Department of Health and Human Services (HHS) and more than 20 federal departments that deliver healthcare services are working to identify appropriate, existing clinical data standards and to endorse them for use throughout the federal sector. This collaboration is an effort to drive adoption of the selected clinical data standards and create a tipping point so the federal clinical data standards become the private sector's de facto standards for the next-generation national health-information network. There are significant public and private forces collaborating in this effort. The resisting forces include the fragmentation and complexity of the healthcare system and the time it takes to move information systems to the new clinical data standards.

- *Tactical Area: Free and Open-Source Software* Free and Open-Source Software (FOSS) refers to a software program in which the source code is available to anyone for use and/or can be modified by anyone, free of any upfront license fee. FOSS gained significant presence in the marketplace through the growth of the Linux operating systems, which set the stage for the growth of FOSS in the infrastructure area of information technology. Progressively, FOSS has migrated from infrastructure to applications in the information technology field. Many experts feel that there is no corporate enterprise software application that is not immune to becoming a commodity because of the power of the community of software developers to create FOSS alternatives to closed-software applications.

FOSS is a central element of the Open Solutions strategy in the Medical Informatics 20/20 Model. The market is growing rapidly across all domains of information technology in both the public and private sectors. Companies such as Boeing, Amazon, Google, and E-Trade use the open-source operating system Linux extensively throughout their enterprises. IBM, Hewlett-Packard, Sun Microsystems, and other leading information technology companies are investing billions of dollars and designing significant aspects of their corporate strategies and business models around Open Solutions.

Healthcare institutions need an affordable comprehensive health-information and clinical information system to meet the Presidential agenda, homeland security requirements, and patient demands for safe, high-quality health care. Open Solutions can offer a cost-effective and viable solution, and healthcare organizations are moving in this direction. VistA Open Office (VOE) for physician offices is an example of how the federal government is using an open solutions approach to support broader access to EHR technology for small medical practices.

The time is right for various healthcare organizations and federal agencies to effectively participate with the Open Software Solutions community and healthcare industry at large, especially given the availability of VistA and the VA Computerized Patient Record System

(CPRS) as an equivalent of Free and Open-Source Software. The steps being taken by VA and HHS to develop and release the VistA Open Office (VOE) system for use in small medical practices is a step in the right direction. Chapter 3 discusses in detail the growth and development of Open Solutions and open-source software in health care. Chapters 6, 7, 8, 9, and 10 expand significantly on VistA, VistA Open Office, and other FOSS options available for health care.

- *Tactical Area: Technology Transfer* Technology Transfer has several dimensions. One focuses on "practical technology transfer" as the process of developing practical applications from the results of scientific research. Another dimension is "technology transfer exchange," which focuses on the sharing or exchange of an actual technology, device, or software code from one organization to another via Web-based sharing or an exchange system. Companies, universities, and government organizations have now dedicated entire departments or programs toward technology transfer. For instance, the U.S. Department of Veterans Affairs (VA) has operated a Health Information Technology Sharing (HITS) office and program for a number of years focused on identifying, tracking, and facilitating the transfer of knowledge and technology between government agencies and the private sector. See Chapter 4 for an expanded case study on this program.

  Think of technology transfer exchange for medical informatics as an eBay for health and medical technology resources such as software code. The best mechanism to facilitate the sharing or sale of open- or closed-software code would be an Internet exchange of some type. eBay is an example of a general-interest and goods-and-services exchange, but it is quite easy to envision an eBay for health and medical technology. Essential tactics to support technology transfer include the use of:

  ○ *Internet and New Media* The use of various technologies such as the Web, instant messaging, and Wiki to facilitate the transfer of technology or software from one organization to another.

  ○ *Technology Exchanges* Where technology is shared or exchanged using a communication medium and information technology system. These are formal sharing locations usually on the Web. Government Open Code Collaborative (GOCC), Avalanche Corporate Technology Cooperative, and Peradigm from Perot

System are three examples of actual software code exchanges that, through sharing, reduce both the cost of information technology and the inefficiencies of duplication. These cases are explored in Chapter 4.

- *Tactical Area: Open Systems* Creating a national health-information network is a complex undertaking within a market-based economy. Such a network could support broad public health, personal health, and national defense goals, as long as the system addresses critical security, fraud, and privacy issues. Open Systems play a vital and irreplaceable role because they allow the seamless communication and interoperability of diverse health-information systems. Open Systems involve hardware and/or software systems that use and/or adhere to open standards. Open Systems are not necessarily Free and Open-Source Software where the source code of the software is available at no cost. Open Systems and open architecture in particular are critical to interoperability. For a national health-information network to be viable, Open Systems and Open Standards must be used to link a diverse ecosystem of closed software and open-source software programs. Any health information or medical informatics computer program must be developed or modified to communicate using Open Standards with any other system within the context of a national health-information network. Major tactics within Open Systems are:
    - *Open Architecture* Is an information technology (IT) architecture with public specifications and a platform for interoperability.
    - *Open Computing* This is a general term used to describe an "open" philosophy in building information technology systems.
    - *Open Grid* Refers to the Open Grid Services Architecture (OGSA) developed by leading government research labs with Globus Alliance protocols to support supercomputing "grid" development and management.

Innovation as a Key Strategy

Within the Innovation component of the COSI strategies, there are three major tactical areas: Innovation Methodologies, Process Improvement, and Applied Knowledge. Within each of these are specific tactics, initiatives, tools, and technologies that support the Innovation strategy. This is

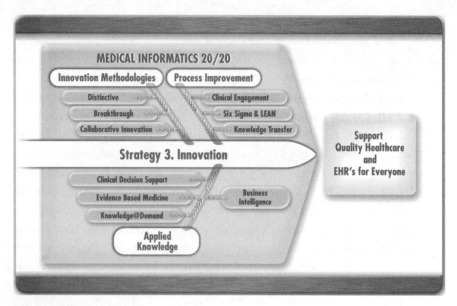

FIGURE 1-5 Tactics Supporting the Innovation Strategy

shown in Figure 1-5. A brief description of each follows, and more information is provided in *Section IV: Toolkit for Medical Informatics Excellence and Quality Improvement.*

- *Tactical Area: Innovation Methodologies* In general, Innovation is the introduction of new ideas, goods, services, and practices that are intended to be useful. As healthcare executives, managers, and clinicians, we must commit to constantly learning how to use new tactics, technologies, and tools that empower our teams to address the challenges before us. There are several primary types of innovation tactics that can be applied in the Medical Informatics 20/20 Model's Innovation Strategy.
  - *Breakthrough Innovation* The invention of a novel, unique process, idea, concept, formula, technology, or tool that promises to change the way people live and work. Breakthrough innovations are leapfrog events such as the invention of television or the invention of the electric lightbulb.
  - *Distinctive Innovation™* A term generally used to describe new but incremental inventions and the application of the innovation to solve a practical problem in a short time frame. Distinctive Innovation is the process of using a rigorous methodology, such

as Six Sigma, to improve something—a process, procedure, product, or invention—that results in a distinctly different outcome than the original. The invention of the electric lightbulb was a breakthrough innovation, but finding a long-lasting filament to make it practical was a Distinctive Innovation.

○ **Collaborative Innovation** The improvement process that involves an extended network of colleagues working together to solve problems using the Internet and collaboration software tools to support connection, communication, and creation. This is a relatively new discipline and is a powerful trend in many industries. Linux and the open-source software movement are examples of Collaborative Innovation. Collaborative Innovation is quite evident in the technology, government, and service sectors. Growth in the healthcare sector is just beginning to accelerate. Two examples of Collaborative Innovation are *IBM's Openness strategy*, which is founded on the principles of Collaborative Innovation, and *Wikipedia*, the world's largest online encyclopedia and an ongoing Collaborative Innovation effort of tens of thousands of people around the world.

Collaborative Innovation is a natural extension of the mission-driven nature of health care and motivations of healthcare professionals to help others. Chapters 12 and 13 expand on this tactic in detail.

• **Tactical Area: Process Improvement** In past years, total quality management (TQM) dominated healthcare improvement efforts. Recently, many leaders have realized that more rigorous and expansive methodologies are needed to map current processes, to assess problems using statistical and other tools, and to develop solutions targeted at the root causes that will have the biggest impact on outcomes. Consequently, Six Sigma and LEAN have become vital tactics and tools in the hands of healthcare organizations seeking to significantly improve behavior and to hold the gains once improvement has been realized.

○ **Clinical Engagement** is crucial for process improvement in healthcare settings. Clinical leaders must lead for quality care to be realized. Healthcare processes can only be transformed with the active commitment and engagement of *all* clinical care and support professionals in a healthcare organization. Quality must come first in thinking and reporting.

○ *Knowledge Transfer* is frequently being seen as the rocket fuel for the diffusion of proven practices that are developed under a quality-improvement program. A multi-year knowledge transfer program with the active support of senior management, integrated with quality-improvement efforts, solves key healthcare organization challenges for rapid diffusion and support of best-practice implementation. *Section IV, Tool Kit for Medical Informatics Excellence and Quality Improvement,* delivers extensive information about the implementation of Knowledge Transfer in healthcare organizations.

○ *Six Sigma* is a quality-management program that measures and improves the performance of an organization by identifying and correcting defects in an organization's procedures, processes, and services.

○ *LEAN* (or Lean Production), originally developed by Toyota, is a methodology that emphasizes "Right." It focuses on getting the right things to the right place at the right time the first time within a context of reducing waste, as well as optimizing processes and embracing changes that support customers.

• *Tactical Area: Applied Knowledge* The three key tactics of Applied Knowledge are:

○ *Clinical Decision Support (CDS),* which involves a variety of systems and processes to support diagnosis and treatment of medical conditions using the most current medical knowledge. From a systems perspective, Clinical Decision Support Systems (CDSS) include interactive computer/Internet information systems that directly assist physicians, researchers, and other healthcare professionals with decision-making tasks related to patient care.

○ *Evidenced-Based Medicine (EBM),* is the application of the scientific method to medical practice. EBM has become a discipline and movement in medicine internationally to bring the latest medical information into clinical practice for patients. It recognizes that many long-established medical traditions are not yet subjected to adequate scientific scrutiny. Community-Based Proven Practices (CBPP) represent practices that have been proven to improve quality within a one or more healthcare organizations, but have not necessarily gone through extensive documentation necessary to be identified as an EBM. Many healthcare organizations are engaged in sharing CBPP to support rapid–cycle improvement.

○ ***Knowledge@Point of Care and Knowledge on Demand,*** are two closely related tactics within the overall field of "open knowledge." Knowledge@Point of Care represents the delivery, through information and communication technology, of the most current evidence base and medical knowledge to assist in the diagnosis and treatment of patients. Knowledge on Demand uses technology to enable information acquisition and deliver knowledge and information at the point of need for a worker or customer. Google, Yahoo, Live.com, and the more advanced Grokker.com are Internet-based services for knowledge at the point of need.

○ ***Business Intelligence (BI)*** is a series of business processes for collecting and analyzing business information. In health care this would include both business and medical information necessary to support the ongoing positioning and success of an organization. The BI discipline also involves the technology used in these processes, and the knowledge, insight, and strategies aggregated through set processes. With the rapid increases in health and medical knowledge on both the clinical and business side of care, extensive amounts of data are being generated. Various tools such as data warehouses, data mining, enterprise application integration, neural networks, artificial intelligence, and other technologies and techniques are used to achieve BI goals and objectives. BI in the 21st century is both a science and an art as large amounts of data are assessed, analyzed, and extracted against goals to realize actionable knowledge.

Applied knowledge in all of its current and future forms is an exciting field within Medical Informatics 20/20 and promises to deliver vital and lifesaving knowledge to professionals and patients from the point of care to before the point of care as preventive care rapidly evolves into "preemptive care."

The three key strategies of the COSI Model, Collaboration, Open Solutions, and Innovation are interlinked in concept and execution within the Medical Informatics 20/20 Model. The various tactics that we have highlighted in Chapter 1 support a more efficient and effective execution of health-information technology deployment in delivery systems today and tomorrow because such tactics—Six Sigma, Facilitated Knowledge Transfer, Collaborative Learning, and the others—address the human factors necessary for medical informatics success.

Section IV: Toolkit for Medical Informatics Excellence and Quality Improvement expands on the themes established in Chapter 1. Other sections of the book expand on the many aspects of Open Solutions in Medical Informatics 20/20. Given the demands for transformation to a patient-centered model, the limited capital resources of many organizations, and the demand for quality, open strategies, tactics, tools, techniques, and technologies are indispensable for success. Chapter 11 delivers expanded descriptions of key tactics within the Collaboration and Innovation strategies of the Medical Informatics 20/20 Model.

The remaining chapters provide a road map for healthcare leaders and organizations to seize this opportunity. Section I establishes a foundation by defining the three key strategies of the COSI Model: Collaboration, Open Solutions, and Innovation. Included in these chapters are the nuts and bolts of these core strategies and their associated tactics and technologies. A high-level review of the status of COSI in business and health care, as well as case-study insights, demonstrate how COSI strategies are being successfully used to improve care. Emphasis is placed on the implementation of EHR systems and their impact on quality of care and concomitant improvements in overall performance by healthcare provider organizations.

It is time to rigorously test the existing processes of our healthcare systems, our hospitals, our ICUs, our physician offices, our nursing homes, and begin to determine how we can provide access to critical medical information in the right place, at the right time. Using Collaboration, Open Solutions, and Innovation, we can analyze health care's complex processes and lay out a plan for moving from the present state to a future state. This web of data networks—from federal and public health agencies to private physician practices—will allow clinicians to care for patients within a true culture of safety, and share clinical information easily, securely, and confidentially. Throughout the book we emphasize people and process enabled by advanced and appropriate technology. That is why we have wrapped "Collaboration" on the front end of "Open Solutions" and "Innovation" on the back end within the context of deploying medical informatics for better care.

CHAPTER 2

Open Solutions in Business—Definitions and Market Expansion

"Always and everywhere, free resources
have been crucial to innovation and creativity."

Lawrence Lessig, *The Future of Ideas: The Fate of the
Commons in a Connected World,* Random House, 2001

"Open Source Everywhere—Software is just the
beginning . . . open source is doing for mass innovation what the
assembly line did for mass production. Get ready for the
era when collaboration replaces the corporation."

Thomas Goetz, Editor, *Wired Magazine,* November 2003

"Linux is everywhere. It's in your Web server.
It's in your data center. It's in your desktop, your laptop,
and handheld. It may soon be in your car and home appliances.
It's being used by NASA to operate the Mars rover."

"What's Next for Linux," *eWeek,* February 2, 2004

Understanding Open Solutions— From "Open Standards" to "Open Collaboration"

In today's knowledge age, the term "open" refers to initiatives whose workings are exposed to the public and are capable of being modified or improved by any qualified individual or organization. "Open" is the opposite of "proprietary" or "closed." In the case of software this would mean that the source code is either open for all to access, such as the Linux operating system, or closed, such as Windows XP where only Microsoft programmers are able to change the source code. The widespread use of the term "open" in different contexts, from Free and Open Source Software (FOSS) and Open Standards to Open Systems and Open Architecture, often causes confusion. "Open Solutions" is the term used to describe a range of "Open" definitions that are becoming vital to many industries around the globe. Following are a series of definitions to aid in the understanding of the various types of "Open Solutions" used throughout this book and in global business today.

Open Solutions—Technology Definitions

1. **Open Standards**—The set of specifications developed to define interoperability between diverse systems. The standards are owned and maintained by a vendor-neutral organization rather than the original commercial developers. Many commercial vendors are asked to comply with these standards.
2. **Open Systems**—Hardware and/or software systems that use or adhere to open standards.
3. **Open Architecture**—An information technology (IT) architecture whose specifications are available to the public and that provides a platform for interoperability.
4. **Free and Open Source Software (FOSS)**—Refers to a software program in which the source code is available for anyone to use. Its original design can be modified by anyone free of any up-front license fee. Most FOSS use is governed by a variety of licensing agreements, but in all cases the source code is available for review and modification by the at-large community generally without cost. The licensing agreements usually address non-financial issues such as recognition, distribution, reuse, ability to expand the code base, etc.

5. **Open Code**—Commercial proprietary software whose source code can be obtained, viewed, and changed within the guidelines of the specific license agreement.
6. **Open Data**—A standard way for describing data formats, per the Open Data Format Initiative (ODFI) and a program to validate that a data file is ODFI compliant.
7. **Open Computing**—A general term used to describe an "open" philosophy in building information technology (IT) systems. It represents the principle that includes architecture and technology procurement policies and practices that align IT with the goals of an open environment. It permits interoperability by using published specifications for APIs, protocols, and data and file formats. The specifications must be published without restrictions to their implementation and without requiring royalties or payments (other than reasonable royalties for essential patents). In the hardware area, plug-and-play interfaces are examples of Open Computing.
8. **Open Grid**—Refers to the Open Grid Services Architecture (OGSA) developed by leading government research labs with Globus Alliance protocols to support supercomputing "grid" development and management that allows users to share computing power, databases, and other online tools securely across corporate, institutional, and geographic boundaries without sacrificing local autonomy.

Open Solutions—Business Process Definitions

1. **Open Knowledge**—An open system of knowledge transfer using the Internet and other information technologies to share best practices, emerging proven practices, knowledge, and innovations within one or more "Community of Performance" or across organizational boundaries.
2. **Open Collaboration**—Involves using open communication circles among diverse stakeholders to solve problems, accelerating commitments and maturation of open standards and facilitating a collaborative incubator for innovation and enhanced processes. Wikipedia is one example of Open Collaboration. At www.wikipedia.org, an international network of volunteer collaborators has created the world's largest online free encyclopedia with more than 2 million entries in ten languages. Another example of Open

Collaboration is the eGovernment effort, which has had multiple sponsors including the Architecture and Infrastructure Committee of the Federal CIO Council, IT R&D Coordination of the White House Office of Science and Technology Policy, the Office of Intergovernmental Solutions, the Office of Citizen Services, and the US General Services Administration (GSA).

3. **Open Innovation**—An open-minded and integrated approach to innovation that harnesses both internal and external sources of new and improved ideas, processes, and technology to synthesize products and services that meet customer needs. The innovation outcomes are shared to the larger community openly with or without the use of a type of open source license agreement.

Open Solutions—Healthcare Definitions

With Open Solutions just emerging in health and medical care, the authors have taken a step forward in defining two key terms:

1. **Open Health**—A formal or informal digitally enabled network of professionals, people and patients who are collaborating to support and improve patient health and wellness. There are numerous initiatives designed to support the use of public domain or Free and Open Source Software in the form of personal health records and other applications. Online patient support networks are one example of the sharing that symbolizes the concept of Open Health. Open Health is also closely aligned with the concept of better public health through collaboration, except that Open Health leverages digital, Internet, and other technology tools to support better health care.

2. **Open Medical**—Focuses on Open Solutions on the business and clinical side of health care where multiple formal and informal networks are collaborating throughout the healthcare industry to research, develop, promote, and facilitate Open Solutions. Many of the efforts of these networks are focused on interoperability, including Open Standards for clinical data exchange in the support of Regional Health Information Organization development, and the overall National Health Information Network. These efforts are also focused on the evolution and promotion of free and open

source and public domain software to help support quality care within a lower cost paradigm.

Based on the many ways "open" is being used, it is clear that the term now goes beyond simply sharing "Free and Open Source Software" within the specification of the open source software license agreements. It is also being applied to many other business domains such as:

a. Medical informatics
b. Personal health
c. Clinical and biomedical research
d. Financial and operations
e. Clinical quality of care
f. Patient safety
g. Training material
h. Policy and regulations
i. Clinical and business processes

The above list of the "open" variants is a foundation for effective communication about next-generation medical informatics and health information technologies necessary to create affordable, quality healthcare services; support interoperability; and address disaster preparedness, patient safety, and other healthcare concerns at a national and global level.

Section II, Collaborating for Quality with Open Solutions, and Section III, Deploying Medical Informatics Open Solutions, will address many of the eight Open Solutions' technology definitions, while Section IV, Toolkit for Medical Informatics Excellence, will examine how collaboration, innovation, and value management can support a better healthcare system in the United States and the world.

Benefits of Open Solutions for Health Care

There are distinct benefits of Open Solutions across the technology, business process, and healthcare arenas. These include:

- ***Open Solutions in the form of Open Standards*** will be essential to support interoperability and clinical data exchange to support EHRs for all Americans.

- ***Open Solutions in the form of Free and Open Source Software (FOSS)*** will play a critical role in improving the quality of software and reducing the cost of health information technology.
- ***Open Solutions in the form of Open Architecture*** will be vital to interconnecting open and closed information technology systems for integrated and lower-cost operations that can support clinical quality, public health, and national defense.
- ***Open Solutions in the form of Open Knowledge, Open Innovation, and Open Collaboration*** will be imperative for organizations to share, reuse, and improve tacit resources and explicit experiences so that within and across organizations people can save time and money by not "reinventing the wheel."
- ***Open Health and Open Medical*** will serve as the nexus for collaboration standards, software code, and business-process knowledge that can improve healthcare business and clinical processes.

There are many dimensions to Open Solutions. The continued development and expansion of all types of "open" will stimulate innovation and competition to improve the quality of care through health information technology and the supporting renovation in the business and clinical processes that must accompany their application. At the core of Open Solutions is Free and Open Source Software, which is demonstrating its benefits through rapid growth in many sectors of the world economy.

A Focus on Free and Open Source Software (FOSS)

One rapidly growing area in the overall information technology world is Free and Open Source Software (FOSS), which is best symbolized by Linux, the FOSS operating system that delivers a direct competitive threat to Microsoft's near-monopoly in the operating system market. Linux is only one of many FOSS initiatives under development or in operation. In 2006, there were more than 129,107 registered FOSS projects with more than 1.3 million registered users at SourceForge.net, a worldwide repository and support service for FOSS. This is a 40% increase in the number of projects over early 2004.

Free and Open Source Software (FOSS) is software available to the public in source code form and usually on a no-cost license basis. FOSS can be licensed under one of 50 or more approved FOSS licensing arrangements that guide the use, modification, or redistribution of the software. Open Source Initiative (www.opensource.org) lists the key attributes of many licensed FOSS arrangements including: free distribution, access to source code, ability to modify code, no discrimination against any users or fields of endeavor, must not be specific to a product, must not restrict other software, and must be technology neutral. Linux is just one example of the many industrial-strength FOSS products available in the marketplace. Within its first year of release, the Firefox browser (from the Mozilla Foundation) reached more than 100 million downloads; this was only five months after achieving 50 million downloads. By 2006, Firefox had achieved nearly a 13% market share of the Internet browser market. Thousands of unpaid software developers and contributors worldwide donated hundreds of thousands of work hours creating, improving, and supporting this acclaimed FOSS product.

While Free and Open Source Software (FOSS) is often called "free software," it may or may not include a charge for packaging, service, support, documentation, training, and so on. It is *free* in as much as the user has the rights to freely use the software, make changes to it, and distribute it. There is generally no up-front license fee and there is no ongoing maintenance fee. Like any other software, FOSS is released under a variety of licenses. Much of Free and Open Source Software is released under the General Public License (GPL), as is the Linux operating system. Although GPL does not restrict the software's use, it does contain restrictions intended to preserve its open-source status: notices of authorship (e.g., it is usually copyrighted), adherence to defined developmental control, and a requirement that additions made to the code are shared with the FOSS community. How that software is distributed and enhanced over time by a Web-based community of developers, not the issue of ownership, is what gives the software its FOSS status. The Free Software Foundation (http://www.fsf.org/) provided Figure 2-1, which illustrates types of software and their relationships. There are more than 50 types of FOSS licenses. All of the licenses result in the code being copyrighted and the source code being available to users, but the various terms related to use, recognition, sharing back code additions, and so on will vary among types of FOSS licenses.

FOSS is similar to Public Domain Software, with three key differences: 1) Public Domain Software is free of charge, without restrictions (e.g., release of VistA under the Freedom of Information Act); 2) Public

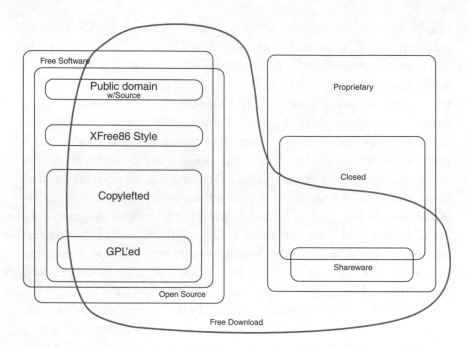

FIGURE 2-1 Universe of Free and Open Source Software Types
Source: Diagram by Chao-Kuei from Free Software Foundation Web site
http://www.fsf.org/licensing/essays/categories.html

Domain Software is not copyrighted; and 3) Public Domain Software may not always come with source code.

A Market Overview of Free and Open Source Software (FOSS)

The Free and Open Source Software (FOSS) market is growing rapidly across all domains of knowledge and information technology in the private as well as public sectors. Efforts in both sectors relate not only to the use of Open Source solutions but also the development of Open Source solutions. Section I of this book highlights developments in the private and public sectors focusing on Open Solutions and FOSS that are applicable in particular to health care.

The Free and Open Source Software (FOSS) movement began many years ago, and it is continuing to accelerate toward both acceptance and viability. In many cases, the FOSS style of software programming can be viewed as a "community barn-raising activity" where neighbors came together to put up a new barn as a nonpaid group activity in a short period of time. The end product was a high-quality barn constructed in a few days as opposed to one built by a family working alone for months. Eric Raymond, in his groundbreaking book *Cathedral and Bazaar—Musings on Linux and Open Source by an Accidental Revolutionary*" (http://www.catb.org/~esr/writings/cathedral-bazaar/), profiles the Open Source movement as the community of programmers who come together voluntarily and without pay to create useful software programs such as Linux or Firefox using a network or a "Bazaar" approach; this approach is the opposite of the traditional top-down, closed, proprietary, work-for-hire programming method, which Raymond refers to as a "Cathedral." The "Bazaar" phenomenon is spreading across all facets of information technology. FOSS products range from operating system upgrades, desktop clients, JAVA-based development kits, and application servers, to an impressive number of applications in virtually every industry, including health care and finance.

In the last several years, the growth in FOSS has accelerated significantly. Key contributing factors for this growth are growing awareness, increased software functionality, increasing adoption, and the ability of certain FOSS applications to operate at the enterprise level, such as Apache Web service and the Linux operating system. The increased functionality has resulted from high-profile alliances and coalitions. The success of Linux and its evolution into a viable, cost-effective, enterprise-ready, secure, and scalable solution are due in part to the contribution of code by the National Security Agency's version of Linux, called Secure Linux (SELinux), which was released in 2000.

Today, many popular FOSS products are available in addition to the Internet backbone products based in FOSS (e.g., TCP/IP, HTTP, Send-Mail, and BIND). They include:

- *Linux Operating System*—It is becoming a mainstream operating system for file and print servers, Web servers, embedded applications (e.g., point of sale terminals and set-top boxes), and scientific applications, and it is moving rapidly into the enterprise application space with strong support from vendors such as HP, Oracle, SAP, and IBM.
- *Apache Web Server*—As of August 2006, it powered nearly 63% of all Web servers on the Internet, more than all other Web servers combined, including Microsoft. Frequently, the Linux operating system is used in conjunction with Apache Web server to power Internet Web sites around the world.

- *Firefox Web Browser*—In its first year of release, consumers downloaded it more than 100 million times.
- *Perl Language*—It is the basis for many Web servers' dynamic content and is widely used for scripting and automation.
- *BSD/UNIX*—Most commercial versions of the UNIX operating system either are based directly on BSD source code or borrowed heavily from its design.
- *OpenOffice*—A comprehensive suite of desktop office applications that provide very similar capabilities as Microsoft Office, it offers the ability to read and modify nearly any MS Office document. OpenOffice runs effectively and natively on Linux and MS Windows and is beginning to be used widely around the world. There have been over 61 million downloads and it's estimated that OpenOffice and it's low cost sister software suite StarOffice have secured 14% of the large enterprise market.
- *My SQL*—It is a FOSS database that offers the full functionality of similar databases such as Microsoft SQL.

During the last several years, there have also been some countervailing forces such as the SCO lawsuit, which claims that part of the Linux code infringes on proprietary, patented lines that the company owned from current UNIX licenses. SCO has not revealed what the exact lines of code are, and many industry experts feel that SCO is just seeking to bully the industry. In the meantime, several industry leaders such as IBM and Red Hat are aggressively contesting the suit and indemnifying any clients that choose the Linux operating system on IBM hardware.

Nevertheless, the international software community has been heavily engaged in a virtual "barn raising" for Free and Open Source Software as it has expanded into all types of software. In September 2006, Source Forge.net, the world's largest Free and Open Source Software development Web site, that delivers a collaborative software development platform, has more than 129,000 hosted projects with over 1.3 million registered users. The number of hosted projects has grown from 36,000 in early 2003 to over 129,000 today. As the number of FOSS projects grows, so do the numbers of corporate enterprises and governments that use FOSS solutions to lower total technology ownership costs, access source code, gain flexibility, take control of modifications, and obtain better security capabilities.

One of the driving forces in the growth in diversity and size of the FOSS community is the proliferation of programmers outside of software companies. Scores of FOSS programmers use software at businesses such as Amazon and Bank of America, as well as federal, state, and local agencies. These programmers develop software to support their operations with solutions offering the lowest ownership cost, the most security, the most flexibility, and source code that is available for easy adaptation.

Key Growth Highlights of Free and Open Source Software (FOSS)

The market growth of FOSS is accelerating across many software sectors including: Internet, operating systems, databases, infrastructure, applications, and desktop. Also, there is significant growth in the quality and number of offerings for "fee" and "free" software support and service. FOSS growth has been seen in all areas of the product life cycle: product development based on FOSS, use of FOSS in daily operations, and service and support for FOSS-based products.

1. **Linux operating system** has seen rapid sales growth and market acceptance. Linux has reached a breakout point in enterprise, according to research firm IDC. Sales of Linux servers jumped 63% in the fourth quarter of 2003 compared to the previous year's fourth quarter, according to IDC. This report is echoed by Gartner's year-end server sales report that measured a 90% increase in the Linux market in 2004.[1] According to TheStreet.com, these results indicate that half of all server shipments from major vendors will eventually come with Linux preloaded.[2] These reports also indicate that the profit margin for these Linux servers is actually increasing. Hewlett Packard reported in January that its Linux-related revenue exceeded $2.5 billion in 2003. IDC projects that the worldwide volume of Linux server shipments is going to increase from around 800,000 in 2003 to 2.5 million in 2007. This data does not include all installations of Linux in preexisting hardware or no-name brand servers. It is clear from all these reports that Linux has reached the mainstream in enterprise and that its adoption will continue to increase. In the

---

[1]James Maguire, *Report: Linux Servers Seeing Upsurge*, February 27, 2004.
[2]Bill Snyder, TheStreet.com, Linux Juggernaut Rolls On, March 30, 2004.

May 2004 issue of *Time* magazine, Gartner predicted that Linux will run 21% of desktops by 2008, taking its market share directly from Microsoft. At the end of 2004, IDC said that Linux server shipments will be 25.7% of worldwide server shipments in 2008, up from 15.6% of worldwide server shipments in 2003. The Open Source Development Labs (www.osdl.org) shown in Figure 2-2 is a great place to start in the exploration of the Linux world.

2. **Apache Web Server** is a FOSS solution that has been the number-one Web server in the world since 1996. In the last several years, Apache market share has increased from 67% in February 2004 to more than 70% by August 2005 and it dropped slightly to 63% by August 2006. In the same period, the number of servers increased from approximately 8 million to 22 million.

3. **OpenOffice** (and StarOffice, a very low–cost version packaged and supported by Sun) is a FOSS suite of business productivity applications. There is mounting evidence that FOSS is moving from the server side of the IT world to the desktop. This movement is accelerating faster outside the United States. The support for FOSS on the desktop is growing. StarOffice (www.staroffice. com) is similar to Microsoft Office. It includes word processing, spreadsheet, and presentation software, as well as a drawing tool

FIGURE 2-2 Open Source Development Labs Home Page
Source: www.osdl.org

and a database. It also includes accurate import filters for other file formats such as Office and WordPerfect. StarOffice is a very low-cost suite of business applications, priced at $52 after rebate versus $374 to $449 (U.S.) for Microsoft Office Professional Edition. StarOffice is based on a FOSS version of OpenOffice (www. OpenOffice.org) and is distributed by Sun Microsystems with limited service and support features. In April 2004, it was reported that Wal-Mart Stores, the world's largest retailer, had begun selling Microtel PCs with Sun's version of the Linux operating system and StarOffice. OpenOffice runs stably and natively on both Linux and MS Windows systems. eWeeks Labs conducted an independent assessment of StarOffice 8 in September 2005 and concluded that "we were pleased with the suite's word processing, spreadsheet, presentation, and database functions. In addition, we experienced generally good results opening and creating Microsoft Office formatted documents with StarOffice . . ." By the end of 2005, Star-Office had been downloaded more than 52 million times.

4. **Firefox Web Browser** is part of the Mozilla project's mission (www.mozilla.org) to preserve choice and innovation on the Internet. The Mozilla Foundation is the facilitator, developer, and provider of the award-winning Firefox Web browser and Thunderbird e-mail software. Mozilla's Firefox is an advanced browser that simplifies and speeds up the browsing experience, and Thunderbird is a stand–alone e-mail and newsgroup application that can be used as a companion to Mozilla's Firefox or by itself. Lightweight, fast, extensible, and featuring sophisticated junk mail filters, Thunderbird sets a new standard for e-mail software. Within a year of release, there were 100 million downloads worldwide. The quality of Mozilla software and the strength of the network of developers indicate that the Open Solutions model of software development can be very cost effective, while creating a compelling product—available for no charge—that rivals and bests comparative closed software Web products.

Growing Corporate Support for FOSS

Major international corporations are supporting the development of Open Solutions, especially Free and Open Source Software (FOSS).

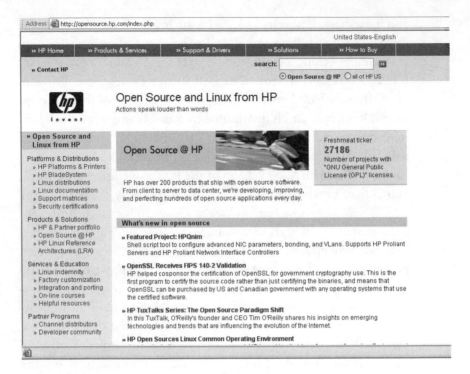

FIGURE 2-3 HP Open Source Web Service
Source: http://opensource.hp.com/index.php

- **Hewlett Packard (HP):** *Sponsors new FOSS projects every week.*
  Martin Fink, vice president of Linux efforts at HP, said in *Linux Insider* (March 19, 2004) that HP is initiating "two to three new open source application development projects per week. That's 100 to 150 [projects] per year, and it's accelerating." He also stated that by 2005, HP expects there will be "17 million users of Linux server software, up from 10 million in 2003." HP, one of the biggest backers of the Linux operating system, announced on June 1, 2004, that it would increase its backing of open source software by being the first large technology company to certify and support programs made by MySQL, AB, and JBoss, Inc. This is viewed as a competitive strike against IBM, which sells its own stack of proprietary middleware software. As of September 2006, HP had over 200 products that ship with open source software.
- **IBM:** *Moves to open source on all desktops, provides $1 billion-plus in FOSS support, and focuses on service and support of FOSS.*

- *Fortune*, in September 2005, published an article titled "IBM Shares Its Secrets" profiling the strategy of CEO Sam Palmisano, a strategy he called "openness," which is focused on a major new "spur to innovation itself." In this approach, IBM shares its secrets, patents, software code, and so on in an effort to increase the overall market and to position its consulting services for collaborating with customers to invent new technologies and improved business processes. In the software field, IBM has been a leading supporter of Linux and other open-source technology. The result has been that all IBM high-growth applications are built on open-source foundations.

- IBM support of Linux and open-source software is very difficult to estimate because it is so intertwined with the company's entire business strategy. In the first few years of the 21st century, it was estimated that FOSS received more than $1 billion in support from IBM, focused on server-side solutions, with a migration over time to desktop solutions. IBM is not only supporting the development of FOSS products, but is also a significant user of FOSS applications. It is estimated that IBM employs more than 600 programmers who support Linux, and the end result for IBM is a world-class operating system at far lower cost based on the open-source model. IBM gets a big bang for its buck, and the company

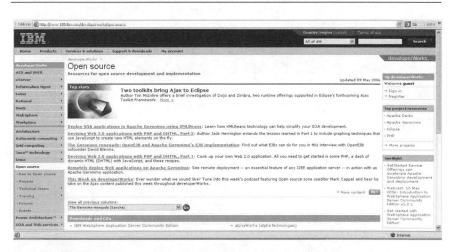

FIGURE 2-4 IBM Open Source Resource Center on the Web
Source: http://www-128.ibm.com/developerworks/opensource

avoids estimated costs in excess of $500 million per year if it were to build and maintain a closed software operating system.

○ A memo from IBM CIO Bob Greenberg stated, ". . . our chairman has challenged the IT organization, and indeed all of IBM, to move to a Linux-based desktop before the end of 2005. This means replacing productivity, Web access, and viewing tools with open standards based equivalents." IBM's support is so strong that significant parts of the organization are now shifting to a service/support function for FOSS as a source of revenue growth.

○ At a conference in 2004, Douglas Heintzman, director of technical strategy for IBM Software Group, said that from IBM's perspective, Open Source offers many benefits: It can drive standards, provide cost-effective access to base components, be a mechanism to allow companies to cooperate in development of common infrastructure technology as a platform for innovation, be a mechanism to drive multi-vendor consistency to enhance value to customers, provide a common and flexible base to support multiple hardware platforms, and drive a critical mass of software development.

○ Eclipse Foundation (www.elipse.org) is an open-source community that focuses on supporting development and applications platforms for building software. IBM has been a key supporter of this effort. Heintzman said that this alliance, which has been supported by IBM with the donation of $40 million worth of soft-

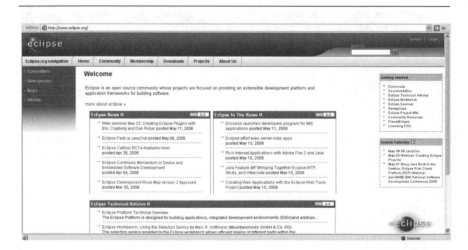

FIGURE 2-5 Eclipse.org Web site
Source: www.eclipse.org

ware, has generated more innovations than could ever be imagined. He elaborated that it was IBM's view that "pragmatic open standards make sound public policy" and that it is not a good idea to "fight the market." He said, "In the past, IBM fought the decline of the mainframe, and it almost led to our demise. Now IBM happily embraces and evolves their whose or what business model." He suggested that the key elements of success—Open Source, Internet technology, and the rapid pace of eBusiness needs—were interrelated and integral to the future of IBM. He said, "Open source and open standards played a key role in the emergence of the Internet and the first-generation e-businesses, and they will continue playing an increasingly important role as we continue evolving the next generation of e-businesses."

○ In a white paper on Open Computing, Heintzman indicated that businesses and governments are embracing open computing, open standards, and some open-source projects because of the many benefits offered by them. IBM has made the strategic decision to embrace these concepts and is aligning its hardware, software, and business services to support its customers on the journey toward "on-demand" information technology services.

- ***Scalability and growth using FOSS.*** Amazon.com is one of the largest users of FOSS. In 1999, it was estimated that 70% of all of the software used at Amazon.com was Open Source; an even larger percentage at Yahoo.com was Open Source. In 2001, Amazon migrated all of its servers to Linux. An article in News.com reported that Amazon.com was able to cut $17 million in technology expenses in a single quarter and decreased technology costs as a portion of net sales by 20%, largely due to the switch to Linux. Today, Amazon continues to be a significant user of FOSS solutions to support its Web site operations. In addition to being able to build and operate its e-commerce platform less expensively and better than with closed software products, Amazon has also been collaborating with customers. Amazon has built a network of millions of contributors—from the people who rate books and share their buying preferences to those who buy books—that helps build a common knowledge base, which assists all shoppers. The information technology framework supports this extensive customer sharing that enhances the browsing and buying experience for all Amazon customers.

FOSS Service and Support Are
Widely Available for "Free" and for a "Fee"

The FOSS support and service environment is increasingly filling with many robust offerings for private enterprises, public organizations, and government agencies. Today, FOSS has the benefit of substantial support from two major support networks:

- *Paid Support*—Major IT organizations (IBM, HP, Oracle, Perot Systems, Red Hat, Novell, and others) are delivering a wide array of service/support programs for FOSS under various financial arrangements. In addition to providing customer support programs, these organizations are making significant financial and time commitments to the growth of the FOSS support infrastructure. Also, tens of thousands of their employed programmers and developers are active contributors to the free community support networks built around FOSS initiatives.
- *Free Community Support*—Developers and programmers participate in an international network to develop and expand FOSS without direct compensation. SourceForge.net is one central place where the diversity of FOSS can be evaluated.

Free and Open Source Software (FOSS) in the
Federal Government: Expanding Development and Use
Across Many Software Classes by Numerous Federal Agencies

Numerous government agencies have been involved in Free and Open Source Software on many different fronts: they have facilitated and supported the development of FOSS with the private sector; they have developed FOSS solutions to meet internal needs; they have been users of FOSS; and in some cases, they have established open standards and policies.

Across a large number of federal agencies, CIOs and their teams are using and benefiting from Free and Open Source Software such as the Linux operating system, the Apache Web server, JBoss application server, open-source content management and e-learning systems, the Mozilla Firefox browser, and MySQL / PostgreSQL (open-source relational databases that use standard Structured Query Language). A significant number of government agencies have authored studies, white papers, and surveys over the last several years to support policy making and to guide deployment of FOSS within the federal IT infrastructure. Figure 2-6, *Federal Government Open*

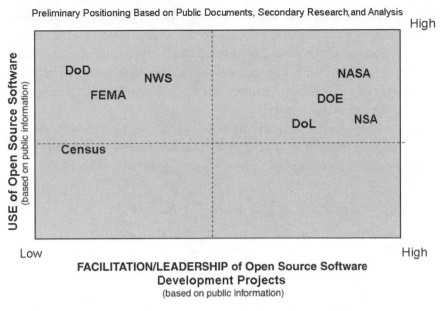

Preliminary Positioning Based on Public Documents, Secondary Research, and Analysis

FIGURE 2-6 U.S. Government Agencies' Open Source Software:
Use & Facilitation

Source Software Use and Facilitation, plots on a grid several government
agencies' use of FOSS compared with the facilitation/leadership in the
development of FOSS projects with the private sector. The growing presence of FOSS is exemplified in the federal government by the following
examples, which illustrate both the use and leadership in development of
FOSS applications by U.S. government agencies.

U.S. Department of Defense (DoD)—FOSS Policies and Roadmap

A January 2003 study by Mitre on the use of FOSS in the DoD highlighted many key aspects: 1) The DoD has 115 different FOSS applications and 251 instances of use; 2) FOSS software performed critical
functions in four areas: infrastructure support, software development,
security, and research; 3) the removal or banning of FOSS would
adversely affect certain types of infrastructure components (e.g.,
OpenBSD) that support network security; 4) the removal would hinder
the demonstrated ability of FOSS applications that support architecture
diversity and that had the capability to be updated rapidly in response to

new types of cyber attack; and 5) banning FOSS would have immediate, broad, and strongly negative impacts on the ability of many sensitive and security-focused DoD groups to defend against cyber attacks. The study also reported that FOSS applications tend to be much lower in cost than the proprietary equivalents, yet they often provide high levels of functionality with good user acceptance.

The Mitre DoD report recommendations were to "develop generic FOSS policies that promote the broader, more effective use of FOSS and encourage use of commercial products that work well with FOSS. The follow-up actions were to:

- Create a "Generally Recognized As Safe" FOSS list.
- Develop generic infrastructure, development, security, and research policies.
- Encourage the use of FOSS to promote product diversity.

The Mitre report led to the 2003 DoD policy memorandum stating that Open Source Software within the DoD is accepted as long as it complies with the same policies for commercial and government off-the-shelf software and meets certain security standards, according to a memo outlining the policy by John Stenbit, Assistant Secretary of Defense and CIO. Although, from the DoD's perspective, the policy statement is neither endorsement of FOSS nor a banning (which is the position that Microsoft aggressively lobbied for) of commercial products, the policy memo is a significant milestone for a government agency's relationship to FOSS. In general, the market has viewed this as a positive development, and many FOSS products have been certified under the DoD and/or government policies. Red Hat's Linux Advanced Server, for example, has the Defense Information System Agency's Common Operating Environment certification, while the SuSE Linux Enterprise Server 8 has the Common Criteria Security certification, required by most federal agencies. In late 2006 a new Department of Defense study, 'Open Technology Road Map' advised

Web–based Resources:
- Use of Free and Open Source Software in the U.S. Department of Defense—Mitre Report (http://www.egovos.org/rawmedia_repository/ 588347ad_c97c_48b9_a63d_821cb0e8422d?/document.pdf)

- Open Source Software in the Department of Defense Memorandum—DoD CIO John Stenbit's policy memo (http://www.egovos.org/rawmedia_repository/822a91d2_fc51_4e6e_8120_1c2d4d88fa06?/document.pdf)
- Presentation Summary of the Mitre Report for DoD (http://gopher.info.usaid.gov/regions/europe_eurasia/cop/free_and_open_source_slideshow.pdf)
- Open Technology Road Map (http://www.acq.osd.mil/actd/articles/OTDRoadmapFinal.pdf)

the DoD to integrate comprehensive open source strategy into procurement and development policies. It advocated the adoption of open technologies, support for open standards, and provided guidance on licensing and governance while advising against proprietary vendor lock-in.

The number of FOSS applications by the DoD continues to grow. Prior to the January 2003 Mitre study, a NASA document on FOSS had

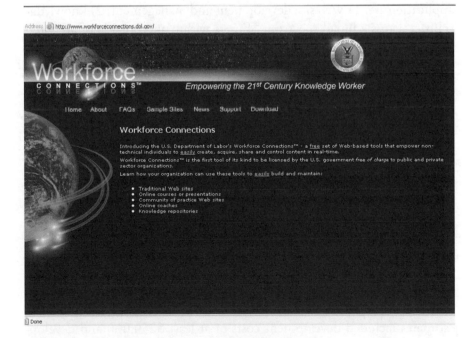

FIGURE 2-7 Workforce Connections Open Source Software Web Site
Source: www.workforceconnections.dol.gov/

identified 110 different DoD applications of FOSS licenses, and a Mitre report included 115.

U.S. Department of Labor (DoL)—
Develops and Releases FOSS Program

Workforce Connections™ is the first software tool of its kind to be trade-marked and licensed by a U.S. government agency free of charge to public and private sector organizations (under a general public license).

The DoL describes Workforce Connections as "a flexible environment that enables personnel without programming expertise to acquire, share, and document knowledge. This knowledge transfer can be presented as a traditional Web site, as an online self-paced course or presentation, or as a community of practice/interest Web site. Workforce Connections is used to administer Web site content using the Internet or Intranets." Examples, links, and agencies using the system are available online at Workforce Connections (http://workforceconnections.dol.gov/).

The primary uses for the Workforce Connections FOSS software application are: 1) Web site development and management; 2) knowledge transfer across a broad spectrum of users within and outside of an enterprise; 3) data-rich reference repository; and 4) the delivery of online courses, presentations, and coaching. It can also deliver a robust series of Web-based collaboration tools to support a very large or a small community of practice.

Workforce Connections addresses common content management needs with the least amount of effort. It is designed so that non-technical users can create and maintain their own content in easy-to-use templates and post or change content online. The toolkit compresses the time and effort necessary to publish content and resources to an Internet Web site or intranet.

OSHA recently used Workforce Connections to develop an important online course for a wide audience. OSHA wanted to develop a 6-to-8-hour online course on workplace violence for many different audiences from OSHA's Workplace Violence Group. The key requirement was that the course conform to Section 508 and SCORM version 1.2. The project estimates included development costs of at least $250,000 and development time of 10 months. However, using Workforce Connections, the course was completed in two and half months at less than $5,000 per instructional hour using internal SMEs, versus $30,000 to $40,000 per instructional hour using an outside contractor.

The following Figure 2-8 is a summary of cycle time and cost savings achieved using Workforce Connections.

Web services built by using Workforce Connections have won three Axiem Awards (an international recognition of excellence for state-of-the-art interactive and media applications). The Workplace Violence Course for OSHA won an Axiem Award for Excellence in Government Programs; and On-Line Coach Technology won two Axiem Awards for Absolute Excellence: Excellence in Technical Achievement and Excellence in Government Programs.

U.S. Department of Homeland Security (DHS)—FOSS Supports Disaster Preparedness

At the March 4, 2004, Open Source in Government Conference held at George Washington University, Barry West, CIO of FEMA, gave a presentation about the use of FOSS in his agency. He stated, "FOSS is a huge piece of our country's disaster preparedness infrastructure within the Department of Homeland Security and National Weather Services." He has advocated the use of Open Source since the early 1990s, while he was the CIO of the National Weather Service, where it became fairly apparent

Training Development Approach	Development Time	Costs per hour	Ongoing Maintenance
Web-based Online Training Development (not SCORM or Section 508 compliant)	9 to 12 months	$30 to $40 K per hour	Requested by SME, performed by contractor
Workforce Connections Web Publishing tool	2½ months	Less than $5K per hour	Performed by SME
Savings using Workforce Connections versus traditional Web development approach	6 to 9 months savings	$25K to $35K per hour	$100/hr contractor maintenance

FIGURE 2-8 Cost Savings of Workforce Connection Web Publishing Tool

to him that FOSS was "better, cheaper, and faster." West said that FOSS encourages:

- Software re-use.
- Cooperation among programmers.
- Better code quality and security.
- Appropriate software review and testing.
- Earlier discovery of software bugs.
- Exposure of poor design.
- Reduction in acquisition costs.
- Seamless integration.

West closed his presentation with a reference to a CIO magazine that stated, "The bottom line is, those CIOs not using Open Source now *will be* in the next 12 to 24 months."

At FEMA, FOSS was chosen as the best-of-breed software framework because: 1) It provided a secure architectural framework, 2) offered improved product performance and scalability, 3) encouraged communications among developers, 4) offered reusable code, and 5) shortened development time. At FEMA, he had to implement mission critical systems, provide a best-of-breed software framework, and eliminate disparate and stove-piped systems development. To address these and other issues, he implemented a FOSS environment by:

- Providing a flexible control layer through the Apache framework, which supports all Intranet and Internet activity.
- Delivering scalability via Linux to be able to address larger disaster preparedness requirements.
- Adhering to Open Standards such as XML, Soap, UDDI, Apache Web services engine, J2EE, and so on.

He stated that factors for his successful use of FOSS were near universal adaptability and acceptance, common architecture framework, cohesiveness, uniformity, lower cost, technology availability, and the availability of many FOSS support vendors. He added that the FOSS "user groups are incredible—with quick responses that are sometimes more accurate than under a vendor support call." West also said, "Microsoft is OK with desktop, but everywhere else, Linux is in use."

Within FEMA some of the current uses of FOSS include:

- Disasterhelp.gov and Ready.gov.
- Disaster Management Interoperability Services (DMIS).

- National Emergency Management Information System (NEMIS) for incident activity management, disaster declaration management, and online disaster victim request.

National Security Agency (NSA)—Collaborates on Selinux

In the late 1990s, the National Security Agency (NSA) undertook a project designed to provide other federal agencies with a highly secure operating system environment. The decision was made early on to use Linux as the platform for this secure system, and they began the project that eventually became Security Enhanced Linux, or SELinux (http://www.nsa.gov/selinux/). It was developed as a research prototype to address persistent problems with mainstream operating systems where discretionary access controls could not provide appropriate security. SELinux was built based on 12 years of the NSA's operating system security research and the application of the NSA's Flask security architecture. The key missing feature from the Linux OS was mandatory access control (MAC) that allowed administratively set security policy to control all processes and objects, as well as make decisions based on all security-relevant information. SELinux addressed the above issues, plus offered strong separation of security domains and separate databases based on confidentiality, integrity, and purpose.

SELinux limits damage from virus, worm, and Trojan horse infection; inhibits virus propagation; eliminates most privilege elevation attacks; and constrains damage from undiscovered holes. The source code for SELinux was publicly released in 2000 to the FOSS community and is now part of the standard 2.6 Linux kernel as one of the key elements of the security module. According to Grant Wagner, technical director for NSA's Secure Systems Research Office, SELinux "delivered direct user benefit and met real security needs. In addition, the growing international user/developer community has made a real contribution back to the NSA. It has been a powerful technology transfer tool" for the NSA (Open Source and Government Conference 2004, March 16, 2004).

National Weather Service—FOSS
Improves Performance and Saves Money and Lives

The Advanced Weather Interactive Processing System (AWIPS), used by forecasters throughout the country to issue weather warnings, advisories, alerts, and forecasts, switched to Linux from a proprietary UNIX-based

HP/UX platform. Since the switch, AWIPS costs have decreased by as much as 75% because Linux requires lower and nonproprietary hardware and needs less maintenance. While director of the National Weather Service, Barry West directed the switch to FOSS Linux on an Intel platform. At the March 2004 conference he stated, "Our [National Weather Service] advanced lead time increased significantly for getting warnings out to the public, and this saves money and lives." West said Open Source has been invaluable in its ability to expand rapidly to cover increased network demand during an emergency.

He also mentioned that the weather service documented a cost benefit ratio of 3 to 1 (i.e., benefits were three times the cost) by going to Linux, and that during Hurricane Isabelle the service handled a record 330 million Web hits using Linux-based Web servers. "Aside from increased efficiency," West said, "Linux works with many different types of hardware environments. We can run the same applications on a supercomputer and take it down to the workstation without recompiling. You cannot do that with other operating systems." Both the www.weather.gov Web site and the National Oceanic and Atmospheric Administration Web site run on FOSS platforms using Linux, Apache, PHP, and other FOSS solutions.

U.S. Census Bureau—Improves Citizen Services Through FOSS

The Census Bureau has not only realized cost savings and operational efficiency, but it has also found FOSS to be easier to use because it is stable, portable, and easily upgradeable. The Census Bureau's in-house-developed systems that assist Americans in obtaining information are based on a series of FOSS tools, including the LAMP suite of Open Source Tools (Linux, Apache, MySQL, Perl, PHP, and Python programming languages).

According to Lisa Wolfisch Nyman from the Census Bureau, FOSS saves tax dollars at her agency with the use of a combination of Linux, Unix, and SGI machines—and even some Windows boxes. She described some operational benefits gained with these FOSS systems, including avoiding procurement process delays as well as efficiency in purchase-order processing, contract processing, and management. She also said that accessing service and support has not been a problem (Newsforge Census Bureau: "Open Source Makes Sense to Deliver Stats on the Web," March

20, 2002; "Managing Technology, More Agencies Pick Free/Open Source Software," *Government Executive Magazine,* December 15, 2003).

National Aeronautics and Space Agency (NASA)—Leads Numerous FOSS Projects

There are significant numbers of successful open source projects at NASA that have received widespread publicity. In April 2003, NASA released a FOSS study, "Developing an Open Source Option for NASA Software,"

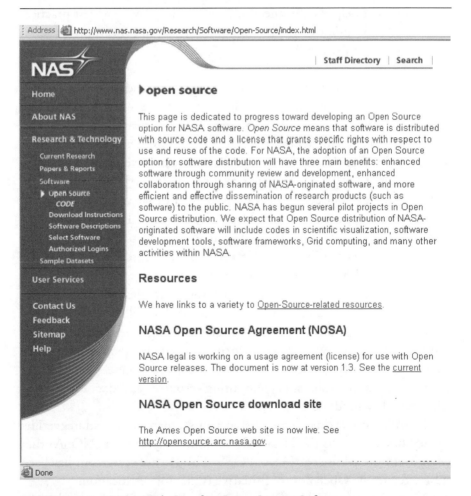

FIGURE 2-9 NASA Web Site for Open Source Software
Source: http://www.nas.nasa.gov/Research/Software/Open-Source/index.html

written by Patrick J. Moran (NASA Ames Research Center, M/S T27A-2, NASA Advanced Supercomputing—Technical Report NAS-03-009). The report identified three important benefits of FOSS for NASA:

1. *Improved software development,* because access to software results in faster evolution of the software and faster resolution of problems
2. *Enhanced collaboration,* in particular across organizational boundaries, supporting NASA's mission to work with other agencies, academia, and industry
3. *More efficient and effective dissemination*—FOSS coupled with Internet helps NASA meet its directive to provide widest practical and appropriate dissemination of information concerning its activities and their results

The April 2003 report concluded with a recommendation that "NASA develop an Open Source option for software developed within the agency" for some, but not all, NASA-developed software. The report also detailed the rationale behind the author's recommendations, reviewed leading FOSS licenses, addressed a series of issues related to Open Source distribution of NASA software, and outlined a series of next steps.

Use of Open Source has also expanded in other areas. The Globus Toolkit is used as a basis for the NASA Information Power Grid (IPG). The Globus project is one of the 11 Open Source collaborations sponsored by the Department of Energy (DOE) that are described later in the DOE highlight. The IPG joins supercomputers and storage devices owned by diverse participating organizations into a single, seamless computing environment. According to the Globus Web site, "IPG will help NASA scientists collaborate to solve important problems facing the world in the 21st century. Just as the Web makes information anywhere available everywhere, the IPG will someday give researchers and engineers around the country access to distant supercomputing resources and data repositories whenever they need them."

NASA is now taking the next step in its Open Source strategy: The agency has developed the NASA Open Source Agreement (NOSA) that will govern the release of NASA's FOSS. This license agreement has been submitted to the Open Source Initiative (OSI) for certification.

One of the primary objectives of the NOSA license is to ensure that the software is available to the community and that any improvements made to the software are contributed back to the community, including the NASA project team that manages the software.

NASA's external software release policy, originally designed in 1997, mandates that all software developed by or for the agency go through a technology reporting process. Before any NASA software is released, it has to be evaluated to determine the government rights, suitability for copyright or patent protection, technology transfer potential, and export control requirements. Following this evaluation, the appropriate method of release is determined in consultation with the project team that is responsible for the software. External release may include copyright or patent protection if the software will be licensed to industry for purposes of commercialization.

NASA also maintains an online resource (see Figure 2-9) focused on supporting advancement for Open Source for NASA software at http://www.nas.nasa.gov/Research/Software/Open-Source/index.html. According to the Web site:

> "The adoption of an Open Source option for software distribution will have three main benefits: enhanced software through community review and development, enhanced collaboration through sharing of NASA-originated software, and more efficient and effective dissemination of research products (such as software) to the public. NASA has begun several pilot projects in Open Source distribution. We expect that Open Source distribution of NASA-originated software will include codes in scientific visualization, software development tools, software frameworks, grid computing, and many other activities within NASA."

At the Web site, NASA maintains links to various Open Source related resources (http://www.nas.nasa.gov/Research/Software/Open-Source/Resources.html), the current version of the NASA Open Source Agreement, and a NASA Open Source download site at Ames Research Center (http://opensource.arc.nasa.gov).

U.S. Naval Oceanographic Office (NAVO)— Research Study Identifies a Series of FOSS Successes

In November 2003, the Commander, Naval Meteorology and Oceanography Command (CNMOC) executed a Cooperative Research and Development Agreement (NCRADA-01-008) to assess the current use of Free and Open Source Software at NAVO and to identify additional opportunities for further implementation of Free and Open Source

Software (FOSS) within NAVO's computing environment. NAVO possesses leading-edge technical and science skills for the application of information technology to the processing of oceanographic data over multiple scientific domains. NAVO produces numerous information products supporting U.S. Navy operations, the Department of Defense, and various commercial, national, and international customers. These NAVO capabilities are critical to developing and maintaining the highest quality oceanographic products for the Navy fleet. NAVO also maintains an extensive library of state-of-the-art scientific application software.

Findings from the research study included the following:

- There is already extensive use of Open Source within NAVO's computing infrastructure.
- Open Source was initially adopted on a limited basis without a formal policy directive or strategy for implementing Open Source.
- Key successes that occurred in the ISS60, UNISIPS, Network Attached Storage Servers, and QA/Monitoring workstation migrations to Open Source
- Key lessons that were learned from these deployments in migration, training, reliability, security, and financial areas

U.S. Department of Energy (DOE)— Sponsors Open Source Development Projects and Harnesses the Power of Linux and Globus (http://www.globus.org/) for Supercomputing

The DOE is sponsoring 11 Free and Open Source Software development projects, according to a 2003 report. Following are some of the key projects included in this report:

- **Globus**—The Globus Project is developing fundamental technologies needed to build computational grids. Grids are persistent environments that enable software applications to integrate instruments, displays, and computational and information resources managed by diverse organizations in widespread locations. Much of the Globus work takes place at Argonne National Laboratories. The technologies can be licensed under an "open source" license but are not on OSI's list of approved licenses.

- **MeshTV**—MeshTV is an interactive graphical analysis tool for visualizing and analyzing data on two- and three-dimensional meshes. It is a general-purpose tool that handles many different mesh types, provides different ways of viewing the data, and is virtually hardware/vendor independent while providing graphics at the speed of the native graphics hardware.

The DOE is also active in the development of the DOE Science Grid, which serves as a system template that can aid in enabling partnerships between public institutions and private companies aimed at creating new products and technologies for business. The effort is a collaboration between IBM's high-performance computing group and the DOE's National Energy Research Scientific Computing Center (NERSC), which will empower researchers to tackle scientific challenges beyond the capability of existing computers. The grid will give scientists access to far-flung supercomputers and data storage in the same way that an electrical grid provides consumers with access to widely dispersed power-generating resources.

Since 2002, there have been a number of additional grid announcements. IBM and several leading universities announced the application of grid computing to solve complex healthcare and environmental research problems. In particular, the University of Oregon, Electrical Geodesics, Inc. (EGI), and IBM announced a new project that uses grid computing, Linux, and IBM supercomputer technology to speed and improve the diagnosis of epilepsy, stroke, and depression. Prior to this, the university completed the ICONIC grid (Integrated Cognitive Neuroscience, Informatics, and Computation), which features IBM servers running Linux, IBM application servers, and the open source Globus Toolkit.

The emerging grids deliver geographically distributed organization platforms to share applications, data, and computing resources. An emerging model of computing grids are built with clusters of servers joined together over the Internet, using protocols provided by the Globus open source community and other open technologies, including Linux. The Globus Alliance is playing an important role in defining specifications for Open Grid Services Architecture (OGSA), an integral part of Globus Toolkit that includes software services and resources for full-scale implementation of OGSA. It was noted that grid computing using the open source Globus Toolkit would improve access to patient data, improve patient security, and enhance accountability. The Globus Alliance will also study neuro-informatics potential for using grid and Linux-based systems to speed and improve brain wave monitoring at hospitals and research centers.

Defense Advanced Research Projects Agency (DARPA)—Supports and Funds Multiple Open Source Projects

DARPA is encouraging vendors to publicly release, under open source licenses, software developed under contract with the agency. Its leading FOSS projects include GForge, Cougaar, and Semantic Web.

- **GForge** is a collaborative software development tool that allows developers to organize and manage any number of software development projects. GForge, which is licensed under the GPL license, is an open source version of the software that powers the SourceForge site. There are at least 93 Web sites worldwide using GForge, including several U.S. government agencies: DARPA (cougaar.org, semwebcentral.org), NASA's Goddard Space Flight Center, NOAA, and the National Science Digital Library.
- **The Cognitive Agent Architecture (Cougaar)** is a Java-based architecture for the construction of large-scale, distributed, agent-based applications. This began as an Open Source research program and has been in development for more than eight years. Cougaar has led DARPA to develop its own form of FOSS license called "Cougaar Open Source License" (COSL), which is a modified version of the OSI-approved BSD License.

One of DARPA's other key FOSS efforts is the Composable High Assurance Trusted Systems (CHATS) program, designed to protect computer systems from constant attack. CHATS and other related technology initiatives will be developed in concert with the unclassified Open Source operating system development community and will have broad applicability to many programs within DARPA and the DoD. These trusted operating system capabilities would be created by engaging the Open Source development community in the development of security functionality for existing Open Source operating systems. Additionally, DARPA will engage the Open Source community in a consortium-based approach to create a "neutral," secure operating system architecture framework. This security architecture framework will then be used to develop techniques for composing Open Source capabilities to support both servers and clients in the increasingly network-centric communications fabric of the DoD. These technologies are critical for defensive information warfare capabilities and are needed to ensure that DoD systems of the future are protected from attack.

U.S. Department of Health and Human Services (HHS)— Supports Development of a Free and Open Source Software (FOSS) Electronic Health Record Through Grants and the Release of VistA-Office EHR

In 2004, the Center for Medicare and Medicaid Services announced it had awarded a $100,000 grant to the American Academy of Family Physicians (AAFP) to develop low-cost, standardized, Open Source electronic medical records. The grant will help the AAFP to develop, implement, and evaluate a pilot project that provides electronic health record (EHR) systems for several medical practices (CMS press release, May, 28, 2004). According the CMS press release:

> The project represents a step toward HHS Secretary Tommy G. Thompson's goal of promoting the use of electronic health records, in order to improve the quality of care provided to Americans. President Bush last month established a national goal of assuring that most Americans have electronic health records within 10 years. Secretary Thompson is pushing to speed up efforts to establish a national, interoperable health information infrastructure that would allow quick, reliable, and secure access to information needed for patient care, while protecting patient privacy.
>
> "Health information technology promises huge benefits for all Americans, including higher quality care at lower costs," Secretary Thompson said. "We're moving aggressively on many fronts to harness the power of health information technology to improve health care in this country. This new pilot project represents a step forward as we encourage the adoption of electronic medical records."
>
> "This project is an opportunity for CMS to further its objective of improving the quality and efficiency of healthcare services provided to Medicare beneficiaries by promoting the adoption of EHR and information technology in small and medium-sized ambulatory care practices," Dr. McClellan said. "This grant will help support technological changes to enable family practice doctors to participate fully in a more modern and efficient health care system," Dr. McClellan said. "Our support of the AAFP initiative is an important part of the Department of Health and Human Services' broader

program to promote the use of information technology to update our health care system and organize it around the best interests of patient care."

In addition to these efforts, CMS is trying to lower the barriers, both financial and regulatory, to the dissemination of health information technologies. For example, CMS is investing in making the U.S. Department of Veterans Affairs (VA) electronic health record (EHR) system available as a low-cost EHR option for non-VA physicians, and has also recently announced a new exception to the Stark regulations for Community-wide Health Information Systems. In all, the AAFP grant represents a commitment by CMS to AAFP's important project, and to the broader goal of improving the quality and efficiency of healthcare delivery.

The results of the AAFP demonstration project were reported in March 2005. The AAFP's Center for Health Information Technology completed an EHR pilot project with six family physician practices in different states. The practices deployed the same EHR software system for six months, and they were studied during that time. The pilot effort evolved after the grant to focus on studying the ASP hosting of an EHR application and not developing a FOSS–based EHR system. AAFP concluded that:

- ASP hosting and remote delivery of the EHR works and has the potential to scale.
- Web-based training is a viable, cost-effective solution for medical practices as they prepare for and implement an EHR system.
- Connectivity of the EHR to external sources of information (e.g., laboratories, hospitals, pharmacies, etc.) is critical to success in small practices.

According to David C. Kibbe, MD, MBA, and principal investigator on the project, "Overall, the pilot project left participants with optimism about the future use of EHRs within family medicine."

Also mentioned in the CMS 2004 press release was the pending release of a version of VistA, the comprehensive health IT system developed and used by the VA. The VA system is being adapted to support EHR deployment in small medical practices as well as large healthcare provider organizations. In 2005, the first version of VistA-Office EHR was released for use by medical practices, with an upgraded version arriving in 2006 and widespread diffusion is targeted for 2007 and beyond. See Chapter 6 for more information on the expanding VistA market; a brief case study on VistA-Office EHR is found in Chapter 5.

More Federal Government FOSS Highlights

The above-listed examples of federal government FOSS activities represent just some of the most prominent uses of FOSS that have implications for the government's future consideration regarding FOSS. There are strong indications that there are thousands and thousands of other successful adoptions and deployments of various FOSS tools throughout all elements of the federal government. Here is one "under the radar" example of financial savings shared on an Internet discussion board when researchers of this working paper were responding to a query from a Workforce Connections development about a reference to the use of JBoss at the Department of Labor.

- **U.S. Department of Labor Saves Money Through FOSS**—"Just thought you'd like to know that the United States Department of Labor's Office of the Chief Financial Officer uses JBoss to process about $3.0M worth of financial transactions yearly in one application alone. There are several other legacy applications scheduled for migration. By using JBoss, we've saved the taxpayers about $100,000 in BEA Weblogic licensing fees and about $10,000 in annual support fees."—*Michael R. Maruya, DOL/ OCFO/OFD/DFAD base.*

Other examples of federal government adoptions as reported by the Setal Foundation and as identified during research for this report include:

- **U.S. Department of Homeland Security, WhiteHouse.gov, and DoD.gov Prefer Open Source**—The United States Department of Homeland Security changed its Intranet and Internet servers from Windows 2000 to Oracle running on Linux in January 2003, stating that its security is preferable to that of commercial software. The White House Web site runs on Linux using Apache, and the DoD Web site runs Netscape-Enterprise/4.1 on Linux.
- **U.S. Navy Moves from Unix to Linux, and Saves Massive Costs**—The U.S. Navy recently replaced proprietary UNIX servers with Linux on some of its ships. The replacement of proprietary hardware and software with Intel and Linux has already resulted in a 10-to-1 cost reduction. In addition, the Navy Web site runs Apache and OpenSSL (http://www.openssl.org/). The OpenSSL Web site states, "The OpenSSL Project is a collaborative effort to develop a robust, commercial-grade, full-featured, and Open Source toolkit imple-

menting the Secure Sockets Layer (SSL v2/v3) and Transport Layer Security (TLS v1) protocols as well as a full-strength general purpose cryptography library. The project is managed by a worldwide community of volunteers that use the Internet to communicate, plan, and develop the OpenSSL toolkit and its related documentation. Why buy an SSL toolkit as a black-box when you can get an open one for free?"

- ***Leading Government Search Engines Are Driven by FOSS (Linux, Apache, OpenSSL)***—The search function at www.firstgov.gov is running Apache and OpenSSL on Solaris 8, and the NTIS (National Technical Information Service) Web site is running Apache on Linux.

- ***U.S. Patent and Trademark Office (USPTO)***—The office has made a decision to base the technologies used in its Systems Development and Integration (SDI) contract on Open Source technologies, primarily Linux, J2EE/JAVA, XML, and a Service Orientated Architecture (SOA). USPTO has in the past released a request for proposal where the key requirement was that its SDI projects had to be developed using open platform. This RFP was a follow-up to its Systems Development and Maintenance (SDM) contract, which included expenditures of $43 million. This is one of the first times a federal government agency has launched such a major initiative based on Open Source technologies. During briefings regarding its RFP, USPTO detailed the great success it has had with Open Source technologies. Some of the successful Open Source applications include the Electronic Filing System (EFS), the Job Application Rating System (JARS), and the Patent Enterprise Application Integration (PEAI) project. USPTO is ready for next-generation projects based on previously used Open Source technologies.

- ***Health and Human Services (HHS) has also developed vital Web-based public health and surveillance solution on public domain software.*** The Epi-X is the Centers for Disease Control and Prevention's Web-based communications solution for public health professionals. Epi-X is based on Epi Info™, a public domain software package designed for public health practitioners that provides for easy form and database construction, data entry, and analysis with epidemiological statistics, maps, and graphs.

- *U.S. General Services Administration Supports Open Solutions Through Long Running Educational Program* Series and Other Initiatives (http://www.gsa.gov/collaborate)—Within the GSA there is an Intergovernmental Solutions Division which promotes more efficient and effective government. Within this group there is a series of activities including the 'Networking among Communities of Practice (CoP)' effort to support high performance. According to the Web site there are three initiatives within this effort:
  - *Communities of Practice*—In this area there are "discussion archives, document repositories, and wiki pages from intergovernmental networks supported by the GSA's Office of Intergovernmental Solutions (OIS)."
  - *Collaborative Expedition Workshops*—There are open, bimonthly workshops on valuable topics that are bigger than any one institution. By facilitating the delivery of knowledge and case studies in this format the GSA hopes to stimulate and support advanced use of technology and processes to improve government functioning.
  - *Data Reference Model Public Forum*—"Commissioned by OMB and the CIO Council, the Data Reference Model Working Group (DRM WG) invites public comment through the DRM Public Forum, to enable broad-based contributions to DRM evolution."

The GSA believes that "high performance requires quality dialogue, openness, and transparency in order to build the trust that leads to credible actions on behalf of communities at local, state, regional, and national levels. For the past four years, the Intergovernmental Solutions Division has offered the Collaborative Expedition workshops as a scaffold to open up conversations toward shared understanding needed by intergovernmental communities separated by geography, jurisdiction, or specialization."

In the summer of 2006 a very useful and insightful workshop was held on the use of Wikis, Blogs, and Web based networking software. The title of the program was 'ExpeditionWorkshop/Open Collaboration Networking Wiki Information Technology at http://colab.cim3.net/cgi-bin/wiki.pl/ and then scroll down until you see the July 18, 2006 program link.

The program featured the Director of CIA's Center for Innovation advocating the creation of a government 'Intellipedia' based on a Wiki that could create a common knowledge repository for all governmental agencies focused on sharing real-time knowledge and intelligence to support homeland security and national defense. This program and many others in the series have served a tremendous role in educating and empowering governmental officials in using various types of open solutions while stimulating collaboration and innovation.

Building the FOSS Business Case Through Leadership in the State and Federal Governments

At the March 2004 Open Source in Government Conference, a new consortium of state governments was announced, Government Open Code Consortium (GOCC). This consortium is led by the Commonwealth of Massachusetts, and its objective is to share the code developed by the members of the consortium. To date, Kansas and Delaware have joined this consortium, and the membership is increasing. The CIO office of Massachusetts (http://www.mass.gov/?pageID=itdhomepage&L=1&L0=Home&sid=Aitd) is serving as a central site. The state has developed some information about various licenses, which will be used by the consortium.

Barry West, a presenter at the conference, has served in prominent IT leadership roles at the Census Bureau, National Weather Service, and Department of Homeland Security's FEMA as CIO. It is evident that his career advancement has been based on solid successes in using technology prudently and wisely to save lives and money, and in particular, the broad adoption and deployment of FOSS to achieve significant cost reductions, efficiencies, and other benefits to solve critical problems facing three federal agencies over the past 10 years. At the March 2004 conference, his suggestions for moving a federal agency to FOSS included:

- Building a solid business case.
- Finding a champion who will take a risk on new approaches.
- Providing internal education and extensive communications.
- Defining a clear focus on the costs and benefits.
- Focusing on effective change management.
- Using an internal technology review board.

FOSS Is Growing Fast Internationally

Many European governments have adopted Free and Open Source Software (FOSS) solutions to lower the cost of technology and make it affordable to their citizens. FOSS is making rapid strides internationally, particularly through direct promotion by governments and government agencies. Several nations have already mandated the use of Open Source in government agencies, including Brazil and South Africa. Recently, the finance ministry of Israel made OpenOffice the default office suite for government agencies.

In Asia, the governments of Japan, China, and South Korea formed an alliance to jointly develop an Open Source operating system based on Linux. Several years ago the Thai government asked several major computer manufacturers to start selling inexpensive Linux-based PCs in order to provide its citizens with computers. The program was such a success that Microsoft was forced to reduce the price of Windows XP and MS Office to $40, less than a tenth of the standard retail price, to remain a viable competitor in the Thai computer market.

Almost every European country has issued major studies, policy papers, and guidelines on Open Source and has either major ongoing Open Source projects or is in the middle of test trials. In Spain, for example, the province of Extremadura has successfully migrated all computers for the state and local government offices to run Linux. In Germany, the city of Munich is migrating to Linux and the Interior Ministry has invested tens of millions of dollars to pay software companies to write Open Source software to secure email and develop a drop-in replacement for Microsoft Exchange.

The Interoperable Delivery of European eGovernment Services to Public Administrations, Businesses, and Citizens (IDABC) (http://europa.eu.int/idabc) has an "Open Source Observatory" site featuring news items as well as an extensive collection of case studies, reports, resources, events, and FAQs. It is an extensive repository of information on international Open Source projects and developments. IDABC was created by the European Commission to facilitate exchange of information and data among members of the commission and to promote the use of open standards and best practices for computers and networking.

The IDABC site links to the studies, reports, and guidelines on Open Source that have been published by almost every European government as well as other governments. IDA has carried out and released an extensive set of reports on Open Source, including a very thorough migration guide for Open Source projects, including a comprehensive spreadsheet that allows administrators to calculate the savings they will achieve by migrating from MS Windows to Open Source.

The European Commission is also funding pilots of Open Source technology for the public sector through the Consortium for Open Source in the Public Administration (COSPA) (http://www.cospa-project.org/about.html). COSPA has 15 European participants from Italy, Hungary, Denmark, the United Kingdom, and Belgium as well as three international "observers" from Canada, New Zealand, and the United Nations Educational Scientific and Cultural Organization (UNESCO). The consortium has launched several pilots to analyze the effects of the introduction of Open Data Standards (ODS) and Open Source (OS) software for personal productivity and document management in European Public Administration (PA), the equivalent of government agencies in the United States. The consortium is aiming at building a leading, effective, and visible success case by:

1. Deploying ODS and OS desktop software solutions in several European PAs, and benchmarking their effectiveness through a cost/benefit analysis;
2. Building a European, multilingual, freely accessible knowledge and experience base by comparing and pooling knowledge, and by building on and complementing current activities in the field; and
3. Disseminating the results and the experiences of the study through a series of workshops at a regional and European level.

UNESCO has a Web portal site (http://portal.unesco.org/ci/en/ev. php-URL_ID=12034&URL_DO=DO_TOPIC&URL_SECTION= 201.html) promoting the development and deployment of Open Source software for underdeveloped nations. The site contains an extensive collection of software, projects, case studies, and lists of organizations that are involved in open source projects.

Veterans Health Administration FOSS information technology system, VistA, has been deployed in numerous countries such as Finland, Mexico, and Egypt. Many other countries are interested in deploying VistA. There are numerous other countries that have been documented and tracked by the VHA Health Information Technology Sharing (HITS) program. Chapter 8 details large-scale deployments of VistA outside of the VA in the United States and worldwide.

Additional FOSS Resources Online

There are additional resources that can assist in evaluating the qualitative and quantitative benefits of FOSS in health care and other industry and government sectors, including:

- **"Why Open Source Software / Free Software (OSS/FS)? Look at the Numbers!"** (http://www.dwheeler.com/oss_fs_why.html)— This paper provides additional background and quantitative analysis of the growth of FOSS. It was written by researcher David Wheeler, also the author of the "Secure Programming for Linux HOWTO" and several other documents. This document provides an extensive listing of quantitative data that indicates that, in many cases, using FOSS is a reasonable or even superior approach to using their proprietary competition. The purpose of the paper is to illustrate the range of factors that should be considered when assessing and acquiring FOSS.
- **The Open Source Reference Book** (http://www.egovos.org/ Resources/Book)—This Web site includes what local and national governments, the defense establishment, and the Global 1000 need to know about open source software.

Forecast: Accelerated Growth of FOSS

Quickly, FOSS is moving from information technology infrastructure, like the Linux operating system, to enterprise applications like Customer Relationship Management (CRM), suites of office productivity software such as OpenOffice, databases like MySQL, ERP like Compiere, and many other software application areas.

In health care, the equivalent is the clinical informatics and EHR market serving over 5,000 hospitals and hundreds of thousands of doctors, where less than 5% are using EHRs and clinical informatics. Here, VistA, in its various forms, is poised to provide a viable alternative to public health organizations, private health systems, and physicians. In Chapter

6, VistA Market Overview, a broad snapshot of the current market and how it is poised for growth is provided. Remember: over 50% of all U.S.-trained physicians have used the VistA system.

According to Larry Augustin, the visionary behind SourceForge.net, the largest Open Source development site on the Internet, "First we made games, and they said, 'Of course people will make games for free. But they won't make anything serious and give it away.' Then we made compilers and developer tools, and they said, 'Of course they will make developer tools. They're developers. But they won't make anything serious, like an operating system.' So, we made an operating system, and they said, 'Of course they made an operating system. They studied Unix in school. But they'll never make applications.' Guess what we're making now—applications. The next wave of Open Source is here."

The view of many experts is that the enterprise software model of big licensing fees, high support costs, and lags in tailoring software to meet clients' needs has resulted in a broken model. With enterprise software today, there is a long sales cycle, it is expensive, and there is a disconnect between license cost and manufacturing cost, in which over 70% of new license revenue goes to sales and marketing. Figure 2-10 shows a comparison of closed source versus Open Source software across key dimensions that are important to the executives and managers who purchase and maintain information systems for their organizations.

This book explores the Open Solutions and FOSS alternative that delivers reduced sales and marketing expenses, offers the opportunity to test and trial before complete install, and provides access to the source code and participation with an extensive network of other users and developers to improve functionality.

More and more corporations are moving to from a purely proprietary closed software model to a hybrid model.

- Novell is marketing its software for the "Open Enterprise™," positioning it as the "only software that makes Open work for you. From desktop and data center to identity management, resource management and collaboration, our flexible combination of open source and commercial software delivers more than you ever imagined."
- Even Microsoft, the leading advocate of "closed" software, is responding with a community and collaborative development effort that it labels "Shared Source" initiative where Microsoft will make

	Closed/Proprietary Software	Open Source Software
Significant License Fee	Frequently, yes	No
Sales Cycle	Long	Short
Availability of Service/ Support	Yes, under service agreement	Yes, free and fee based service available
Enterprise Ready	Yes	Yes, in many categories of infrastructure and applications
Install Time	Long (months)	Short (weeks)
Ability to Customize Source Code	No	Yes

FIGURE 2-10 Comparison of Closed Source vs. Open Source Software

its source code available to select customers and developers under specific contractual relationships to solve customer problems and create economic opportunities.

The reality is that Free and Open Source Software (FOSS) information technology infrastructure and now applications are here to stay. In the near future, every proprietary software application will have a viable FOSS alternative.

CHAPTER 3

Growth of Open Solutions in Health Care

"The history of the medical community's understanding of the importance of sharing discoveries is a paradigm for what has been more recently developing in the Free/Open Source Software community."

—*Medical Enterprises and Open Source* by Daniel L. Johnson, MD

Open Solutions in Health and Medical Care

Open Solutions and Free and Open Source Software (FOSS) are an increasingly important trend in health care today. When exploring the topic of FOSS healthcare solutions, there are two critical dimensions to understand: *use* and *development* of FOSS. The number of FOSS solutions currently available has grown to be quite substantial. The number of FOSS healthcare products under development is equally impressive.

It is important to recognize that a wide range of FOSS solutions are already in use in health care, generally consisting of business applications such as Linux, Apache, OpenOffice, mySQL, Firefox, and many more utilities and administrative software solutions. In addition, there are a large number of healthcare-specific FOSS solutions that are being widely deployed, including OSCAR, FreeMed, MedLine, BLAST, Epi-X, SaTScan™, and VistA. For instance, Lucene (an open source search engine—http://lucene.apache.org/java/docs/) is being used in health care by clinicians, while SaTScan™ (a free software tool focused exclusively on health care—http://www.satscan.org/) is used to identify disease clusters early in an outbreak. Many of these FOSS products used in healthcare settings are listed or profiled in more detail in later sections of this book.

It is vital, as well, to recognize the ongoing development of many new FOSS healthcare software applications continues to come about from the collaboration of a growing global network of FOSS programmers. They are constantly releasing many new solutions or enhancements to existing FOSS products under one or more Open Source license arrangements that allow healthcare providers to acquire and use them at no cost. These include enhancements to Open Source EHR systems such as VistA and OpenMed, personal health record solutions like My Health*e*Vet and VIA Online Medical Records, health information exchange solutions, genomic systems, and many more medical specialty software solutions.

Open Solutions Milestones in Health Care

The following are recent milestones in the development of Open Solutions and Free and Open Source Software (FOSS) in health care:

- *"Free and Open Source Software (FOSS) Analysis: Profile of Increasing Use and the Opportunity in Information Technology and the Health Care Enterprise"* **(June 2002)**—Back in 2002, Douglas Goldstein, in his enterprise *e-strategy* work for the Veterans Health Administration, identified Free and Open Source Software (FOSS) in health care as an "under the radar" emerging information technology trend that would continue to grow as the use of FOSS gained market share across most major computing arenas. This led to the development of a subsequent white paper for the CIO of the Veterans Health Administration (VHA) entitled "Free and Open Source Software (FOSS) Analysis: Profile of Increasing Use and the Opportunity in Information Technology and the Health Care Enterprise" (June 2002) that highlighted a number of healthcare FOSS development projects of potential interest to the VHA.
- *Free and Open Source Software in Health Care a Top IT Trend*—FOSS gained significant visibility when Healthcare Informatics declared FOSS as one of the nine Tech Trends for 2004, in the article

"Inroads in the Right Places—Open Source." The key growth factors noted outside and inside health care at that point in time were:

○ *IBM's support of Linux* $100M+ contributions to the FOSS alliance Ellipse.org and IBM's efforts to migrate from Windows to Linux. IBM also makes software that runs on Linux, and operates a portal focused on open source developers.

○ *Growth of Linux* on the desktop in Europe and Asia with United States deployments ramping up.

○ *Viability of FOSS* due to the growing support and service market and other resources including www.SourceForge.net and www. freshmeat.net.

○ *The Pacific Telehealth & Technology Hui* (www.pacifichui.org) based in Honolulu, Hawaii, created an open source version of the VistA electronic health information system that is freely available on the Web. Private vendors used this version of VistA as the basis for their implementation projects in Hawaii, American Samoa, Texas, and elsewhere.

○ *UCLA Medical Center, Los Angeles,* a large non-government user of Open Source, whose clinical system runs on a Linux-based operating system from CliniComp International, San Diego, and utilizes open source Apache servers.

○ *Capital Cardiology Associates (CCA), Albany, New York,* uses an online EMR called "escribe," which was developed by Lille Corp (www.lillecorp.com), an entirely Linux-based, thin-client system using eight Open Source programs. CCA treats 40,000 patients a year, while handling 30,000 diagnostic procedures. Lille found a Linux believer in their CEO Dr. Martin Echt, a longtime UNIX fan, who wanted a new IT system that would connect CCA's seven hospitals and 18 locations cost-effectively.

• *Veterans Health Administration & Open Source—Market Update*—In 2004, an internal white paper was prepared for the Office of the CIO within the Veterans Health Administration (VHA) entitled "Veterans Health Administration & Free and Open Source Software (FOSS)—Market Update, Open Source Business Models Analysis and Implications for VHA and VistA." This study identified the extensive use and development of FOSS by many different federal agencies, profiled FOSS business models, and gave

Open Solution implications and recommendations for VHA's public domain health information technology system known as VistA.

FOSS in health care is getting attention and recognition at important conferences across the country and around the world, including:

- *HIMSS and TEPR*—At the annual Health Information Management Systems Society (HIMSS) conference in 2004, there were five FOSS-related sessions. These included two by the Military Health System on "Military Health System Information Management and Technology Direction: Now and Into the Future" and "Creating an Electronic Medical Record That Supports a Military Medical Workforce." There were also other FOSS sessions on network management and international FOSS developments. The 2004 conference was also the first by Towards the Electronic Patient Record (TEPR) to hold a dedicated Free and Open Source Software track dedicated to exploring successful deployments of FOSS within medical practices and hospitals. In 2005, HIMSS sessions were dominated by education sessions on implementing EHRs and clinical informatics solutions with information technology, which hinges on Open Standards, collaboration, and interoperability strategies and tactics. Open Standards is the DNA that will make EHRs interoperable and effective in improving quality and reducing costs.

- *AMIA 2005*—Thirty presentations and papers at the American Medical Informatics Association (AMIA) Annual Symposium addressed Open Solutions in some respect. Thirty percent of the papers described the development of new medically related Free and Open Source Software and the rest talked about using existing FOSS in the development of a medical application related to issues such as sydromatic surveillance, consumer health vocabulary, clinical informatics, and statistical analysis. One of AMIA's papers identified 179 clinically related Free the Open Source Software development efforts in the 2003–2004 timeframe. The titles of the 2005 AMIA papers that involved Open Source are shown in Table 3-1.

- *VistA-Office EHR (VOE) is released by the U.S. Department of Health and Human Services (HHS) in Late 2005*—HHS's Physician Focused Quality Initiative extends Centers for Medicare & Medicaid Services (CMS) strategies and programs to 1) assess the quality of care for key illnesses and clinical conditions that affect

Table 3-1 American Medical Informatics Association List of Papers Involving Open Source

* A Study of Clinically Related Free/Open Source Software Projects
* An Open Source Model for Open Access Journal Publication
* Live Demonstration of the Capabilities of the VistA Free/Open Source Stack EHR/EMR
* LexGrid Editor: Terminology Authoring for the Lexical Grid
* Reviewing Managing Syndromic Surveillance SaTScan Datasets using an Open-Source Data Visualization Tool
* An Open Source Environment for the Statistical Evaluation of Outbreak Detection Methods
* Redesigning an Infection Control Application to Support an Enterprise Model
* Linking Primary Care Information Systems and Public Health Vertical Programs in the Philippines: An Open Source Experience
* AMPATH—Medical Record System (AMRS): Collaborating Toward an EMR for Developing Countries
* Building an Internationalized Content Delivery Architecture: Lessons Learned
* Acceptability of an Internet Treatment Decision Support Program for Men with Prostate Cancer
* Architecture for Remote Training of Home Telemedicine Patients
* Creating a Vaccine Adverse Event Ontology for Public Health
* EM Clustering Analysis of Diabetes Patients Basic Diagnosis Index
* Protégé-OWL: Creating Ontology-Driven Reasoning Applications with the Web Ontology Language
* YPED: A Proteomics Database for Protein Expression Analysis
* A Web-Based Prototype System for Patient Use Confirming Taiwan Electronic Medical-Record Templates
* A Wireless, Handheld Decision Support System to Promote Smoking Cessation in Primary Care
* Applying Hybrid Algorithms for Text Matching to Automated Biomedical Vocabulary Mapping
* Key Design Elements of a Data Utility for National Biosurveillance: Event-Driven Architecture, Caching, and Web Service Model
* Knowledge-Based, Interactive, Custom Anatomical Scene Creation for Medical Education: The Biolucida System
* Automating Tissue Bank Annotation from Pathology Reports—Comparison to Gold Standard Expert Annotation Set
* Identifying Consumer-Friendly Display Names for Health Concepts
* Semantic Clinical Guideline Documents
* 802.11 Wireless Infrastructure to Enhance Medical Response to Disasters
* MASCAL: RFO Tracking of Patients, Staff and Equipment to Enhance Hospital Response to Mass Casualty Events
* Missing Prenatal Records at a Birth Center: A Communications Program Quantified
* Of Mice and Men: Design of a Comparative Anatomy Information System
* SPIN Query Tools for De-identified Research on a Humongous Database
* Using Concept Relations to Improve Ranking in Information Retrieval

many people with Medicare, 2) support clinicians in providing appropriate treatment of the conditions identified, 3) prevent health problems that are avoidable, and 4) investigate the concept of payment for performance. This initiative includes the Doctor's Office Quality (DOQ) Project, the Doctor's Office Quality Information Technology (DOQ-IT) Project, the Vista-Office EHR (VOE) Project (http://www.vista-office.org), and several demonstration projects and evaluation reports. VistA-Office EHR (VOE) will be an EHR that will be available under a no-license-fee arrangement because the software is in the public domain and has been developed and paid for by tax dollars. VistA is in essence a de facto Open Solution now available to healthcare providers. Section II, Chapters 5 and 6, contains additional information on VOE. It is anticipated

---

Veterans Heath Information Systems and Technology Architecture (VistA)—Selected Awards and Recognition Received in 2006

The Department of Veterans Affairs' (VA) model system of electronic health records and clinical information system—VistA, developed with extensive involvement of front-line healthcare providers, has won the prestigious "Innovations in American Government Award." The annual award, sponsored by Harvard University's Ash Institute for Democratic Governance and Innovation at the Kennedy School of Government and administered in partnership with the Council for Excellence in Government, honors excellence and creativity in the public sector.

VA hospitals last year scored higher than private facilities on the University of Michigan's American Customer Satisfaction Index, based on patient surveys on the quality of care received. The VA scored 83 out of 100; private institutions, 71. Males 65 years and older receiving VA care had about a 40% lower risk of death than those enrolled in Medicare Advantage, whose care is provided through private health plans or HMOs, according to a study published in the April 2006 edition of Medical Care.

VA's complete adoption of electronic health records and performance measures have resulted in high-quality, low-cost health care with high patient satisfaction. A recent RAND study found that the VA outperforms all other sectors of American health care across a spectrum of 294 measures of quality in disease prevention and treatment. For six straight years, the VA has led private-sector health care in the independent American Customer Satisfaction Index.

The VistA system is a free public domain software or FOSS, and information is available through VA's Web site (http://www.va.gov/vista_monograph/) and from other sources mentioned throughout the book.

Additional information on the awards is available by visiting the Web site (www.innovations.va.gov)

that VistA will become one of the leading Open Source EHR packages deployed by physicians and healthcare provider organizations as they work to implement EHR systems over the next decade. Figure 3-1 is the Web site for the Physician Quality Initiatives from HHS.

In the Open Solutions standards area, Health Level Seven (HL7) has been very active across a number of fronts as it relates to clinical data exchange.

- HL7's mission as an international community of healthcare experts and information scientists is to collaborate in the creation of "standards for the exchange, management, and integration of electronic healthcare information. HL7 promotes the use of such standards within and among healthcare organizations to increase the effectiveness and efficiency of healthcare delivery for the benefit of all." HL7 is one of several American National Standards Institute (ANSI) accredited standards development organizations (SDO) that produce standards (e.g., specifications or protocols) for a particular healthcare domain such as pharmacy, medical devices, imaging, or insurance (claims-processing) transactions. HL7's domain is clinical and administrative data. HL7 is a not-for-profit volunteer organization where the members represent all public and private sectors in health care and have an interest and experience in the development of clinical and administrative standards for health care.

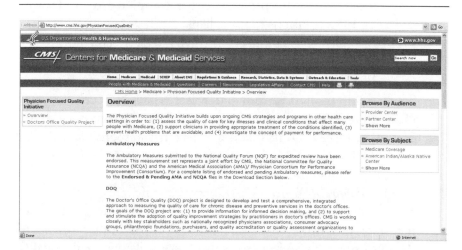

FIGURE 3-1 HHS-CMS Physician Focused Quality Initiative
Source: http://www.cmshhs.gov/physicianfocusedqualimits/

FOSS Support Organizations in Health Care

Critical to Open Solutions and Free and Open Source Software (FOSS) development is the existence of formal and informal networks of developers, companies, and individuals that are supportive of development. Many clinical FOSS projects may be supported by only a few developers, while others could have dozens, hundreds, or thousands. Often times, the larger clinical FOSS initiatives have dedicated not-for-profit entities coordinating and facilitating development. The healthcare community now has several growing not-for-profit entities focused on advocating the use of Free and Open Source Software and Open EHR solutions. For example:

- *OpenEHR Foundation* (http://www.openehr.org/) is a not-for-profit company, limited by guarantee. Its founding shareholders are University College London, United Kingdom, and Ocean Informatics, Australia. The foundation currently sponsors a number of open source EHR projects around the world.

- *Canada Health Infoway* (http://www.infoway-inforoute.ca/en/home/home.aspx) is an independent, not-for–profit organization that has as its membership Canada's 14 federal, provincial, and territorial deputy ministers of health. Infoway invests with public sector partners across Canada to implement and reuse compatible health information systems that support a safer, more efficient healthcare system. Launched in 2001, Infoway and its public sector partners have over 100 projects, either completed or underway, delivering EHR solutions to Canadians.

- *FreeMED Software Foundation* (http://www.freemed.org/) is a nonprofit corporation promoting the development and acceptance of FreeMED and other GPL and LGPL software from the Open Source community. The foundation is a vehicle for such development through contracting and using grants for the continued development of FreeMED. Its board of directors is responsible, through the CEO, for the disbursement of funds and completion of contracted or granted project work.

- *VistA Software Alliance (VSA)* (www.vistasoftware.org) is a nonprofit trade organization that promotes the distribution and implementation of Open VistA, VistA-Office EHR, and other variants of the VistA system. VSA recognizes that VistA will enhance the quality of care provided, lower costs, and improve patient safety. Two primary goals of VSA are: 1) to harness the resources of the members to promote and facilitate adoption of VistA, and 2) to serve as a trade organization that can work with public and private sector healthcare providers and IT vendor organizations to promote and facilitate adoption of VistA across the country and around the world. The VSA Web site contains a list of many of the VSA's member companies that provide VistA implementation and support services such as Novell, InterSystems, SAIC, Hewlett Packard, DSS Inc., MedSphere Systems Corporation, Perot Systems, Fidelity, Blue Cliff, Oleen Healthcare Management, GE Healthcare, MELE Health Information Systems, Proxicom, and others. (http://www. vistasoftware.org/about/members.html).

- *WorldVistA* (www.worldvista.org) is a nonprofit, tax exempt organization that "seeks to make healthcare information technology more affordable and more widely available worldwide. In particular, WorldVistA is focused on further developing and supporting the growing global VistA user community. WorldVistA seeks to help those who choose to adopt the VistA system to successfully master, install, and maintain the software for their own use. WorldVistA will strive to guide VistA adopters and programmers toward developing a community based on principles of open, collaborative, peer review software development and dissemination." WorldVistA has a number of development efforts aimed at adding new software modules such as pediatrics, obstetrics, and other functions not used in the veterans' healthcare setting.

  In 2004, WorldVistA was award a contract by the U.S. Department of Health and Human Services to be the VistA Vendor Support Organization (VVSO) for the VistA-Office EHR (VOE) initiative. WorldVistA is also focused on supporting a full-scale Open Source version of VistA that can be used by any physician office, hospital, or other healthcare provider organization. It has played a key role in the development and evolution of the Open Source VistA solution that can run on an Open Source stack, which includes the GT.M programming platform and Linux operating system.

Sources of Information on Clinical FOSS Solutions

Aside from many of the traditional IT magazines and journals such as *CIO Magazine, Health Informatics, Government Health IT News, The*

Journal of the American Medical Informatics Association, and *Virtual Medical Worlds,* there are several that focus specifically on Open Source solutions. The following are a number of these sources on the Web that specifically deal with Open Source solutions in medicine.

- ***American Academy of Family Physicians (AAFP)*** lists resources from the AAFP's Center for Health Information Technology about a variety of Free/Open Source Software projects that focus specifically on electronic health records and other medical-related issues. (http://www.centerforhit.org/x337.xml and http://search.aafp.org/htdigsearch/htsearch?words=open+source)
- ***EMRupdate.com*** is touted as the most frequently visited site for unbiased and independent EMR information. The site was designed to share a clinician's research on electronic medical records (EMR), which were evaluated as part of a search for "the perfect" electronic medical record system for a 10-doctor group practice. (http://www.emrupdate.com)
- ***Journal of Open Source Medical Computing*** is an electronic forum for disseminating information on Free and Open Source medical computing. (http://www.josmc.org/)
- ***LinuxMedNews*** is an online newspaper on Free and Open Source Software in medicine. (http://www.linuxmednews.com/)
- ***NewsForge*** is the online newspaper for Linux and Free and Open Source Software. (http://www.newsforge.com/search.pl?query=medical)
- ***SourceForge.net*** is the world's largest Open Source software development Web site, hosting more than 129,000 projects and over 1.3 million registered users with a centralized resource for managing projects, issues, communications, and code. (http://www.SourceForge.net)
- ***US: The Open Source Reference Book*** provides detailed information on Open Source solutions. It is aimed primarily at government IT officials, but it's useful to everyone interested in the topic. (http://www.egovos.org/Resources/Book)
- ***Medical Informatics 20/20*** The authors of this book will be posting updates and expanding information related to medical informatics and the topics in this book, with resources, updated information, and blogs on appropriate use of technology to improve the quality and cost-effectiveness of health care in the United States and around the globe. (http://www.medicalinformatics2020.com)

- *GPL Medicine* This Web site's goal is "to promote software using the General Public License (GPL) in the medical software arena." In particular, the Web site focuses on medical practice management software, hospital management software, and electronic health records. Over time, the Web site will be developed to enable finding GPL-based electronic health records and open source–based practice management software systems. (http://www.gplmedicine.org/)
- *WebRing—Free and Open Source Software in Medicine* There is an ever-expanding network or WebRing devoted to FOSS in medicine. This is a very useful place to check up on the developments and new applications available to support quality health and medical care. (http://l. webring.com/hub?ring=freeandopensourc)
- *VistA(r) and Open Healthcare News* (www.openhealthcare.info) which is edited by Roger A. Maduro. This is a Web site that is focused on news about open solutions in healthcare. This includes news about VistA, HuiOpenVistA as well as other solutions that at either open source software or follow the principles of open solutions. The site provides regular news summaries and analysis of items of interest as well as a wealth of materials and commentary on the subject. There is also an e-newsletter that can be subscribed to so that open solutions updates are sent directly to an email inbox.

Continued Growth in FOSS Healthcare Projects

"A Study of Clinically Related Free and Open Source Software Projects" by Michael A. Hogarth, MD, and Stuart Turner, DVM, MS, Biomedical Informatics Research and Consulting Service, UC Davis School of Medicine, Davis, California, AMIA 2005 Conference Papers. This study identified 179 clinically related Free and Open Source Software projects in some stage of development in the 2002–2003 time frame, and the numbers of projects are escalating. The study revealed the following preliminary observations:

- Clinical information systems and imaging systems account for nearly half of all Free and Open Source Software discovered in this study.
- If a project delays releasing a deliverable more than 100 days beyond the first announcement, it is unlikely to ever produce one.
- A fraction of clinical open source projects "die on the vine" without producing a viable software product.

The authors of the study concluded that additional questions had to be asked and research conducted to further assess the status and quality of clinical FOSS. The existence of a clinical FOSS project doesn't necessarily mean that the software works and is cost-effective. The next phase of their planned research is to more fully assess the effectiveness, viability, and sustainability of the identified clinical FOSS projects. Those findings will be very useful.

The inventory of available FOSS solutions in health care is now quite large. Products include Free and Open Source Software utilities, EHR systems, imaging solutions, free medical knowledge databases, and much more. The following is just a short sample listing of some of the Free and Open Source clinical software solutions, utilities, and knowledge databases that are already accessible. U.S. federal and state governments have paid for the development of many of these solutions, which are now available in the public domain. More detailed lists and profiles of many other selected products are given in Sections II and III of this book.

A Sampling of Clinical FOSS Solutions

AMPATH Medical Record Systems (AMRS) is an international open source project that has built a scalable, flexible electronic medical record system built on open standards. (www.amrs.iukenya.org and http://openmrs.org/wiki/)

BLOX is one of a number of other MedIC technology projects. The purpose of the project is to develop a quantitative medical imaging and visualization program for use on brain MR, DTI, and MRS data. It is a joint project of the Kennedy Krieger Institute and Johns Hopkins University's Psychiatric Neuroimaging Lab. There have been 22 developers involved in this effort. In addition, the MedIC service from Johns Hopkins provides access to a variety of other free medical software at the MedIC Web site. (http://medic.rad.jhu.edu/download)

CARE2X integrates data, functions, and workflows in a healthcare environment. It currently contains four major components: HIS (Health-service Information System); PM (Practice [GP] Management); CDS (Central Data Server); and HXP (Health Xchange Protocol). (http://www.care2x.org/ and www.liferecord.com)

CAREWare is a scalable software application, from stand alone system to the Internet, developed by HRSA for managing and monitoring HIV care. (http://hab.hrsa.gov/careware/)

ClearHealth claims to be the first Free and Open Source Practice Management System to address the big five features: medical billing, medical accounts receivable, scheduling, access control, and EMR. (http://www.clear-health.org)

Clinic Assessment Software Application (CASA) is a tool for assessing immunization practices within a clinic, private practice, or any other environment where immunizations are provided. (http://www.cdc.gov/nip/casa/Default.htm)

ClinicalTrials.gov was developed by the U.S. National Institutes of Health (NIH), through its National Library of Medicine (NLM), to provide patients, family members, and the public with current information about clinical research studies. (http://www.clinicaltrials.gov/)

Drug Abuse Warning Network (DAWN) is a national public health surveillance system that monitors trends in drug-related emergency department visits and deaths. Various reports can be generated from its online database. (http://www.dawninfo.net/)

Epidemiology Info/Map **Epi-X** , **Epi Info, and Epi Map** are public domain software packages designed for the global community of public health practitioners and researchers. (http://www.cdc.gov/epiinfo/)

FreeMed is Open Source practice management and an electronic and computer records system. It allows the tracking of medical data, in detail, with preservation of not just the diagnosis but the reasons for medical encounters. (http://www.freemed.org)

Healthcare Cost and Utilization Project (HCUP) generates statistics using data from the Nationwide Inpatient Sample (NIS), the Kids' Inpatient Database (KID), and the State Inpatient Databases (SID) for states that participate. (http://www.ahrq.gov/hcupnet/)

ImageJ is a public domain Java image-processing program. It runs, either as an online applet or as a downloadable application, on any computer with a Java 1.1 or later virtual machine. (http://rsb.info.nih.gov/ij/docs/index.html)

jEngine has built a world-class open source enterprise integration engine. Users of jEngine include healthcare systems and hospitals using HL7 interface engine, and integration of HL7 with EMR and Practice Management systems. This latest release qualifies jEngine as a viable, real-world solution for small to medium hospitals and software vendors requiring HL7 integration. (http://www.jengine.org)

MedQuest Clinical Data Collection Design System is a suite of software tools that enables the user to quickly design a medical data collection system and to then collect data using that system. (http://cms.hhs.gov/medquest/default.asp)

Medscribbler Lite is a fully implemented, free EMR that facilitates creating a handwritten EMR using a tablet PC. It includes a robust, secure client server application for a network or desktop environment. (http://www.medscribbler.com/)

MedWatch is the FDA's Safety Information and Adverse Event Reporting Program, serving both healthcare professionals and the medical product–using public. It provides important and timely clinical information about safety issues involving medical products, including prescription and over-the-counter drugs, biologics, medical and radiation-emitting devices, and special nutritional information. (http://www.fda.gov/medwatch/)

myPACS is a Web-based medical image content management system designed to help clinicians share their knowledge. MyPACS.net is a free service offered to the international radiology community. (http://www.mypacs.net or http://www.mypacs.net/enterprise/)

National Health Card Project (NHCP) of Brazil was started in 1999 by the government of Brazil to create a national patient identification and information system. The goal of this project is to collect information on patient treatments and aggregate it into a national repository of health records. (http://dtr2001.saude.gov.br/cartao/index_cns.htm)

NHLBI Palm OS Applications is a series of Palm OS applications and treatment guidelines created by the U.S. National Institutes of Health, which is releasing them into the public domain. (http://hin.nhlbi.nih.gov/palmapps.htm)

NetEpi, or "Network-enabled Epidemiology," is a project focused on developing a suite of free, open source tools for epidemiology and public health practice. The application NetEpi Case Manager is a tool for securely collecting through the Internet structured information about cases and contacts of communicable diseases important for public health. The driving force for the development NetEpi Case Manager has been the challenge of collecting a rapidly changing set of data items from many sources in the event of an outbreak of a communicable disease, such as SARS or a deadly avian influenza. The application allows data to be collected from authenticated users of the system, who can be located anywhere in the world, and loaded into a centralized database. (http://www.netepi.org)

Open Infrastructure for Outcomes is a shared and free infrastructure that supports the creation of Web-forms as plug-and-play modules for medical information systems with integrated statistical reports generation. These forms can be weaved together into sophisticated applications through user-composable workflows and schedules. The two major components are the Internet-accessible OIO Server and OIO Library. The OIO Server is a Web-based data management system that manages users, patients, and information about patients, while the OIO Library is a metadata repository that facilitates the sharing of metadata between users and between OIO Servers. The OIO Library hosts a database of open source medical software projects and related documents. The ultimate goal of this project is to facilitate pooling of expertise, create assessment instruments, and perform data management, training, and quality assurance. This also offers reporting tools to reduce the cost of customization and maintenance of medical information systems and outcome assessments. This project is led by Andrew P. Ho, MD, assistant clinical professor in the Department of Psychiatry, Harbor–UCLA Medical Center. (http://www.txoutcome.org)

Public Health Laboratory Information System (PHLIS) is a PC-based software application for use in public health laboratories. (http://wonder.cdc.gov/wonder/sci data/misc/type txt/phlis.asp)

SaTScan is software that supports analysis of spatial, temporal, and space-time data. The functions available through this open source soft-

FIGURE 3-2 SaTScan Web Site
Source: http://www.satscan.org/

ware are to test statistically significant geographical surveillance of disease; detect spatial or space-time disease clusters; test the disease distribution over space and time; evaluate the statistical significance of disease cluster alarms; and perform repeated time-periodic disease surveillance for the early detection of disease outbreaks.

This free software has been under development and enhancement since 1997. Financial support for SaTScan was received from the National Cancer Institute, the Alfred P. Sloan Foundation, and the Centers for Disease Control and Prevention. (http://www.satscan.org/)

Statistical Export and Tabulation System (SETS) gives data users the tools to access and manipulate large data files on their personal computers. This tool and several large data sets are made available by the National Center for Health Statistics. (http://www.cdc.gov/nchs/sets.htm)

The Reminder Database: A Tool for Quality was developed by the Cedar Rapids Medical Education Foundation as a tool to improve quality of care by providing reminders to clinicians. According to the New England Journal of Medicine, only 24% of hypertensive patients have their blood pressure controlled, despite regular annual visits to their doctors. In addition, patients frequently fail to return for follow-up visits for diabetes, lipid management, pap smears, and mammograms. Consequently, doctors who want to provide effective care and management of their patient populations have a need for software to track and recall such patients. In managed care settings, physicians who can produce data showing quality care may also have a competitive advantage. The program is available online at the following Web site in an effort to support educational and clinical use in promoting quality care of practice populations. (http://www.crmef.org/reminder.html)

Vaccine Adverse Event Reporting System (VAERS) is a cooperative program for vaccine safety of the CDC and FDA. This free Web site provides a nationwide mechanism by which adverse events following immunization may be reported, analyzed, and made available to the public. (http://vaers.hhs.gov/)

VistA is the comprehensive health information technology system that supports the Veterans Health Administration (VHA), which is the largest healthcare system in the United States. The entire VistA information technology system is available in the public domain—more than 140 software modules of infrastructure and applications. VistA is also the foundation for VistA EHR, which is a comprehensive EHR system available in the public domain. Variants of the system include RPMS, VistA-Office

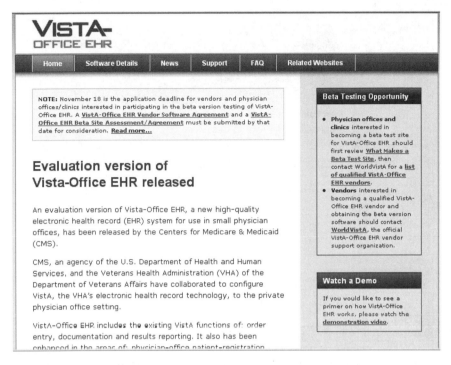

FIGURE 3-3 VistA Office EHR Web Site

EHR (VOE), and OpenVistA. See Sections II, III, and IV for more details. Online sources include http://www.vista-office.org/ and http://www.doqit.org. The VA leads for the sixth year running in 2005 Veterans Health Care Outscores Private Sector—Again in patient satisfaction according to the American Customer Satisfaction Index. (Source: http://www1.va.gov/opa/pressrel/PressArtInternet.cfm?id=1069). The Veterans Health Care system is based on the Public Domain—Free and Open Source Software—VistA Health Information System and Technology Architecture which has served as the foundation of VistA EHR and which we explore extensively in Sections II and III in this book.

FOSS Rationale and Benefits for Healthcare Organizations

There are an increasing number of resources available on FOSS in health care. Some additional resources to examine, as you evaluate the qualitative and quantitative benefits of FOSS in health care, include:

FIGURE 3-4 Open Source Software: A Primer for Health Care Leaders
Web Page
Source: http://www.chef.org/topics/view.cfm?itemid=119091

- ***Open Source Software: A Primer for Health Care Leaders*** The
  California Healthcare Foundation (CHCF) has released a report
  on open source solutions in health care. The report examines the
  development and distribution of open source software, a well-
  established software development model—and a potential solution
  to the looming challenges of integration—characterized by collaboration among individuals and organizations with common interests,
  sharing intellectual property, and a commitment to standards.
  (http://www.chcf.org/topics/view.cfm?itemid=119091)
- ***"Why Free and Open Source Software and Free Software (FOSS/
  FS)? Look at the Numbers!"*** This document by David Wheeler provides an extensive listing of quantitative data indicating that in many
  cases using FOSS is a reasonable or even superior approach to using
  other proprietary solutions. (http://www.dwheeler.com/oss_fs_why.
  html)

- ***Six Barriers to Open Source Adoption*** This article by Dan Farber lists significant barriers that still need to be overcome for broad acceptance of open source across enterprises. (http://techupdate. zdnet.com/techupdate/stories/main/Six_barriers_to_open_source_ adoption.html)

Major organizations such as the California Healthcare Foundation have joined the effort to educate leaders. Significant growth is now occurring in both the use and the development of FOSS applications using: Linux, MYSQL, Apache, openSSL, and other open source utilities and tools. There is significant growth in international networks of healthcare programmers organized around an increasing number of healthcare ini-tiatives to build and evolve Free and Open Source Software (FOSS) solutions. These efforts range from Open Source VistA, led by the not-for-profit, 501c3, WorldVistA and the VistA Software Alliance, to BLOX, an initiative whose purpose is to develop an open source quantitative medical imaging and visu-alization program for use on the brain sponsored by the Kennedy Krieger Institute and Johns Hopkins University's Psychiatric Neuroimaging Lab.

Doug Heintzman of IBM, in his paper "The Role of Open Comput-ing, Open Standards, and Open Source in Public Sector," describes goals of "openness," which are applicable to the healthcare market as well. He indicates that the goals of 'openness' include:

- Ensuring flexibility.
- Ensuring interoperability.
- Avoiding vendor lock-in.
- Avoiding imposing technology decisions on the citizenry.
- Driving cost-effectiveness.
- Ensuring future access to information.
- Ensuring a level playing field for competition.
- Maximizing freedom of action.

Heintzman says that most major companies and governments have embraced the concept of open computing. Healthcare institutions in par-ticular are beginning to catch on to the idea of adopting FOSS solutions. The rationale for FOSS in health care, in addition to the above-mentioned goals, includes support of the *global* public/private healthcare community by making tools available that are not based on proprietary solutions, wherever appropriate.

Given the emerging trend in FOSS, the increasing cost of commercial software, and the limited funding available to healthcare institutions, all healthcare organizations need to evaluate FOSS solutions and related benefits as part of their information technology and clinical excellence strategy. The evaluation should take note of:

- *Significantly lower and quantifiable total cost of ownership (TCO)* when comparing Free and Open Source Software (FOSS) against proprietary vendor solutions in key software product categories.
- *Enhanced security and interoperability* (e.g., meeting HIPAA, emerging CHI, and NHII standards) relative to many proprietary software applications and frameworks.
- *Growing weight of global public and private support* around FOSS products and solutions, including collaborative organizations like Open Source Development Labs (OSDL), WorldVistA, Free Software Foundation, and the Open Source Health Care Alliance.
- *Rapidly growing FOSS implementations and success stories* in federal, state, and local governments and in the private healthcare sector.
- *Evolving federal trends, mandates, and executive recommendations,* including the DoD FOSS policy, the President's Information Technology Advisory Council 2000, Consolidated Health Informatics efforts, Technology Transfer, the presidential mandate that most Americans obtain an electronic medical record in the next 10 years, and others.
- *Extensive growth in FOSS availability, and functionality* in areas including servers, middleware, development tools, and the desktop.
- *Demonstrable improvement in system performance and reliability* based on comparable workloads in a growing number of application areas.
- *Reduction in ongoing staff support* for manpower requirements to support fixes, patches, moves, adds, changes, and other ongoing maintenance tasks.

Open Solutions and Free and Open Source Software (FOSS) in health care are growing rapidly. FOSS will gain increasing recognition over this next decade as an essential part of any cost–effective solution to implement clinical data exchange or electronic health record (EHR) systems needed to support high-quality care in private and public healthcare organizations around the world.

Collaborating for Quality with Open Solutions

"We can't treat EHR as a competitive advantage that we keep for ourselves. We have to spread it around as widely as possible."

Frank Hayes, "Network Effect," ComputerWorld

"It is not the strongest of the species that survive, nor the most intelligent, but the one most responsive to change."

Charles Darwin

"Collaboration is the fuel that allows common people to attain uncommon results."

Anonymous

Section Overview: Medical Informatics 20/20 emphasizes the COSI strategies of Collaboration, Open Solutions, and Innovation. The focus of this section of the book is on the first of these key strategies, Collaboration. Interest by healthcare organizations in the public and private sector in collaborating on the development of health information systems has increased significantly. These organizations are seeing the benefits of pooling resources to work on mutually beneficial health technology sharing initiatives in such areas as medical informatics standards, electronic health records (EHRs), personal health records (PHRs), health information exchange (HIE), and public health information systems.

Chapter 4, Establishing a Health Information Technology Sharing Program, delivers a detailed description of a health information technology sharing (HITS) program and business process that can be established by a healthcare organization to proactively identify potential collaborative health IT sharing opportunities that save time and money in implementing technology. It is based on the highly successful HITS program that was established within the Veterans Health Administration (VHA) to support its HealthePeople strategy. In addition, three other short profiles are presented of other information technology collaborations by organizations such as Perot Systems, PÉRADIGM™ Software Sharing Community, Medtronics, Best Buy, Thomson, and a network of government agencies.

Chapter 5, Profiles of Collaboration Projects in EHRs, Standards, and Health Information Exchanges, highlights a series of profiles on selected collaborative projects and activities in medical informatics architecture and standards, electronic health records (EHRs), personal health records (PHRs), health information exchange (HIE), and public health information systems. Links to many other collaborative organizations, projects, and activities in each of these major areas are also given for readers to further explore on their own. In addition, extensive lists of collaborative projects across all the dimensions are provided in a series of detailed tables.

Chapter 6, The VistA Market—Today and Tomorrow, highlights the many collaboration activities related to the deployment of VistA health information technology and EHR systems throughout the world, from a private healthcare facility in Midlands, Texas, to federal agencies such as the Veterans Administration (VA) and the Indian Health Service, to state-run healthcare facilities in Hawaii and

Oklahoma, as well as international implementations of VistA in Mexico, Egypt, and other countries. It describes key organizations and their activities related to implementation of this Free and Open Source Software solution in various forms such as VistA–Office EHR, the Pacific Hui OpenVista, and other variants supported by WorldVistA and the VistA Software Alliance. In-depth knowledge on how major health information technology companies are stepping up to support VistA outside of the VA is shared along with links to key sources of information on open solutions in health care.

Chapter 7, National Health Information Network (NHIN), Regional Health Information Oganizations (RHIO), and the Federal Health Information Exchange (FHIE), discusses the National Health Information Network (NHIN) and the formation and activities of Regional Health Information Organizations (RHIOs) across the country. These are major public and private sector collaborative efforts aimed at putting in place key components of the National Health Informatics Infrastructure in the Unites States. The chapter also gives a detailed profile of the highly successful Federal Health Information Exchange (FHIE) project as well a listing of other selected health information exchange (HIE) initiatives that are now underway.

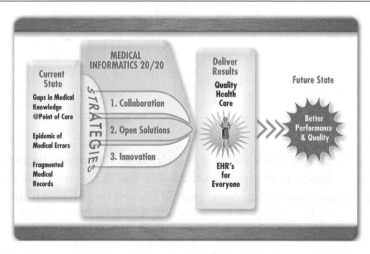

FIGURE II-1 Tactics, Tools, and Technologies Supporting Collaboration and Medical Informatics 20/20

CHAPTER 4

Establishing a Health Information Technology Sharing Program

"The history of the medical community's discovery of the importance of sharing discoveries is a paradigm for what has been more recently developing in the free software or open source community."

—*Medical Enterprises and Open Source* by Daniel L. Johnson, MD

Transforming by Sharing Knowledge and Technology

In the book *2020 Vision* written in the early 1990s, authors Stan Davis and Bill Davidson discussed the movement toward interorganizational initiatives. They were still searching for a more specific label to better fit this emerging movement. Today we have multiple labels to describe these interorganizational activities, such as *partnering, alliances, collaboration, facilitated knowledge transfer,* and, the most simple and direct word, *sharing.* This book has organized the strategies and tactics associated with these terms into a powerful Medical Informatics 20/20 model to guide leaders in transforming the healthcare industries of the world.

Interest by healthcare organizations in the public and private sector in collaborating on the development of health information systems has increased significantly over the past few years. These organizations have begun to see the benefits of pooling resources to work on mutually beneficial medical informatics and health information technology sharing initiatives in such areas as medical informatics standards, electronic health records (EHRs), personal health records (PHRs), health information exchange (HIE), and pubic health information systems.

This chapter focuses on the experience of the Veterans Health Administration (VHA) in creating a health information technology sharing (HITS) program. The chapter concludes with highlights of several examples of the sharing of information technology by other organizations in the form of software and other intellectual property in a modified Open Solutions model. The initiatives highlighted include Perot Systems' PÉRADIGM™, the Avalanche Corporate Technology Cooperative, and the Government Open Code Collaborative (GOCC).

In 2001, the Veterans Health Administration (VHA), which is an agency within the U.S. Department of Veterans Affairs (VA), developed a long-range information systems strategy aimed at pursuing collaborative partnerships with public and private sector organizations. The goal was to help foster open, interoperable health information systems with common architectures and standardized data and communications components that could be used to improve health care for veterans and others across the country. The HITS program within the VHA Office of Information (OI) was established to provide support for the Health*e*People long-range collaborative strategy.

Specific objectives of Health*e*People and the HITS program included:

- *Standards*—Developing and adopting common solutions and standards for architecture, data, communications, security, technology, and systems. Adopting common clinical data, terminology, and communications standards, and sharing data from multiple agencies to be used for public health purposes.
- *Sharing*—Seeking appropriate opportunities for sharing existing health information systems and technologies.
- *Joint Development*—Seeking appropriate opportunities for joint procurements, development, or operation of health information systems.
- *Health Information Exchange*—Seeking appropriate opportunities for improved health information exchange to support interoperability across the public sector and provide leadership for the private sector.

- *Convergence*—Working with partners toward convergence on high-performance health information systems.

The HITS program proved to be very successful. Appended to this chapter is a table listing some of the major accomplishments and activities of VHA's HITS program at the end of its fourth year of operation.

The creation and execution of a successful HITS program is a multi-phased process. This chapter provides well-defined steps to follow for your organization to succeed in systematically identifying and implementing collaborative initiatives. This process is modeled on the successful efforts of VHA's Health IT Sharing (HITS) program.

Phase I: Identifying High Potential Sharing Opportunities

Step 1: Build the Foundation

To successfully execute collaborative projects and information exchange with other organizations, your organization may need to establish and staff a Health Information Technology Sharing (HITS) program. The number of staff would vary depending on the size of your organization. The program could be staffed by as few as one to two people. The HITS staff would perform a number of ongoing activities designed to help your organization identify potential health IT sharing opportunities that might be worth pursuing. The staff should begin by identifying internal organizational needs that lend themselves to health-related IT sharing. They should also identify external organizations where mutually beneficial HITS opportunities might likely exist. Some of these ongoing HITS activities might include:

- Networking at meetings and conferences (both governmental and nongovernmental).
- Responding to high-level mandates (e.g., legislation, corporate policy) pertaining to health IT sharing.
- Participating in regularly scheduled meetings with management counterparts across your IT organization.
- Monitoring your organization's monthly CIO management reports, IT plans, IT architecture, and other pertinent documents.

- Monitoring public and private sector health IT systems, plans, and architecture (e.g., via the Internet).
- Meeting with potential health information and technology sharing partners.

Step 2: Gather the Information

HITS program staff should continuously collect information on potential health IT sharing partners, public and private sector health IT systems, key organizational contacts, major IT sharing initiatives, IT portfolios, and IT development or acquisition plans. A HITS database should be established to enable staff to collect and store large amounts of data related to health information systems and to monitor potential and current sharing activities. This data should be updated routinely and should include, at a minimum, information such as project/system ID; project/system name, description, and sharing category (e.g., intra-organization, interorganization, government, non-government, international); project start/end dates; key partners;

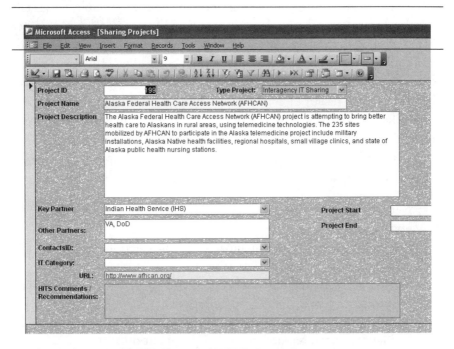

FIGURE 4-1 Health IT Sharing (HITS) Database

points-of-contact; URL; and internal HITS comments or recommendations. The database may need to be made available to both internal offices and external organizations. Figure 4-1 is a sample screen from a "Sharing Projects" file within a HITS database.

Step 3: Analyze the Information

Once the information has been gathered, the next step is to identify potential sharing opportunities that may help address some internal operational needs. To do this, the HITS program staff should conduct a periodic high-level analysis of health information sharing opportunities based on the data collected and stored in the HITS database. The data should be sorted and viewed in a number of ways during this analysis phase. For example, it could be sorted by categories such as electronic health record (EHR), personal health record (PHR), architecture and standards, health information exchange (HIE), and public health information system. The data could also be sorted by organization and many other variables as the staff looks for meaningful clusters and findings on which to base recommendations to senior management about which health information sharing opportunities to pursue.

Some other factors affecting a decision to pursue a health information systems sharing relationship include:

- Awareness of internal organizational needs that lend themselves to potential opportunities for health information systems sharing.
- A mandate from a higher authority, such as Congress or the chief executive officer (CEO), that provides the impetus to pursue an information systems sharing initiative.
- Identification of an opportunity that mutually benefits all partners based on an objective analysis of planned information system implementation and existing organization portfolios of health information systems.

When assessing opportunities with potential partners it is important to prioritize sharing opportunities for further study based on cost-benefit estimates, the potential for near-term success, the probability for a win-win outcome that will meet the operational needs of all potential partners, and whether the joint effort will delay progress of other major informations systems initiatives that may already be underway. In addition, it is imperative to ensure that the potential sharing opportunities align with the mission and goals of the partnering organizations. These priorities should be evaluated on at least an annual basis. If the assumptions of the program and/or organizational needs change in the middle of the project, it should be analyzed immediately to determine next steps.

Step 4: Select the High Opportunity

HITS program staff may want to use an objective decision support tool to assist them in deciding which sharing opportunities to recommend and in which priority. For example, they may build a prioritization matrix that measures each opportunity against such factors as meeting critical mission goals, enhancing provided services, and delivering highest potential return on investment. Once the analysis is complete, the HITS program management staff should submit their official report on potential health IT sharing opportunities with key findings and recommendations to the chief information officer (CIO).

The CIO would review the findings and recommendations presented in the report and set the priorities of the potential health information sharing opportunities to be pursued. The HITS staff should stand ready to provide support during this decision-making process as needed. They might be tasked to bring in potential partners, operational staff, and other senior staff to meet with the CIO; gather additional information as follow-up on key issues; or prepare additional briefing packages or materials for the CIO and other decision makers.

Step 5: Develop the High Potential Opportunity

Once the CIO has selected the health IT sharing initiatives to pursue, the HITS management and program staff should begin to work with the appropriate internal offices to initiate the next steps to establish formal contacts between the potential key stakeholders in each of the partnering organizations. When a potential sharing opportunity becomes a project and is formally approved and funded, a project manager (PM) should be appointed from the appropriate office within your organization. The HITS staff will continue to track the progress of the sharing project over time and provide limited support, as needed.

Phase II: Establishing the IT Sharing Project

Step 1: Make Initial Contact

Once the health IT sharing initiatives have been selected and approved for further action, the HITS program management staff should draft an initial contact message to be conveyed to each potential partnering organization through e–mail (preferred), phone, or memorandum. This message ought to contain, at a minimum, the following information:

- Introduction of the HITS program manager and a brief description of the HITS program.
- Summary of the proposed health information sharing initiative.
- Inquiry about interest in pursuing the proposed health information sharing initiative.
- Request for a point-of-contact from each potential partnering organization, including name, e–mail address, and phone number.

Each contact should be documented in the HITS database, including any "go/no go" decisions and the rationale for the decisions.

Step 2: Convene Face-to-Face Meetings

If the potential partners agree to proceed with further evaluation of the proposed health information sharing initiative, an initial meeting or conference call should be scheduled. Participants should include proposed business users of the information system from each organization and high-level decision makers that can authorize whether to proceed, based on the outcome of the initial meeting. If results of the initial meeting are positive, a follow-up meeting should be scheduled with expanded participation to include key business managers and executives from the CIO's office. The HITS program director, with support from the HITS program staff, should facilitate these meetings. Agenda items might include:

- Overview and goals of the potential sharing arrangement or health IT collaboration.
- Overview of the required resources to support the initiative.
- Capability of each potential partner to support the sharing arrangement or IT collaboration.
- Benefits of the potential sharing arrangement or IT collaboration.

- Potential barriers and risks of the sharing arrangement or IT collaboration.
- Compatibility of the partners (e.g., organizational business culture).

If appropriate, on-site demonstrations of key systems might be arranged. Meeting minutes should be recorded, including a "go/no go" decision and rationale.

Step 3: Identify Champions

If after this second meeting the potential partners agree to further pursue the proposed health information sharing initiative, each partnering organization ought to identify a "champion" who will be expected to provide leadership on behalf of his or her organization. The champion's role will be to:

- Establish a sense of urgency for the project.
- Create a guiding coalition.
- Develop a vision and strategy.
- Prepare and present the business case.
- Communicate the vision and business case.
- Identify short-term wins.
- Anchor new approaches in the organization's culture.

Identifying a champion is crucial to the success of any major project that will have a significant effect on existing clinical and business practices.

Step 4: Develop Formal Documentation

The purpose of this next step is to further define the roles and responsibilities of the HITS program management staff in support of the champions and/or respective leaders of the partnering organizations. The HITS staff may need to provide support in:

- Developing the formal documentation, including the:
  - Business case, as required for any major projects. These documents demonstrate good project management practices and provide a strong business case for the investment and define the proposed cost, schedule, and performance goals if funding approval is obtained.
  - Sharing Agreements (e.g., memorandum of understanding [MOU], memorandum of agreement [MOA], inter-agency agreement, or

selling agreement). These formal agreements, signed by senior management officials, spell out the terms of the IT sharing partnership. The following are suggestions of what might be included in the sharing agreement, based on the needs of an individual project:

–Lead agencies/organizations
–Background information
–Roles and Responsibilities
–Purpose and scope of agreement
–Guiding policy and principles
–Contributions of each sharing partner
–Executive oversight or governance structure
–Project management team
–Interagency working groups
–Major project milestones
–Performance metrics
–Amendment of Agreement
–Dispute resolution method(s)
–Period of performance
–Approval(s)

- Obtaining necessary approvals for funding this mutually beneficial health IT sharing initiative; preparing a preliminary list of potential funding sources.
- Scheduling follow-up meetings: The HITS program management staff may help to initially identify working group members, track accomplishments, and suggest scheduling frequency based on tracking of the tasks/accomplishments.
- Establishing joint working groups: Identify the technical issues best addressed by working group(s); effective methods for managing communication among members (teleconferencing may not always be a viable option); and assignment of subject matter experts. The working groups may help define the span of responsibilities.
- Documenting technical, legal, and policy constraints and requesting exemptions, as appropriate.
- Facilitating the submission of the packet of information for the IT sharing initiative for approval within the organization. Information may include a revised analysis, MOU, or business case. If the project is disapproved, the HITS program management staff should document the reasons in the HITS database. If the project is approved,

the HITS staff should then begin to disengage and simply monitor the progress of the sharing initiative.

Step 5: Establish Project Governance

A formal governance structure is strongly recommended when establishing an interorganizational health information sharing project. The structure might include:

- An executive oversight committee (e.g., board of directors or executive committee) composed of senior management officials with specific responsibility and authority to make major decisions affecting the project.
- Key interorganizational working groups to address financial, contracting, and legal issues, at a minimum.
- A project manager (PM) who possesses strong leadership and negotiation skills and has a clear understanding of the culture and environment of all partnering organizations. Managing programs that cross organizational boundaries can be challenging in terms of line authority over the staff, personnel performance appraisals, coordination and control, obtaining office space, equipment, training, and other issues.
- A project management team composed of members from each partnering organization and that may include both employees and contract staff.

At this point, the PM for the sharing project assumes most of the responsibilities for seeing the project through to completion. However, the HITS program management staff may remain in contact to document progress, provide liaison services, as needed, and share lessons learned from other projects. They can also help to ensure that both internal and external stakeholders play positive influencing roles in the IT sharing arrangement, creating "win-win" relationships.

Phase III: Planning for the Health IT Sharing Project

Step 1: HITS Program Staff Activities

During the project planning stages, the HITS program staff might continue to provide limited support to the project manager (PM) and respective leaders of the partnership, upon request. In an effort to facilitate a "win-win" result for all sharing partners, the HITS program management staff should stay informed about project activities in order to communicate progress to the CIO and other senor managers. Additional activities may include:

- Briefing the PM on the history of the health information sharing initiative.
- Preparing responses to internal and external inquiries concerning the health IT collaboration.
- Supporting the evaluation and capture of lessons learned throughout the duration of the sharing project.
- Suggesting project management communication vehicles (e.g., weekly conference calls, e-mail groups, meetings) for effective information flow.

Step 2: Project Management Activities

It is the PM's responsibility to develop the project management plan, which formally documents all the components necessary to ensure a thorough and shared understanding of the collaborative project from start-up and planning, through execution, to close out. Some of the benefits of developing the project plan include:

- Ensures that each partner's requirements are met.
- Identifies major goals, objectives, and milestones early in the process.
- Encourages a positive, shared group mind-set that the partners have achievable goals.

The following questions may assist the sharing partners, stakeholders, and the PM in identifying the major tasks and activities and resolving issues prior to proceeding with the project work:

- Is the activity focused on customer needs and expectations?
- Is the activity within the agreed-upon project scope?
- What are the internal and external constraints?
- When is it due to be completed?
- What is the time duration?
- What agency resources are required?
- What is the overall cost of the project?

Phase IV: Implementing the IT Sharing Project

The PM is responsible for overseeing the implementation of the project management plan by following the many generally accepted best practices associated with project management through the life cycle of the project. In this leadership role, the PM facilitates negotiations to obtain resources across the matrix of partnering organizations. The HITS program manager, upon request, continues to provide advice and support to the PM for a smooth transition from project planning to project implementation. The examples in Table 4-1 offer insight into the types of Phase IV supportive activities the HITS program manager may be asked to become involved in:

Table 4-1 Project Management and HITS Program Staff Implementation Tasks

	Implementing the IT Sharing Project
Key Project Manager Tasks	**HITS Program Management may provide support by:**
Schedule interagency project milestones and major activities by taking into account the individual partner's needs and outcome goals	Alerting the PM to significant changes in priorities or budgets of partnering agencies that could affect the sharing project
Coordinate the partners' readiness and their IT systems' functional and technical requirements	Helping to facilitate identifying points of contact and obtaining needed information to complete functional and technical requirements
Develop reasonable timeframes for major sharing activities or milestones with input from the project team and partnering agencies	Monitoring the partnering organizations timelines throughout project implementation and offering guidance, as needed, on how to better achieve reasonable time frames
Survey and identify any sharing partners' special requirements that could affect scheduling, such as acquiring special hardware, developing or customizing data processes, or changing systems and IT policies	Helping to facilitate identifying points of contact to obtain needed information
Layout and track progress of major tasks through the use of effective management tools, such as Gantt charts, network diagrams, milestone charts, checklists, and project management software	Monitoring and reporting major achievements or problems to senior management, as needed
Communicate and promote the project's success to all stakeholders	Helping to develop project marketing materials as needed Ensuring that all communication and promotional activities are coordinated between relevant offices in each partnering organization.

Phase V: Expanding and Transferring Knowledge

As a health information sharing project nears completion, the IT sharing partners' and HITS program management staff need to shift their focus to evaluating the success of the project, compiling and sharing lessons learned, and determining if there should be any follow-up on project activities. The lessons learned may be used to modify existing IT project development, prioritization, and control processes; guide future interorganizational sharing initiatives; and contribute to improvements in inter-agency project management. Overarching questions to consider include:

- How effective was the sharing arrangement in meeting the original objectives?
- How well did the sharing project meet the planned implementation dates?
- Were the original business assumptions that prompted the sharing arrangement validated?

The post-implementation activities for health IT sharing projects should include:

- Evaluating the success of the IT sharing project.
  - Use standardized evaluation tools and techniques to collect, record, and analyze data (e.g., performance-based management and information technology performance measures).
  - Survey users' perceptions and identify positive and negative sharing project experiences.
  - Assess tangible benefits that can be assigned a dollar value (e.g., personnel costs, IT costs to purchase/modify/upgrade system equipment).
  - Use a multi-functional team approach to determine how well the project goals and objectives were met from each organizations' perspective.
  - Include both qualitative and quantitative performance measures that measure customer satisfaction (surveys), on-time task completion within budget task completion, service improvement, and cost savings.

- Compare expected project results against actual benefits and returns.
- Compiling and sharing lessons learned.
  - Solicit feedback from the sharing partners during the course of the project and after project implementation.
  - Document positive and negative lessons learned during the project's life cycle.
  - Compile a final "lessons learned" report.
- Determining if the health IT sharing project should be expanded.
  - Consider replicating the project at additional sites, if needed.
  - Consider bringing in new partners who could benefit from this type of sharing project.
  - Consider increasing the amount of information flowing between partners.

Health Information Technology Sharing (HITS) Program Checklist

Phase I: Identify High Potential Sharing Opportunities

- ☐ Assess internal agency needs and identify any unmet needs
- ☐ Periodically review the health IT systems and plans of external organizations
- ☐ Gather information on major health IT sharing initiatives of interest
- ☐ Gather and enter data on potential sharing activities/partners into a HITS database
- ☐ Analyze the data and identify potential sharing opportunities and partners
- ☐ Perform a preliminary cost/benefit and risk analysis of high-priority opportunities
- ☐ Arrange initial meetings and system demonstrations, as appropriate
- ☐ Identify all potential stakeholders
- ☐ Identify and prioritize potential health IT sharing opportunities to pursue
- ☐ Present preliminary findings and recommendations on sharing opportunities to the CIO
- ☐ Arrange high-level meetings or briefings for the CIO, as needed
- ☐ Await CIO's selection of sharing initiatives to pursue

Phase II: Establish the HITS Project

- ☐ Contact each potential organization to discuss the sharing opportunity
- ☐ Establish a point-of-contact for each organization
- ☐ Schedule and conduct initial meetings with interested organizations
- ☐ Schedule and conduct follow-up meeting(s) with expanded participation
- ☐ Ensure a "champion" is identified in each partnering organization
- ☐ Help formalize the partnership agreement (e.g., memorandum of understanding/agreement)
- ☐ Help put in place an appropriate governance structure for inter-organizational sharing projects

(continues)

FIGURE 4-2 Health Information Technology Sharing Program Checklist

FIGURE 4-2 *continued*

☐ Ensure a project manager (PM) is appointed

Phase III: Plan for the HITS Project

☐ Brief the project manager on the history of the sharing initiative
☐ Prepare responses to internal and external inquiries concerning the health IT relationship
☐ Suggest project management communication vehicles (e.g., weekly conference calls, e–mail groups, meetings) for effective information flow
☐ Help to develop and obtain necessary approvals for the project plan and budget
☐ Help put together the project management team

Phase IV: Implement the HITS Project

☐ Ensure the inter-organization project management team has all needed background information
☐ Monitor and report on achievements, obstacles, and scheduling delays
☐ Report significant changes in project plans to senior management and other key parties
☐ Offer guidance, as requested, to help achieve objectives in reasonable time frames
☐ Facilitate and track resolution of support issues and keep track of lessons learned

Phase V: Expand and Transfer Knowledge

☐ Evaluate the success of the sharing project through application of measurable performance metrics
☐ Document the process and all lessons learned before officially completing the project
☐ Ensure that all public announcements about the project are reviewed and approved by all of the partnering organizations before being released
☐ Support and promote knowledge sharing based on outcomes of the IT sharing project

---

Health IT Sharing Program

Summary of Major Accomplishments and Ongoing Activities
[2001–2004]

The following are just some of the many major VHA Health IT Sharing (HITS) accomplishments and activities with other federal, state, local, and tribal governments, in addition to private sector and international organizations.

• *Federal Health Architecture (FHA) and the Consolidated Health Informatics (CHI) Federal eGov Initiatives*—The VHA is actively participating in these multi-year, interagency initiatives aimed at achieving systems convergence and agreement on architecture and standards for health information systems across federal government agencies (e.g., HHS, DoD/ Military Health, VHA, IHS). Federal agencies participating in CHI adopted more than 12 standards to support interoperability (e.g., HL7, LOINC, NCPDP, DICOM, and X12).

- *Federal Credentialing System and VetPro*—This is a collaborative partnership between HRSA and VA with other federal agencies on a standardized, electronic credentialing system and databank that meets JCAHO standards. (http://bhpr.hrsa.gov/dqa/fcp.htm)
- *Interagency Memorandum of Understanding (MOU) and VHA*—The VHA has put in place a number of MOUs with federal agencies, such as the FDA, NLM, and NCI, to support collaboration on a National Drug File, sharing drug information, developing terminology standards, and other purposes.
- *Interagency Committees/Work Groups*—VHA staff currently participate on key federal healthcare information committees such as the Quality Interagency Coordination Task Force (QuIC), National Committee on Vital and Health Statistics (NCVHS), and various National Health Information Infrastructure (NHII) work groups.
- *National and International Health Information Standard*—Continued involvement by the VHA and the IT Architects in national and international nongovernment organizations (NGO) working on the development and adoption of many healthcare information and communications standards (e.g., HL7, LOINC, DICOM, X12).
- *National SNOMED License*—The VA, the DoD, and the HHS collaborated on an agreement with the College of American Pathologists (CAP) to license the college's standardized medical vocabulary system (SNOMED) and make it freely available throughout the United States.
- *VA/DoD Electronic Health Record (EHR) System*—This is a large umbrella initiative involving the VA/DoD collaboration on an EHR system involving a Clinical/Health Data Repository (C/HDR) and other components such as pharmacy, laboratory, and scheduling.
- *VA/DoD Planned Joint Demonstration Sites*—The FY 2003 National Defense Authorization Act, Section 722, requires at least three more VA/DoD sites for the conduct of specific collaborative IT solutions focusing on budget and financial management, coordinated personnel staffing and assignment, and medical information and technology solutions. This is in addition to the existing VA/DoD joint venture healthcare sites with shared IT systems that are operating at seven locations: Albuquerque, NM; El Paso, TX; Las Vegas, NV; Anchorage, AK; Miami, FL; Honolulu, HI; and Fairfield (Martinez), CA.

- **Federal Health Information Exchange (FHIE)**—FHIE provides historical data on separated and retired military personnel from the DoD's Composite Health Care System (CHCS) to the FHIE Data Repository for viewing by VA clinicians in VistA. FHIE was successfully deployed across all VA medical centers beginning in June 2002. A new, related initiative, the **Bi-Directional Health Information Exchange (BHIE)**, is now underway.
- **VA/DoD Laboratory Data Sharing & Interoperability (LDSI) Project**—This was a successful multi-year, joint VA/DoD initiative to develop a national solution to allow the department's healthcare facilities to send lab test orders and receive lab test results to and from any site, as needed.
- **VA/DoD Consolidated Mail Outpatient Pharmacy (CMOP) Project**—The departments collaborated on an application that supports the VA's refilling of outpatient prescription medications from the DoD's military treatment facilities at the option of the beneficiary. Testing was successfully completed.
- **VA/DoD eHealth Portals**—The departments are collaborating on the development and enhancement of their eHealth portal systems, TRICARE Online, and My HealtheVet. Both departments acquired the health and wellness content for their Web sites.
- **TRAC²ES**—This successful joint VA/DoD development effort was aimed at integrating all assets (medical and transportation) required to facilitate the decision process of evacuating military casualties from a combat theater to a VA or DoD source of definitive medical care within the Continental United States (CONUS).
- **VistA & D.C. Government**—VHA staff provided limited technical assistance to the D.C. government over the past year as they successfully implemented the VistA system in two of their major outpatient clinics.

Additional sites are planning to use VistA in the coming year(s).

- **VistA and American Samoa**—VA staff at headquarters and the Honolulu VAMC provided limited technical assistance to the American Samoan government over the past few years as they successfully implemented the VistA system in the LBJ Tropical Medical Center.
- **VistA and National Hansen's Disease Centers**—With VHA assistance, the National Hansen's Disease Programs (NHDP), based in Baton Rouge, Louisiana, brought up the VistA system in 1989 and updated their infrastructure in 2000. They have a patient database size of 16,082 patients.
- **VistA and State Government Health Departments**—VHA staff have received numerous calls from state and local government representatives expressing an interest in possibly acquiring and using the

VistA/CPRS system. Briefings and demonstrations have been arranged, as needed. Examples include:

○ West Virginia, Texas, Hawaii, Louisiana, Michigan, and several other states that have expressed an interest in acquiring and implementing VistA and CPRS, in addition to several major cities and counties.

- **VistA and State Veterans Homes**—VHA staff are working with representatives from state veterans homes, the Geriatrics Program, the VISNs, VAMCs, and cyber security on this initiative. More than 70 sites have been given secure CPRS read-only access to date.

- **VistA and Indian Health Service (IHS)**—The VA and the IHS signed a new inter-agency MOU in support of health information sharing efforts (e.g., CPRS, VistA Imaging). The agencies will continue to work on developing and adopting common health information standards and new technical solutions.

- **VistA and AAMC/Affiliated Medical Schools**—The VHA has academic affiliations with 107 medical schools and more than 1,200 other educational institutions. VHA OI selected several pilot sites to test collaborative health information solutions in FY 2005/06.

- **VistA and Veterans Service Organizations (VSO)**—The VHA has made VistA and CPRS read-only available to authorized patient representatives in Veterans Service Organizations (VSO) over the past year (e.g., VFW, DAV, PVA, and American Legion).

- **VistA and Public Health and Biosurveillance**—The Department of Health and Human Services (HHS) has numerous public health systems and databases that capture data on specific diseases, deaths, incidents, and other events. Initial efforts were started in FY 2004 involving the transmission of de-identified patient data from the VHA to the HHS's Centers for Disease Control and Prevention (CDC).

- **VistA and International Healthcare Communities**—A number of countries have either implemented VistA or have expressed an interest in possibly acquiring and implementing the system. These include Finland, Egypt, Germany, and Mexico. Representatives from many other countries have contacted VHA and have been briefed and/or given demonstrations of the VistA system.

- **VistA and Mexico**—The Instituto Mexicano del Seguro Social (IMSS) is moving forward with testing and implementing the VA's VistA system. It has successfully implemented a Spanish version of VistA in more than ten hospitals and hope to implement it in up to 100 hospitals by the end of 2006.

- **VistA Sharing and the Open Source Healthcare Communities**—Under the Freedom of Information Act (FOIA), the VA has released copies of VistA software to the open source community and many other healthcare providers and health IT vendors (e.g., OSHCA and WorldVistA).

- **VistA Office EHR and HHS/CMS**—The Department of Health and Human Services (HHS), the Centers for Medicare & Medicaid Services (CMS), and the Veterans Health Administration (VHA) are collaborating on an initiative to transfer VistA, the VHA's electronic healthcare record (EHR) system, to the private physician office setting. Targeted for release July 2005, the VistA-Office EHR (VOE) system will be available to individual practices and the EHR industry.
- **VistA and the Vendor Community**—The VistA Software Alliance (VSA) was formed to allow a collaboration between government and private businesses to facilitate the implementation of VistA within healthcare organizations outside of the VA. A growing number of major software vendors have joined the VSA (e.g., HP, EDS, Perot Systems, and InterSystems).
- **Bi-Directional Web Connections**—In an attempt to create a more comprehensive and tightly coupled online community of information sharing for veterans on the Internet, HITS staff have worked with the federal, state, and local veterans and healthcare organizations to put in place hyperlinks between their Web sites and the VA's.
- **National 211 Project**—Local VA Medical Centers are collaborating with efforts at the state and local community levels across the United States on their implementation of health and human services information and referral (I&R) telephone call centers accessed by dialing "211."
- **Knowledge Exchange and the Healthcare Community**—VHA staff have met with senior representatives from numerous major healthcare provider organizations (e.g., Kaiser Permanente, CHRISTUS, Adventist Health) to share knowledge related to health IT systems.

These are just some of the many health IT sharing activities the VA is collaborating on with other organizations.

Examples of Health IT Sharing for Quality and Safety by Other Organizations

Recent developments in the National Health Information Infrastructure/ Network within the United States highlight the importance of how technology and knowledge transfer techniques can offer a major breakthrough in implementing the much needed electronic health record systems and health information exchange systems. There needs to be a concerted effort to formalize health information technology sharing programs within the federal and other public sectors. In addition, a major collaborative focused on health information technology transfer across public-private sectors is also needed. The VA's HITS program is one of many successful programs. There are other examples of technology transfer and sharing in an Open Solutions and modified Open Solutions model. Several examples follow:

- Avalanche Corporate Technology Cooperative in the private sector.
- Government Open Code Collaborative Cooperative in the public sector.
- PÉRADIGM™ by Perot Systems in health care.

These collaborative initiatives are going beyond knowledge transfer to the actual sharing and transfer of software code and other intellectual assets within a collaborative modified Open Solutions environment. The efforts are modified Open Solutions because they focus on sharing intellectual assets among a membership network that is based on fees and other factors. An overview of these collaborative initiatives follows.

The Avalanche Corporate Technology Cooperative— Sharing Intellectual Property for Lower Costs and Better Service

This effort was incorporated in early 2004, and as of 2006 there were 13 member partners. Avalanche is a private exchange that enables its members to contribute, collaborate, and legally distribute intellectual property such as software including all source code and other property to other members. Avalanche is considered a gated/closed community, because only members can share software/technology. Members can donate any in-house software to the Avalanche library, turning over legal ownership of the code to Avalanche. Members potentially benefit from additional improvements made to the program, which is coordinated through the Avalanche collaborative software development process. All software code in the library is free to members. The oversight for Avalanche operations and growth is provided by the board of directors and CEO. Currently, annual membership fees are $30,000, which allows members to partner on research, standards documents, and software development. The expectations of the cooperative are:

- Save money on upfront licensing fees and maintenance fees, and ownership of information technology assets, but not on installation and ongoing development.
- Access to tested technology solutions, intellectual property, and experienced resources.
- Access to other members' ideas and knowledge for critical business and IT issues.
- Affordable membership fees that represent less than .01% of the expected software budget.
- Control of products and services including budget, product functionality, release schedules, and investment in new products.

Avalanche began as a project funded by some of the world's leading corporations, including Medtronics, Thomson, Jostens, Best Buy, Imation, and Cargill. It was designed to research open source concepts, collaboration approaches, and business structures that support a member group of companies. The end result was a business charter that outlined the basic structure, approach, and business model of a company that would provide a corporate collaboration and exchange environment. In many ways this effort is a modified Open Solutions business model in that the cooperative aggregates, develops, and enhances software for members within a "demand chain framework." Figure 4-3 illustrates the six founding members of the cooperative and also lists the current software and intellectual property available. For more information visit http://www.avalanche.coop/

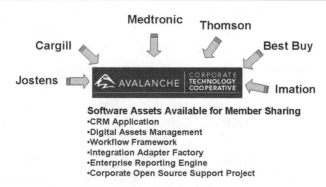

FIGURE 4-3 Avalanche Corporate Technology Cooperative

Government Open Code Collaborative (GOCC)— Sharing Software Code for Lower Costs

The Government Open Code Collaborative (GOCC), launched in June 2004, is an example of a voluntary collaboration between public sector entities and nonprofit academic institutions that encourages the sharing of computer code where the redistribution of this code is allowed. They define open code as "code that is licensed for reuse under an OSI Approved License or any other open source license deemed acceptable under the GOCC operating rules (e.g., Open Source Software, Free Software)." The GOCC's overriding objective is to allow government entities (federal, state, and local government, an authority, or other sub-national public sector entities in the United States) to transfer code they develop to other government operations, at no cost, without the usual barriers or legalities. The donated code and content (i.e., documentation, technical information, etc.) is accessible through a Web-based repository, with different access privileges for "members," "academic members," and "observers." Members and academic members sign an operating agreement through an authorized representative that allows them to appoint additional members within their entities to deposit/withdraw code and participate in GOCC meetings. Observers opt out of the agreement, although member sponsorship permits them to download code and participate in group discussions without a vote. The general public may also download code if members who donated the code grant public access. See http://www.gocc.gov/docs/about_GOCC/ for details.

The University of Rhode Island hosts the GOCC repository, which consists of MySQL database, Z Object Publishing Environment Application Server, Apache Web server, OpenLDAP authentication service for storing membership data, and the Debian Linus operating system running on an Intel-based rack-mounted server. Members can access the Big Brother Administrator's Guide at http://www.gocc.gov/groups/MA_ ITD/stateprojects/bigbro or its next-generation GPL replacement, the Hobbit, at http://hobbitmon.sourceforge.net to monitor networks for available resources.

Initial membership in the GOCC included 11 government agencies (http://www.gocc.gov/docs/about_GOCC/launchannouncement) from Massachusetts, Rhode Island, Pennsylvania, Utah, Kansas, Missouri, West Virginia, and Virginia. At the time of this writing, the GOCC Web site listed 45 members and 92 observers. It appears that healthcare agencies are participating in the GOCC as observers only and have not requested member status. Examples of member and observer contributions include a GOCC Listserv (New York's attorney general's office), application development for the repository (secretary of state of Rhode Island), and donation of code (Harvard and MIT). An example of the software available on the GOCC.gov site is Election Tally, contributed by the city of Newport News, Virginia. Election Tally is a parameter-driven Web-enabled application written in Python that utilizes ModPython and MySQL. It generates an election tally report by extracting files from the state Board of Elections and produces a video simulcast. Supporters of the GOCC hope that every state government will eventually join and begin to leverage existing technology from across the country. The faster membership grows, the more likely members (and taxpayers) will reap some of the following benefits:

- Reduce duplication of effort in custom-built software, particularly in routine areas of automation involving tax collection, real estate assessment, budget preparation, finance/accounting, public safety, election tally, and so on.
- Lower taxpayer costs associated with costly computer software research and development.

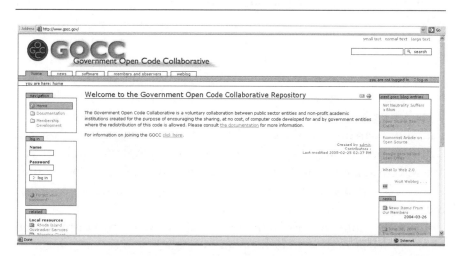

FIGURE 4-4 Government Open Code Collaborative
Source: http://www.gocc.gov

- Increase the availability and accessibility of code that meets the specific needs of government agencies.
- Eliminate the time-intensive state-to-state negotiation needed for each code-sharing arrangement.
- Shorten time frames associated with bringing new products to market.
- Increase consistency in services, standardization, and cohesiveness across government entities.
- Increase interoperability and connectivity between databases across the country.
- Increase innovation and quality of IT products.
- Heighten accountability.

The GOCC promotes its policy of no affiliation with professional or private sector entities or acceptance of financial or in-kind assistance from any private sector company as an advantage. For more information visit GOCC at http://www.gocc.gov.

PÉRADIGM™—Supporting Rapid Cycle Solution Development Through Open Solutions

This software-sharing service from Perot Systems is an industry-first collaborative technology program focused on supporting the transformation in healthcare information technology. It is structured in a modified Open Solutions model where there are no upfront license fees for outsourcing customers relative to healthcare applications, community-shared solutions and Perot Systems–produced applications. The technology seeks to leverage the open source movement and end proprietary models and high license fees by creating communities of users who share upgrades and enhancements. At the core of the effort is an open source "stack" (LAMP) that includes Linux (operating system), Apache (Web server), MySQL (database), and Perl, PHP, and Python (languages). Over time PÉRIDIGM plans to expand and move up the so-called software stack to include middleware and other applications.

In one example of PÉRADIGM™ use, the Stanford Hospitals and Clinics (SHC) needed to develop an expanded Web service capability and, hopefully, in the process reduce the operating costs that they would incur if they used a closed source software model from a third-party vendor. Stanford selected two "no license fee" applications from the Community Pass library of PÉRADIGM software that included a content manager and the portal application framework. The end result was that an independent SHC Web site was developed and launched utilizing applications from PÉRADIGM's open source model library, which saved approximately $450,000. The savings were realized from elimination of vendor software license, upgrade, and maintenance fees.

Perot Systems is adapting the PÉRADIGM™ model for different components of health care, including Payer PÉRADIGM enterprise solution to support a variety of health plans from U.S.-based and international plans to Medicaid and Medicare, including Part D prescription drug coverage. For instance Payer PÉRADIGM's library of software applications is targeted to streamline and simplify back-office functions for health plans in their operations using a service-oriented architecture (SOA). Examples of other software applications to be shared include:

- Personal Health Record (PHR)
- Workflow Manager
- Patient Billing Account Receivables
- Healthcare Information Portal (HIP) [*payer*]
- Enterprise PERspective Knowledge Manager
- Performance Dashboard
- Denials Management
- HR Management System
- Inventory Material Management System

To conclude, bringing together a community with common interests to develop various types of Open Solutions is the ultimate in "collaboration." Healthcare organizations should establish or participate in a health information technology sharing (HITS) program that assists in the rapid and effective deployment of clinical informatics to support better patient care. Only by fostering further collaboration and involving all customers and stakeholders will we see the healthcare industry move forward more rapidly toward achieving the vision of performance excellence and quality care through an electronic health record for every person in the world come 2020.

CHAPTER 5

Profiles of Collaboration Projects in EHRs, Standards, and Health Information Exchanges

"The universal use of EHRs will create a
quantum leap in the quality of patient care."

Dr. Munsey Wheby, President, American College of Physicians

After the president announced his plans for every American to have an Electronic Health Record (EHR) in 10 years, Dr. Brailer, the National Coordinator for Health Information Technology at the time, said that our healthcare issues could not be solved by either the government or private industry working on their own. He said that all public and private sector stakeholders would have to work together to attack the challenges facing our healthcare industry. Secretary Leavitt, of the Department of Health and Human Services (HHS), then followed up by establishing the American Health Information Community (AHIC) in an effort to bring key leaders in the public and private sector together to address the healthcare information technology issues and challenges facing health care today.

Healthcare organizations in the public and private sector have accepted this challenge and have begun collaborating on the development of a wide variety of health information solutions over the past few years. These organizations have begun to see the benefits of pooling resources to work on mutually beneficial health IT sharing initiatives. Scans of various open source Web sites including SourceForge.net and LinuxMedNews.com uncovered more than 300 international Open Source collabortaive software development initiatives in health care that were clinical and business related. The AMIA annual meeting 2005 paper "A Study of Clinically Related Open Source Software Projects" identified 179 clinically oriented efforts. This chapter will highlight some of these major collaborative health IT projects, especially ones related to open source software solution. These projects and activities are grouped into the following categories:

- Health Informatics Architecture and Standards.
- Electronic Health Records (EHR).
- Personal Health Records (PHR).
- Health Information Exchange (HIE).
- Public Health Information Systems.
- Health Information, Education, and Knowledge Sharing.
- Health IT Specialty Systems.

Finally, information on a number of public and private sector organizations that encourage collaborations on health IT systems in each of these areas, as well as many additional links to other collaborative projects related to selected medical specialty areas, are also presented in this chapter.

Profiles of Selected Health IT Collaboration Projects and Activities

IT Architecture, Standards, and Infrastructure

The following are brief descriptions of some of the many collaborative projects, activities, and organizations with a focus on health IT architecture and open standards.

Health Level Seven (HL7)

Health Level Seven (HL7) is one of several American National Standards Institute (ANSI) accredited Standards Developing Organizations (SDO) operating in the healthcare arena. It is a not-for-profit volunteer organization. Its members consist of healthcare providers, vendors, payers, consultants, government groups, and others. Their aim is to develop and advance the clinical and administrative standards for healthcare information systems. (http://www.hl7.org/)

Consolidated Health Informatics (CHI) eGov Initiative

The Department of Health and Human Services (HHS) has partnered with 23 other federal agencies and/or departments involved in health care on a multi-year federal eGov initiative to identify and adopt health IT standards. This has been an effort focused on adopting a portfolio of existing health information interoperability standards (health vocabulary and messaging) enabling all agencies in the federal health enterprise to "speak the same language" based on common enterprise-wide business and information technology architectures. These federal agencies will then build these adopted standards into their health IT architecture. All of the adopted standards can be accessed through the White House e-Gov link at the end of this paragraph. CHI is aimed at achieving health information systems convergence as well as agreement on standards for EHR systems. CHI goals have been incorporated into the FHA and activities coordinated through the Office of the National Coordinator for Health Information

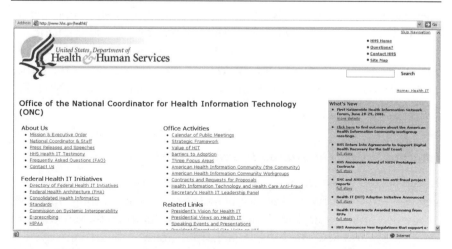

FIGURE 5-1 Office of the National Coordinator for Health Information Technology (ONCHIT) Web Site
Source: http://www.hhs.gov/healthit/

Technology (ONC) (http://www.hhs.gov/healthit/). The CHI effort laid a foundation of standards for clinical data interoperability by the public sector in an effort to accelerate acceptance in the private sector of these clinical data standards in the private sector so that EHR interoperability can be achieved within the context of the National Health Information Network. (http://www.whitehouse.gov/omb/egov/c-3-6-chi.html)

National Health Information Infrastructure (NHII) and the National Health Information Network (NHIN)

Many federal healthcare organizations have provided subject matter experts to help develop the National Health Information Infrastructure (NHII) plan prepared by the National Committee on Vital and Health Statistics (NCVHS). The plan laid the foundation for a program aimed at developing a national consensus providing guidance in eight key areas: 1) research and population health, 2) homeland security, 3) consumer health, 4) financial incentives, 5) safety and quality, 6) standards and vocabulary, 7) architecture, and 8) privacy and confidentiality. The NHII Strategic Plan was developed based on extensive input over several years from public and private sector organizations and individuals. (http://aspe.hhs.gov/sp/nhii/Documents/NHIIReport2001/toc.htm)

The Office of the National Coordinator for Health IT (ONCHIT) is charged with providing leadership for the development and implementation of the plan, with specific emphasis on development and implementation of an interoperable National Health Information Network (NHIN). The place to access information on NHIN and related topics is the Office of the National Health Information Technology Coordinator (ONCHIT) referenced above.

Internet2/Next Generation Internet (NGI)

Internet2 is a consortium being led by 205 universities working in partnership with industry and government to develop and deploy advanced network applications and technologies, accelerating the creation of tomorrow's Internet. The Next Generation Internet (NGI) initiative is a multi-agency federal research and development program that is developing advanced networking technologies, developing applications that require advanced networking, and demonstrating these capabilities on test beds that are 100 to 1,000 times faster end-to-end than today's Internet. The federal agencies that have participated in NGI include DARPA, NSF, DoE, NASA, NIH, NLM, and NIST. Key Internet2 and/or NGI projects include initiatives in the following fields of health care: radiology, orthopedic surgery, telehealth, medical education, and medical imaging. (http://www.internet2.edu)

Systematized Nomenclature of Medicine (SNOMED)

SNOMED® International is a division of the College of American Pathologists (CAP) and is focused on advancing excellence in patient care through the delivery of SNOMED. SNOMED is a dynamic and sustainable, scientifically validated terminology and infrastructure that enables clinicians, researchers, and patients to share healthcare knowledge worldwide, across clinical specialties and sites of care. Developed in collaboration with the United Kingdom's National Health Service, SNOMED CT's controlled healthcare terminology includes comprehensive coverage of diseases, clinical findings, therapies, procedures, and outcomes. It provides the core general terminology for an EHR, containing more than 357,000 concepts with unique meanings and formal logic-based definitions organized into hierarchies. SNOMED CT is considered to be the most comprehensive multilingual clinical reference terminology available in the world. (http://www.snomed.org/)

Electronic Health Records (EHR)

The following are brief descriptions of just some of the many collaborative projects, activities, and organizations involving the development and implementation of EHR systems. The primary focus will be on those projects that involve Open Solutions.

AMPATH Medical Record Systems (AMRS)

This is an international open source project that has built a scalable, flexible electronic medical record (EMR) system based on open standards. It is a collaborative effort involving the Regenstrief Institute, the Indiana

Table 5-1 Health IT Architecture and Infrastructure Links

Other Examples of Collaborative Health IT Standards, Architecture, and Infrastructure Projects and Activities

Collaboratory for High Performance Computing & Communication
http://collab.nlm.nih.gov/

Common Open Source Medical Objects (COSMO)
http://sourceforge.net/projects/cosmos/

Connecting For Health
http://www.markle.org/markle_programs/healthcare/

Consolidated Health Informatics (CHI) Project
http://www.whitehouse.gov/omb/egov/c-3-6-chi.html

DICOM
http://medical.nema.org/

EHCR-SupA Framework IV
http://www.chime.ucl.ac.uk/HealthI/EHCR-SupA/

eHealth Initiative (eHI)
http://www.ehealthinitiative.org/

EHR Collaborative
http://www.ehrcollaborative.org/

Federal PKI Initiative
http://www.cio.gov/fpkisc/

Free Software Foundation Europe
http://www.fsfeurope.org/

GeoSpatial OneStop eGov Initiative
http://www.fgdc.gov/

GLOBUS Project
http://www.globus.org/

Good European Health Record (GEHR) Project
http://www.chime.ucl.ac.uk/HealthI/GEHR/

Government Open Code Collaborative (GOCC)
http://www.gocc.gov/

GovernmentForge.org
http://www.governmentforge.org/

Healthkey Project
http://www.healthkey.org/

HL7
http://www.hl7.org/

Internet2 MedMid
http://middleware.internet2.edu/medmid/

LOINC
http://www.loinc.org/

Minnesota Health Data Institute (MHDI)
http://www.mhdi.org/

NCPDP
http://www.ncpdp.org/

OpenEMed
http://www.openemed.org/

PICNIC
http://www.medcom.dk/picnic/

Project SafeCom
http://www.safecomprogram.gov/SAFECOM/

Public Health Data Standards Consortium
http://www.cdc.gov/nchs/otheract/phdsc/phdsc.htm

SNOMED International
http://www.snomed.org/

SNP Consortium
http://snp.cshl.org/

SPECIALIST Project
http://lhncbc.nlm.nih.gov/cgsb/research/nls/

SPIRIT Project
http://www.euspirit.org

VA HealthePeople Initiative
http://www.va.gov/vhaitsharing/

University School of Medicine, Moi University in Kenya, Columbia University, and Partners in Health (Boston, MA). The AMPATH Medical Record System (AMRS) was created as an EMR initially focused on supporting the IU-Kenya Program's project to target the prevention and treatment of HIV/AIDS in Kenya. (http://www.regenstrief.org/intranet/Regenstrief/medinformatics/amrs/ or http://openmrs.org/wiki/Main_Page)

CARE2X

CARE 2X is an international Open Source Software initiative for hospitals and healthcare organizations to integrate existing information systems into one single efficient health information system. Its objective is to solve commonly found problems in a network of multiple programs incompatible with each other. It is designed to integrate almost any type of services, systems, departments, clinics, processes, data, and communications that exist in a hospital. Its design also allows it to handle nonmedical services or functions such as security, maintenance, and so on. It uses a standard SQL database format for storing and retrieving data; it is modular and highly scalable. It can be Web-based so it can be accessed by any browser running on any operating system and does not require special user interfaces. CARE2X has won several awards including the 2003 Linux Medical News Achievement Award and PHP architect 2003 grant award. It is available under the GPL license. (http://www.care2x.com)

FreeMED

FreeMED is an open source practice management and electronic medical records system. It is a multi user, multi tasking Web-based medical management system that has been deployed in the United States, Europe, and South America. FreeMED is primarily supported by the FreeMED Software Foundation, Inc., a nonprofit corporation promoting the development and acceptance of FreeMED and other GPL and LGPL software from the open source community. (www.freemed.org and www.freemed software.org)

National Health Card Project of Brazil (NHCP)

This initiative was begun in 1999 by the government of Brazil to create a national patient identification and information system. The goal of this project is to collect information on patient treatments and ultimately aggregate it into a national repository of health records. In order to ensure its interoperability with all existing health systems, it was developed using a smartcard with Java and XML software running on HTTP (Web server). A pilot was carried out in 44 cities in 11 states covering 13 million people (out of a total population of 180 million). The pilot was successful, and in early 2003 the project began a rollout to a total of over 500 cities that will cover more than 100 million patients. As a result of this project, health managers now have an accurate and reliable source of health information all the way down to municipalities. The information, which can be obtained and mapped with the click of a button, includes data on prescribed drugs, exams, epidemiological control, disease tracking, fraud detection, and auditing.

The application was written to run in remote localities that lack reliable electricity or telephone service. In parallel with the pilot project, 80 million people have been uniquely identified in the NHCP database, and interoperability with external systems and vendors is operational through XML documents. The project won Sun Microsystem's annual Duke Choice Award for Java applications at the 2003 JavaOne conference. From the outset, the NHCP had the objective to avoid vendor lock-in or proprietary technology. Java technology and the XML data format were chosen for that specific reason. (http://dtr2001.saude.gov.br/cartao/index_cns.htm)

Open Source Clinical Applications and Resources (OSCAR)

OSCAR is an open source Web-based electronic patient record system for delivery of evidence resources at the point of care. The software was developed under the auspices of the Department of Family Medicine at McMaster University in Hamilton, Ontario, Canada. The system has been deployed at several Canadian community health centers, and the Vancouver Coastal Health Authority is supporting the project financially. It is available under the GNU Public License (GPL). (http://www. oscarmcmaster.org/)

OpenEMR

OpenEMR is a free, open source practice management, EMR, and billing application. Thanks to the global efforts of physicians and developers, OpenEMR is claimed now to be the most widely distributed open source EMR system used in the world by small practices. It can be installed on Windows, Linux, UNIX, or Macintosh OS X systems. Implementation and support services are provided by several vendors. (www.open emr.net and http://sourceforge.net/projects/openemr)

VistA-Office EHR

The Department of Health and Human Services (HHS), the Centers for Medicare and Medicaid Services (CMS), and the Veterans Health Administration (VHA) are collaborating on an initiative to make a version of the widely used VistA electronic health record (EHR) system available for use in the private physician office setting. The first version of VistA–Office EHR (VOE) was released to selected facilities in August 2005. After beta testing in early 2006 by a number of facilities and practices, it's anticipated that by the end of 2006 the full production version 2 will be available for use by clinicians across the country and world. Visit www.vista-office.org and also see Chapters 6 and 12 in this book for more information on VOE.

OpenVistA and Hui OpenVistA

There are several, closely related open source versions of the VistA electronic health record (EHR) system that run on a Linux platform. They are based on the public domain version of the U.S. Department of Veterans Affairs (VA) VistA system that runs on the commercially available MS Windows or

FIGURE 5-2 VistA-Office EHR Web Site
Source: http://www.vista-office.org/

VMS operating system platforms. See Chapter 6 for more discussion on the VistA system. (http://sourceforge.net/projects/openvista)

Personal Health Records (PHR)

The following are brief descriptions of just some of the many collaborative projects, activities, and organizations involving the development and implementation of personal health record (PHR) systems. A primary focus will be on those projects that involve open source solutions.

The personal health record (PHR) differs from the EHR. It is an electronic, lifelong record of health information that is maintained by individual citizens. These individuals own and manage the information in the PHR, which comes from *both* their healthcare providers and the individuals themselves.

Table 5-2 Electronic Health Record Links

Other Examples of Collaborative Electronic Health Record (EHR) Organizations, Projects, and Activities

Canada Health InfoWay
    http://www.infoway-inforoute.ca
	Pacific HUI Open VistA
	    http://www.pacifichui.org/OpenVista/

BPHC Central Valley Health Network EMR
Project
    http://bphc.hrsa.gov/chc/CVHNinfo.htm
	Open Source Health Record—xChart
	    http://www.openhealth.org/index.htm

ClearHealth
    http://www.clear-health.org
	OpenEHR
	    http://www.openehr.org/

CottageMed
    http://mtdata.com/~drred/cottagemed/
    about.htm
	Phoenix PMS
	    http://www.ruralcommunityhealth.org/
	    projects/phoenix.html

Doctors' Office Quality Information
Technology (DOQ-IT)
    http://www.qualitynet.org
	"tkFP"
	    http://tkfp.sourceforge.net/

FREEMED Project
    http://www.freemed.org/
	The Medical Record (TMR)
	    http://dmi-www.mc.duke.edu/dukemi/
	    research/research.html

GnuMed
    http://www.gnumed.org/
	SQL Clinic
	    http://www.sqlclinic.net/

Michigan Electronic Medical Record Initiative
(MEMRI)
    http://www.memri.us/home.html
	VA VistA
	    http://www.va.gov/vista_monograph

MirrorMed
    http://www.mirrormed.org
	VistA Office EHR
	    http://www.vista-office.org

Open Source EHR— AAFP & MedPlexus
    http://www.aafp.org/x19365.xml
	OpenVistA
	    http://worldvista.sourceforge.net/
	    openvista/index.html

AHIMA myPHR

The American Health Information Management Association (AHIMA) is a national nonprofit professional association, founded in 1928, dedicated to the effective management of personal health information needed to deliver quality health care to the public. It has put together a Web site with a set of procedures and forms you can use to construct your own personal health record. (http://www.myphr.com/)

Eastern Maine Healthcare and MyOnlineHealth

MyOnlineHealth is a secure Internet service designed to give residents, patients, and consumers a way to better manage their health care. Eastern Maine Healthcare and its member hospitals began providing this service in 2002, free to consumers. (http://www.myonlinehealth.com/)

iHealth Record

The iHealth Record was released in May 2005 by Medem. It is a joint venture of the American Medical Association (AMA) and six other medical societies. Key features include:

- No cost to patients. The service is funded by physician and hospital groups who license the service for their patients.
- Online consultations for patients paid for by health plans.
- It has the capability to include e–mail capabilities between doctors and their patients.
- It includes current medical conditions, medications, past surgeries and allergies, and end-of-life directives.
- Health information is securely stored on the Medem network and cannot be sold or provided to any third parties without a patient's permission.
- Additional resources include education programs, automated reminders regarding medications, and other services.
- Patients decide which physicians will have access to view the record, and for what period of time that access is granted.

Visit http://www.ihealthrecord.org/.

My HealtheVet

My HealtheVet (MHV) is the gateway to veteran health benefits and services. It has been developed and deployed by the U.S. Department of Veterans Affairs (VA) and provides access to trusted health information, links to federal and VA benefits and resources, the Personal Health Journal, and now online VA prescription refill. In the future, MHV registrants will be able to view appointments, co-pay balances, key portions of their VA medical records online, and much more. It has been deployed at all VA medical centers across the country, and hundreds of thousands of veterans are now using this PHR system. (http://www.myhealth.va.gov/)

Health Information Exchange (HIE)

The following are brief descriptions of just some of the many collaborative projects, activities, and organizations focused on Health Information Exchange (HIE) systems. The primary focus will be on those projects that involve open solutions.

Connecting for Health

Connecting for Health is a public–private collaborative designed to address the barriers to development of an interconnected health information infrastructure. Connecting for Health was created by the Markle Foundation.

FIGURE 5-3 My HealtheVet Web Site
Source: http.//www.myhealth.va.gov/

Table 5-3 Personal Health Record (PHR) Links

**Other Examples of Personal Health Record (PHR)
Collaborative Projects and Activities**

AHIMA myPHR
  http://www.myphr.com/
Comprehensive Health Enhancement Support
Systems (CHESS)
  http://www.engr.wisc.edu/ie/research/
  facilities/chess.html
Dr. I-Net
  http://www.drinet.com/default.asp
Eastern Maine Healthcare and
MyOnlineHealth
  http://www.myonlinehealth.com/
eCureMe and MyHealth Chart
  http://www.ecureme.com/index.asp
GCAP RelayHealth Project
  http://www.relayhealth.com/
iHealth Record
  http://www.ihealthrecord.org/
iValley
  https://www.siouxvalley.com/iValley/
  index.cfm

My HealtheVet
  http://www.myhealth.va.gov/
My Family Health Portrait
  http://www.hhs.gov/familyhistory/
PCASSO
  http://medicine.ucsd.edu/pcasso/
PersonalMD Online Medical Records
  http://www.personalmd.com/medrecord
  intro.shtml
VIA Online Medical Records
  http://www.vwsvia.org/
Profile MD
  http://www.e-medtools.com/profilemd.
  html
Patient-Driven, Open-Source Digital Health
Records Platform (PING)
  http://www.ping.chip.org/
MediCompass
  http://www.medicompass.com/

More than 100 leading private and public organizations are now collaborating on this initiative. The ability to deliver medical information where and when it is needed via a trusted health information exchange solution will help to improve the quality of care, reduce medical errors, lower costs, and empower patients. (http://www. connectingforhealth.org/)

eHealth Initiative

The eHealth Initiative is an independent, nonprofit organization that brings together multiple stakeholders to improve the quality, safety, and efficiency of health care through the use of information and information technology (IT). It has focused its growing set of resources and tools to support states, regions, and communities across the nation who are engaged in establishing health information exchange (HIE) solutions. See Chapter 12 for more information on the eHealth Initiative. (http://www. ehealthinitiative.org/)

Federal Health Information Exchange (FHIE)

The Federal Health Information Exchange (FHIE) program is a federal government health IT initiative aimed at facilitating the secure electronic one-way exchange of patient medical information between the Department of Defense (DoD) and the Department of Veterans Affairs (VA). The success of this initiative has given rise to a new project called the Bidirectional Health Information Exchange (BHIE) project. This project offers a two-way exchange of clinical information between the participating agencies. (http://www1.va.gov/vha_oi/docs/Interagency_Health_Information_Exchange.pdf)

Indiana Health Information Exchange (IHIE)

The Indiana Health Information Exchange (IHIE) is a nonprofit, collaborative venture backed by a group of healthcare institutions in Indiana. Their strategy is to create a common, secure, electronic infrastructure that expands communication and information-sharing among participating providers, hospitals, public health organizations, and other healthcare entities in Indiana. Their vision is to use information technology and shared clinical information to:

- Improve the quality, safety, and efficiency of health care in Indiana.
- Create unparalleled research capabilities for health researchers.
- Exhibit a successful model of health information exchange for the rest of the country.

See http://www.ihie.com/.

Santa Barbara County Care Data Exchange

CareScience formed a partnership with the California Healthcare Foundation, an independent nonprofit philanthropy, to test the concept of community-wide shared information services. The Santa Barbara County Care Data Exchange is a collaboration among a collection of medical groups, hospitals, clinics, laboratories, pharmacies, payers, and other healthcare organizations committed to exchanging clinical data at the point of care. The Santa Barbara County Care Data Exchange is an operational patient record exchange solution currently involving 75% of all providers in California's Santa Barbara County, hospitals, independent practices, and local laboratories. (http://www.carescience.com/healthcare_providers/)

Massachusetts Health Data Consortium (MAHD) and the New England Health EDI Network (NEHEN)

The MAHD coalition was founded in 1978 by the state's major public and private healthcare organizations to serve as a neutral agency to collect, analyze, and disseminate healthcare information. One of the goals of the consortium is to improve the region's healthcare information infrastructure by fostering the growth of a variety of health information networks, building on systems already in place, while encouraging collaboration and standardization among these networks. The MAHD coalition helped develop the New England Health EDI Network (NEHEN), a secure and innovative electronic-commerce solution for reducing administrative costs in health care.

State of New Mexico Rapid Syndromic Validation Project (RSVP)

This project is a coordinated effort between a number of state, local, public, and private institutions including Sandia National Laboratories (SNL), Los Alamos National Laboratory (LANL), the University of New Mexico Department of Emergency Medicine, the New Mexico Department of Health Office of Epidemiology, six local hospitals and local physician organizations, as well as the open source software community. RSVP provides early warning and response to emerging biological threats as well as emerging epidemics and diseases. The system supplies real-time clinical information to the provider and other potential users, such as the state's Department of Health, about current patient symptoms, disease prevalence, and location.

Southeast Michigan e-Prescribing Initiative

This project is sponsored by the "Big 3" automakers to improve health care for their employees, retirees, and their families. Physicians providing care to these people will access medication history of the patient and will be provided decision support tools to ensure the safety of their patients. As a by-product, the automakers expect to reduce their healthcare costs while improving the quality of care.

Tennessee Volunteer eHealth Initiative

This is a funded by the state, Vanderbilt University, and an AHRQ (Agency for Healthcare Research and Quality) grant. The objective of this project is to create operational core data exchange to support a longitudinal record summary including all providers and care settings, with a special focus on Medicaid population. This will improve coordination of care for patients who see multiple physicians or who migrate between home care and nursing facilities or hospitals.

Public Health, Disease Registries, and Biosurveillance

The following are brief descriptions of just some of the many collaborative projects, activities, and organizations focused on public health and biosurveillance information systems.

Global Outbreak Alert and Response Network

The World Health Organization has established the Global Outbreak Alert and Response Network (GOARN), a technical collaboration of existing institutions and networks that pool human and technical resources for the rapid identification, confirmation, and response to outbreaks of international importance. (http://www.who.int/csr/outbreak network/en/)

National Electronic Disease Surveillance System (NEDSS)

NEDSS is an initiative that promotes the use of data and information system standards to advance the development of efficient, integrated, and interoperable surveillance systems at federal, state, and local levels. It is a major component of the Public Health Information Network (PHIN). This broad initiative is designed to:

- Detect outbreaks rapidly and to monitor the health of the nation.
- Facilitate the electronic transfer of appropriate information from clinical information systems in the healthcare system to public health departments.

Table 5-4 Health Information Exchange Links

Other Examples of Health Information Exchange (HIE) Collaborative Projects and Activities

Connecting Communities
http://www.connectingcommunitiespro
gram.org/communities/
Connecting Colorado
http://ccbh.ehealthinitiative.org/Awardee_
ConnectingColorado.mspx
Cooperative Exchange Association
http://www.cooperativeexchange.org/faq.
html
Alabama Dynamic Online Event Reporting
System
http://www.connectingcommunities
program.org/communities/states.aspx
Electronic Death Registration (EDR)
http://www.cdc.gov/nchs/about/major/
dvs/elecdeathcert.htm
Electronic Verification of Vital Events (EVVE)
Project
http://www.naphsis.org/
eHealth Initiative
http://www.ehealthinitiative.org/
E-Vital
http://www.whitehouse.gov/omb/egov/
c-2-4-evital.html
Federal Health Information Exchange (FHIE)
http://www1.va.gov/vadodhealthitshar
ing/page.cfm?pg=13
Greater Cincinnati HealthBridge
http://www.healthbridge.org/
Hawaii Health Information Exchange
http://www.hhic.org/
Healthcare Collaborative Network
http://www.connectingforhealth.org/
resources/HCN_24.html
HealthConnect —Australia
http://www.health.gov.au/healthconnect/
Indiana Health Information Exchange (IHIE)
http://www.ihie.com/
Indianapolis Network for Patient Care (INPC)
http://www.regenstrief.org/medinformatics/
inpc/
Inland Northwest Health Services
http://www.inhs.org/
MA-SHARE Projects
http://www.mahealthdata.org/
Mendocino SHARE
http://www.ruralcommunityhealth.org/
projects/msp.html
Minnesota Health Information Network
(MN-HIN)
http://www.mn-hin.org/

N.C. Emergency Department Information
System
http://www.ncedd.org/WhatsNew_Reports.
html
National EMS Information System
http://www.nemsis.org/
National Immunization Registry Clearinghouse
http://www.cdc.gov/nip/registry/
National Vital Statistics System
http://www.cdc.gov/nchs/nvss.htm
New England Healthcare EDI Network
(NEHEN)
http://www.nehen.org/
New Jersey Primary Care Association—EMR
Project
http://ccbh.ehealthinitiative.org/
communities/states.aspx
North Carolina Emergency Department
Database (NCEDD)
http://www.ncedd.org/
Patient Safety Institute (PSI)
http://www.ptsafety.org/default.asp
RxHUB
http://www.rxhub.net/index.html
Santa Barbara County Care Data Exchange
http://www.sbccde.org
Santa Cruz County Health Information
Exchange
http://www.axolotl.com/press/20041201/
Sisu Medical Systems
http://www.sisunet.org/
SureScripts Electronic Prescribing System
http://www.riqi.org/projects.htm
Taconic Health Information Network and
Community
http://www.taconicipa.com/info/press.cfm
Utah Health Information Network
http://www.uhin.com/
VHA/DoD Laboratory Data Sharing Project
http://www1.va.gov/vadodhealthits
haring/page.cfm?pg=4
WEDi
http://www.wedi.org/
Wisconsin Health Information Exchange
http://ccbh.ehealthinitiative.org/profiles/
Wisconsin.mspx

- Reduce provider burden in the provision of information.
- Enhance both the timeliness and quality of information provided.

Visit http://www.cdc.gov/nedss/

National Biosurveillance Data System

An initial pilot solution has been developed and put in place to extract and feed data from the Veterans Health Administration (VHA) VistA system to the Centers for Disease Control and Prevention (CDC) within the Department of Health and Human Services (HHS). VHA collaborated with CDC to transmit de-identified patient data from the national VA Austin Automation Center to the CDC. VHA is now planning on transmitting additional segments of data extracted from VistA to other federal public health and disease surveillance systems maintained by HHS.

Real-Time Outbreak and Disease Surveillance (RODS)

The RODS Laboratory is a collaboration between researchers at the University of Pittsburgh and the Auton Lab in Carnegie Mellon University's School of Computer Science. The laboratory was founded in 1999 to investigate methods for real-time detection and assessment of disease outbreaks. Current research interests of the faculty include algorithm development, assessment of novel types of surveillance data, natural language processing, and analyses of detectability. The laboratory is now home to four large projects that work with health departments to create surveillance systems: RODS software development, the Public Health Data Center, the National Retail Data Monitor (NRDM), and the BioWatch Support Program. As of late 2005, there were 481 participating facilities with 217 connected in real–time. (http://www.health.pitt.edu/rods/)

WHO HealthMap

The Public Health Mapping and GIS program has become a global partnership involving WHO Regional and Country Offices, WHO Member States, infectious disease programs, UN agency and bilateral partners, research institutes, WHO collaborating centers, and the private sector. The Public Health Mapping and GIS program has developed tools and

Table 5-5 Public Health and Biosurveillance Links

**Other Examples of Public Health and Biosurveillance
Collaborative IT Projects and Activities**

American Bone Marrow Donor Registry
http://www.charityadvantage.com/abmdr/
Home.asp
American Public Health Association (APHA)
http://www.apha.org/
Disaster Assistance ePortal
http://www.disasterhelp.gov/
Drug Abuse Warning Network (DAWN)
http://www.dawninfo.net/
European Early Warning & Response System
(EWRS)
https://webgate.cec.eu.int/ewrs/
Global Outbreak Alert and Response Network
http://www.who.int/csr/outbreaknetwork/en/
Health Alert Network (HAN) Project
http://www.phppo.cdc.gov/han/
Models of Infectious Disease Agent Study
(MIDAS)
http://www.rti.org/page.cfm?nav=423&
objectid=BD00FB88-D7BD-424E-
975F88C0E1498194
National Electronic Disease Surveillance
System (NEDSS)
http://www.cdc.gov/nedss/
North Carolina Healthcare Info and
Communications Alliance
http://www.nchica.org/

Partners in Information Access for Public
http://phpartners.org/
Health Project
http://phpartners.org/
Project BioShield
http://www.whitehouse.gov/bioshield/
Public Health Informatics Institute
http://www.phii.org/
Public Health Information Network (PHIN)
http://www.cdc.gov/phin/index.html
Public Health Foundation
http://www.phf.org/
Real-Time Outbreak and Disease Surveillance
(RODS)
http://www.health.pitt.edu/rods/
StatePublic Health.org
http://www.statepublichealth.org/
St. Louis Emergency Patient Tracking System
(EPTS)
http://www.raystl.com/eptsinfo/epts_
home.asp
VACMAN
http://www.cdc.gov/nip/vacman/default.
htm
WHO HealthMap
http://www.who.int/csr/mapping/en/

applications allowing the global partners to respond to critical information needs of infectious disease and public health programs. These tools are based on recent advances in GIS technologies, mapping, and remote field data collection tools such as handheld global positioning systems, mobile mapping units, and Internet connectivity. (http://www.who.int/csr/mapping/en/)

Health Knowledge, Information, and Education

The following are brief descriptions of some of the many collaborative projects, activities, and organizations focused on sharing health information, educational materials, and other knowledge and lessons learned about medicine and health care.

2-1-1 Project

The 2-1-1 nationwide project is being spearheaded by United Way and comprehensive and specialized information and referral agencies in states and local communities. 2-1-1 is an easy-to-remember three-digit dialing system (similar to 9-1-1) that makes a simple, but critical connection between individuals and families who are seeking healthcare services or volunteer opportunities, or have a need to contact another appropriate community-based organization or government agency. A robust 2-1-1 system can be an integral crisis response tool for communities across the country. In widespread emergencies like an attack, flood, tornado, fire, or health crisis, not only does this valuable service alleviate the strain on systems like 9-1-1, but it is also there for people who don't know where to turn for help in everyday circumstances. (www.211.org)

Federal Credentialing System and VetPro

This initiative involves a collaborative partnership between HRSA and the VA along with other federal agencies on a standardized, electronic credentialing system and databank that meets JCAHO standards. (http://www.quic.gov/workforce/enhance/finalrpt.htm)

GrantsNet

GrantsNet is an Internet application tool created by the Department of Health and Human Services (HHS) Office of Grants Management and Policy (OGMP) for finding and exchanging information about HHS and other federal grant programs. GrantsNet serves the general public, the grantee community, and grant-makers (i.e., state and local governments, educational institutions, nonprofit organizations, and commercial businesses. (http://www.hhs.gov/grantsnet/)

Health Education Assets Library (HEAL)

The Health Education Assets Library is a digital library that provides freely accessible digital teaching resources of the highest quality that meet the needs of today's health science educators and learners. Using state-of-the-art Internet technologies, HEAL enables educators across the country to efficiently search and retrieve teaching resources from a variety of sources.

HEAL was established in 2000 as a joint effort of three health science institutions in the United States: the David Geffen School of Medicine at UCLA, the University of Utah Spencer S. Eccles Health Sciences Library, and the University of Oklahoma Health Sciences Center. (http://www.healcentral.org/)

National Guideline Clearinghouse™

The National Guideline Clearinghouse™ (NGC), a public resource for evidence-based clinical practice guidelines, is an initiative of the Agency for Healthcare Research and Quality (AHRQ), which is an agency of the U.S. Department of Health and Human Services. NGC was originally created by AHRQ in partnership with the American Medical Association and the American Association of Health Plans. (http://www.guideline.gov)

National Library of Medicine (NLM) MedlinePlus

MedlinePlus brings together authoritative information from NLM, the National Institutes of Health (NIH), and other government agencies and health-related organizations. Pre-formulated Medline searches are included in MedlinePlus and give easy access to medical journal articles. MedlinePlus also has extensive information about drugs, an illustrated medical encyclopedia, interactive patient tutorials, and the latest health news. (http://medlineplus.gov)

WHO Health Information Network Project

The Health InterNetwork was created to bridge the "digital divide" around the world in health, ensuring that relevant information—and the technologies to deliver it—are widely available and effectively used by health personnel: professionals, researchers and scientists, and policy makers. Launched by the secretary general of the United Nations in September 2000 and led by the World Health Organization, the Health InterNetwork has brought together public and private partners under the principle of ensuring equitable access to health information. The core elements of the project are content, Internet connectivity, and capacity building. (http://www.healthinternetwork.net)

Table 5-6 Health Information, Education, and Knowledge Sharing Links

**Other Examples of Health Information, Education, and Knowledge Sharing
Collaborative Projects and Activities**

Health Information

2-1-1 Project
http://www.211.org/
AskMe3
http://www.AskMe3.org/
California Nursing Home Search
http://www.calnhs.org/
Consumer Health Vocabulary Initiative
http://www.consumerhealthvocab.org/
DrugRef.org
http://www.drugref.org/
Health On The Net (HON)
http://www.hon.ch/
Healthy Milwaukee
http://www.cuir.uwm.edu/HM/links.html
MedMarx
http://www.usp.org/
NNLM - MedLine
http://www.nlm.nih.gov/
N.C. Advanced Healthcare Directive Registry
http://www.secretary.state.nc.us/ahcdr/
PAHO Virtual Health Library
http://www.bireme.br/bvs/I/ihome.htm
Rx for Ohio
http://www.rxforohio.org/
Science.gov ePortal
http://www.science.gov/
WHO—Health Information Network Project
http://www.healthinternetwork.net/

Education and Training

eTraining Portal
http://www.golearn.gov/
Health Education Assets Library (HEAL)
http://www.healcentral.org/
TrainingFinder
http://www.train.org/DesktopShell.aspx

Knowledge Sharing

National Guideline Clearinghouse™ (NGC)
http://www.guideline.gov/
Knowledge Management—KM.GOV
http://www.km.gov/
Healthcare Cost and Utilization Project
(HCUP)
http://www.ahrq.gov/data/hcup/hcupnet.
htm
Vaccine Adverse Event Reporting System
http://vaers.hhs.gov/

**Research, Disease Registries, and Online
Databases**

AMA Online Databases
http://www.ama-assn.org/ama/pub/
category/2997.html
Bioinformatics Research Systems & Projects
http://bioinformatics.org/
The Biomedical Informatics Research Network
(BIRN)
http://nbirn.net/AU/index.htm
Cancer Biomedical Informatics Grid (caBIG)
http://cabig.nci.nih.gov/
Combined Health Information Database
(CHID)
http://chid.nih.gov/
GrantsNet
http://www.hhs.gov/grantsnet/
Healthcare Cost and Utilization Project
(HCUP)
http://www.ahrq.gov/hcupnet/
National Electronics Clinical Trials and
Research (NECTAR)
http://nihroadmap.nih.gov/clinical
research/overview-networks.asp
National Center for Biotechnology Information
http://www.ncbi.nlm.nih.gov/
SEER Project
http://www-seer.ims.nci.nih.gov/
Statistical Export and Tabulation System
(SETS)
http://www.cdc.gov/nchs/sets.htm

Health IT Specialty Systems

The following are brief descriptions of some of the many collaborative health IT projects, activities, and organizations focused on selected specialty areas such as emergency management, patient safety, and genomics. The primary focus of these collaborative projects is on Open Solutions.

Healthcare Cost and Utilization Project (HCUP)

The Healthcare Cost and Utilization Project (HCUP) is a family of healthcare databases and related software tools and products developed through a federal-state-industry partnership and sponsored by the Agency for Healthcare Research and Quality (AHRQ). HCUP databases bring together the data collection efforts of state data organizations, hospital associations, private data organizations, and the federal government to create a national information resource of patient-level healthcare data (HCUP Partners). HCUP includes the largest collection of longitudinal hospital care data in the United States, with all-payer, encounter-level information beginning in 1988. These databases enable research on a broad range of health policy issues, including cost and quality of health services, medical practice patterns, access to healthcare programs, and outcomes of treatments at the national, state, and local market levels. (http://www.hcup-us.ahrq.gov)

Human Genome Nomenclature (HUGN) Database Project

HUGN is a nonprofit body that is jointly funded by the U.K. Medical Research Council, the U.S. NHGRI grant P41 HG003345, and the Wellcome Trust (U.K.). It operates under the auspices of the Human Genome Organization (HUGO), with key policy advice from an International Advisory Committee (IAC). The value of the human genome sequence will depend crucially on the quality and accessibility of the annotation of the genome. Providing an approved symbol for each gene is a small but important part of this process. As of 2005, HGNC has already named more than 20,000 genomic objects of which more than 17,000 are functional genes. Their current priority is assigning nomenclature to genes submitted from the Human Genome Project. (http://www.gene.ucl.ac.uk/nomenclature/)

MNSTAR

Minnesota is just one of many states that have developed a statewide emergency medical system (EMS). Many of these states have been working with the National EMSC Data Analysis Resource Center and based their systems on their National EMS Information System (NEMSIS). (www.nedarc.org/Position_papers/default.htm). Also visit the State EMS

Systems Web site at http://www.nedarc.org/nedarc/emsDataSystems/index.html.

myPACS

myPACS is a free international service that links together thousands of radiologists from 1500 institutions in 75 countries who use it to create their cases online. By 2005, the service had logged more than 10,000 teaching file cases with more than 40,000 images. All that is needed to participate is a free account and a Web browser to start sharing cases over this network. This free service to the international community is a Web-based medical image content management system. Its mission is to help clinicians share knowledge through the use of content management technology. MyPACS has become the largest collaborative repository of radiology cases on the Internet since it was launched in 1999. (http://www. mypacs.net)

Patient Safety Reporting System (PSRS)

The Patient Safety Reporting System (PSRS) is a learning program being jointly developed by two federal agencies: the Department of Veterans Affairs (VA) and the National Aeronautics and Space Administration (NASA). NASA is using its experience from developing and running its highly successful Aviation Safety Reporting System (ASRS). NASA developed and has been running this system for the Federal Aviation Administration (FAA) since 1976. (http://www.psrs.arc.nasa.gov)

Universal Credentialing DataSource

Developed by the Council for Affordable Quality Healthcare (CAQH), the Universal Credentialing DataSource is a single, national process that eliminates the need for multiple credentialing applications. Through this innovative online service, providers complete one standardized application to meet the needs of all participating health plans and other healthcare organizations. CAQH also has expanded the service to allied health providers in 30 fields, including nursing, optometry, and physician assistants. (http://www.caqh.org/ucd.html)

Table 5-7 Health Specialty Links

Links to Collaborative Health IT Organizations and Special Health IT Projects and Activities

Emergency Management
DEEDS—Data Elements for Emergency Department Systems
http://www.cdc.gov/ncipc/pub-res/deedspage.htm
Delaware EDIN System
http://www.nedarc.org/Position_papers/default.htm
MEMSIS
http://www.nedarc.org/Position_papers/default.htm
MNSTAR
http://www.nedarc.org/Position_papers/default.htm
N.C. PreMIS System
http://www.nedarc.org/Position_papers/default.htm
Ohio EMSIRS System
http://www.nedarc.org/Position_papers/default.htm
State EMS Systems
http://www.nedarc.org/State_data/state_data_map.htm

Genomic Information Systems
American Society for Human Genetics (ASHG)
http://genetics.faseb.org/genetic
BLAST
http://www.ncbi.nlm.nih.gov/BLAST/
Entrez Gene
http://www.ncbi.nih.gov/entrez/query.fcgi?db=gene
GeneCards project
http://bioinfo.weizmann.ac.il/cards/index.html
GeneTests
http://www.geneclinics.org/
Genetic Alliance
http://www.geneticalliance.org
Genomic Messaging System (GMS)
http://www.haifa.il.ibm.com/projects/software/imr/gms.html
Human Genome Project
http://www.ncbi.nlm.nih.gov/genome/guide/human/
Human Genome Nomenclature (HUGN) Database
http://www.gene.ucl.ac.uk/nomenclature/
Human Genome Organization (HUGO)
http://www.gene.ucl.ac.uk/hugo/

Online Mendelian Inheritance in Man™
http://www.ncbi.nlm.nih.gov/entrez/query.fcgi?db=OMIM

Commercial Health Information Sharing Solutions
My HealthDirective
http://www.MyHealthDirective.com/
VitalChek
http://www.vitalchek.com/?clicked=1
National Council for Prescription Drug Programs
http://www.ncpdp.org
MedicAlert
http://www.medicalert.org

Patient Quality and Safety
Foundation for Health Care Quality
http://www.qualityhealth.org/
Healthcare Cost & Utilization Project (HCUP)
http://www.ahrq.gov/data/hcup/
Health Legacy Partnership (HELP)
http://www.healthlegacy.org/help/
LeapFrog Group
http://www.leapfroggroup.org/
National Patient Safety Foundation
http://www.npsf.org/
Patient Safety Institute (PSI)
http://www.ptsafety.org/
Patient Safety Reporting System (PSRS)
www.psrs.arc.nasa.gov
QIS/QuIC Initiative
www.quic.gov
QualityNet Exchange
http://www.qnetexchange.org/
Quality Health Foundation
http://www.mpqhf.org/
Universal Credentialing DataSource
http://www.caqh.org/ucd.html
Vaccine Safety Datalink Project
http://www.cdc.gov/nip/vacsafe/vsd/
Vaccine Management System
http://www.cdc.gov/nip/vacman/Default.htm
VetPro Credentialing System
http://datacenter.cit.nih.gov/interface/interface226/vetpro.html

(continues)

Table 5-7 *continued*

Links to Collaborative Health IT Organizations and Special Health IT
Projects and Activities

Telehealth

Alaska Federal Health Care Access Network
(AFHCAN)
  http://www.afhcan.org/
American Telemedicine Association (ATA)
  http://www.atmeda.org/
Association of Telehealth Service Providers
  http://www.atsp.org/
Home Telehealth Pilot—Canada
  http://hth.marchnetworks.com/atlantic_
  project.asp
Missouri Telehealth Network (MTN)
  http://www.muhealth.org/~telehealth/proj/
  oat.html

Pacific Telehealth and Technology HUI
  http://www.pacifichui.org/
Project Touch
  http://hsc.unm.edu/touch/
State Telehealth Projects
  http://www.hlthtech.com/states/states
  index.html
TeleHealth for Kansans Project
  http://www2.kumc.edu/telemedicine/
  programs/telehealthforkansans.htm

Health IT Organizations

The following is a short list of some of the many other organizations in the public and private sectors collaborating on health IT projects and activities that may not have been previously mentioned.

Open Source, Collaborative Consumer Health Vocabulary Initiative

This open collaborative is working to address a vital need in translating medical terminology into a form understandable by consumers and patients. Consumer health vocabularies provide a methodology to link everyday words and phrases about health (e.g., "heart attack") to more technical terms used by doctors, nurses, and other healthcare professionals (e.g., "myocardial infarction"). With over 100 million Americans searching for health information on the Internet, it is frequently difficult for them to remember the technical name of a disease or medicine. According to the initiative's Web site, health care is a public good and vital issue so that consumer health vocabularies need to be open source to encourage widespread use and further development. (http://www.consumerhealthvocab.org)

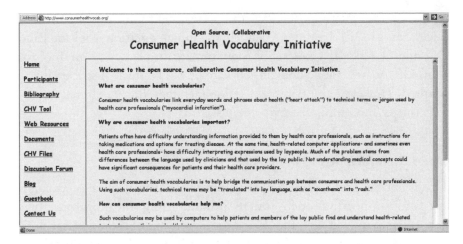

FIGURE 5-4 Consumer Health Vocabulary Web Site
Source: http://www. consumerhealthvocab.org/

U.S. National Heart, Lung, and Blood Institute of National Institutes of Health—Applications

The U.S. National Heart, Lung, and Blood Institute (NHLBI) has created a series of Palm OS applications and treatment guidelines and that are free to use and available as public domain software. The only requirement for use is to appropriately credit NHLBI. Initial applications include: 1) Act in Time to Heart Attack Signs—Physician Quick

FIGURE 5-5 National Heart, Lung & Blood Web Site
Source: http://hp2010.nhlbihin.net/palmapps.htm

Reference Tool for Palm OS, 2) Asthma Treatment Guidelines, 3) a BMI calculator, 4) OEI Treatment Guidelines Implementation Tool for Palm OS, and 5) ATP III Cholesterol Management Implementation Tool for Palm OS. As free public domain software, it can be freely distributed and adapted. However, the treatment guidelines may not be altered in any way. (http://hin.nhlbi.nih.gov/palmapps.htm)

Open Bioinformatics Foundation

This is not-for-profit, tax-exempt organization that is focused on expanding and supporting open source programming in bioinformatics. According to its Web site, the "foundation grew out of the volunteer projects Bioperl, BioJava, and Biopython and was formally incorporated in order to handle our modest requirements of hardware ownership, domain name management, and funding for conferences and workshops."

The foundation and its Web site simply provide the administrative support for organization member projects. The foundation is a central resource for the facilitation of the following open source software projects: BioPerl, BioJava, BioPython, BioRuby, BioPipe, BioSQL/OBDA, MOBY, and DAS. (http://open-bio.org)

FIGURE 5-6 Open BioInformatics Web Site
Source: http://www.open-bio.org/wiki/Main_Page

Table 5-8 Collaborative Health IT Organizations Links

Health IT Collaborative Organizations

American Health Information Management Assoc. (AHIMA)
  http://www.ahima.org/
American Medical Informatics Association (AMIA)
  http://www.amia.org/
California HealthCare Foundation
  http://www.chcf.org/
College of Healthcare Information Management Executives
  http://www.cio-chime.org/
Community Health Information Technology Alliance (CHITA)
  http://www.chita.org/
Government Open Code Collaborative
  http://www.gocc.gov/
Health Information and Mgmt. Systems Society (HIMSS)
  http://www.himss.org/ASP/index.
HealthTech
  http://www.healthtech.org/

International Medical Informatics Association
  http://www.imia.org/
Joint Healthcare Information Technology Alliance (JHITA)
  http://www.jhita.org/
The Leapfrog Group
  http://www.leapfroggroup.org/index.html/
Markle Foundation
  http://www.markle.org/index.stm
National Association of Health Data Organizations
  http://www.nahdo.org/
National Alliance for Health Information Technology (NAHIT)
  http://www.nahit.org
National Assoc. for Public Health Statistics and Info. Systems
  http://www.naphsis.org/
National Business Coalition on Health
  http://www.healthsmart.org/
Robert Wood Johnson Foundation
  http://www.rwjf.org/index.jsp

Summary

The list of collaborative projects, activities, and organizations provided above is comprehensive, but by no means complete. It provides the reader with practical information and links that will save a lot of time as you explore the possibilities of collaboration. While the links provided were current at the moment of publication, some of them will change over time. If a link in the book is found to not work then do a search in a major search engine on the Web and, frequently, the updated links and information on the topic or subject will be found. Collaboration for a safer, higher quality healthcare system is a rapidly expanding field of endeavor and new resources are being developed and shared every day.

CHAPTER 6

The VistA Market—
Today and Tomorrow

"The VistA system helps to put more science
into the practice of medicine."

The Washington Monthly, January/February 2005

"The Electronic Health Record in the Department of Veterans
Affairs is the best in the United States, absolutely the
best at large scale, and probably the best in the world."

John Glaser, Ph.D., Vice President &
CIO Partners (Harvard) HealthCare System, October 2003

The VistA system created by the U.S. Department of Veterans Affairs
(VA) is one of the most successful examples of an integrated health information technology system. It includes an electronic health record (EHR)
module the VA refers to as the Computerized Patient Record System
(CPRS). Developed by the VA from a clinical perspective, VistA has
been continuously enhanced over the past 25 years. It has been successfully deployed and utilized by administrative and clinical staff working in
VA medical centers, clinics, and nursing homes across the country, and is
now being widely deployed in private health systems, public hospitals,
and medical offices in the United States and internationally. Visit
http://www.va.gov/vista_monograph/ for a detailed description of the
VistA system.

The VistA system has become one of the largest efforts in the world to date bringing a public domain health information technology and EHR solution to users in the public and private sector as an Open Solutions option, through the Freedom of Information Act (FOIA). In essence the world's largest and most highly regarded health information technology and EHR system was developed to serve American veterans, was paid for by U.S. taxpayer dollars, and is now available to any healthcare organization without requiring software license fees. This is what the Institute of Medicine had to say:

> "VHA's integrated health information system, including its framework for using performance measures to improve quality, is considered one of the best in the nation."*

This does not mean that installing VistA is without costs. There are still costs associated with acquiring needed hardware, the reengineering of clinical business processes, training, implementation, telecommunications, and other costs. It just means that the overall costs of acquiring and implementing a comprehensive EHR system can be significantly reduced since the software is free and doesn't require recurring licensing fees. VistA is now being used outside of the VA, both in the United States and overseas. For instance, Midland Memorial Hospital, a four-hospital system in Texas, has successfully implemented a version of VistA called OpenVistA. Chapter 9 presents more information on Midland's and other doctors' offices, hospitals, and healthcare organizations across the world that are opting for a proven high-quality information technology system and EHR system. They are bringing to life the Medical Informatics 20/20 vision and the strategies of Collaboration, Open Solutions, and Innovation.

The Need for Affordable Health Information Technology (HIT) Systems

Advanced care management health information technology systems, including Computerized Physician Order Entry (CPOE) and EHR systems, should no longer be considered optional for healthcare organizations. They are essential for those institutions that wish to survive in the competitive market and provide requisite quality of care to their patients.

Institute of Medicine (IOM) Report, "Leadership by Example: Coordinating Government Roles in Improving Health Care Quality (2002)"

In 1991, the Institute of Medicine first focused heavily on the issue of EHRs in its publication "The Computer-Based Patient Record: Essential Technology for Health Care." The initial definition of the computer-based patient record has evolved over the years to electronic medical record (EMR), electronic health record (EHR), and now includes the evolving personal health record (PHR).

The EHR system is really a concept that involves a multi-step process, achieved over time by implementing multiple health information systems and connecting them together to create a common information environment that can be readily accessed by caregivers. Connecting these multiple systems has been a challenge for most organizations. Private sector healthcare organizations have been spending billions of dollars each year on information technology (IT), but very few have a working EHR system. Even after several decades, very few commercial health IT vendors offer comprehensive, integrated EHR systems to healthcare provider institutions that are easy to use and affordable.

As an alternative to high-cost commercial solutions, a number of Free and Open Source Software (FOSS) health IT solutions have begun to emerge, some of which were discussed in Chapter 5. Of these, perhaps the most famous and widely used Open Solution is the VistA system developed by the U.S. Department of Veterans Affairs (VA).

The VistA System

VistA is a comprehensive and integrated EHR system that has been deployed in VA medical centers, outpatient clinics, and nursing homes across the country. Table 6-1 VistA Software Modules lists in detail all the software applications and programs in the VistA comprehensive health information and electronic health record system. The U.S. Indian Health Service (IHS) acquired and has implemented a variation of the VistA system in a wide range of healthcare facilities serving Native Americans. IHS's system is known as RPMS and has a number of enhancements to VistA that have made this an effective tool in treating its patient population, which includes large numbers of women and children normally not seen in VA healthcare settings. Several other federal and state healthcare organizations are also using the VistA system to varying degrees, including the DoD, state veterans homes, and a rising number of state-level healthcare organizations.

Table 6–1 The VistA Software Modules

VistA Software Packages

Health Data Systems
Automated Medical Information Exchange
    (AMIE)
Incident Reporting
Lexicon Utility
Occurrence Screen
Patient Representative

Registration, Enrollment, and Eligibility Systems
Patient Registration
Admission, Discharge, Transfer (ADT)
Clinical Monitoring System
Enrollment Application System (EAS)
Hospital Inquiry (HINQ)
Income Verification Match (IVM)
Record Tracking
Resident Assessment Instrument/Minimum
    Data Set (RAI/MDS)
Veteran Identification Card (VIC)

Health Provider Systems
Care Management
Clinical Procedures
Computerized Patient Record System (CPRS)
CPRS: Adverse Reaction Tracking
CPRS: Authorization/Subscription Utility (ASU)
CPRS: Clinical Reminders
CPRS: Consult/Request Tracking
CPRS: Health Summary
CPRS: Problem List
CPRS: Text Integration Utilities (TIU)
Dentistry
Hepatitis C Case Registry
Home–Based Primary Care (HBPC)
Immunology Case Registry (ICR)
Intake and Output
Laboratory
Laboratory: Anatomic Pathology
Laboratory: Blood Bank
Laboratory: Electronic Data Interchange (LEDI)
Medicine
Mental Health
Nursing
Nutrition and Food Service (N&FS)
Oncology
Pharmacy: Automatic Replenishment/
    Ward Stock (AR/WS)
Pharmacy: Bar Code Medication Administration
    (BCMA)
Pharmacy: Consolidated Mail Outpatient
    Pharmacy (CMOP)
Pharmacy: Controlled Substances
Pharmacy: Drug Accountability/Inventory
    Interface

Pharmacy: Electronic Claims Management
    Engine
Pharmacy: Inpatient Medications
Pharmacy: Inpatient Medications—Intravenous
    (IV)
Pharmacy: Inpatient Medications—Unit Dose
    (UD)
Pharmacy: National Drug File (NDF)
Pharmacy: Outpatient Pharmacy
Pharmacy: Pharmacy Benefits Management
    (PBM)
Pharmacy: Pharmacy Data Management
    (PDM)
Pharmacy: Pharmacy Prescription Practices
    (PPP)
Primary Care Management Module (PCMM)
Prosthetics
Quality: Audiology And Speech Analysis and
    Reporting (QUASAR)
Radiology/Nuclear Medicine
Remote Order Entry System (ROES)
Scheduling
Social Work
Spinal Cord Dysfunction
Surgery
Surgery: Risk Assessment
VistA Imaging System
VistA Imaging: Core Infrastructure
VistA Imaging: Document Imaging
VistA Imaging: Filmless Radiology
VistA Imaging: Imaging Ancillary Systems
Visual Impairment Service Team (VIST)
Vitals/Measurements
Women's Health

Management and Financial Systems
Accounts Receivable (AR)
Automated Information Collection System
    (AICS)
Beneficiary Travel
Compensation and Pension Records
    Interchange (CAPRI)
Current Procedural Terminology (CPT)
Decision Support System (DSS) Extracts
Diagnostic Related Group (DRG) Grouper
Engineering
Equipment/Turn-In Request
Event Capture
Fee Basis
Generic Code Sheet
Incomplete Records Tracking (IRT)

(continues)

Table 6-1 *continued*

Integrated Funds Distribution, Control Point Activity, Accounting, and Procurement (IFCAP)	*Cross-Cutting Monographs* Duplicate Record Merge
Integrated Patient Funds	Health Level Seven (HL7)
Integrated Billing (IB)	VistA Kernel
Patient Care Encounter (PCE)	VistA Kernel ToolKit
Personnel and Accounting Integrated Data (PAID)	List Manager MailMan
Voluntary Service System (VSS)	Master Patient Index (MPI) and Master Patient Index/Patient Demographics (MPI/PD)
Information and Education Systems	My HealtheVet Personal Health Record
Automated Safety Incident Surveillance Tracking System (ASISTS)	Network Health Exchange (NHE) Patient Data Exchange (PDX)
Library	Remote Procedure Call (RPC) Broker
Police and Security	VA FileMan
	VistALink

VistA is a proven product and can be readily adapted for use in acute care, ambulatory, and long-term care settings. It has been used in public and private healthcare provider organizations across the United States and in a number of international settings (e.g., Egypt, Germany, Finland, Samoa, and Mexico). VistA software has been released to non-VA users under the Freedom of Information Act (FOIA) for several decades. There have been many thousands of downloads of the FOIA-VistA software over the years. The VistA software suite has also been made available via the VistA Hardhats organization (www.hardhats.org) and the World VistA organization (www.worldvista.org) and there have been thousands of copies of the VistA system downloaded from their sites. Visit http://www.va.gov/vista_mono graph/ for a detailed description of the VistA system.

Over the past decades, the VA's VistA system has been adopted by a number of other non-VA healthcare provider organizations across the country. The following are some examples of these:

The *Department of Defense (DoD)* and the Department of Veterans Affairs (VA) have a long–standing tradition of health information and technology sharing spanning the past several decades. In 1983, the DoD was first provided copies of the VistA application software. In 1987, two DoD facilities, March Air Force Base and Fitzsimmons Army Medical Center, began extensive testing of the VistA software. In 1988, SAIC was awarded a $1 billion, eight-year contract to design, develop, and implement its solution, which involved modifying the VistA system to meet DoD requirements for what is known as the DoD Composite Health

Care System (CHCS). CHCS is now used at all major military treatment facilities around the world.

The *Indian Health Service (IHS)* and the VA also have a long–standing tradition of health information and technology sharing spanning several decades. In 1984, the IHS began implementation of 60 systems using VistA software. They refer to their system as the Resource and Patient Management System (RPMS). Many components of the RPMS health information system are still based on the VistA system. The system is an integrated solution for the management of clinical and administrative information in hundreds of IHS healthcare facilities of various sizes and orientations around the country. Over the years, a number of key RPMS software modules have been incorporated back into the VA VistA system including "Health Summary" and "Women's Health."

The *Presbyterian Health Service* in Albuquerque, New Mexico, has installed RPMS, which is based on VistA, to support their healthcare services. The RPMS system interfaces with commercial ancillary systems.

The *National Hansen's Disease Program (NHDP)*, based in Baton Rouge, Louisiana, is primarily responsible for inpatient and outpatient care and treatment of Hansen's disease. In addition to the clinical programs in Baton Rouge, the NHDP center also coordinates outpatient care for Hansen's disease patients throughout the United States at BPHC grant–funded clinics as well as private physician offices. NHDP first brought up the VistA system in 1989 and updated its VistA infrastructure in 2000. It currently has a patient database size of 16,082 patients.

The state of *Oklahoma* has acquired and implemented VistA and its EHR component (CPRS) in its seven intermediate and long-term care state veterans homes at Norman, Claremore, Talihina, Clinton, Ardmore, Sulphur, and Lawton. Their architecture involves a centralized system using a single VistA database residing in Oklahoma City. The state awarded a contract to Hewlett Packard (HP) and MedSphere Corporation to implement VistA in early 2004. The first facility was up and running by May 2004 and the project was successfully completed well ahead of schedule in the summer of 2005, with all seven healthcare facilities using VistA.

VistA and American Samoa working with the Honolulu VA Medical Center and VA's National Office of Information staff provided limited technical assistance to the American Samoan government as it successfully implemented the VistA system in its LBJ Tropical Medicine Hospital. A more detailed profile of this collaborative project is provided in Chapter 9.

Others Activities Across the United States—Washington, DC, Washington state, California, and Hawaii have implemented VistA systems in a limited number of facilities. At the time of this writing, West Virginia, Texas, Louisiana, Michigan, and several other states were exploring the acquisition and implementation of VistA. The VA has also given VistA and CPRS (see Figure 6-1) read-only secure access to authorized providers at more than 70 state veterans homes across the country. The VA has also received numerous calls from local city and county governments expressing an interest in acquiring and using the VistA system. As interest grows, the number of commercial vendors willing to support VistA implementations has increased, and they have now formed a trade organization known as the VistA Software Alliance (VSA). For more information, visit www.vista software.org. An expanded discussion of VSA can be found in Chapter 3 and later in this chapter.

International Activities—VistA software modules have been installed in healthcare institutions around the world, including Mexico, Finland, Germany, Nigeria, Egypt, and Samoa. Many healthcare organizations in other countries have contacted the VA and are evaluating the

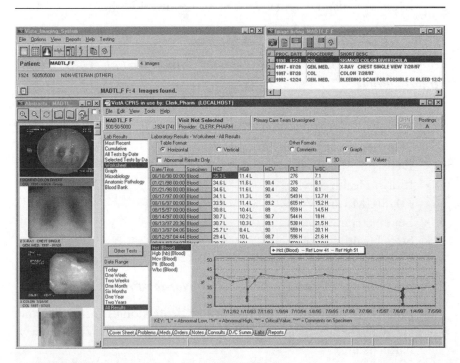

FIGURE 6-1 VistA Imaging and CPRS Screen

possibility of using VistA (e.g., Panama, India, and Jordan). The Open Source community has begun to embrace VistA and an organization called World–VistA has emerged which is focused on further developing and supporting the growing global VistA community.

Major Derivations of VistA

Throughout the world, there are currently six major branches of VistA that have emerged including:

- The VistA system as released by the VA under the Freedom of Information Act (FOIA).
- The RPMS system used in Indian Health Service (IHS) healthcare facilities.
- The Composite Health Care System (CHCS) used in DoD facilities.
- Open Source VistA collaboratively developed and released by the Pacific Hui and WorldVistA.
- VistA as modified and released by vendors such as MedSphere, DSS, and other companies.
- International variants of VistA as modified or customized by Mexico, Finland, Germany, Nigeria, Egypt, and others.

Major VistA Communities Of Interest

Government: Federal, State, Local, and Tribal Government Organizations

The following are some of the major federal, state, tribal, and local government organizations across the country that have embraced VistA.

- Department of Veterans Affairs
- Department of Defense
- Indian Health Services
- HHS/CMS and VOE
- State Veterans Homes
- State Health Departments
- City and County Health Departments

Nongovernment Organizations (NGOs): Not-for-Profit

- HardHats is a virtual community of professionals interested and active in the deployment of both VA VistA and OpenVistA. (www.hardhats.org).

- VistA Software Alliance is an alliance of leading health IT companies that support the implementation of VistA in the public and private sectors. (www.vistasoftware.org).
- WorldVistA is committed to making health IT systems more affordable and widely available across the world, with an emphasis on VistA and open source solutions. (www.worldvista.org).
- Pacific Telehealth and Technology Hui conducts research, develops prototypes, and then disseminates and institutionalizes telehealth applications in support of the medical needs of beneficiaries in the Pacific (e.g., Hawaii, American Samoa, and Guam). (www. http://www.pacifichui.org).

Nongovernment Organizations (NGOs): For Profit

- Hewlett Packard (HP) is one of the major information technology vendors in the world. It offers many products in information technology and medical technology for the healthcare market. HP won the contract to implement VistA in the Oklahoma state veterans homes.
- MedSphere Systems Corporation is a health IT company actively involved in migrating VistA to an open platform. It has recently implemented VistA in public and private healthcare facilities in Oklahoma and Texas.
- Document Storage Systems (DSS) offers middleware that integrates COTS products with VistA. Its intimate knowledge of the VistA system has made it an important player in the growing VistA marketplace.
- Intersystems Corporation's products include the Caché post-relational database and "M" language platform used by VA medical centers across the United States.
- SAIC is a Fortune 500 company providing IT solutions to the private and public sectors, including the DoD Composite Health Care System (CHCS).
- EDS is a major information services player in public and private sectors, and provides development and maintenance services to the VA for its VistA system.
- Daou Systems, recently purchased by Proxicom, is an IT consulting and management services company actively involved in the design and development of the VistA Office EHR solution.

- Oleen Healthcare Information Management is a health IT services company with extensive experience in systems implementations and the "M" language environment used by VistA.
- Other large IT companies, including IBM, Sun, Novell, Red Hat, and Northrop Grumman, are strong supporters of Open Source Software and Open Solutions such as VistA.
- Other small and mid-size companies and consultants offer a variety of VistA implementation and support services, such as Blue Cliff, Mele Associates, Metro Computer Systems, Sea Island Systems, and Informatix Laboratories.

International Community

VistA has been deployed to varying degrees in a number of countries such as Mexico, Germany, Finland, Nigeria, and Egypt, as well as in American Samoa. Many healthcare organizations in other countries have expressed interest in exploring the possibility of deploying VistA, including Jordan, India, Panama, and Malaysia. Over time as countries implement and embrace VistA, the systems tend to become unique variants of the original VistA systems. Screens and system prompts are translated into local languages. The 'look and feel' are changed to reflect the culture of the country using the system. New modules and changes to the business rules embedded in VistA make the system better fit the new, international environment where it is being used. It may be that by 2020 the Hispanic version of VistA implemented by Mexico may dominate in Central America and be the largest deployed version of VistA in the world.

Key VistA System Advocacy and Support Organizations

VistA Software Alliance (VSA) is a nonprofit organization whose purpose is the promotion of VistA as a healthcare IT solution that improves quality of care, lowers costs, and improves patient safety. This trade organization and its members are committed to supporting achievement of the National Health Information Infrastructure (NHII) and the associated National Health Information Network (NHIN) in the United States through the intelligent use of a proven health information open solution, VistA. The two primary goals of the VSA are

1) to harness the resources of the members to promote and facilitate adoption of the VistA electronic health record (EHR) system, and

2) to serve as a neutral party representing multiple vendors that want to collaborate with the VA and other federal, state, or local government agencies in order to promote and facilitate the widespread adoption of VistA by healthcare providers around the world.

The VSA serves as a neutral party representing the many health IT vendors that provide VistA support, maintenance, development, and implementation services. Potential customers who want to find out more about VistA and the companies that support it can contact the VSA before communicating with any specific vendor.

The founding members of VSA are the leading VistA implementation and support organizations that support both public and private sector deployments of VistA. They include Hewlett Packard, InterSystems, Perot Systems, SAIC, Oleen, MedSphere, Novell, and Document Storage Systems. (http://www.vistasoftware.org/resources/index.html)

WorldVistA was incorporated on March 18, 2002, as a nonprofit corporation in California. It was formed to help make healthcare information technology more affordable and widely available both within the United States and around the world. More specifically, WorldVistA seeks to extend and further enhance the functionality of the VistA system developed by the VA. These efforts include developing additional VistA software modules for pediatrics, obstetrics, patient billing, and other hospital services not normally used in veterans hospitals. WorldVistA will also help adopters successfully master, install, and maintain the system. As the group of VistA adopters and programmers grows, WorldVistA will work to weave them into a collaborative, consensus-based, open-source community.

A priority project for the WorldVistA and the larger community is the development and deployment of an open source solution known as OpenVistA. In order to run VistA, it has been necessary to pay certain software licensing fees for the "M" programming language compilers and the underlying operating systems (e.g., MS Windows/NT or VMS). The OpenVistA project eliminates these fees by allowing VistA to run on the GT.M programming environment and the Linux operating system, both of which are free, open source products. By reducing software purchase and licensing costs, OpenVistA becomes a viable alternative solution for many providers who could not otherwise afford to acquire and implement an electronic health record (EHR) system. The collaborative OpenVistA project involving both WorldVistA and the Pacific Telehealth and Technology Hui seeks to provide healthcare organizations with the software, documentation, and training materials, in addition to helping build long-term mutual support relationships facilitating the transfer of needed knowledge and expertise to successfully implement VistA. Visit World VistA at http://www.worldvista.org and the Pacific Hui at http://www.pacifichui.org/.

VistA Business Models

Over the past few years, three primary business models have emerged in the VistA marketplace:

- **Application Service Provider (ASP)** delivers an ASP solution to serve small offices from a remote location under a management service agreement. The clients avoid the capital expense associated with technology and simply budget monthly fees for health information technology services. The actual Open Solution software is hosted off-site by the service bureau company.
- **Maintenance and Support** is implemented in the client organization, and the organization contracts with an information technology services company to provide ongoing support. This involves providing implementation and ongoing support for VistA for mid–range to large–scale healthcare provider organizations.
- **Consultative Services and Knowledge Transfer** is where the healthcare information technology services company provides advice related to planning, feasibility, and implementation through a combination of consulting and knowledge transfer service solutions. Over time the healthcare organization or public healthcare system develops its internal support infrastructure with local talent developed cooperatively.

In addition to pursuing one or more of these models, the VSA member companies have each developed additional value–added products that can be interfaced to VistA in such areas as billing, pediatrics, and imaging, which may not be included in the current open source VistA solutions.

The Market

There is a tremendous market for both COTS and Open Source health information technology and EHR solutions. The market includes:

- Government hospitals, nursing homes, and clinics (federal/state/local).
- International governments and their healthcare facilities/systems.
- Private sector hospitals and nursing homes.
- Private sector clinics and physician offices.
- Other healthcare organizations such as research and public health.

As of early 2006, only a small percentage of hospitals and medical practices worldwide had implemented person-centered medical informatics systems that include EHRs, CPOE, and many other necessary clinical and business modules.

The Competition

Some of the major vendors of other commercial health information technology systems include:

- McKesson: http://www.mckesson.com/homeflash.html
- Siemens Medical Solution (SMS): https://www.smed.com/default.asp
- Epic Systems Corporation: http://www.epicsystems.com
- Meditech: http://www.meditech.com/
- IDX: http://www.idx.com/
- Cerner: http://www.cerner.com/public/
- Healthcare Management Systems: http://www.hmstn.com/
- Eclipsys: http://www.eclipsys.com/

Unfortunately, the cost of acquiring their software and paying the recurring licensing fees often put their products out of reach of many physician offices and midsized healthcare delivery organizations across the country and around the world.

The Future—Continued Growth of VistA Worldwide

VistA use outside of the VA continues to accelerate ever more rapidly. WorldVistA and the Open Solutions community are starting to contribute many additional Free and Open Source Software modules to VistA. Many innovative enhancements to the VistA system will come over time, not from the VA, but from the larger VistA community. For example, the numerous companies that make up the VistA Software Alliance will be offering commercial-off-the-shelf (COTS) add-ons to VistA. Other countries such as Mexico, Finland, and Nigeria will also be contributing new tools and software that will benefit all of the collaborating VistA communities. In addition to the Computerized Patient Record System (CPRS), VistA Clinical Imaging, and the Master Patient Index, many other new VistA modules are in various stages of development by the VA, including a health data repository (HDR) and a personal health record (PHR). The VistA development community is also working on the conversion of VistA software modules to Java, an enhanced Web front end, and many other new features that will be released and shared. What we are seeing is that the "open source" VistA system can successfully compete with any of the other major information technology companies and their COTS EHR solutions they are selling in the marketplace.

CHAPTER 7

National Health Information Network (NHIN), Regional Health Information Organizations (RHIO), and the Federal Health Information Exchange (FHIE)

RHIOs are not a dance. RHIOs are not a place.
A RHIO is an interoperable clinical information
exchange that is being rolled out in communities to meet
patient needs and the public health needs of society.

Douglas Goldstein and Peter Groen

This chapter discusses the National Health Information Network (NHIN) and the rapid formation and activities of Regional Health Information Organizations (RHIO) across the country. These are major public and private sector collaborative efforts aimed at putting in place key components of the National Health Informatics Infrastructure in the

United States. The chapter also provides listings of many other selected Health Information Exchange (HIE) initiatives. In addition, two case studies profiling operational health information exchanges are discussed: the Federal Health Information Exchange (FHIE) and the Cancer Biomedical Informatics Grids (caBIG).

NHIN and RHIO

The Office of the National Coordinator for Health Information Technology (ONCHIT) and the National Committee on Vital and Health Statistics (NCVHS) have clearly stated that the long-range strategy for a National Health Information Infrastructure (NHII) requires a national health information network (NHIN) that can provide low-cost, secure data movement. They have stated that a NHIN is needed, along with a public–private oversight or management function to ensure adherence to public policy objectives. Development of this infrastructure is considered a vital national priority.

On July 21, 2004, the U.S. Department of Health and Human Service (HHS) released *Framework for Strategic Action, The Decade of Health Information Technology: Delivering Consumer-centric and Information-rich Health Care*. It presented four goals and associated strategies to achieve the vision of utilizing information technology (IT) solutions to reduce costs, avoid medical errors, and improve health care in America:

- Inform clinical practices with use of electronic health records (EHR).
- Interconnect clinicians so that they can exchange health information using advanced and secure electronic communication.
- Personalize care with consumer-based personal health records (PHR) and better information for consumers.
- Improve population health through advanced biosurveillance methods and streamlined collection of data for quality measurement and research.

With regards to health information exchange (HIE) systems, ONCHIT believes that a key component of the goal to interconnect clinicians is to promote interoperability, that is, the ability to exchange patient health information among clinicians and other authorized entities in a timely manner and under consistent security, privacy, and other protections.

On November 15, 2004, in an effort to gain broad input regarding the best mechanisms to achieve nationwide interoperability to meet the goal of interconnecting clinicians so that they can exchange health information, ONCHIT released a request for information (RFI). The RFI encouraged the public to explore the role of the federal government in facilitating deployment of a nationwide health information network (NHIN); how it could be governed, financed, and operated; and how it could be supported by and coordinated with regional health information exchange projects.

The "Summary of Nationwide Health Information Network (NHIN) Request for Information (RFI)" of June 2005 identified the following concepts that emerged from the majority of RFI respondents:

- A NHIN should be a decentralized architecture built using the Internet linked by uniform communications and a software framework of open standards and policies.
- A NHIN should reflect the interests of all stakeholders and be a joint public/private effort.
- A governance entity composed of public and private stakeholders should oversee the determination of standards and policies.
- A NHIN should be patient-centric with sufficient safeguards to protect the privacy of personal health information.
- Incentives will be needed to accelerate deployment and adoption of a NHIN.
- Existing technologies, federal leadership, prototype regional exchange efforts, and certification of EHRs will be the critical enablers of a NHIN.
- Key challenges will be the need for additional and better-refined standards; addressing privacy concerns; paying for the development and operation of, and access to, the NHIN; accurately matching patients; and addressing discordant inter- and intra state laws regarding health information exchange.

The "Summary of Nationwide Health Information Network (NHIN) Request for Information (RFI)" (http://www.hhs.gov/healthit/rfisumma ryreport.pdf) also stated:

The potential value of the interoperable exchange of health information among disparate entities is substantial. A recent study that estimated a net savings from national implementation of fully standardized interoperability between providers and five other types of organizations could yield $77.8 billion annually, or approximately 5% of the projected $1.7 trillion spent on U.S. health care in 2003. Other studies estimate that between 20–30% of our healthcare spending, or up to $300 billion each year, is for treatments that do not improve health status, are redundant, or are not appropriate for the patient's condition. Administrative inefficiencies (e.g., paper handling) have been separately estimated to be of similar magnitude. While more work is needed to validate these savings estimates, all-available evidence suggests that implementation of interoperable health information exchange will result in significant savings.

Other potential benefits identified included the following:

- Consumers could consult clinicians more easily without fear of losing their records, repeating tests, or having to recall complex histories for each clinician.
- Payers could benefit from the economic efficiencies, fewer errors, and reduced duplication of effort.
- Clinicians could benefit from having easier access to complete problem lists, procedure histories, allergies, and medication histories at the point of service.
- Interoperability may also lead to meaningful public health reporting, bioterrorism surveillance, quality monitoring, and advances in clinical trials.

Implementing the National Health Information Network

When discussing operational considerations, many respondents recommended that the NHIN follow an evolutionary path, with a gradual rollout. Many respondents stated that an incremental approach that integrates existing networks and builds momentum around early successes is more likely to succeed in the United States.

Most respondents who discussed technical considerations envisioned a NHIN as a decentralized network built around regional exchanges of information run by a Regional Health Information Organization (RHIO). In a decentralized architecture, RHIOs could handle the day-to-day operations of regional health exchange and facilitate integration into a NHIN. Respondents also stated that standards would be needed to facilitate interoperability.

According to Eric G. Brown, vice president of Forrester Research, in his presentation at a Healthcare Information and Management Systems Society (HIMSS) conference on "Building Regional Health Information Networks," public and private sector organizations will need to collaborate and build the trusted Regional Health Information Networks (RHIN). The National Health Information Network (NHIN) will then tie the RHINs together. The challenge is for 100 to 200 regions to build the needed RHINs during the next 5 to 10 years, connecting more than 6,000 hospitals and hundreds of thousands of clinicians.

On December 12, 2005, *Health IT World News* reported that Accenture, Cisco, IBM, Microsoft, Northrop Grumman, Oracle, and Sun were among the wide range of technology and consulting companies tapped to design a $18.6 million NHIN for the U.S. Department of Health and Human Services (HHS). According to the report, the NHIN will be designed and rolled out through four consortia, each consisting of several IT, consulting, security, and healthcare companies and organizations.

According to the eHealth Initiative (eHI) Foundation's "Second Annual Survey of State, Regional, and Community-Based Health Information Exchange Initiatives and Organizationss" released in 2005, the number of health information exchange (HIE) efforts actively exchanging data had tripled over the past year. There are now more than 100 HIE projects underway in 45 states. A brief sampling of these initiatives include:

- Delaware Health Information Network
- Florida Health Information Infrastructure
- Indiana Health Information Exchange
- Maine Health Information Network Technology
- Maryland/DC Collaborative for Healthcare IT
- Mesa County Health Information Network (CO)
- Michigan Health Information Infrastructure
- Santa Barbara County Care Data Exchange (CA)
- Taconic Health Information Network and Community (NY)
- The Wisconsin Health Information Exchange Project
- Tri-Cities Care Data Exchange Project (TN)
- Whatcom Health Information Network (WA)

A detailed listing can be obtained by viewing the eHI's report, which can be found at http://www.ehealthinitiative.org. Also, visit http://aspe.hhs.gov/sp/nhii/statelocal.html

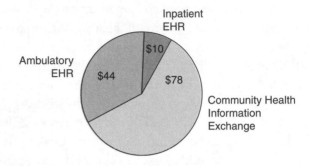

Where will the savings come from?

Net estimated annual savings: $132 billion

FIGURE 7-1 Savings from Health IT Systems
Source: Center for Information Technology Leadership/Forrester

Case Study: Federal Health Information Exchange (FHIE)

The U.S. Department of Veterans Affairs (VA) and the Department of Defense (DoD) have already developed and put in place a networking solution that allows them to exchange patient information between their two electronic health record (EHR) systems, VistA and CHCS. This solution, originally referred to as the GCPR Framework Project, is now known as the Federal Health Information Exchange (FHIE).

The Veterans Health Administration (VHA), the Military Health System (MHS), and the Indian Health Service (IHS) collect and maintain health information on their extensive patient populations in separate EHR systems. The Government Computer-Based Patient Record (GCPR) Framework Project was originally envisioned as an electronic interface that would allow physicians and other authorized users at the VA, DoD, and IHS health facilities to access data from any of the other agencies' health facilities. GCPR was never intended to be a separate computerized health information system, nor was it meant to replace the VA's, DoD's, and IHS's existing health information systems.

By the end of 2000, the prototype solution was completed, and pilot testing of data transfer among selected facilities successfully demonstrated that the GCPR technology solution worked, although significant issues in

FIGURE 7-2 VA/DoD Health IT Sharing Web Site
Source: http://www. 1.va.gov/vadodhealthitsharing/ and http://www.1.va.
gov/vadodhealthitsharing/page.cfm?pg=13

translating and sharing comprehensive patient records had yet to be fully addressed. Senior IT management at the VA and the DoD decided to re-baseline the project and focus on some "early deliverables" of immediate applicability to the VA's and the DoD's missions. The partnering agencies set a priority to allow VA healthcare providers to view DoD health data by the end of September 2001. Unfortunately, this interim effort largely excluded the IHS. Once this interim effort was achieved, however, the CIOs planned to resume the broader GCPR Framework Project goals—establishing a link among all three partner agencies' health information systems.

In 2002, the GCPR Framework Project was renamed the Federal Health Information Exchange (FHIE). Nationwide deployment of the first version of FHIE was completed by the VA on July 17, 2002. This first version enabled the one-way transfer of data from the DoD's existing healthcare information system to a separate database that VA hospitals could access. Subsequent phases would further enhance FHIE to include the exchange of additional domains of patient data and work toward a long-term solution involving the Bi-directional Health Information Exchange (BHIE) amongst partnering agencies. These federal agencies are already well on their way toward being key players in the United States' efforts to put in place a NHIN.

Background

The VA and the DoD, combined, provide healthcare services to approximately 12 million veterans, military personnel, and dependents at an annual cost well in excess of $40 billion. The VHA and the MHS collect and maintain patient health information in separate systems. The Gulf War of the early 1990s exposed many deficiencies in these systems and highlighted the need for the VA and the DoD to be able to readily access and transfer accurate health data on their respective populations. In December 1992, Congress asked the GAO (the federal General Accounting Office, renamed in 2004 to the Government Accountability Office) to report on how the VA and the DoD, along with the IHS, could share IT and patient medical information to provide greater continuity of care, accelerate VA eligibility determinations, and save on software development costs.

In November 1997, the president called for the two agencies to start developing a "comprehensive, life-long medical record for each service member." This led to the establishment of the Government Computer-based Patient Record (GCPR) Framework Project the following month. Given its long tradition of collaborating with other federal agencies on health IT systems, the IHS was also invited to participate in the GCPR project. In early 1998, a project manager was appointed, the interagency project management team was formed, interagency working groups were put in place, and contracts were awarded to a number of vendors to begin work on the proposed system.

There were to be four phases associated with the project:

- Preliminary Start–up Phase (FY 99)
- Phase I: Prototype Development and Testing (FY 99)
- Phase II: Pilot System Development and Testing (FY 00)
- Phase III: Phased Deployment and Enhancements (FY 01-04)
- Phase IV: Ongoing Operations and Support (FY 05+)

The GCPR Framework Project, now referred to as the Federal Health Information Exchange (FHIE), was completed as planned, but not without overcoming some major obstacles. The first version of FHIE was successfully deployed nationwide by the end of July 2002. In September 2003, enhancements to FHIE were completed and deployed that added to the base of health information made available to VA clinicians from the DoD. The system transitioned into "steady state" and ongoing operational support starting in FY 2005.

Major Project Activities and Accomplishments

The GCPR Framework Project, now known as FHIE, was set up as a formally funded interagency project in FY 1998. The project was a joint effort involving the VA, DoD, and IHS. Costs of the project were to be borne by all three partners, with the precise share to be determined as the project proceeded.

From its inception, the GCPR, or FHIE, was all about working together, sharing costs, and leveraging agency and technological resources. However, most of the individuals assigned to the project by the VA, DoD, and IHS had little previous experience working on collaborative interagency projects.

GCPR was envisioned as an electronic interface that would allow physicians and other authorized users at VA, DoD, and IHS health facilities to access data from any of the other agencies' health facilities. The interface was expected to compile requested patient information in a "virtual" record that could be displayed on a user's computer screen. GCPR was never intended to be a separate computerized health information system, nor was it meant to replace the agencies' existing systems.

One of the first steps taken was to put in place a signed interagency memorandum of agreement (MOA). A board of directors was established to set GCPR programmatic and strategic priorities and secure project funding from the VA, DoD, and IHS. An executive committee was also formed to set tactical priorities, oversee project management activities, and ensure that adequate resources were made available. The committee membership consisted of senior managers from the VA, DoD, and IHS.

The GCPR Framework Project was managed on a day-to-day basis by an interagency project office staffed by personnel from the VA, DoD, IHS, and the project's prime contractor. An interim project manager was also appointed to head up the team. Litton/PRC was selected as the prime contractor and was responsible for building, shipping, installing, configuring, and operating the GCPR Framework and providing needed site training. Battelle Memorial Institute of Columbus, Ohio, was awarded contracts for developing medical "reference models," which would allow for the exchange of data among different systems without requiring extensive standardization efforts.

The project also established a number of government-led working groups, which consisted of VA, DoD, and IHS employees along with Litton/PRC staff. There were working groups addressing acquisition, finance, legal, marketing, telecommunications, and clinical practices. The project called for extensive collaboration between multiple public and private sector organizations, which was a totally new way of doing business for many of the partners.

There were four phases associated with the project:

- Phase I, involving the development of the prototype for the GCPR Framework, proceeded throughout 1999. Final acceptance testing of the prototype was conducted in March 2000. Clinicians and technicians applied a vigorous, scripted testing process to demonstrate and validate the GCPR components, including architecture and technology; secure data request and retrieval functions; functional interfaces; message handling and trigger events; and the ability to conduct population studies. Both the clinical and technical testing of the prototype were successful.

- Phase II involved the development and testing of a pilot system by the prime vendor, Litton/PRC, at selected sites. The pilot tests of data transfer among selected VA facilities was completed by the end of 2000 and demonstrated that the GCPR Framework solution worked. However, it became clear that significant issues in translating and sharing comprehensive patient records had not been adequately addressed. A number of project management issues surfaced that placed the project in some jeopardy. These were documented in a GAO report to Congress in April 2001. As a result, senior IT management of the partnering agencies stepped forward to provide additional oversight and guidance.
- Phase III was scaled back and re-baselined. The senior IT management team decided to focus on some "early deliverables" of immediate applicability to their missions. The partnering agencies set a priority to allow VA healthcare providers to view DoD health data by the end of September 2001. This interim effort largely excluded IHS. Once this interim effort was achieved, however, the CIOs hoped to resume the broader GCPR Framework project goals: establishing a link among all three partner agencies' health information systems. The project was also renamed the Federal Health Information Exchange (FHIE) at this point in time.

The FHIE near-term solution was rapidly developed and began alpha testing on November 14, 2001, at the San Diego VA Medical Center with a sample of DoD patients from the Naval Medical Center San Diego. A clinical quality assurance assessment of beta test results was completed in March 2002. Beta testing of the FHIE near-term solution at five sites was completed in April 2002: Anchorage, El Paso, San Diego, Seattle, and Washington, DC.

On May 3, 2002, the Deputy Secretary of the Department of Veterans Affairs and the Under Secretary for Personnel & Readiness at the Department of Defense signed a Memorandum of Agreement (MOA) on the Federal Health Information Exchange (FHIE) Governance and Management. This MOA:

- Replaced original GCPR agreements signed in 1998.
- Renamed GCPR as the Federal Health Information Exchange (FHIE).

- Designated the VA as the lead agency for FHIE.
- Revised and clarified goals and objectives of the project.
- Committed executive-level support necessary to adequately support the project.

On April 26, 2002, the CIO for the VA chaired a review of the FHIE system and test results to determine whether the first version of FHIE was ready for deployment. Based on the results of this review, he determined that FHIE was ready to deploy on May 27, 2002. Deployment of the first version of FHIE was completed by the VA on July 17, 2002.

In September 2003, enhancements to FHIE were completed and deployed that added to the base of health information available to VA clinicians from the DoD. It included discharge summaries, allergy information, consultation results, and other selected patient data.

- Phase IV involved completing a FHIE post-implementation review and the transition into ongoing operations and support starting in 2005. This was successfully achieved well ahead of schedule. The VA and DoD are now moving forward with a new project called the Bidirectional Health Information Exchange (BHIE) that builds on the accomplishments of the highly successful FHIE solution.

Lessons Learned from FHIE

This major interagency collaboration project taught the agencies many valuable lessons that will be extremely valuable in working on future interagency initiatives. The project helped define and put in place business models that can be replicated in the future with regard to governance structure, interagency working groups, cross-agency funding mechanisms, and acquisition strategies.

From the outset, decision-making and oversight were blurred across several management entities, compromising GCPR's progress. The roles and responsibilities of these entities and the relationships among them were not clearly spelled out in the original MOA among the GCPR partners, and no one entity exercised final authority over the project. The GCPR board of directors and the executive committee did not follow sound IT business practices—such as ensuring agency commitment, securing stable funding, and monitoring the project's progress—as dictated by federal requirements. Without agency commitment and sufficient oversight, the project team has been limited in its ability to manage

GCPR effectively or efficiently. Unstable funding forced GCPR project managers to develop and issue multiple short-term contracts for work that could have been covered by a single longer-term contract.

Much of this was recorded in an April 2001 report by the GAO to Congress on the status of the project. The GAO noted that the project was experiencing schedule and cost overruns and was operating without clear goals, objectives, and consistent leadership. The GAO recommended that the participating agencies: 1) designate a lead entity with final decision-making authority and establish a clear line of authority for the GCPR Framework Project, and 2) create comprehensive and coordinated plans that included an agreed-upon mission and clear goals, objectives, and performance measures, to ensure that the agencies could share comprehensive, meaningful, accurate, and secure patient healthcare data. The VA, DoD, and IHS agreed with their findings and recommendations and made a number of changes.

As a result, senior IT management of the partnering agencies stepped forward to provide additional oversight and guidance. For example, the project was scaled back and re-baselined. The senior IT management team decided to focus on some "early deliverables" of immediate applicability to their missions. The partnering agencies set a priority to allow VA healthcare providers to view DoD health data by the end of September 2001. The project was also renamed the Federal Health Information Exchange (FHIE) at this point in time. A permanent project manager was also finally appointed.

In March 2002, the GAO again reported that the project was continuing to operate without clear lines of authority or a lead entity responsible for final decision-making. Further, the project continued to move forward without detailed plans, proper coordination, and full cooperation among partnering agencies, or an agreed-upon mission with clear goals, objectives, and performance measures. This led to the signing of the new MOA for the Federal Health Information Exchange (FHIE) Project, replacing the original GCPR agreements. The new agreement revised and clarified the goals and objectives for the FHIE project, and designated the VA as the lead agency for FHIE. These changes, coupled with the earlier re-baselining and scaling back on the scope of the project, allowed the partners to successfully complete the nationwide deployment of FHIE by July 2002.

Based on the many lessons learned, the VA and its partners are now much better prepared to work on future interagency initiatives. The agencies have learned to deal with the major challenges to collaborative, interagency projects, such as budgeting, joint acquisitions, joint operations, joint development, legal issues, cultural issues, and interagency communications.

Existing FHIE System

FHIE allows electronic data from separated service members contained in the DoD's Composite Health Care System (CHCS) to be extracted and transmitted to an FHIE data repository maintained by the VA. Clinicians in VA medical centers and outpatient clinics across the country can access this data through the remote data view component of the Computerized Patient Record System (CPRS) in VistA. This patient information is normally made available for access via FHIE about six weeks after the service member's separation.

FHIE now provides current, near real-time data feeds electronically from CHCS I and CHCS II to the FHIE repository node for active duty, retired, and separated service members. Current data are being sent in Health Level Seven (HL7)–like messages. The following categories of DoD medical data currently being transferred to FHIE are:

- Patient demographics
- Pharmacy data
- Radiology reports
- Laboratory results
- Allergen information
- Discharge summaries
- Consultation reports
- Standard Ambulatory Data Record (SADR) information
- Inpatient Admission/Discharge/Transfer (A/D/T) information

In 2003, FHIE was capable of accommodating up to 800 queries per hour, with an average response rate of four seconds per query. In September 2003, VA clinicians made more than 1,900 authorized queries to the database. FHIE has provided clinicians at the VA with the capability of having almost instantaneous display of DoD patient data in the same format as other local patient data on veterans is displayed in CPRS.

Program management officials stated that the repository presently contains data on almost 2 million patients as of the end of 2003. This

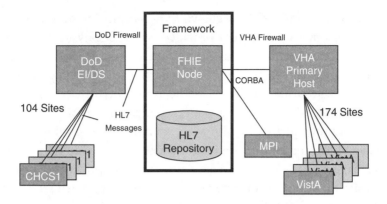

FIGURE 7-3 FHIE Architectural Overview

includes clinical data on almost 1.8 million personnel who separated from the military between 1987 and June 2003. The data consist of over 23 million laboratory records, 24 million pharmacy records, and 4 million radiology records. Access to complete patient information from the DoD is still somewhat limited because CHCS II, the DoD's new and more comprehensive health information system, is still being developed and deployed. CHCS II was renamed Armed Forces Health Longitudinal Technology Application (AHLTA) in late 2005.

Benefits

The one-way transfer of healthcare data from the DoD to the VA using FHIE has already allowing clinicians in VA medical centers to make faster, more informed decisions through ready access to information on almost 2 million patients, thereby improving their level of healthcare delivery.

In testimony to Congress on December 15, 2003, FHIE program officials and physicians cited various clinical and other benefits from using information provided via the FHIE data retrieval capability. In elaborating on the specific benefits, they reported the following:

- *Enhanced standardization and continuity of health care*—FHIE has enhanced the standardization of care by enabling VA physicians to review and apply approaches used by DoD physicians for diagnosing and treating particular illnesses or injuries. This capability has improved coordination by allowing the VA physicians to understand the outcomes of treatment provided by DoD physicians while the patients were on active duty, thus contributing to the continuity of health care, and improving the quality of care for each patient.

- *Improved clinician satisfaction*—The availability of electronic records has enabled physicians to spend less time searching for patient records and has provided them with more complete health information for diagnosing and treating patients' illnesses. Prior to FHIE, VA physicians had to rely on the veterans themselves to provide their military health records to the medical facility or request separated service members' paper records from the VA Medical Records Center or the DoD National Personnel Records Center, both located in St. Louis, Missouri. Using FHIE's data retrieval capability, however, physicians are able to retrieve veterans' medical information within approximately four seconds. Further, program officials stated, as a result of having the electronic medical information, fewer repeat tests are necessary for some patients, thus freeing healthcare resources for other medical needs.

- *Improved patient satisfaction*—Veterans seeking medical care at VA facilities have greater confidence that their electronic medical information is secure and well preserved. Unlike paper files, which are subject to loss and destruction during transfer and storage, electronic medical information is available to the VA physicians when needed.

In addition, during a demonstration of FHIE's capabilities at VA's Washington, DC, medical center, the chief of staff noted that the availability of healthcare information on separated service members has proven particularly valuable for treating emergency room and first-time patients.

Future FHIE Plans and Activities

The VA and DoD are proceeding with a joint, long-term strategy involving the two-way exchange of clinical information. Under the Health*e* People strategy, the VA and DoD plan to seek opportunities for sharing existing systems and technology and explore the convergence of VA and DoD health information applications consistent with mission requirements. The departments are proceeding with projects that are expected to result in a limited two-way exchange of health data by the end of 2005. Development of the Bi-directional Health Information Exchange (BHIE)

FHIE—Use Case

December 2005 A service member's injury in Iraq in 2005 left him disfigured and requiring substantial medical attention after his separation from active military service. He was a young man in his early 20s and was applying for health benefits and compensation from the VA that he was entitled to by law.

The VA administrative staff at the VA facility he where he was scheduled to be evaluated wondered if there was any DoD electronic medical information that could be made readily available to assist their clinical staff during their upcoming evaluation of him. The VA staff were apparently having difficulties getting copies of his paper medical record information.

They decided to test the newly installed Bi-directional Health Information Exchange (BHIE) capability of the VA/DoD FHIE system. By using the Remote Data View function in the VA Computerized Patient Record System (CPRS), within 25 seconds they were able to pull up a health summary with all of his recent clinical results: radiology text reports and prescription information from the Army medical center where he had been treated. The VA staff were very pleasantly surprised. They said this was "wonderful" and they would have the VA physician look at this data as part of his clinical evaluation of the young man in the coming week.

This was just one example of the awesome power of the interagency IT work by the VA and DoD, work that has great meaning for this brave young man.

The Path to Interoperability

FIGURE 7-4 FHIE and the Path to Interoperability

Key References and Web Sites

Federal Health Information Exchange (FHIE): http://www.va.gov/vadod healthitsharing/

Veterans Health Administration: http://www.va.gov/health_benefits/

Military Health System: http://www.ha.osd.mil/

Indian Health Service: http://www.ihs.gov/

---

solution is already well underway. Pilot tests at a limited number of sites have already shown the system works well. Deployment at additional VA and DoD sites will begin in 2006.

The VA and DoD are also proceeding with development of interoperable data repositories that will support the bidirectional exchange of computable data between the DoD Clinical Data Repository (CDR) and the VA Health Data Repository (HDR), known as Clinical Data Repository/ Health Data Repository (C/HDR). In September 2004, the VA and DoD successfully demonstrated a C/HDR pharmacy prototype in a computer laboratory setting. The departments are actively developing C/HDR for production and anticipate completing development and testing of the initial interface in 2006.

Finally, HealthePeople is a long-range collaborative strategy of the Veterans Health Administration (VHA) aimed at increasing availability and use of high-performance, interoperable health information systems to improve health of veterans within their communities across the country. The strategy focuses on seeking a national Health Information Exchange (HIE) solution conforming to the architecture of the National Health Information Network (NHIN) and supporting a comprehensive, longitudinal electronic health record (EHR) and personal health record (PHR) for veterans.

Case Study: Cancer Biomedical Informatics Grids

Biomedical Informatics Grid (caBIG™)

The Cancer Biomedical Informatics Grid (caBIG) is an example of a voluntary biomedical informatics network or grid that virtually connects individuals and institutions, enabling them to effectively share data and research tools in an open environment with common standards. caBIG is a World Wide Web of cancer research and development providing a common unification that accelerates understanding of the disease and delivers new approaches for the prevention, early detection, and treatment of cancer. Its goal is to create more global opportunities to make important new cancer-related findings, quickly and efficiently. Over 600 individuals have contributed to the caBIG initiative and more than 24 new products are expected to be available to the caBIG and cancer research communities through the grid during 2005. caBIG is being developed under the leadership of the National Cancer Institute's Center for Bioinformatics (NCICB).

A three-year pilot program was launched in July 2003 at the request of the cancer research community, which was struggling to manage and manipulate the complex data sets produced in biomedical studies. Disparate standards and lack of interoperability among systems were major impediments to solving the detection and treatment of cancer, resulting in duplicated efforts, unshared data, and wasted time, effort, and lives. The pilot program involves 50 National Cancer Institute (NCI)–designated cancer centers. As part of the activities in building the grid, these centers are developing specific biomedical research tools to

FIGURE 7-5 Screen shot of caBIG Web site
Source: http://cabig.nci. nih.gov

include standards- and components-based clinical trial management systems, tissue banks and pathology tools, and a collection of integrative cancer research applications. Related data sets within these domain areas will also be available through the grid. Standards and tools will support common usage of vocabularies, data elements, and the formation of a unifying architecture, which will ensure interoperability of tools across the grid, facilitate collaboration and data sharing, and streamline cancer research activities across the spectrum. The caBIG Web site reports that during its first year, they launched more than 75 projects, including the first iteration of the caBIG Compatibility Guidelines and end-to-end solutions like caARRAY and genePattern that provide microarray tools at both ends of the process, or cytoscape and caWorkbench that provide analysis capabilities for molecular pathways.

caBIG is built on the principles of open source, open access, and open development. By definition, this means that this shared environment is readily available to anyone in biomedical research. Rather than operating in a vacuum, NCI believes that caBIG will not only redefine how *cancer* research is conducted, but it will change how *all* future health-related research is conducted. caBIG has several strategic-level working groups: strategic planning, data sharing, and intellectual capital and training. It also has five primary workspaces that support collaboration:

- Clinical trial management systems.
- Tissue banks and pathology tools.
- Integrative cancer research.
- Vocabularies and common data elements.
- Architecture.

The following list includes applications/tools, infrastructure, and data sets from the NCICB and participating cancer centers that are used to support the caBIG initiative. For instance, the "Applications in Alphabetical Order" outlines the applications and software tools that support caBIG architecture, facilitate data collection, and support data analysis and integration. In "View Applications by Workspace," it describes the various technology tools that are applicable to which workspaces. The "Infrastructure" area provides key underlying caBIG infrastructures including ontologies, common data elements, and object models. Finally, the "Data Sets" section contains a collection of biomedical research data available through the caBIG consortium and resources. The three major components of the caCORE infrastructure are caBIO, caDSR, and EVS, which are available under an Open Source licensing agreement.

- **Cancer Bioinformatics Infrastructure Objects (caBIO)** creates models of biomedical objects to facilitate the communication and integration of information from the various initiatives supported by the NCICB.
- **Cancer Data Standards Repository (caDSR)** stores the Common Data Elements developed by NCI-sponsored organizations.
- **NCI Enterprise Vocabulary Services (EVS)** contains standard vocabularies for a variety of settings in the life sciences. The EVS project produced the NCI Thesaurus (provided under an open content license) and the NCI Metathesaurus (based on NLM's Unified Medical Language System Metathesaurus supplemented with additional cancer-centric vocabulary).

caCORE components are powered by open source software represented by a series of Apache projects.

caBIG participants include approximately 500 people from 50 NCI-designated cancer centers and hospitals, universities, and other organizations. For a complete listing, visit the caBIG Web site at https://cabig.nci.nih.gov/ and click on "caBIG participants" at the top of the page.

Although cancer patients are the most important beneficiaries of the caBIG, its infrastructure and tools have broad utility outside the cancer community. Regional Health Information Organizations (RHIOs) can learn valuable lessons from NCI's work on caBIG. Currently there are

FIGURE 7-6 PITAC Diagram
Source: http://www.nitrd.gov/pitac/reports/20040721_hit_report.pdf

between 200 and 300 RHIOs being developed in the United States, with approximately 20 of them already exchanging information. However, there are still a large number of patient records dispersed throughout the healthcare community in hospitals, physician offices, labs, and so on. The caBIG offers important solutions to exchanging clinical data among organizations and improving health care through information sharing and collaboration. caBIG also successfully demonstrates how open solutions can facilitate communication between organizations and allow for free flow of information in a secure and private environment. Visit https://cabig.nci.nih.gov/ for more knowledge and resources.

In conclusion, Figure 7-6 from a report to the president from the President's Information Technology Advisory Committee best sums up the equation to realize better health care for people throughout the world.

Deploying Medical Informatics 20/20 Open Solutions

The free software movement has become a serious challenge to big, global software players. Just about any kind of software can now be found in open source form.

Thomas Friedman, *The World Is Flat*, 2005.

Open source is nothing more than peer-reviewed science.

Marc Andreessen, the creator of first Web browser— Mosaic and Netscape

Section Overview: The Medical Informatics 20/20 model embraces the COSI strategies of Collaboration, Open Solutions, and Innovation as the way to implement new technology, products, and services effectively and efficiently. The focus of this section of the book is on the implementation of Open Solutions as it examines the acquisition, deployment, and use of EHR systems in different settings. It includes detailed profiles on various open source software

EHR systems that have been implemented by large and small healthcare provider organizations around the world.

Chapter 8, **Acquiring and Implementing EHR Systems**, delivers a detailed account on how to implement an EHR system in a healthcare provider organization. Many of the steps in the process can be applied to open source software EHRs or closed/proprietary types of EHRs. The chapter explores the rationale, planning deployment, and post-implementation processes. It also discusses various benefits of acquiring and implementing an EHR along with some major issues, for example, privacy, security, and clinical "champions." See Figure 1-3.

Chapter 9, **Case Studies of VistA Implementations—United States and International**, includes a broad spectrum of case examples of leading healthcare organizations around the world that have taken advantage of the VistA health information technology system. It provides specific case studies on the implementations of the VistA health information technology and EHR system in mid-size and large-scale healthcare organizations from a private healthcare facility in Midlands, Texas, to federal agencies such as the VA and the Indian Health Service, to state-run healthcare facilities in Hawaii and Oklahoma, as well as international implementations of VistA in Mexico, Egypt, and other countries. The VistA system was developed by the U.S. Department of Veterans Affairs (VA) and is in the public domain and available for use by other organizations without license fees, similar to Free and Open Source Software (FOSS).

Chapter 10, **Profiles of Leading Open Solutions EHRs**, provides a series of short profiles on notable open source EHR solutions that are available and are being implemented in small- to mid-size healthcare organizations around the world. Some of the EHRs discussed includes the AMPATH system, which is focused on international application in developing countries, and OpenEMR, OSCAR, and FreeMED, which have been deployed in developed countries.

CHAPTER 8

Acquiring and Implementing EHR Systems

"I am convinced that the medical revolution of our children's lifetime will be the application of information technology to health care."

Tommy Thompson, Former Secretary,
U.S. Department of Health and Human Services

Introduction

This chapter will serve as a short, practical guide to acquiring, implementing and operating an electronic health record (EHR) system in a healthcare facility or provider organization based on the experiences of Chief Information Officers (CIOs) and developers of electronic health records. The target audience is healthcare executives and clinicians about to embark on the challenging experience of automating a healthcare organization or facility for the first time with medical informatics and EHRs.

Why EHR Now?

Even though the importance of EHRs has been well recognized by many for the past several years, its implementation across healthcare organizations has not been very common. To date only a minority of hospitals and health systems have implemented fully integrated EHRs within their overall health information technology framework. Meanwhile, only 4% to 8% of physicians have implemented EHRs in their offices, where most people's medical records begin.

Physicians have been able to operate their offices on paper-based systems for many years. So, they question as to "What is wrong with the current process? Why should we consider implementing EHRs and incur additional cost?" The healthcare industry is changing and so is practice of medicine.

The following are some of the key benefits associated with the use of EHRs:

- *Improved quality of care and reduced errors* by migrating from paper-based systems; EHRs provide timely information about patients so care decisions are based on latest information.
- *Medical and medication safety* with easy access to historical information
- *Improved workflow* as EHRs facilitate migration of the workflow from reactive to proactive.
- *Satisfying reporting requirements* by many organizations such as regulatory agencies, internal stakeholders, and external stakeholders.
- *Qualifying for "pay-for-performance" programs* because technology will help measure the performance.
- *Ease of sharing information* for everyone involved in providing care to the patient.
- *Ability to extract public health and biosurveillance information.*
- *Increasing focus on the importance of electronic health records by the federal government.*
- *Saving time and administrative hassle* by reducing the paper process related to administrative activities.
- *Enhanced revenue* through timely and appropriate billing and focusing on complete revenue cycle process.
- *Intrinsic satisfaction* for clinicians in their care delivery.
- *Reduction in overall healthcare cost* because even the use of partial toolsets such as e-prescribing and e-orders have been modeled to save the U.S. healthcare budget approximately $44 billion per year. Full EHRs could expand that savings, for society at large, to several hundred billion dollars per year.

One reason physicians have held back on the adoption of EHRs is because they have not seen the tangible benefits of EHRs and have not understood the true value of making a significant investment in health information technologies. Many healthcare organizations have been lagging behind in the use of EHRs for many reasons, such as lack of quantifiable benefits, competing priorities, and lack of organizational commitment.

However, more information is becoming available. In the past two to three years, several studies have quantified benefits of technology in selected areas:

- Electronic health record (EHR).
- Decision support tool to deploy evidence-based medicine at point of care.
- E-prescribing.
- Computerized provider order entry (CPOE).
- Creation of regional health information organizations (RHIO).

Several other areas are being analyzed in detail. A more in-depth discussion on return on investment (ROI) and value measurement is presented in Section IV.

Moving Away from Paper: How to Begin

With more than 400 vendors of electronic health record (EHR) systems in the marketplace today, moving from paper to a digital system is far more than a purchase decision: It is a process, a product, and an operational change. EHR-based medicine will change workflow, and in some cases will change the very nature of how clinicians practice medicine. EHR systems will affect their practices, while increasing patient satisfaction and laying the foundation for the right kind of 21st-century medical practices that will improve reimbursement while enhancing quality and patient care.

A critical success factor for an effective EHR implementation is using a disciplined process to set the right expectations, select the right tool, and make sure all stakeholders are involved in the process. This is a multiphased process that begins with proper planning.

So You Want to Acquire and Implement an EHR System

Healthcare organizations also typically acquire and implement office automation and business systems in addition to their EHR system; however, the focus of this chapter is specifically on EHRs. Typically, an organization's health IT systems consist of a collection of modules that might include

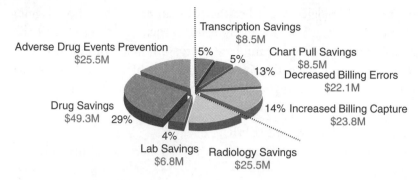

FIGURE 8-1 EHR Net Benefits Chart. The net benefits of EHR over five years is estimated to be $86,400 per provider and are accrued by several stakeholders.
Source: Samuel J. Wang, et al., Cost and Benefit Analysis of Electronic Medical Records in Primary Care *American Journal of Medicine*, 2003, Vol. 114, p. 397.

patient registration, clinic scheduling, inpatient admissions/discharge/transfer (ADT), pharmacy, laboratory, radiology, nursing, surgery, dietetics, order entry, clinical decision support, and other sub-systems. These modules are normally integrated into a comprehensive EHR system.

As your healthcare organization or facility makes a decision to acquire and implement an EHR system, it is important to understand the driving factor behind this decision. It may be a desire to improve patient care; to save money; to cut staff; to keep up with your competition; because you have been directed to do so as a result of legislation; or for one of many other reasons. The reason behind the EHR implementation will give you an indication of the level of commitment, support, or resistance you can expect to encounter as you continue to move forward with this endeavor.

The decision as to what system to acquire and implement is a story in itself. Following the traditional systems development lifecycle approach, the organization will have spent some time looking into the cost/benefit of the system, the desired functional capabilities, and various technical designs. Chapter 13 has a more detailed discussion about cost/benefit analyses and return-on-investment (ROI).

See Chapter 10 for more detailed information on various open source EHR solutions such as:

- Open EMR
- AMPATH
- OSCAR
- FreeMED

- CHLCare
- CottageMed
- PhoenixPM
- Open VistA

Historically, there have been two basic options available with regard to the acquisition and implementation of an EHR. Organizations could buy a commercial off-the-shelf system or develop a system of their own from scratch. In the 1970s, the only real option was to develop your own system. In the 1980s and 1990s, purchasing a commercial off-the-shelf system was often seen as the best option. In the 21st century, selection of an open source software solution has emerged as a very reasonable third option. There are numerous pros and cons for each of these approaches. In this book, our focus will be on the experiences of organizations that choose to acquire and implement Open Source solutions, although many of the steps are also applicable to organizations implementing a commercial off-the-shelf solution.

If you are the individual charged with leading the effort to acquire and implement the EHR, carefully take stock of your capabilities, strengths, weaknesses, and what is driving you to take on this effort. This will become important as you start working on your overall project plans, set up the organization you need, make hiring decisions for key staff, and take other major steps forward. To be successful in this long-range undertaking you will need to be committed to working on this effort for some years. Being driven by a desire to do good, to overcome huge obstacles, to have fun, to make a real difference in improving patient care—these are what it should be about.

Getting Started

Let's say the decision to acquire and implement an EHR system for your organization has been made. Once this management decision is made, the next step is to define project governance. This involves many key tasks. Some of them are:

- Assignment of a project manager to lead the effort. In selecting the person to lead this effort, the person should have the requisite technical and management skills needed to implement a complex, computerized EHR system.

- Assignment of physician "champion" to obtain support from this critical group.
- Set up a project organization to include oversight committee and various working groups focusing on operational processes such as medication management, clinical documentation, laboratory integration, and others.
- Set up the project team to include dedicated staff from all appropriate departments such as nursing, medical technicians, and others.
- Most importantly, focus on process improvement and change management to leverage EHR rather than fitting the new system to old processes.

The person selected to serve as the project manager should be a professional with the requisite technical and management skills needed to implement a complex, computerized EHR system in a healthcare environment. One does not normally hire a pharmacist to design and build office buildings. One does not hire an insurance agent with an interest in medical cases to perform surgery. One should not hire a surgeon or some other unqualified individual who simply has an interest in computers to head up this monumental information technology (IT) project management effort. To effectively lead this effort, the individual selected will need to draw upon a wide array of management and technical skills he or she acquired over time on related information systems management projects.

After the project manager has been selected and he or she has had a little time for orientation within the organization, the focus should shift to developing a detailed plan. This is more than a simple project plan. Because your healthcare organization may not have had any previous experience with computers, you need to put together a strategic plan that captures the long-range vision and goals with regard to the acquisition and implementation of a comprehensive EHR system. A mid-range or tactical plan is also needed to identify the major objectives you are setting out to achieve in the next two to three years with some degree of detail on budget projections and major milestones. Finally, a short-range operational plan that lays out the requisite organizational structure needed, immediate staffing levels, operational budgets, other resource requirements, and major upcoming tasks over the next year also need to be developed. The CIO should ensure that the plans are continually reviewed and updated so they remain relevant and useful to the organization.

As soon as the plans are developed, they need to be presented to the senior management of the organization for their input and "buy in." This may take several months of interaction to make sure everyone clearly understands what you are planning, what is needed, when, how much it is going to cost, and so on. One can't emphasize enough the need to keep presenting the plan to all the key senior management officials and stakeholders until you are sure everyone truly understands, agrees to it, and that they can not plead ignorance when you need to call upon them for support.

Similarly, there is a need to keep presenting the plans to the senior clinicians in the organization for their input and "buy in." Ultimately, it will be the clinician community that will be most affected by your efforts to implement an EHR system, and they will be the ones who will need to be won over for the effort to truly succeed. Identifying "champions" within the clinical community who support your plans and will help lead the way is crucial to success. These champions may be physicians, nurses, or technicians drawn from the various clinical services in your facility. If they take ownership of the system, you're well on your way to success.

Setting Up Your Health IT Organization

As your EHR plans are approved and you continue to move forward, the next step will be to start setting up a health information technology (IT) organization and start hiring key staff needed to initially acquire and implement the planned systems. In the early stages, your organization may be so small (say two to four people) that the organizational structure is very simple. You may have a single box on an organization chart called Health Information System (HIS) in which you may have the systems manager and two to three well-rounded staff who can do it all. Over time the organization may evolve through stages to include a small section that works on hardware, another section that focuses on software, and a third on telecommunications. Additional sections may be added in the future to include customer support, administrative support, and other areas depending on the size of the healthcare organization and the success of your EHR effort. A lot of this also depends on your organization's decisions on contracting out the work or bringing it in-house.

HIS Organization Structure

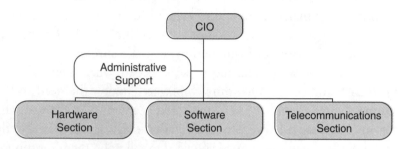

FIGURE 8-2 Health Information System Organization Structure

When you first get started and set up your health IT organization you want to hire the most talented staff you can get with a wide range of skills. As the project leader, you also want to look for people who complement your capabilities and offset weaknesses you may have. Again, the decisions you make may be influenced by the degree to which one contracts out for the needed systems and support. You will be looking for aggressive multi-talented staff that understand hardware, software, management, contracting, healthcare, and a slew of other things. In other words, hire people willing to do whatever is needed to ensure the success of the EHR project and the organization. Initially, anticipate that the health IT organization will be tightly staffed until it proves its worth. You might want to see whom you can recruit from within the existing healthcare organization before looking elsewhere. Your personnel department will normally guide you through the accepted hiring practices the rest of the organization normally uses. A good source for young, low-cost talent is nearby community colleges.

As stated above, over time your organization structure will need to evolve. Staffing levels will grow. Specialization will occur. Technicians who troubleshoot and repair hardware are very different from programmers who patch existing systems and develop new software applications. Telecommunications network staff require a completely different set of knowledge and skills. Management staff that understand planning, budgeting, personnel management, contracting, and other administrative activities will also be needed.

Again, your IT organization will evolve over time, the staffing levels will grow, and skill needs will change. You need to prepare for this.

Building the Infrastructure

If you are starting from scratch, one of your first concerns will probably be setting up a computer room to house the computers running the EHR system. This all depends on the current status of your technology infrastructure. If there are engineering staff in your organization who can help you design a computer room and adjoining spaces, by all means tap into their expertise. You are going to want to build a computer room that is adequately sized for both short-term and long-term needs. You will have to get into identifying electrical requirements for the equipment going into the room, environmental systems (e.g., air conditioning and heating), raised flooring, physical security, fire protection systems, lighting, telecommunications closets, uninterruptible power supplies (UPS), and many other areas where the assistance of an architect/engineer will be helpful. Building a computer room can take one to two years given the planning, budgeting, architectural work, contract awards, and then the actual construction phase.

Co-locating the health IT staff offices next to the computer room is something to consider. Since there will be a lot of work the staff will have to do that requires ready access to the computer room, you will find that co-location will save time, make life easier all around, and provide a form of additional security around the computer room. In addition to office space for the staff, you need to provide for a computer training room, space to repair hardware, and secure storage space. Furniture will also need to be acquired for your staff's offices as well as the training room, repair room, and storage room.

The EHR system you acquire will no doubt include a number of computer systems or servers, disk drives, tape drives, telecommunication routers and hubs, consoles, printers, and other peripherals that will need to be securely housed in the computer room. Then come the hundreds of workstations and printers that will need to be placed around the healthcare facility for your users. The hardware will need to be stored until it can be placed into the identified work areas around your buildings. The placement of the equipment is contingent on knowing where it needs to be installed and ensuring that electrical outlets are handy, telecommunication lines have been run to the workstation locations, and furniture is in place, all tied to the implementation planning schedule. Space for replacement and broken devices will be needed. Don't forget you will also need a set of tools for installing or repairing equipment.

With regard to the system software, you will need to acquire, install, and configure the operating systems software for the main computer systems and file servers. Then comes the acquisition, installation, and configuration of your application software. When the software is delivered, you will have not only the medium the software is on (e.g., disks, tapes) but also a fair amount of system documentation and manuals that you will need to store and have handy for ready use. You need to make sure you have the needed number of licensed copies of the software, that you keep copies stored in a secure place if you need to reinstall the software, and that you have arranged for ongoing support to include needed patches and enhancements to the software. This will be addressed in more detail in the next section.

Telecommunication networks are an extremely important part of the EHR system. The telecommunication networks can be broken down into local area networks (LAN) and wide area networks (WAN). The LAN is what allows the users within your facility to access the main computer systems and file servers. The LAN includes the cabling plant or all the wiring in the facility from the computer room to all the workstations and printers. You might have fiber-optic cable running from the computer room to small telecommunications closets located around your facility on each floor. From these closets you will probably have copper wiring (CAT-5) running to outlets in the various rooms on each floor where the workstations are placed. In addition to the cabling plant, some network devices will be needed to connect all the wires together, using punch down blocks, hubs, or switches. You will also have some form of software that will be used to manage the LAN and the devices connected to it. Putting in a cabling plant where one does not already exist, or even revamping existing cabling, is a major undertaking and can take quite some time. You may need to get specialized advice before proceeding. You also want to consider wireless network requirements and capabilities.

The WAN allows users on the LAN to connect to other computer systems around the world. A WAN telecommunications line is normally installed by a major communications company to your facility and connected to a switch or router in your computer room. This might take some time to order and get installed. This hardware coupled with networking software is used to set up the capability for users to connect to computers at other healthcare facilities or to the Internet. There are a lot of issues related to WANs such as bandwidth, speed, encryption, firewalls, and other details you will need to study. Here too you may need specialized advice before proceeding too far. Some additional details will be provided in the next section.

Acquiring and installing all of this needed infrastructure requires funding. This can easily run into millions of dollars for a large facility. Given your organization's budgeting process, plan on getting your needs to management perhaps a year before you plan on acquiring and installing anything. Also, remember you are going to need a steady flow of supplies to keep your systems running, for example, ink cartridges, paper, and labels. You will need an operating budget to keep the infrastructure up-to-date and adequate to support your existing and planned health IT environment.

Even as you acquire and install the infrastructure you need, technological changes will be occurring. For example, your organization might find a need to implement wireless devices or decide to use flat screen monitors, switch from the traditional telephone service to voice-over-IP systems, or implement video-conferencing technology. All of these changes have a domino effect and may in turn affect your cabling plant or computer room space requirements. Working with an EHR system is an experience of never-ending changes and challenges.

Hardware and Software Acquisition, Development, Maintenance, and Support

At some point, you will have identified the specific EHR system you are going to acquire and implement. When that time comes, you will know what hardware platform is needed to run the system and can start to put in place the exact electrical outlets, power sources, air conditioning, and other components that will be needed. The company you purchase the hardware from will normally have technical representatives to provide you with specifications to prepare the computer room to house its systems. Once you know what systems are coming, you can also arrange to enroll yourself and your staff in the training courses needed to operate and maintain the hardware and operating systems you will be installing.

Hardware installation does require some thought. You will need to look at the footprint or space the equipment will take up in the computer room. You need to make sure that electrical outlets are handy, that there is space on all sides of the equipment to do repairs, that there is an unobstructed flow of air conditioning, that you have furniture or hardware racks to mount the equipment, and so on. If you have several computer systems, you'll want to cluster the consoles in an area where you can work on multiple systems at one time. A printer should be connected to the consoles and should be handy to print out error reports and needed console messages. Placement of disk and tape drives also needs to be thought out. Other things to consider include leaving room for growth and installation of ramps to facilitate the movement of equipment into and out of the room. Protecting the hardware assets by installing solid doors with locks, taking note of fire extinguishers, and having plastic sheeting on hand to cover and protect the equipment from water damage are all things to consider. Finally, make sure you have a maintenance and support contract in place and get to know your vendor's on-site support person well.

Software to be installed as part of your EHR system may include the operating system software, software utilities such as database management packages and network management software, as well as the healthcare software applications you intend to install, such as patient registration, clinic scheduling, pharmacy, and laboratory. You will need to ensure that you have multiple copies of the software stored in both the computer room and a secure off-site location in case you need to restore the systems after a major failure. Similarly, you will need to have multiple copies of the software technical manuals that will need to be referred to often when performing specialized system operations or maintenance activities. Space and cabinets to store the software and manuals in the computer room need to be arranged. You need to make sure you have the needed contracts in place to cover the licensed software, help desk support, and ongoing maintenance. When your hardware has been installed and it comes time to do the initial installation of all the needed software, you and/or your staff need to be there and be actively involved in the process whether you contract out work on the system or not. The more you know about your system, the better.

It is important to plan on setting up three separate environments for the application software: production, development, and training. The production environment is where you will run the application to support day-to-day business operations. The development environment is where you will customize the system, develop reports, and test new software and software patches to see if there are going to be any problems that might affect your production system. The training environment typically mirrors the production system and will be used to train end users on application functionality before it is migrated into the production environment. When laying out your computer room and purchasing hardware and software, plan on the acquisition and installation of these three system environments.

Telecommunications is a key part of your system. Having a large, well-organized telecommunications closet in the computer room to house and cross connect all computer system equipment located throughout your facility is a must. Plan on it housing hubs, switches, and routers for your LAN and WAN, as well as punch-down blocks and connectors for the fiber-optic and copper cable coming into the computer room. Similarly, you need to get familiar with all of the communications closets throughout your facility that house your telecommunications cable distribution and cross-connection points. Some organizations now combine the operation of their computer and telephone cabling plans and systems operations. You will need to test all the connections and keep a database of all the cables in your facility and what is connected to each one. Your telecommunications networking systems include software to be used to manage the networks, monitor performance, troubleshoot, arrange connections to different devices, and so on.

You most likely will be charged with the management of many other systems besides the EHR system. These include the office automation systems (OAS), numerous personal computer (PC) systems located around your facility, business transaction systems, fiscal systems, and management information systems. In addition, as one of the leaders for your organization you may ultimately be charged with taking over responsibility for the computerized telephone system (PBX), televideo-conferencing systems, satellite communications, microwave connections, wireless personal digital assistants (PDAs), and many others. However, that is a subject for a different book.

Implementing the System Over Time

Implementing an EHR system is a multi-year effort. Once the initial EHR solution has been selected, you need to get started on further refining the detailed project plan, laying out all the many tasks that will need to be done over the next one to two years to ensure initial success in implementing the system and set up an ongoing project management process.

Key tasks in the system development and implementation lifecycle include:

- **Implementation planning**—This involves planning of the process, setting up tools to help the team, and many planning activities.
- **Requirements definition**—This is where you define your organizational requirements that need to be supported by the EHR. It would be important that you not customize the new system to meet your processes. Rather, you should focus on how your processes can be changed to leverage the new system offering.
- **Build and test the system**—This is where you would customize and/or tailor the system to meet your organizational needs and test it. The testing is a multi-phased process. First comes the *initial system testing* of delivered hardware and software to make sure that it performs according to the documentation. Then comes *modular testing* by programmers for each functional software component they are developing and/or modifying that make up a larger application module such as pharmacy or nursing. Then comes the more complex *application testing* where system functionality for a specific module such as patient registration is tested along with any interfaces to other applications. Finally, *system testing* is conducted for the complete collection of hardware and software that is going to be placed into production. This testing must address scalability, security, all key hardware and software components, and complete system functionality.
- **Training**—This is where you would train your end users. It is important to provide multiple levels of training to ensure that your users understand the complete system, how their operations fit in with the system, and how the system integrates with their operational processes.
- **Installation and conversion**—This is where you actually switch the system from testing mode to production mode. This needs to be a process that is carefully sequenced and orchestrated to ultimately achieve a comprehensive EHR system.
- **Post-implementation review**—After the system has been implemented, you should assess the system's effectiveness, determine if the

users are using its functionality to support their daily operation, and identify issues that are causing users to create work–arounds. The list of issues needs to be addressed and resolved.

Use of an automated project management tool to help lay out major tasks and track progress is strongly recommended. There are commercial project management packages you can use like MS Project, or you might want to consider using a free and open source project management tool such as GanttProject (www.ganttproject.sourceforge.net) or GanttPV (www.pureviolet.net/ganttpv). You will need to assign tasks to key staff and stay on top of the project by checking your progress against the plan most every day. You must remain firmly committed to the plan and the major milestones you have set, although some flexibility can be built into it to handle major contingencies or shifts in priority.

Keep in mind that, with all best intentions, you can never eliminate all risks associated with implementation of a complex system like an EHR. Therefore, your project plan and monitoring need to focus on mitigating potential risks. It is recommended that you develop a risk mitigation plan focusing on timely resolution.

As the plan is developed, make sure you are keeping all stakeholders, such as senior management, clinical staff and others, involved in the process. They have to be continually briefed on the plan, changes to it, and its current status when it starts to move forward. You need to look for champions among the senior management and clinical staff that will help guide, defend, and fund the project. You will also need to find champions or "super users" in the various departments you will be automating to help smooth the implementation process.

Even as you are going through the early stages of systems acquisition, construction, and installation needed just to set up the basic infrastructure, you need to start identifying and prioritizing the areas and/or functions of the organization or facility that you will be automating. You need people from these areas in the working ranks that have an interest in computers and know the department, its business processes, and the people that will be affected by the EHR project. You will need to identify these people and provide them with some orientation training well before you start implementing the system. It is recommended to develop a communication plan to parallel with key milestones in the project to keep everyone informed about the system implementation and to manage their expectations.

Converting to a New EHR System

Figure 8-3, Clinical Informatics Foundations for Quality, illustrates key modules around the EHR system that work together to support quality care.

Whether starting up from scratch or converting from an existing system to a new system, there is a rough order that should be followed when implementing the many modules that collectively make up an EHR system:

- The first application you will need to implement is *Patient Registration*. You need to start populating your EHR system's database with the basic demographic information on your patients, for example, name, address, age, and sex. All of the other clinical and business applications (e.g., Patient Billing, Clinic Scheduling, Pharmacy, Laboratory, Radiology) will be keying off the patient registration file and the patient demographics it contains.

- Once you have entered the basic demographic data on your patients, you can proceed with the implementation of the next clinical applications based on their relative importance to your organization. *Patient Billing, Outpatient Clinic Scheduling,* and *Inpatient Admissions/*

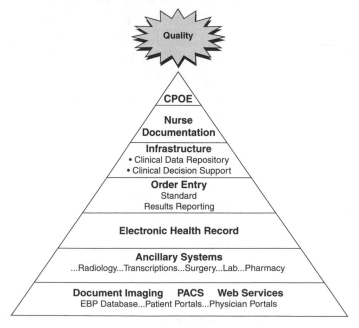

FIGURE 8-3 Clinical Informatics Foundations for Quality

Discharge/Transfers (ADT) are typically the next areas to be implemented. They have the highest returns on investment (ROI).

- These applications are then normally followed by the *Laboratory* and *Pharmacy* modules. At this point you will have laid the foundation needed by any EHR system.
- Then comes the long list of *other clinical software applications* in whatever prioritized order you wish, for example, *Radiology, Dietetics, Surgery, Medicine,* and *Nursing.*

Even as the first modules are being implemented, the pharmacy or laboratory departments should be preparing for the time they will automate their day-to-day business operations. Champions and/or "super users" need to be identified, and they need to start familiarizing themselves with the new system. Workstations and printers need to be installed where needed. Paper, labels, ink cartridges, and other supplies need to be ordered. Basic files will need to be set up and the software configured to work effectively. You will need to enter authorized provider names, lab test names, and drug names and doses; connect laboratory instruments; connect drug-dispensing machines; provide basic training to the staff; and so much more. In the pharmacy you might want to start with the automation of the outpatient pharmacy before moving to the inpatient pharmacy. For the laboratory you might want to start with chemistry, and then work your way through the laboratory section by section. Then set the target date to go live, and stick to it.

It will take many months for these initial areas to settle down. However, it is at the point when pharmacy and laboratory go online that you will truly have a basic EHR system up and running. Clinicians will finally be able to start using the system and will be able to get useful clinical information on patients.

You must remember that your patients are some of the major keys to success for the process. Communicating with your patients about the upcoming change is critical. Months in advance, you need to start informing them and other stakeholders about your plans to computerize their health records. Use all of the means at your disposal to prepare them for the upcoming event. They will want to know what you are doing with their data. When you switch to the new system, there will be an initial slowdown in processing that will affect them. Take the time to educate them about what the EHR systems project will mean to them in the future, as Web-based personal health record (PHR) systems emerge.

Law of New Systems Acceptance: The louder and more frequently a person talks about how they love *the idea* of using a new system, the harder it is going to be to get this person to use it. The more the person talks about how hard it is going to be to adapt and use the new system, the easier they are really going to be about using it.—**Peter Groen, MPA**

Implementing an EHR system in an organization that has never had such a system is a major business and cultural change. However, a number of excellent EHR systems now exist and many organizations have successfully implemented them over time. Healthcare organizations often invest many years implementing health information software applications before making the successful transition into the use of an overarching EHR system. Along the way you will find that some of the older staff might get frustrated and never complete the journey with you.

As you continue to implement addition modules, the quantity and quality of clinical data available through the EHR increases. A major step forward comes when you move toward online order entry by clinicians. Then comes the implementation of clinical imaging, clinical alerts, clinical decision support tools, and an almost unending list of many other modules that will continually improve health care.

Differences in COTS vs. Open Solution Implementations

While many of the tasks, assignments, and risks associated with implementing EHR systems are similar for both commercial-off-the-shelf (COTS) and Free and Open Source Software (FOSS) solutions, there are some differences worth noting. For example:

- Users of open source solutions tend to gather in online communities and share their experiences. They feel free to ask for help, discuss their successes and failures, and to seek out partners to collaborate on developing needed enhancements to the system. COTS users rely on the vendor and vendor-sponsored user groups to share information and knowledge that sometimes is not timely.
- In FOSS EHR applications there are two support networks: 1) the formal relationship with a company such as HP, Medsphere, Perot

Systems, and others to support the FOSS solution, and 2) the ability to obtain software help from a larger international network of open source developers.

• Internal IT support staff for COTS solutions can be small because they don't need to have detailed knowledge of the software code. For open source solutions, the internal staff may take on more responsibility with regard to developing unique system enhancements that require knowledge of the application code.

• User expectations have to be managed appropriately. With COTS solutions, users appreciate the fact that the vendor may only make selected changes requested, and in all cases you will be billed for the work. Under the open source solution approach, users may be able to have the IT staff or the "open development community" make many of the changes to the system that they want over time at less cost.

• Finally, under an open source solution scenario, care should be taken to ensure that a very stringent testing and quality-assurance process is followed becasue there may not be a vendor legally liable for assuring the quality of code.

The open source community has a different feel to it that you might find refreshing. Developers and users of open source software solutions tend to gather in online collaborative communities and share their experiences. They feel free to ask for help, discuss their successes and failures, and seek out partners to collaborate on developing needed enhancements for the system. The new and innovative ideas that emerge from this type of global community can be amazing. Figure 8-4, Tactics Supporting the Open Solutions Strategy, describes the different dimensions of Open Solutions. For more information on this strategy examine Chapter 11 and for definitions, refer back to Chapter 2.

Ongoing Operational Issues

There are many recurring day-to-day operational issues that need to be addressed as you go about implementing the EHR system. There are many administrative tasks, such as health IT budgets to be prepared, funds to be accounted for, contracts to be awarded, staff to be managed, time cards to be filled out, overtime to be tracked, work schedules to be set up to provide

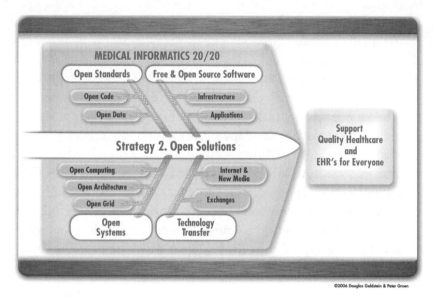

FIGURE 8-4 Tactics Supporting the Open Solutions Strategies

24/7 coverage, leave to be approved, management reports to be generated, supplies to be ordered and distributed, meetings to attend, and so on.

There are also many mundane but very necessary systems management tasks that need to be performed, such as setting up accounts for new users, arranging and attending computer training, maintaining inventories of hardware and software, keeping track of all telecommunications lines and devices connected to them, regularly monitoring and tracking systems performance and resource availability, checking computer system logs for errors, checking computer audit logs for security breaches or problems, keeping hardware repair logs, fixing or replacing workstations, performing daily system backups, testing the backups, testing and installing needed software patches, and many more tasks. As discussed previously, the organizational structure and staffing levels will need to be adjusted as time passes to effectively perform these tasks and provide high-quality service. Some of the more technical issues you will be facing day-to-day are addressed in the next section of this chapter.

Electrical systems and environmental controls need to be monitored. Line conditioners and uninterruptible power supply equipment housed in your computer room is a must. Emergency power provided by backup generators to selected outlets used by workstations crucial to hospital operations in case of a major power failure need to be identified. Environmental controls for your computer room also need to be installed and monitored, especially during off-hours to prevent system failures due to overheating. Physical security controls need to be put in place, such as motion detectors and electronic keypad locks that track entry into the computer room.

System access and security, especially under the new HIPAA regulations, is of major concern. You need to set up a process for employees to obtain access to the systems. Before setting up a user account and issuing passwords, you need to get the user to fill out a form with needed identifier information and have his or her supervisor let you know what information or options he or she should be allowed to have. You also need to get a signed user agreement to be kept on file in which users acknowledge their understanding of their responsibilities, especially with regards to privacy and security. The new users should also be given training on the use of the system. If the person is going to occupy a position of trust that gives them extensive access to the system, a background check should also be performed.

Other tasks that need to be performed that may not be immediately obvious include walking around your facility to get to know the people, seeing for yourself what is really happening, and getting feedback you might not otherwise receive. Preparing and conducting an annual user-satisfaction survey with which you can track performance over time is useful. Then there are community events that the CIO needs to attend as part of the management team to stay in touch with the patients and other stakeholders who may be affected by the new system. You should also be warned that there will be bond drives, charity drives, and other activities that will consume your time.

Technical Issues

As the EHR system becomes operational, many technical issues and functions need to be addressed by the CIO and/or systems manager. Computer systems need to be managed. Whether you run your own systems or have signed a contract for a company to do this for you, your organization still has a responsibility to ensure the systems are managed properly and not put at risk.

From a systems management point of view, your goal should be to have the system operational and available for use 100% of the time. In actuality,

Mystery in the Surgery Department: The computer support staff at the hospital had tried for months to fix a problem with computer workstations in the surgery department that kept failing intermittently all day long. One day, while going to replace the workstation again, the technician noticed that the computer had failed several times while he was standing there, each time when the nearby elevator went by. Apparently the powerful electrical motors on the elevator were interfering with the computer each time it went by the floor. Mystery solved.

there will be times when you need to take the systems down for maintenance, install new software, fix a major problem, recover from a power failure, or some other problem. If you have contractor-run systems, you will want to put these performance targets into the contract as well as penalties for failing to meet the target. To monitor systems performance, you will want to regularly run systems performance monitors that are usually a part of your operating system software utilities to track central processing unit (CPU) usage, disk drive usage, average system response times to users, number of users, number of active jobs/sessions, and so on, especially during your peak business hours. You also want to log all downtime and the reasons for it. By capturing these statistics and analyzing them, you will be able to see trends that will guide you in tuning your systems or making decisions to acquire additional computer resources before you have a major problem.

There are many systems maintenance tasks that need to be performed also. For example, you should have a daily backup of your database. Over time, your database may grow to be far more valuable to your business than all your investment in computer equipment. In addition to a daily backup, a file should be recording all transactions throughout the day so that in case of a massive failure, you can go to your last backup and read in the file of all the transactions that occurred up to the moment of failure, bringing you as up to date as possible on your restored backup system. In addition to daily backups, a monthly backup should also be done and permanently stored in a secure, fireproof, remote location. The backups should be checked every month or so to make sure they are working. Sometimes a parameter is changed, and some facilities have found the backups they thought they were doing were of no use.

Software patches to correct minor problems need to be installed in the test account and then moved into production to keep the system up to date and working correctly. In addition, new versions of the various software modules will need to be installed periodically, as well as totally new modules. These need to be installed on the test system first in order to see how long it takes, what changes users can expect, and if any unexpected problems occur before moving it into the production environment. In some cases, the EHR system may need to be taken out of production for major software upgrades. In that case the date and time for taking the system down should be coordinated with the user community and scheduled late at night on a weekend in order to minimize the impact on patient care and productivity. Remember, if you are running an open source solution, you won't need to purchase new software licenses or pay for upgrades.

The patient database needs to be properly protected. The software should come with various audit logs and features that you may have to activate and monitor regularly. In addition to patient privacy and database security, one also needs to take steps to monitor the quality of the data being entered into the database. This may be an activity that needs to be done by the various departments responsible for inputting data into the system. Making sure names and titles are entered correctly and consistently in the patient, physician, and user files becomes extremely important over time. Names of drugs, lab tests, ward locations, clinics, and many other variables must be constantly monitored and corrected to reduce the potential for errors. Remember, the database may ultimately be of far greater value to the organization over time than the cost of all other computer resources combined.

The type of workstations and printers to be acquired and used may be more complicated than one thinks at first blush. Depending on the needs of the users, they might need to use a standard PC workstation, a more robust clinical-imaging PC workstation, a thin client workstation, a dumb terminal, a wireless PC, a personal digital assistant (PDA), or some other device. Printers are also not that simple. The facility may need high-speed printers for large-volume print jobs, label printers, laser printers, desktop ink jet printers, dot matrix/impact printers, or some other specialized printing device. There are also many other issues that will emerge related to workstations. For example, if workstations are placed in the laboratory or kitchens, special protective covers may be needed. Also, wireless radio frequency (RF) devices will need to be checked to ensure they do not interfere with pacemakers.

> **A Mouse?** One of the older physicians in the hospital just learning how to use a PC with a mouse wanted to know why when he picked up the mouse and spoke into it, it didn't type what he was saying. He assumed it worked like his dictating machine. Don't assume everyone knows how to use a computer.

There are a lot of technical issues associated with your telecommunications systems that one also needs to address. Use of fiber-optics between buildings on a large campus should be considered to avoid problems with lighting strikes and power surges that can otherwise destroy large numbers of workstations if they were connected to copper-wire lines. Installing a high-speed segmented LAN should be considered to handle heavy traffic, especially once one starts transmitting clinical images. Redundant lines and pathways should be designed into your network layout in case lines get severed. WANs should be designed to handle increasing data traffic over time as you move into video conferencing, clinical imaging, and heavy Internet usage. Extensive security on the incoming WAN lines and any modems needs to be seriously addressed given the growing threats from hackers and virus attacks.

A Plan for Continual Change and Quality

Remember, the end goal is transforming the care process for high quality. EHR system deployment is an important tool in the process. EHR implementation is not over when your organization starts using the system for the first time. It is a continuous improvement process to support changing operational needs and leveraging technology/application as it improves.

Even as you are implementing the new system, business requirements are continually changing and there are emerging technologies that may require

> **Understanding the system from the patient's point of view!** One of the training exercises for my key computer staff involved checking in to the hospital as a patient and seeing the system from their point of view. It really led to better understanding and empathy with the patient. Also, some good programming changes and ideas for new systems emerged.

> ## WHO Resource
>
> After writing this chapter, the authors came across a document developed by the World Health Organization (WHO) entitled "Guidelines for the Development of Health Management Information Systems." These guidelines were developed based on practical experience in Western Pacific countries on the acquisition, development, implementation, operation, and maintenance of health information systems. The guidelines are aimed at helping health authorities and senior managers think through all steps of the planning process before any decisions are made or resources committed. The authors of this book highly recommend this document. Much of what we have presented in this chapter is also addressed in that document, validating many of our findings and recommendations. (http://www.wpro.who.int/publications/pub_9290611065.htm)

you to update your tactical and operational plans. Personal health records (PHR), clinical imaging systems, Web-based clinical reference materials, secure e–mail exchange between physicians and patients, linkages to insurance and pharmacy networks, wireless technologies, and community health information exchange (HIE) systems are just some of many new requirements and emerging technologies that you will want to consider adopting.

To keep from getting overwhelmed by these changes, the EHR plans need to be constantly reviewed, updated, and then adhered to in order to operate in a proactive rather than a reactive mode. Establishing a steering committee to help keep the plan up to date, prioritize requests for change, and help make key decisions should seriously be considered. This committee should be composed of senior management officials and clinicians from across the organization. Remember, if you have implemented an open source solution, you will not normally need to purchase new software licenses, pay for upgrades, or purchase new modules.

In addition to the EHR plan, an IT architecture document should be prepared to provide a technical framework to promote a technology vision across the healthcare organization so that all systems and components are interoperable. Identifying health informatics standards to be followed is a key component of the architecture. The architectural framework should be designed to be flexible and should be updated as new needs are identified.

CHAPTER 9

Case Studies of VistA Implementation— United States and International

> "VHA's integrated health information system, including its framework for using performance measures to improve quality, is considered one of the best in the nation."
>
> *Institute of Medicine (IOM) Report,*
> "Leadership by Example: Coordinating Government Roles in Improving Health Care Quality, 2002"

Introduction

The U.S. Department of Veterans Affairs (VA) has developed and implemented a comprehensive health information system and EHR system known as VistA, which was built from the ground up with a clinical focus. Many of the commercial off-the-shelf (COTS) health information systems in the private sector today were designed from a financial perspective and now are being reengineered to address medical and clinical informatics requirements. The VistA system is a proven product and can be readily adapted for use in acute care, ambulatory, and long-term care settings. It has been used in public and private healthcare provider organizations across the United States and in a number of international settings.

Table 9-1 VistA Software Modules

VistA Software Packages
Health Data Systems
Automated Medical Information Exchange
  (AMIE)
Incident Reporting
Lexicon Utility
Occurrence Screen
Patient Representative

Registration, Enrollment, and Eligibility Systems
Patient Registration
Admission/Discharge/Transfer (ADT)
Clinical Monitoring System
Enrollment Application System (EAS)
Hospital Inquiry (HINQ)
Income Verification Match (IVM)
Record Tracking
Resident Assessment Instrument/Minimum
  Data Set (RAI/MDS)
Veteran Identification Card (VIC)

Health Provider Systems
Care Management
Clinical Procedures
Computerized Patient Record System (CPRS)
CPRS: Adverse Reaction Tracking
CPRS: Authorization/Subscription Utility (ASU)
CPRS: Clinical Reminders
CPRS: Consult/Request Tracking
CPRS: Health Summary
CPRS: Problem List
CPRS: Text Integration Utilities (TIU)
Dentistry
Hepatitis C Case Registry
Home–Based Primary Care (HBPC)
Immunology Case Registry (ICR)
Intake and Output
Laboratory
Laboratory: Anatomic Pathology
Laboratory: Blood Bank
Laboratory: Electronic Data Interchange (LEDI)
Medicine
Mental Health
Nursing
Nutrition and Food Service (N&FS)
Oncology
Pharmacy: Automatic Replenishment/Ward
  Stock (AR/WS)
Pharmacy: Bar Code Medication
  Administration (BCMA)
Pharmacy: Consolidated Mail Outpatient
  Pharmacy (CMOP)
Pharmacy: Controlled Substances
Pharmacy: Drug Accountability/Inventory
  Interface
Pharmacy: Electronic Claims Management
  Engine

Pharmacy: Inpatient Medications
Pharmacy: Inpatient Medications—
  Intravenous (IV)
Pharmacy: Inpatient Medications—
  Unit Dose (UD)
Pharmacy: National Drug File (NDF)
Pharmacy: Outpatient Pharmacy
Pharmacy: Pharmacy Benefits Management
  (PBM)
Pharmacy: Pharmacy Data Management (PDM)
Pharmacy: Pharmacy Prescription Practices (PPP)
Primary Care Management Module (PCMM)
Prosthetics
Quality: Audiology and Speech Analysis and
  Reporting (QUASAR)
Radiology/Nuclear Medicine
Remote Order Entry System (ROES)
Scheduling
Social Work
Spinal Cord Dysfunction
Surgery
Surgery: Risk Assessment
VistA Imaging System
VistA Imaging: Core Infrastructure
VistA Imaging: Document Imaging
VistA Imaging: Filmless Radiology
VistA Imaging: Imaging Ancillary Systems
Visual Impairment Service Team (VIST)
Vitals/Measurements
Women's Health

Management and Financial Systems
Accounts Receivable (AR)
Automated Information Collection System
  (AICS)
Beneficiary Travel
Compensation and Pension Records
  Interchange (CAPRI)
Current Procedural Terminology (CPT)
Decision Support System (DSS) Extracts
Diagnostic Related Group (DRG) Grouper
Engineering
Equipment/Turn-In Request
Event Capture
Fee Basis
Generic Code Sheet
Incomplete Records Tracking (IRT)
Integrated Funds Distribution, Control Point
  Activity, Accounting, and Procurement
  (IFCAP)
Integrated Patient Funds
Integrated Billing (IB)
Patient Care Encounter (PCE)
Personnel and Accounting Integrated Data
  (PAID)
Voluntary Service System (VSS)   *(continues)*

Table 9-1 *continued*

Information and Education Systems	List Manager
Automated Safety Incident Surveillance Tracking System (ASISTS)	MailMan
Library	Master Patient Index (MPI) and Master Patient Index/Patient Demographics (MPI/PD)
Police and Security	My HealtheVet Personal Health Record
Cross-Cutting Monographs	Network Health Exchange (NHE)
Duplicate Record Merge	Patient Data Exchange (PDX)
Health Level Seven (HL7)	Remote Procedure Call (RPC) Broker
VistA Kernel	VA FileMan
VistA Kernel Toolkit	VistALink

VistA software is in the public domain and has been available to non-VA users under the Freedom of Information Act (FOIA) for several decades. Like open source software, the application code is made available to anyone requesting a copy of the system. Therefore, in the paradigm we have discussed in this book, VistA falls under the broad term of Free and Open Source Software (FOSS). There have been many thousands of downloads of the FOIA–VistA software over the years.

The VistA software suite is available from the VA at http://www.va.gov/vha_oi.

It has also been made available via the VistA Hardhats organization (www.hardhats.org) and the WorldVistA organization (www.worldvista.org). Also, leading information technology companies such as HP, Perot Systems, and IBM, and rapid-growth firms such Medsphere Corporation, DSS Inc., and Mele Associates are actively supporting implementations in the United States and around the globe.

This chapter is divided into two parts. Part A, for the most part describes VistA implementations by public and private sector healthcare provider organizations across the United States. In Part B of this chapter,

Table 9-2 VistA Implementations

Part A: United States	Part B: International
• Department of Veterans Affairs	• Samoa
• Midland Memorial Hospital, Texas	• Egypt
• Indian Health Service	• Mexico
• Department of Defense	• Germany
• HHS and VistA–Office EHR	• Finland
• National Hansen's Disease Center	• Nigeria
• State of Hawaii	
• District of Columbia (DC)	
• State Veterans Homes	
• Oklahoma	

implementations of VistA around the world are presented. Of special note is Mexico, where the government has already successfully deployed VistA in more than 40 hospitals, with many more facilities slated for VistA deployments in the coming months. There are many more examples of VistA implementations underway in Hawaii, West Virginia, California, Louisiana, and other locations around the world that are not profiled here.

Part A: United States

Profiles of selected VistA implementations in small, mid-size, and large-scale healthcare organizations in the United States

U.S. Department of Veterans Affairs (VA) VistA System

The Veterans Health Administration (VHA) operates the nation's largest medical system. It provides care to approximately 4.5 million veterans out of an eligible population of 25 million. The VHA currently employs approximately 180,000 healthcare professionals at 170 hospitals, more than 800 community and facility-based outpatient clinics, over 135 nursing homes, 43 domiciliaries, 206 readjustment counseling centers, and various other facilities. In addition, the VHA is the nation's largest provider of graduate medical education and a major contributor to medical and scientific research. VA medical centers are affiliated with more than 152 medical and dental schools, training more than 80,000 health-related students and residents each year. More than half of U.S. practicing physicians have received training in VA hospitals. The VA is the second largest funder of biomedical research in the United States. The VA also provides healthcare services to active military personnel during wartime and the general population in times of national disasters.

The VA began deploying its VistA system in all of its medical facilities starting around 1984. The system was originally known as the Decentralized Hospital Computer Program (DHC) system. The "initial core" system that was deployed consisted of a limited number of clinical and administrative software modules, which included patient registration, outpatient clinic scheduling, inpatient admission/discharge/transfer (ADT), pharmacy, laboratory, and radiology. Over the years many additional software modules were added, and the DHCP system was eventually renamed VistA

Links to Key Web Sites and Documentation

- VHA Office of Information Web Site—www.va.gov/vha_oi/
- VistA System Web Site—www.va.gov/vista_monograph

Links to Key Articles on VistA

- VistA—U.S. Department of Veterans Affairs National Scale Healthcare Information Systems, *International Journal of Medical Informatics,* February 2003.
- The Veterans Health Administration: Quality, Value, Accountability, and Information as Transforming Strategies for Patient-Centered Care, *The American Journal of Managed Care,* November 2004.
- Comparison of Quality of Care for Patients in the Veterans Health Administration and Patients in a National Sample, *Annals of Internal Medicine,* December 2004.
- The Best Care Anywhere, *Washington Monthly,* January/February 2005.

(Veterans Health Information Systems and Technology Architecture). With the subsequent release of the Computerized Patient Record System (CPRS) for clinicians in 1997 and the deployment of VistA Imaging in the late 1990s and early 2000s, the VistA system emerged as one of the most advanced health information systems in the world. (http://www.va.gov/vista_monograph/)

The VA plans to continue using VistA and will continually improve the system over time. For example, planned enhancements to VistA include:

- My Health*e*Vet, a personal health record (PHR) module.
- National VistA Health Data Repository (HDR).
- Federal Health Information Exchange (FHIE) enhancements to include the Bi-directional Health Information Exchange (BHIE).
- Building a Web-enabled VistA front end.
- Other IT architectural enhancements and new technologies.

Midland Memorial Hospital and VistA

Midland Memorial Hospital is a 371-bed community hospital that operates three campuses in Midland, Texas. Midland provides a full range of acute-care services including emergency medicine, cardiovascular surgery, and advanced radiological and oncology services and serves as a regional referral center for other communities throughout west Texas and southeast New Mexico. The Midland "OpenVista Implementation Project" represented a formidable challenge on multiple fronts. For example, it was the first nongovernment, acute-care hospital in the United States to adopt a VistA-based electronic health record (EHR); it has a community-based physician staff representing all major specialty areas; and they wanted a "best of breed" software environment that would leverage investments in current solutions that needed to be interfaced to VistA. The contract for the project was awarded to Medsphere Systems Corporation.

Guiding Principles and Major Project Objectives

The following are some of the guiding principles and major objectives associated with the Midland OpenVista Implementation Project:

- Enhance patient safety, increase clinical efficiency, and improve healthcare quality.
- Standardize the delivery of care across the continuum (acute, ambulatory, and rehabilitation) and multiple geography locations of care (hospitals and clinics).
- Reduce medical errors and wasteful costs associated with the delivery of health care.
- Build upon the proven success and experience of the VA in the implementation of its comprehensive VistA EHR system for Midland.
- Leverage the OpenVista EHR system as a differentiating factor in helping recruit and retain patients, physicians, and staff.
- Leverage the OpenVista solution to reduce overall systems lifecycle costs for Midland.

Project History

In 2003, Midland Memorial Hospital determined to replace their "sunsetting" pharmacy and laboratory systems. This review prompted IT steering committee members to rethink their best-of-breed strategy and take the opportunity to evaluate a single, integrated solution to meet their clinical, administrative, and financial needs. During the course of their evaluation of traditional healthcare IT companies, they were unable to overcome the $20 million price barrier to implement the comprehensive solution they envisioned. They became aware of VistA through their interaction with the Big Springs VA Medical Center; from Texas Tech medical residents who rotated through the VA center; a general increase in articles in health IT magazines and journals about the VistA system; a growing awareness of the open source community; and the realization that there were multiple commercial vendors supporting the VistA solution.

Midland next engaged in a rigorous 12-month evaluation of the technology, product, and health IT service providers. After attending several national conferences, completing multiple site visits, and a series of intense product demonstrations to its staff, Midland determined to move forward with a comprehensive enterprise assessment of the issues related to implementing the OpenVista solution (Medsphere's commercial version of the VA VistA system). This assessment was completed in August 2004. In January 2005, Midland's IT steering committee unanimously approved the recommendation to begin the OpenVista implementation project.

With OpenVista serving as the platform of innovation, a six-month software development effort ensued to ensure that the product would meet some of the unique functional specifications of Midland. A primary objective of this effort was to complete the required interfaces to share patient demographic information, the event points where charges could be captured, and the seamless sharing of information among 13 disparate information systems Midland wanted to retain. This process was successfully completed by a talented team of VistA engineers who had a thorough knowledge of the system and leveraged standard VA design concepts, improved existing software tools, and developed new integration utilities to accomplish the work. These efforts proved highly successful and set the stage for the next step, the clinical configuration of the system.

Clinical configuration of the system begin in earnest in the summer of 2005, with the training of six newly hired registered nurses who formed the core of Midland's clinical information technology (IT) team. These individuals, under the direction of a Midland nurse informaticist, were trained to become "super users" of the graphical user interface to VistA, known as the Computerized Patient Record System (CPRS). This training gave them the knowledge needed to create templates, order sets, and clinical reminders; set clinical rules; and configure other VistA clinical modules. Staff from Medsphere augmented their staff during the design, configuration, training, and deployment of the VistA system. The goal of the training program was designed to allow Midland to become a self-sufficient organization that would not be dependent on a vendor for many of the ongoing operational and maintenance tasks.

Multiple committees were convened under the direction of the IT steering committee to ensure a smooth transition to the OpenVista EHR.

These multi-disciplinary subcommittees included Computerized Provider Order Entry, Bar Code Medication Administration, Forms, Pharmacy, Medical Records, and Ancillary Department committees. The various subcommittees reported up to the IT steering committee, which would meet monthly for the duration of the project.

Midland and Medsphere also established a joint project governance structure with regular project communication and issue resolution meetings.

Systems Architecture

The enterprise architecture chosen by Midland Memorial Hospital included a centralized server cluster with a single VistA database residing at Midland's main campus facility. Midland selected InterSystems Cache product for its "M" language and database environment due to its robust capabilities, proven scalability, and rich management tool set, which had been deployed in large-scale clinical settings. The multi-campus enterprise is the first acute-care hospital to deploy the OpenVista EHR solution on a Red Hat Linux infrastructure. A high-availability cluster, using multi-processor x86 servers and clustering software, was installed and configured by Hewlett-Packard (HP). This technology configuration provided Midland with an affordable, high-performance, and completely redundant solution using a mix of open source tools, proven application servers, and commodity x86-based hardware.

Software Solution

Midland's best-of-breed software environment presented some challenges for a fully integrated solution like OpenVista. Medsphere was required to develop several enhancements and interfaces to present a unified solution within the VistA framework. Midland currently uses McKesson's Precision 2000 Health Information System. Precision serves as the authoritative source of patient demographics, registration, scheduling, master patient index, and other master files. It is also the primary source of order entry by the ward clerks for laboratory, cardiopulmonary, dietetics, and related consults. Once patients are registered, the information is sent to OpenVista by standardized Health Level Seven (HL7) messages where it is then "filed" away in the appropriate places within OpenVista. From here, at key steps of the clinical-care process, various "events" trigger the charge capture engine to fire off a charge-related message to the Precision system. After the clinical course of care has ended, the Precision system generates a bill and manages the revenue cycle from that point forward. Medsphere developed a unique technology solution to assist with both the filing and the charge capture component of this interface.

The primary VistA modules initially deployed at Midland included the following:

- FileMan
- Kernel
- MailMan
- Patient Information Management
- Master Patient Index (MPI)
- Inpatient Pharmacy
- National Drug File
- Outpatient Pharmacy
- Laboratory
- Radiology and Nuclear Medicine
- Computerized Patient Record System
- Adverse Reaction Tracking
- Authorization/Subscription Utility
- Clinical Reminders
- Consult/Request Tracking
- Health Summary
- Problem List

Medsphere OpenVista Enhancements Developed for Midland

The above packages provided the foundation of the OpenVista solution. From here, Medsphere was required to make the following modifications. This list is not comprehensive, but is representative of the types of changes required to adapt VistA technology in a non-VA setting.

GENERAL:
- Fee Tables in OpenVista linked to a foreign system's Charge Master File
- Common Physician Identifier
- Protocol Event Points for charge capture with HL7 interfaces
- Options to populate User (NEW PERSON) file from a foreign registry

PATIENT REGISTRATION:
- Creation of a common Medical Record Number
- Creation of Account Number file and corresponding field in Visit file
- HL7 interface from authoritative medical manager to VistA

(continues)

PHARMACY:
- Charge capture for real-time or batch transmission to foreign billing system
- High Dose Alerts
- Pharmacokinetic Dosing
- Link Lab Results to Inpatient Med Order

LABORATORY:
- Charge capture for real-time or batch transmission to foreign billing system
- HL7 interface for intake of lab orders
- HL7 interface for reporting out of lab orders
- Tracking Specimen Transfers between Facilities
- Faxing of Laboratory Results
- Creating multiple interfaces for Blood Bank

RADIOLOGY:
- HL7 interface for intake of radiology orders
- HL7 interface for reporting out of radiology orders
- HL7 interface for intake of radiology result reports
- Radiology procedure file populated and updated automatically from Charge Master file

IMAGING:
- Developed document scanning enhancement

Future Enhancements

As Midland has gained more familiarity with the OpenVista product, it has initiated several product enhancement requests. These requests have been funneled into the Medsphere product development roadmap and include:

- Nurse Flowsheets.
- Physician Dashboard.
- Improved, "active" templating.

Project Challenges

As the first commercial enterprise deployment of OpenVista, Midland and Medsphere both learned significant lessons during the project. Some of the many issues and challenges being addressed during the Midland project include:

- This was as much a clinical business transformation initiative, as much as it was a health IT systems implementation project.
- Hardware and Infrastructure Enhancements:
  - Upgrade of existing network infrastructure to accommodate users needs.
  - Upgrade of existing hardware needed for improved reliability and performance.
  - Upgrading clinician work spaces to provide more access and ergonomic feasibility.
- Interface challenges of integrating more than 15 disparate information systems.
- Implementation challenge of training 1,500 users on a mission-critical application for an organization that operates 24/7/365.
- Project management challenges of moderating expectations, managing personnel, and developing a repeatable deployment methodology with no commercial precedent.
- Developing an internal support function that meets the needs of the organization and the end users; integrating customer support with vendor support of the application.

Project Summary

As of 2006, Midland had successfully deployed the foundational Open-Vista modules: Patient Information Management, Pharmacy (inpatient and outpatient), Laboratory, Dietetics, Order Entry/Results Reporting, Radiology, National Online Information Sharing, and Document Imaging. The successful integration of 15-plus other disparate information systems was also completed, and the project remained on budget and on schedule. The physician and clinician "go-live" date was scheduled for the end of January 2006. Implementation of a Bar Code Medication Administration was slated for spring 2006.

The deployment of VistA at Midland represents a seminal event within healthcare IT and positioning of OpenVista as one of the leading EHR platforms involving public–private collaboration and investment. The implementation of a mission-critical, VistA-based solution in the commercial setting by a value-added professional open source technology company for less than half the price of commercial alternatives represents a new paradigm with significant and long-range ramifications for the healthcare industry.

IHS Resource and Patient Management System (RPMS)

The Resource and Patient Management System (RPMS) run by the Indian Health Service (IHS) is an integrated solution for the management of clinical and administrative information in healthcare facilities of various sizes and orientations. Flexible hardware configurations, more than 50 software applications, and network communication components combine to provide a comprehensive clinical, financial, and administrative solution.

Background

The IHS is charged with administering the principal healthcare program for American Indians and Alaskan Natives and provides comprehensive health services through a system of Federal IHS-, tribal-, and urban-operated facilities and programs. These facilities and programs provide health services to 1.4 million American Indians and Alaskan Natives through 144 service units composed of more than 500 direct healthcare delivery facilities, including 49 hospitals, 190 health centers, 7 school health centers, and 287 health stations, satellite clinics, and Alaskan village clinics.

The IHS and the VA have a long–standing tradition of health information and technology sharing spanning the past several decades. In 1984, the IHS began implementation of 60 systems using VistA software, then referred to as DHCP. Many components of the RPMS health information system are still based on the VistA system. A number of RPMS software modules have also been incorporated into VistA over the years.

Resource and Patient Management System (RPMS)

RPMS is a decentralized automated information system of over 50 integrated software applications. Many RPMS applications can function in a stand–alone environment if necessary or appropriate. The system is designed to operate on micro- and mini-computers located in the IHS or tribal healthcare facilities. RPMS software modules fall into three major categories: 1) administrative applications that perform patient registration, scheduling, billing, and linkage functions; 2) clinical applications that support various healthcare programs within the IHS; and 3) infrastructure applications.

Administrative Applications The RPMS administrative applications support the business of healthcare provision. Applications in this category are used to collect, store, and report patient demographic information;

manage the scheduling, admission, discharge, and transfer of patients in inpatient facilities; create claims and handle both manual and electronic billing and accounts receivables; and electronically manage resource requests and supplies.

Clinical Applications The RPMS clinical applications directly support the provision of health care. Applications in this category generally collect all patient-related information gathered during patient contacts into one comprehensive, centralized data file to support healthcare planning, delivery, management, and research. The Patient Care Component provides for entry of visit data that forms the core data set used by most of the RPMS applications. Other applications in this category support patient care and include Laboratory, Radiology, Inpatient and Outpatient Pharmacy, Allergy Tracking, Immunology, Dental, and Women's Health.

Infrastructure This category of applications comprises and supports the RPMS environment with management, development, and communication tools. The MailMan application is an electronic messaging system. VA Kernel software provides a portability layer between the underlying operating system and application code and provides a Kernel Toolkit that supplements the Kernel software package with development and quality-assessment tools, capacity management tools, and system management utilities. The VA FileMan is the RPMS database management system (DBMS).

The Division of Information Resources (DIR) distributes the RPMS application suite to headquarters and each IHS area office. The area office then releases the RPMS application suite to the healthcare facilities within its area. Different facilities use different configurations of RPMS applications, depending upon the types of services they provide.

Technical Environment

- The RPMS suite runs on mid-range to personal computer hardware platforms. Typical configurations range from two RS 6000 computers for large facilities to one Intel-based Windows NT computer for small facilities.
- RPMS applications operate individually and as an integrated suite. Using the HL7 protocol, RPMS applications can be interfaced with a variety of commercial-off-the-shelf software products.
- RPMS information can be exchanged over a local area network (LAN) within a single facility, a wide area network (WAN) with other facilities, and the Internet with other providers and medical researchers.

Other Plans and Activities RPMS software is in the public domain, making it a cost-effective choice in software applications for others to consider using. The IHS recently signed a memorandum of understanding to share the RPMS software with the National Aeronautics and Space Administration (NASA).

The IHS plans to continue to enhance RPMS over time, adding an electronic health record, a clinical imaging module, and other software modules. In addition, the IHS and the Veterans Health Administration plan to continue their long–standing practice of collaborating on various software development projects related to health information exchange, health informatics standards, personal health records, VistA–Office EHR, and other initiatives.

Key Reference Web Sites

- http://www.ihs.gov/Cio/RPMS/index.cfm
- http://www.ihs.gov/cio/ehr/

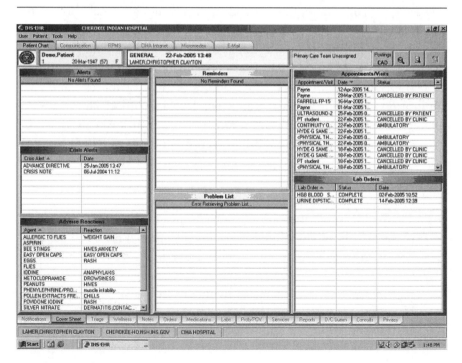

FIGURE 9-1 RPMS: An Example of an EHR Screen Developed for Use Within the IHS

DoD Composite Health Care System (CHCS)

The Composite Health Care System (CHCS) is an automated information system supporting the administration and delivery of health care at Department of Defense (DoD) Medical Treatment Facilities (MTF) throughout the world. Operational support is provided not only to fixed MTFs, but also to mobile fleet hospitals, hospital ships, and at pier-side.

Background

CHCS supports over 130,000 providers and staff in the delivery of health care to MHS beneficiaries at MTFs worldwide. It provides essential, automated information support to Military Health System (MHS) providers, enabling improved quality of care for 8.9 million beneficiaries at more than 700 DoD hospitals and clinics around the world.

The DoD and the Department of Veterans Affairs (VA) have a long-standing tradition of health information and technology sharing spanning the past several decades. In 1983, the DoD was first provided copies of the VistA application software (then known as DHCP). In 1987, two DoD facilities, March Air Force Base and Fitzsimmons Army Medical Center, began extensive testing of the VistA software. In 1988, SAIC was awarded a $1 billion, eight-year contract to design, develop, and implement its system, which involved modifying the VA VistA system to meet DoD requirements for use in all major MTFs around the world.

Composite Health Care System (CHCS)

CHCS provides automated support to all areas of healthcare operations and patient care via modules including these functionalities:

- Patient Administration
- Patient Scheduling
- Pharmacy
- Radiology
- Laboratory
- Nursing QA
- Medical Record Tracking
- Managed Care Program
- Clinical and Administrative Report Generation

Eligibility, enrollment, and data synchronization are supported by the National Enrollment Database (NED) application. Third-party collections are supported through Ambulatory Data Coding, Ambulatory Patient Visits, and Outpatient Itemized Billing interfaces.

CHCS Clinical Practice Support is enhanced through interfaces to specialized clinical systems. Those systems include:

- Digital Imaging Network—Picture Archiving and Communications System (DIN-PACS)
- Collaborative Medical Systems Anatomic Pathology (CoPath)
- Defense Dental Scheduling Application (DDSA)
- Clinical Information System (CIS)
- Defense Enrollment and Eligibility Reporting System (DEERS)
- Defense Blood Standard System (DBSS)
- Executive Information/Decision Support (EI/DS)
- Integrated Clinical Database (ICDB)

For patients, the CHCS allows quicker diagnostic test results resulting in reduced wait time and increased access to medical and professional resources. For providers, using CHCS allows increased communication among physicians, nurses, clinicians, technicians, ancillary services, and administrators.

The CHCS II is the military computer-based patient record that is accessed through a provider-developed graphical user interface. It facilitates outpatient management of health information requirements for the U.S. Armed Forces and, along with CHCS, it provides MHS beneficiaries with a lifelong military medical record. CHCS II was recently renamed Armed Forces Health Longitudinal Technology Application (AHLTA).

Future Plans

The VA and DoD health IT staff are continuing to collaborate on a large, umbrella electronic health record (EHR) initiative. This is part of the HealthePeople (federal) strategy. Specific collaborative projects related to this initiative include development of a Clinical/Health Data Repository (C/HDR), testing of the Bi-directional Health Information Exchange (BHIE) system, and replacement or enhancements to the agencies' Pharmacy, Laboratory, Clinic Scheduling, and other software modules used in both VistA and CHCS.

Key Reference Web Sites

- http://www.saic.com/integration/chcs.html
- http://www.tricare.osd.mil/peo/citpo/projects.htm

VistA–Office EHR

Introduction

The Centers for Medicare and Medicaid Services (CMS), an agency of the U.S. Department of Health and Human Services (HHS), and the Department of Veterans Affairs (VA) are collaborating on an initiative to transfer the VA's electronic healthcare record (EHR) suite of software, known as VistA, to the private physician office setting. The VistA–Office EHR project combines the strengths of both agencies as they aim to make available a high-quality, public-domain EHR solution that can be used in both clinics and physician offices.

The CMS allocated funds in 2005 to modify the VA VistA software into an "office version" to be made available for public use. They also provided initial funds to provide limited end-user support, installation procedures, training materials, system documentation, help desk support, and other needed assistance. Contracts were awarded to the Iowa Foundation for Medical Care (IFMC), Daou Systems, and the WorldVistA organization to support this initiative.

Functional Overview

The functional capabilities contained in the current VistA software suite will serve as the basis for the VistA–Office EHR system. Additionally, modifications are being made to the existing software to augment and support the diversity of patient care provided by a family physician. The VistA–Office EHR system is being made available in the public domain and will provide the capability to transfer outpatient data between the physician office and the Quality Improvement Organization (QIO) clinical warehouse. The initial focus of the VistA–Office EHR program is the family physician practice of four to eight physicians in a small, community-practice setting.

Product Architecture The VistA–Office EHR product adheres to the architecture of VHA's VistA FOIA release. VistA FOIA is designed in a three-tier hierarchy consisting of:

- Cache database
- VistA FOIA software
- VistA/CPRS graphical user interface (GUI) software

Organizations will still need to purchase servers, workstations, and telecommunications (LAN); staff the project; and buy licenses for selected commercial off-the-shelf (COTS) products that might be needed. In other words, while the VistA software is free, approximately 75% of typical systems lifecycle costs will still need to be funded by the healthcare provider organization. VistA–Office EHR will be released to run on the Microsoft Windows operating system.

Product Functionality/Features

The predominant clinical application within VistA that directly supports the healthcare provider is the Computerized Patient Record System (CPRS). VistA–Office EHR will provide a desktop application that offers CPRS ambulatory functionality to the family physician's office. CPRS's ambulatory applications encompass the complete patient-care process, from initial patient registration and scheduling, to physical exams and documentation, treatment, medications, vital signs, and laboratory. Additionally, the administrative functions contained within the VistA system work synergistically with CPRS to support the basic business functions of the office. VistA–Office EHR is being designed so that any existing external interfaces will be preserved, and connectivity to other office software applications will not be precluded. The following are some of the key features it includes:

- The system uses the complete VA VistA FOIA suite of health information systems.
- It also includes Pediatric and Obstetrics and Gynecology modules.
- The system provides the ability to register patients and record patient demographics.
- The system provides the ability to schedule ambulatory encounter patient visits.
- The system shall provide the ability to record billing and health insurance information.
- Claims validation and submission will be performed by third-party products, such as a claims clearinghouse.
- Patient account and receivables management will be addressed by third-party products external to VistA–Office EHR.

- The system provides the ability to record and document the complete clinical encounter for each patient visit. This may include, but is not limited to:
  - Physician's orders
  - Nursing orders
  - Physical examination
  - Patient history and physical
  - Vital signs and measurements
  - Laboratory orders
  - Pharmacy orders
  - Radiology orders
  - Treatments and procedures
  - Referrals
  - Diagnosis and prognosis
  - Plan of care
  - Health summary
  - Problem list
  - Immunizations
  - Allergies
  - Adverse reactions
- The system provides the ability to print any or all parts of the medical record.
- The system supports data entry and retrieval by all physician office personnel, with appropriate access controls.
- The system supports and complies with all governing privacy, security, and confidentiality standards.

Implementations and Current Status

Early on, the CMS recognized the need to provide some limited technical support for initial installation and technical problem resolution with the software. The CMS has reached out to companies that have already expressed a strong interest in providing implementation and support services to healthcare organizations that intend to use VistA–Office EHR. Many of these companies are members of the industry trade association known as the VistA Software Alliance (VSA).

The first version of the VistA–Office EHR software suite was released in August 2005. It was deployed at a limited number of facilities during the first year of its release. This will allow the many companies supporting VistA to become more familiar with this particular variant of the VistA system, even as additional functionality is identified and added to the system for the next release of the product in 2006. Additional resources on the Web to learn more about VistA–Office EHR are:

- VistA–Office EHR Distribution Point: http://www.vista-office.org/.
- WorldVistA, the VistA–Office Support Organization: http://www.worldvista.org/vvso/.

- VistA Software Alliance, an international network of large and small corporations and a network of developers working to enable the deployment of VistA throughout the world: www.vistasoftware.org.
- Center for Health Information Technology sponsored by the American Association of Family Practitioners: http://www.centerforhit.org/x1442.xml.

National Hansen's Disease Center and VistA

The National Hansen's Disease Programs (NHDP), based in Baton Rouge, Louisiana, is primarily responsible for inpatient and outpatient care and treatment of Hansen's disease (leprosy). In addition to the clinical programs in Baton Rouge, the NHDP also coordinates outpatient care for Hansen's disease patients throughout the United States at BPHC grant funded clinics as well as private physician offices.

Health information systems (HIS) are essential to the record-keeping functions and clinical care management of a medical center and its associated patient care programs. For over decade the NHDP has been using a version of the U.S. Department of Veterans Affairs (VA) VistA health information system to meet its needs.

Background

In 1994, the World Health Organization estimated that there were 2.4 million cases of Hansen's disease worldwide with 1.7 million cases registered on treatment. In the United States there are approximately 6,500 cases on the registry, which includes all cases reported since the registry began and still living. The number of cases with active disease and requiring drug treatment is approximately 600. There are 200 to 250 new cases reported to the registry annually with about 175 of these being new cases diagnosed for the first time. The largest numbers of cases in the United States are in California, Texas, Hawaii, Louisiana, Florida, New York, and Puerto Rico.

The National Hansen's Disease Center at Carville, Louisiana, started as a state institution in 1894 named Louisiana Leper Home, treating leprosy, one of the most misunderstood and stigmatized diseases of all time; developed into a highly respected world famous hospital for the treatment, rehabilitation, research, and training in the field of leprosy under federal sponsorship in 1921; and in 1999, had evolved to cover three campuses at Baton Rouge and Carville. It operates within the Department of Health and Human Services, Public Health Service, Health Resources and Services Administration, Bureau of Primary Health Care, Division of National Hansen's Disease Programs. The site at Carville was placed under the National Register of Historic Places in 1992 as part of the Carville Historic District.

The National Hansen's Disease Programs (NHDP) in Baton Rouge, Louisiana, is the only institution in the country exclusively devoted to Hansen's disease. In addition to the clinical programs in Baton Rouge, the NHDP also coordinates outpatient care for Hansen's disease patients throughout the United States at Bureau of Primary Health Care (BPHC) grant funded clinics as well as private physician offices. The NHDP conducts professional education programs for U.S. and international healthcare workers, providing basic information that is not provided in standard medical curricula. The NHDP also operates state-of-the-art, world-renowned laboratory research programs dedicated to improved detection, treatment, and prevention of Hansen's disease.

The U.S. Department of Veterans Affairs (VA) has developed and continues to maintain the VistA healthcare information system to provide a high-quality medical care environment for veterans of the U.S. Armed Forces. Designed from the beginning to focus on clinical aspects of healthcare, the VistA applications share a common set of files such as the patient and provider files. The NHDP chose to adopt and begin installing the VistA system in its institutions in the mid-1980s.

Current Situation

The initial installations of VistA, then known as DHCP, was performed at the Gillis W. Long Hansen's Center. In-house staff were added with the expertise needed to implement and maintain the system. With the loss of staff over the years, much of the needed expertise has been lost and the VistA system has not been updated. The last major upgrade to the system was in 2000. They are running on the last version of MSM v.4.0, the Kernel, and the "full core" set of VistA applications. They have a patient database size of 16,082 patients. The VistA system is in daily use within the program, and the breadth and complexity of its functionality require that a better support infrastructure be put in place.

A study group assigned to conduct a failure mode analysis reported a need to upgrade the VistA system and implement the VA Computerized Patient Record System (CPRS). The committee reported that interdepartmental communication would be enhanced, patient safety would improve, and medication errors would be reduced as a result of implementation of the CPRS. A notable improvement in patient outcomes is expected due to access of health information among healthcare practitioners located at NHDP and the regional health centers.

Implementation of the system would integrate the ordering, dispensing, and administration of medication to the patient. The system alerts the physician, nurse, and pharmacist to allergies and provides a tracking system for the administration of medication. The electronic record is available to healthcare providers at any location where a computer is available. This would eliminate problems with the transportation and tracking of the record at multiple sites. An added benefit of the system is the availability of patient data for clinical investigations. The integrated record will improve communication among health professionals and decrease the space required for record storage.

NHDP Plans

In 2004, the NHDP contacted the VA to discuss how best to proceed with upgrading its system. Apparently, the NHDP plans to maintain and enhance its VistA system. It also plans to implement the VA Computerized Patient Record System (CPRS) module. To accomplish this, they plan on moving from their existing MSM operating system environment to the InterSystems Cache solution currently favored by the VA. Other major objectives include:

- Updating the existing VistA system with current patches or upgrades.
- Implementing many additional VistA applications and utilities.
- Hire trained IT staff to support the VistA system.
- Obtain additional contract support for the system as needed.
- Modify and enhance the VistA system as needed to better meet NHDP needs.
- Provide needed training to administrative and clinical staff on the use of VistA and CPRS.
- Transition to a "paperless" electronic health record.

Unfortunately, budget constraints in FY 2005–06 may preclude them from pursuing the planned enhancements to their VistA system over the short term. However, it appears they will continue to use the currently installed system. It still meets their basic needs for Pharmacy, Medical Records, Clinical, Lab, and Engineering Work Orders. When funding becomes available, they will move forward with the planned enhancements.

Hawaii and VistA

Introduction

Hawaii has been a hotbed of activity with regard to the VistA system. Not only has VistA been used by the VA Medical Center and its clinics in Hawaii, but Tripler Army Medical Center uses a system called CHCS, which is an offspring of VistA. The Pacific Telehealth and Technology Hui has taken VistA and modified it slightly to run on a Linux open source platform. Their VistA open source solution is known as Hui OpenVista. The Hui helped American Samoa implement VistA at the LBJ Tropical Medical Center and is now working with a number of private companies to deploy VistA in a number of hospitals and clinics across the state of Hawaii.

Pacific Hui and OpenVista

The Pacific region has a varied economic infrastructure. Proprietary solutions that are easily affordable to some areas are economic hardships for other areas. Because enterprise-wide healthcare information systems based on VistA are available and in the public domain through the Freedom of Information Act (FOIA), economic factors do not limit its deployment. Making taxpayer-funded software freely available for use by the general public fits in well with the Hui's mission to improve the quality, accessibility, and cost-effectiveness of healthcare services to people living in remote areas of the Pacific.

The Pacific Hui's OpenVista technology transfer initiative is the outcome of a research project funded and managed by the Hui, building on the strengths of the U.S. Department of Veteran Affairs (VA) VistA system. Unfortunately, the VA VistA system currently runs on proprietary operating systems and "M" language compilers that require somewhat costly licensing fees. The Linux-based Hui OpenVista solution is now available to the public in a nonproprietary open source version that avoids these costs. The Pacific Hui's OpenVista project was a collaborative development effort involving WorldVistA, Medsphere, Sanchez/GT.M, the Pacific Hui, and the contributions of countless others in the larger VistA and open source global community.

On June 6, 2003, the Pacific Hui officially released OpenVista. The system operates on a Linux platform and is now available to hospitals and clinics worldwide in a nonproprietary, open source version. One can obtain the software from the SourceForge.net Web site, which is a well-known open source software development site. An updated version was expected to be posted in late 2005.

The initial release of Hui OpenVista encompassed the following functional modules from the VA VistA system:

* Patient Information Management System (Patient Registration and Bed Control)
* Clinic Scheduling
* Pharmacy System
* Laboratory System
* Radiology System

* Computerized Patient Record System (CPRS)
  ○ Cover Sheet
  ○ Problem Lists
  ○ Medication Lists
  ○ Patient Notes
  ○ Consults
  ○ Discharge Summaries
  ○ Electronic Orders
  ○ Results Reporting

On August 1, 2003, the Pacific Telehealth and Technology Hui reported that more than 230 healthcare, software development, and medical research organizations had executed licenses and downloaded the Pacific Hui OpenVista software from the organization's Web site at www.pacifichui.org in the first 60 days since its release. That number has since grown significantly.

OpenVista ASP Solution

After release of the OpenVista system, the Pacific Hui recognized a need to provide OpenVista services to small hospitals, remote clinics, and nurs-

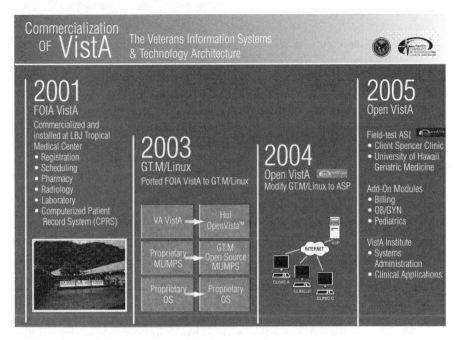

FIGURE 9-2 Commercializing VistA in Hawaii

ing homes in Hawaii that did not have the needed information systems resources to install, operate, and maintain a stand–alone system.

In order to accommodate these types of healthcare facilities, the Pacific Hui developed and tested a prototype of an OpenVista application service provider (ASP) solution. In the ASP configuration, OpenVista is maintained on servers at a central location from which healthcare organizations can access the system via computer workstations. This provides the small, remote sites with access to a fully integrated healthcare information system that has been configured to meet their specific needs. It is equivalent to having an OpenVista system on-site without the need to hire a technical staff to maintain it. Based on tests of the prototype, the Pacific Hui was able to demonstrate that OpenVista can be configured as an ASP solution that uses a single set of OpenVista routines to maintain separate, secure databases for different clients.

The next step was to validate the OpenVista ASP in an operational environment. Once the OpenVista ASP was fully tested and validated at pilot client sites, it could be transferred to private commercial or non

---

Links to Key Web Sites and Documentation

- Pacific Hui: http://www.pacifichui.org/
- VistA System Web Site: http://www.va.gov/vista_monograph/docs/vista_monograph2005_06.doc
- WorldVistA Organization: http://www.worldvista.org/
- VistA Software Alliance: http://vistasoftware.org/

---

profit organizations through the Hui's technology transfer program. As of June 2005, all was proceeding well with the Hui's pilot test of the OpenVista ASP approach with the Clint Spencer Clinic and the University of Hawaii's Geriatric Clinics. A company called BlueCliff, Inc. was established in mid-2005 aimed initially at marketing the OpenVista ASP solution in Hawaii. Another company, Mele Associates, works closely with the Pacific Hui and Blue Cliff on these OpenVista initiatives.

In another related effort, the Pacific Hui collaborated with the University of Hawaii in 2005 to establish the VistA Institute to help promote the development, use, and sustainability of VistA and OpenVista systems. The institute will provide systems applications and administration training and create a VistA library of user manuals and other technical documentation. They are sharing their experience and work with the WorldVistA organization and others involved with the national VistA–Office EHR initiative.

Hawaii, and the Pacific Telehealth and Technology Hui in particular, has proven to be a true "Center of Excellence" for VistA-related activities taking place in the United States and around the world.

D.C. Department of Health and VistA

In the summer of 2002, the District of Columbia (D.C.) Department of Health approached the U.S. Department of Veterans Affairs (VA) about possibly acquiring and pilot testing the use of the VA Computerized Patient Record System (CPRS) in several of its clinics. CPRS is one of the major modules within the more comprehensive VA health information system known as VistA. What emerged was a very successful collaborative effort resulting in the successful deployment of VistA and CPRS in selected pilot test sites by the D.C. Department of Health (DOH).

Following several demonstrations of the system by the VA, management at every level of the D.C. government, from the Mayor's Health Policy Council to the community clinic directors, readily saw the many potential benefits to be derived from choosing to deploy VistA and CPRS. The fact that the system had been successfully deployed in a mix of large, medium, and small healthcare facilities within the VA, DoD, and the Indian Health Service (IHS), and that the healthcare providers using the system were very satisfied with the technology, reinforced their confidence in the decision to move forward with the pilot. The fact that it was available at no cost under the Freedom of Information Act (FOIA) was also a big plus.

The acquisition and implementation of VistA and CPRS by the D.C. DOH became the primary focus of the three-year Technology Opportunities Program (TOP) project. Some of the desired outcomes specifically sought by the TOP project included:

- Improved administration of medical records processes and associated cost savings.
- Improved provider satisfaction with the administrative and clinical care processes.
- Improved patient satisfaction with waiting times and communications with providers.
- Improved patient safety and quality of care as more complete medical records are made readily available to providers.

A combination of DOH staff, contractors, and VA technical support staff were used to identify detailed functional and technical requirements and to configure and install the servers, workstations, and local area networks (LAN). Training was provided to DOH technical and clinical staff by the VA and various vendors such as Cisco and Hewlett-Packard.

The location for the servers used to run the VistA software was centrally located at DOH, near the selected clinics implementing the system. Each of the initial clinic sites was connected to the VistA servers at DOH point-to-point by T1 telecommunications lines. Although the VA provided the VistA and CPRS software, some customization was necessary to adapt the systems to accommodate business rules and functional requirements specific to DOH. A combination of DOH clinical staff, vendors, and VA technical support personnel worked on the installation, setup, and tailoring of the newly installed software to meet the specific needs of the clinics.

The D.C. TOP project encountered many challenges along the way such as the closure of the NPCC and Community Medical Care, Inc. Nevertheless, at the conclusion of the D.C. TOP project, pediatric providers at Mary's Center for Maternal and Child Care were using the VistA CPRS in combination with the paper medical chart. Some observations and results of the implementation of the pilot system include:

- Providers perceived the VistA CPRS module as more legible and more secure than the paper record.
- The online prescription medications list was perceived as very helpful.
- The programmed encounter form was expected to enhance compliance with Medicaid well-child standards over time.
- Problem lists, not always kept current in paper records, were automatically updated in the VistA CPRS.
- Providers were dissatisfied that the initial arrangement required duplicate entry of information to VistA and other existing systems; however, the VistA billing interface and laboratory connectivity will eliminate much of the double-entry by administrative staff and providers.
- The Laboratory Electronic Data Interface (LEDI) module in VistA needed modifications that were not identified and planned for up front.

DOH is looking to possibly replicate VistA's initial successful implementation in other D.C. clinics and healthcare facilities beyond the first pilot sites. Expanded use of VistA and CPRS across other DOH facilities will bring a number of anticipated benefits such as:

- Creating a more reliable, accessible, and centralized medical record.
- Improving quality, effectiveness, and continuity of patient care.
- Enhancing overall patient safety.

As the DOH looks to the future, many new health information technology and business needs may also start to emerge. These might include needs for the following:

- Interfacing other commercial off-the-shelf (COTS) modules such as Patient Billing and Pediatrics.

- Implementing the VistA Health Data Repository (HDR) and Personal Health Record (PHR) modules.
- Implementing a generic health information exchange (HIE) capability
- Adding biosurveillance or disease-reporting capabilities.
- Acquiring and installing wireless network solutions, support for PDAs, and a secure VPN.

State Veterans Homes and VistA

In October 2003, the secretary of the U.S. Department of Veterans Affairs (VA) and the under secretary for health issued guidance to its healthcare facilities across the country on a nationwide initiative to make the VA VistA and Computerized Patient Record System (CPRS) available for use by all interested state veterans homes (SVH). The SVH program is the oldest federal–state partnership and represents a sizeable commitment by the VA to states for shared construction costs and ongoing per diem payments for veterans' care in long-term settings. This effort is part of the VA Health*e*People long-range strategy to pursue collaborative partnerships with other healthcare organizations in the public and private sectors. Specific goals of this SVH initiative were to:

- Contribute to improved health care provided to veterans by both the VA and state veterans homes.
- Improve communication among providers between different levels of care.
- Support continuity of care by making medical record information seamless and transparent to clinicians responsible for care provided at both the VA and state veterans homes.
- Enhance interagency (federal and state) sharing of healthcare information and technology.

Background

The U.S. Congress first authorized federal cost-sharing for state veterans homes in 1888. There are currently about 23,000 residents at more than 120 state veterans homes in 47 states and one U.S. territory. Residents are typically incapacitated or unable to earn a living and require long-term nursing care. Residents are normally military veterans who have generally already received care at VA healthcare facilities. However, residents can sometimes include veterans' spouses.

Of the many state veterans homes, some are physically located on the grounds of a VA Medical Center (VAMC). This close physical proximity led naturally to clinical staff at many SVHs requesting access to the VA VistA and CPRS systems, which are used at all VA healthcare facilities across the country. Within a healthcare setting, automation of medical records has been generally found to improve communication and quality of care by clinicians. It was concluded that providing secure access to VistA for selected staff at the SVHs would better facilitate requests for consultations and associated clinical procedures and improve turnaround time for feedback about results.

Planning and Analysis

The primary business office responsible for overseeing any sharing arrangements with SVHs is the Geriatrics and Extended Care Strategic Healthcare Group (GEC-SHG). In 2002, this office convened a task force to examine in depth the issue of providing access to VistA and CPRS for selected staff at the state veterans homes. They determined that there would be a number of benefits both to the VA and the state veterans homes if secure access to patient data contained in these systems was granted. These benefits included:

- Improved patient care by both institutions.
- Enhanced productivity by professionals at both institutions.
- A reduction in administrative and healthcare delivery costs.
- Increased clinical and health services research.
- Support for future developments in healthcare technology, standards, policy, and management.

Two primary alternatives were identified for sharing VistA and CPRS functionality and data with state veterans homes:

- Alternative 1: State veterans homes could obtain the VistA and/or CPRS software from the VA and operate their own systems using state or contract technical staff.
- Alternative 2: VA Medical Centers could grant state veterans homes with secure read-only access to patient data in the VistA and CPRS systems. The read-only option meant that SVH staff could not write entries into the VA medical record.

A more detailed analysis into the feasibility of providing VistA and/or CPRS read-only access to the state veterans homes was conducted in January 2003. Some of the other issues and major concerns surfaced by this study included:

- Complying with various accreditation requirements such as JCAHO.
- The need to build additional security features into CPRS to handle queries from an authorized external entity.
- The need to address potential physician credentialing and privileging issues.
- Affects on VA help desk and technical support staff.
- Possible VistA software modifications that might be needed.
- Privacy and security requirements such as HIPAA and Privacy Act.
- User access and background checks.
- Legal or contractual requirements.

Based on a survey of state veterans homes completed in June 2003, there were eight states that expressed some interest in possibly acquiring and installing VistA for use as their own health information system. However, over 90% of the states expressed a clear desire to simply have CPRS read-only access for a small number of key staff at their facilities. In addition, the survey found that approximately 30 state veterans homes had already been given CPRS read-only access as a result of local sharing agreements.

Over a period of approximately six months, staff from the Office of Information, General Counsel, CyberSecurity, Geriatrics and Long Term Care, Medical Records Administration, and others helped to develop an implementation plan and detailed guidance needed to address these concerns. In October 2003, the Under Secretary for Health authorized moving forward with this initiative, and this guidance was transmitted to the field.

Systems Implementation

An implementation plan was developed and a VHA Office of Information (OI) program manager was assigned to provide support to the Geriatrics and Long Term Care SHG in moving this national effort forward. Specific objectives for the SVH initiative included the following:

- Provide limited support needed to complete implementation of VistA/CPRS for the SVHs in a selected state, e.g., Oklahoma (pilot test), by the end of FY 2003

- Complete implementation of VistA/CPRS read-only access for a limited number of SVHs in selected state(s) by January 2004.
- Ensure that all states wishing to obtain VistA/CPRS read-only access in their SVHs achieve this by the end of FY 2006.
- Monitor and regularly report to management on the progress of this initiative.

CPRS Read–Only Access

The states that have obtained CPRS read-only access to date for their SVHs are listed below: 20 states, Puerto Rico, the District of Columbia, and more than 70 facilities. Numerous sites in other states are in the process of being connected. There are a total of 128 SVHs in 47 states with more being opened.

VistA Implementations

The Oklahoma Department of Veterans Affairs worked with Hewlett-Packard and Medsphere to implement VistA in its seven SVHs (Norman,

---

Table 9-3 State Veterans Homes and VistA

All Homes with Read-Only Access	Some Homes with CPRS Read-Only Access	No Homes with CPRS Read-Only Access
Alabama	Florida	Arkansas
Arizona	Georgia	Colorado
California	Idaho	Illinois
Connecticut	Massachusetts	Maine
District of Columbia	Michigan	Mississippi
Indiana	Minnesota	Nevada
Iowa	Montana	New Hampshire
Kansas	Nebraska	New Jersey
Kentucky	New York	New Mexico
Louisiana	Ohio	North Dakota
Maryland	Pennsylvania	Tennessee
Missouri	South Carolina	Virginia
North Carolina	Texas	
Oklahoma	Washington	
Oregon	Wisconsin	
Puerto Rico		
Rhode Island		
South Dakota		
Utah		
Vermont		
West Virginia		
Wyoming		

Claremore, Talihina, Clinton, Ardmore, Sulphur, and Lawton). The VA provided some limited consultative expertise through the local VA Medical Centers. The VistA has been successfully installed in every SVH in Oklahoma. The system has received excellent satisfaction ratings from Oklahoma system users and administrators.

Conclusion and Future Scenarios

This collaborative initiative between the VA and SVHs has proven to be very successful. In fact, it is a model for others to follow when attempting to pursue federal and state government partnerships. The VA was able to share its systems with the states and did not have to expend significant resources in doing so. The SVHs provided the funding and resources needed to implement and use the VA systems. The veterans who received healthcare treatment at both the VA and state facilities ended up being the real winners.

As a result of Oklahoma's successful acquisition and implementation of the VistA system for its own use, it is anticipated that several other states may choose to follow suit in the coming years. It is also expected that over time, those SVHs that have CPRS read-only access may want to work with the VA on next steps to take to obtain the ability to place orders and have other interactive VistA and/or CPRS system capabilities. Over the long term, whether the state veterans homes are using VistA or a commercial electronic health record (EHR) system, it is anticipated that they will one day want the ability to share or exchange information on patients receiving care at both the VA and the state homes.

Oklahoma State Veterans Homes and VistA

In 2003, the Oklahoma Department of Veterans Affairs (ODVA) initiated its project to acquire and implement the VistA electronic health

---

Key Web Links

- Armed Forces Veterans Home Foundation:
  http://www.vethomesfoundation.org/frameset.htm

- VA Geriatrics and Extended Care Program:
  http://www.va.gov/geriatricsshg/

record (EHR) system in its seven healthcare facilities, including the state veterans homes (SVHs) in Norman, Claremore, Talihina, Clinton, Ardmore, Sulphur, and Lawton.

Project History

Here is a brief overview of the project time line:

- Hewlett-Packard (HP) was selected as the prime contractor for the ODVA project.
  - HP has been a key partner with the VA for more than 20 years.
  - HP subcontracted with Medsphere for VistA software application expertise.
- Norman was the first facility to implement VistA. Much work was put into customizing VistA to meet the needs of the Oklahoma SVHs. Standardization, documentation, database configuration, and development of training materials and programs were going to be crucial to the overall success of the project and implementation at the future sites.
- VistA was implemented at Norman, a 300-bed facility, in May 2004.
- Claremore was the second site. It was also a 300-bed facility. VistA was successfully implemented there by the end of August 2004.
- Talihina was the third site to go live in September 2004.
- As of June 2005, all seven Oklahoma SVHs were using VistA.
- The project was completed at the beginning of June 2005. Deployment was completed three months ahead of schedule and at a significant cost-savings to ODVA.

Guiding Principles and Major Project Objectives

The following are some of the guiding principles, major objectives, and other planned activities associated with the Oklahoma VistA implementation project:

- Utilization of the proven VA VistA and CPRS software solutions.
- Implement VistA and CPRS in all seven of Oklahoma's SVHs.
- Improve quality of veterans' health care at the Oklahoma SVHs.

- Focus on software deployment, not software development.
- ODVA will stay aligned with the VA VistA system and future plans.
- ODVA will seek to leverage the VA for selective VistA software development and support.

Systems Architecture

The IT architecture chosen for Oklahoma was a centralized one, using a single VistA database residing in Oklahoma City at the ODVA central office. Each of the seven facilities is represented as a division within the overall system and its database. There is a disaster recovery configuration in Norman. Given a disaster occurring at the central site in Oklahoma City, the system at Norman could be brought online to support the production environment.

Project Benefits

The following were some of the major benefits to be derived from the Oklahoma VistA system implementation project:

- Move toward standardization of care across ODVA facilities.
- Implementation of a single, seamless medical record across ODVA facilities.
- Improved access to patient information by ODVA healthcare providers.
- Reduced occurrence of medication errors, and other improvements in patient safety.
- Potential sharing of patient records between ODVA and the VA in the future.
- Reduced costs as funds were focused on software deployment, not software development.
- VistA will help ODVA become HIPAA-compliant.

Project Challenges

Some of the many issues and challenges addressed during this ODVA project to implement VistA included:

- VistA consists of two environments that currently must be implemented: "Roll and Scroll" and the Windows GUI environments.

- Identifying subject matter experts (SME) and/or "champions" in each ODVA facility.
- VistA for ODVA needed some customization for long-term care facilities.
  - Seek a balance between VistA's capabilities and ODVA's requirements.
  - Some reengineering of ODVA processes were needed to meet VistA design.
- Hardware and infrastructure enhancements.
- Upgrade of existing network infrastructure to accommodate users needs.
- Upgrade of existing hardware needed for improved reliability and performance.
- Increasing the number of desktop PCs and printers at ODVA facilities.
- Migration of existing ODVA patient data into VistA.
- Keeping VistA software at ODVA facilities up-to-date and patched.
- An intergovernmental agreement between ODVA and the VA for some degree of software support was needed.
- Centralized IT staff were needed in ODVA to support the seven remote locations.
- Providing 24/7 customer support for the ODVA users of VistA.
- Customized reports needed to be developed for ODVA at the central administration and hospital levels.

VistA Foundation Software Modules

The basic VistA software modules initially implemented by ODVA included:

- Patient Registration
- Admission/Discharge/ Transfer (ADT)
- Inpatient Pharmacy
- Outpatient Pharmacy
- Laboratory
- Master Patient Index (MPI)
- National Drug File
- Patient Demographics
- Radiology and Nuclear Medicine
- Clinic Scheduling

Additional VistA Software Modules

Other VistA software modules to be implemented by ODVA as soon as possible to take advantage of using the VA Computerized Patient Record System (CPRS) include:

- Adverse Events Tracking
- Clinical Guidelines and Reminders
- Consult Requests and Reminders
- Discharge Summaries
- Graphical Lab Trending and Results
- Health Summaries
- Order Entry
- Problem Lists
- Progress Notes
- Vitals and Other Measurements

Additional VistA Software Modules Desired

Other VistA software modules ODVA wants to possibly implement in the future include:

- Controlled Substances
- Dietetics
- Incident Reporting
- Long-Term Care (Accu-Care)
- Mental Health
- Nursing
- Patient Intake and Output
- Social Work
- Volunteer Timekeeping

New Customized Software Modules Needed

There were a number of additional software modules that needed to be acquired and implemented by ODVA that were not a part of the VistA system, such as:

- Patient Billing and Banking
- Nurse Scheduling
- MDS (Accu-Care)
- Selected Lab Device Interfacing

Future Enhancements

A list of long–range enhancements sought by ODVA include the implementation of the following VistA software modules:

- Bar Code Medication Administration (BCMA)
- Claims and Benefit Management
- Vista Imaging (Document and Medical)

The VHA Office of Information (OI) continues to provide updated versions of VistA software and patches to ODVA. Oklahoma has moved on to the next stage of addressing ongoing operations and moving on implementing planned enhancements to its system. This has been a highly successful public-private collaborative initiative implementing an innovative, open source solution.

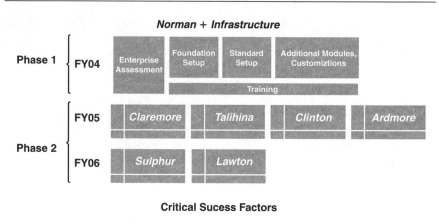

FIGURE 9-3 Oklahoma and VistA Success Factors

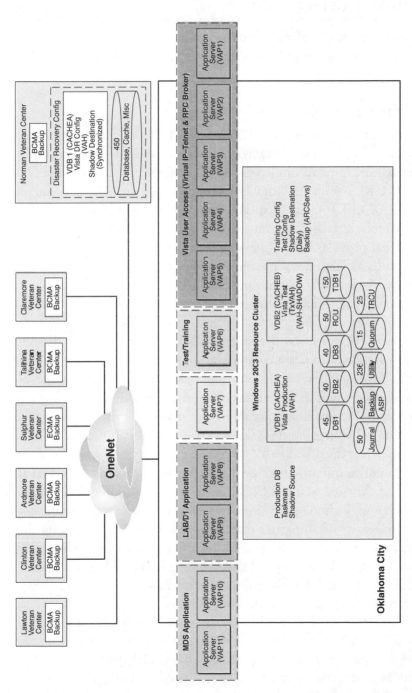

FIGURE 9-4 Oklahoma and VistA System Topology

Part B: International

The following section of this chapter contains profiles of selected VistA system implementations in healthcare organizations around the world.

American Samoa and VistA

The Lyndon Baines Johnston (LBJ) Tropical Medical Center in American Samoa recently completed a highly successful collaborative project involving the acquisition and implementation of VistA, the electronic health record (EHR) system developed by the U.S. Department of Veterans Affairs (VA). LBJ Tropical Medical Center is located in Pago Pago and is the only medical facility in American Samoa. The facility is a 160-bed hospital that provides health care to approximately 70,000 people. It has services such as laboratory, pharmacy, dietetics, radiology, dialysis, and mental health. Before it implemented the VistA system, LBJ had no computer system at all and all record keeping was paper-based, which resulted in a loss of revenue and duplication of many medical services.

LBJ management knew they did not have the resources to develop their own system or to buy a commercial solution. Their CEO and board members went to Honolulu, Hawaii, and talked to the director of the VA Medical Center about the possibility of acquiring and using the VistA system, a comprehensive healthcare information system that has been made available to other organizations for many years through the Freedom of Information Act (FOIA). The VA recognized that military veterans would benefit from this initiative because the VA has no clinics in Samoa and all veterans are treated at the LBJ Tropical Medical Center. The Pacific Telehealth and Technology Hui in Hawaii helped to coordinate the collaborative efforts of all parties that ultimately worked on making this project a success. Some of these other organizations included the Tripler Military Hospital, University of Hawaii, U.S. Air Force, National Guard, PEACESAT, WorldVistA, the governor of Samoa, the American Samoa congressional delegate, and several corporations.

The VistA Patient Information Management System (PIMS) module was implemented first so that basic demographic data on most patients could be entered into the computer database. LBJ then proceeded to implement a series of clinical applications based on their relative importance to the organization. These included the Clinic Scheduling, Pharmacy, and Laboratory software modules. These were the areas that formed the foundation needed in order to effectively implement the VA Computerized Patient Record System (CPRS). Over time, a prioritized list of additional software modules was developed for subsequent implementations in Samoa, such as Radiology, Dietetics, Billing, Surgery, Medicine, and Nursing.

Overall, the implementation of the VistA system went quite well and the employees are enthusiastic about using the system. Very few calls have had to be made by the LBJ Tropical Medical Center to the Honolulu VA Medical Center for help or assistance. The small servers donated by the University of Hawaii have performed extremely well for the 50 or so simultaneous users of the VistA system installed and used by the LBJ Tropical Medical Center. This collaborative effort to implement the "free" suite of software modules that make up the VistA electronic health record (EHR) system was truly successful. It has been very rewarding to the staff to see patient care begin to improve almost immediately once the system was implemented. For example:

- Use of the Patient Information Management module has led to improvements in tracking of discharges, admissions, and transfers (ADT) and the creation of up-to-date in patient rosters.
- Use of the Clinic Scheduling module has led to improvements including better coordination between clinics and medical centers getting records to the clinic, identification and verification of LBJ patient names and ID, and improved reports on clinic workloads.
- Use of the Laboratory module has led to more timely reports, improved tracking of historical lab results, and improved controls on identifying false LBJ patient ID numbers.
- Use of the Radiology module has improved the legibility of the report now that results are typed. Also, workload reports can be readily produced for better management of the department.
- Use of the Pharmacy module has improved its ability to process prescriptions in a timely manner and has also given the center a tool to monitor drug usage and workload. The staff has also seen a significant reduction in duplicate prescriptions.
- The Computerized Patient Record System (CPRS) module allows clinicians to now submit electronic orders to laboratory, radiology, and pharmacy. It also provides the ability to keep progress notes and

Overview of VistA/CPRS and ILC Billing/Collections Information Systems

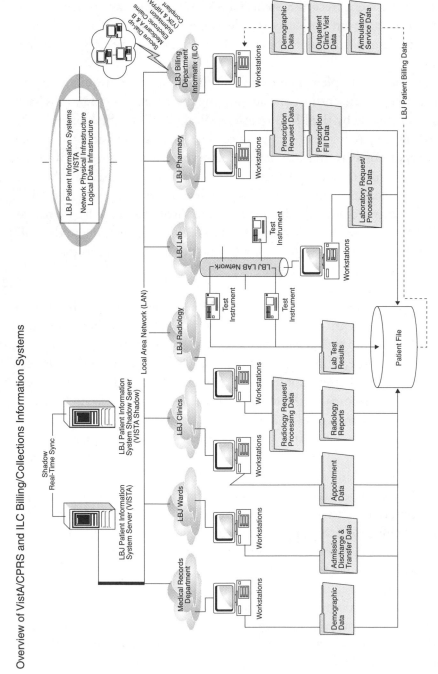

FIGURE 9-5 VistA System Deployed in American Samoa

other defined electronic digital documents associated with a patient, and to view all data associated with a patient, from lab results to medications that have been prescribed and dispensed.

- Use of the Informatix (ILC) Billing/Accounts Receivable module has resulted in dramatic improvements in billing and/or cost recovery. This third-party billing system was added in 2003. Due to the improvement of record keeping, the percentage of earnings from nonresidents increased from 1% to 26%.

Currently there are no plans to further enhance the VistA system in American Samoa. The LBJ Tropical Medical Center will simply continue to use the standard system released by the VA and will keep it patched and up-to-date. The VA VistA and Computerized Patient Record System (CPRS) appear to be more than adequate to meet the long-term needs of the center. However, over time, one would expect that VistA clinical imaging, wireless technology, and other cost-effective enhancements may be made.

Egypt and VistA

National Cancer Institute (NCI)

In 1990, a project was launched to implement a Hospital Management Information System (HMIS) at the National Cancer Institute, Cairo University (NCI-CU). NCI-CU is the leading cancer center in Egypt, delivering cancer care for about 12,000 new cancer cases every year, more than half free of charge.

VistA, formerly known as DHCP, was adopted as the Health Information System. Customization and conversion to Arabic of many parts of VistA was achieved in-house, with cooperation from VA staff and staff from the University of Wurzburg in Germany. Applications used included Patient Registration, Inpatient Admissions/Discharges/ Transfers (ADT), Surgery, Laboratory, Pharmacy, Radiology, Record Tracking, Nursing, Engineering, and a test version of the Clinical Imaging module.

NCI updated the original VistA system running on DataTree "M" into Cache in 2000. The original data was migrated to Cache, which included patient data collected since 1992. NCI has also started working on a GUI interface for ADT, Lab, Radiology, and others. Some of this software is in Arabic, some in English, and some mixed.

Nasser Institute Hospital—An Overview

Nasser Institute Hospital (NIH) was opened in July 1987, encompassing an area of about 35 acres. The main hospital is an eight-floor building with two basement levels. It used to be part of Cairo Curative Organization, but it was moved to the custody of the Ministry of Health and Population (MOHP) in late 1997. NIH is the largest tertiary reference center for MOHP. It consists of 885 beds distributed over more than 40 medical specialties and sub-specialties ranging from ordinary medical and surgical services to the most sophisticated BMT and open heart surgery. Other statistics include:

ICU beds:	68	Total number of ER patients:	20,241
Operating rooms:	23		
Dialysis machines:	53	Total number of outpatients:	201,535
Number of inpatients:	21,347		
Average occupancy %:	98.3%	Number of major operations:	13,509
Average length of stay:	14.6 days		
Average bed turnover:	5.2 times/ year	Number of cardiac catheterizations:	2,474
		Total number of lab tests:	48,969
Average daily admissions:	58.5 p/day	Total number of radiology tests:	31,442
		Total number of dialysis sessions:	18,092
		Total number of mortalities:	1,109

HMIS Project Implementation

The Hospital Management Information System (HMIS) project in Egypt started in 1997. The aim was to establish an HMIS in up to four hospital members of the CCO group and at headquarters. The Nasser Institute Hospital (NIH) joined the project in late 1997. Since about 1994, NIH had been using stand–alone PC workstations set up with a prototype system to provide some financial and statistical data. NIH joined the CCO/MOHP USAID project and implemented HMIS in early 1999, later than the other hospitals in the CCO. This delay entering the project motivated NIH to try to run the activities of the implementation faster to keep up with the other MOHP hospitals. The CIO and other senior management and clinical staff regarded the project from the first as the best chance to join the future of health care and to make the best use of scarce resources. The staff had the medical experience, and with the VistA implementation project they hoped to learn all about information management.

It took about a year from joining the project to the complete cabling of the facility. During this start–up period they had a limited network solution in place to demonstrate the capabilities of the system and to train the hospital staff. In early 2000, network cabling was finished.

The concept of a universal patient number was also implemented for the first time in Nasser Institute Hospital with this project. This concept not only revolutionized its statistics but it was a new start for its future electronic health record (EHR) system.

Maximus played a key role providing support for this joint USAID and Egyptian government project. Maximus provided a training program for a team of programmers, system administrators, troubleshooters, and hardware support staff. The Egyptian staff closely shadowed their counterparts on the Maximus team. For every task in the project performed by Maximus, NIH assigned one of its project team to be trained on that task so they would be able to carry out the job at the end of the project. This knowledge-transfer approach was initiated by Maximus at the outset of the project. Some tasks were completely carried out by NIH staff that were supervised by Maximus. (http://www.maximus.com/corporate/pages/adminhealthsyssvs.asp)

Maximus trained the following number of NIH staff:

- Programmers/Analysts   7
- System Administrators   7
- Help Desk   22
- End Users   376
- Trainers   20
- Application Coordinators   32

For every VistA software application module, NIH had a member of the HMIS department and a member from the department of specialty coordinate the system's implementation. These staff were trained by Maximus. They in turn later shared the responsibility of providing the training to others. They ensured that the transfer of knowledge to end users was successfully accomplished. This approach, plus creating backup or a second line of trained counterparts, ensured the smoothness of the flow of work and gave the staff self-confidence in their ability to achieve their goals.

The NIH team members were always questioning the end users about their opinions on the customization of the VistA packages to meet their needs. Aside from their regular assignments, the team trained more than 300 employees on basic PC skills using a computer-training laboratory set up with the assistance of Maximus. This PC literacy campaign was one of the most successful efforts in the history of the hospital. It was a success as a propaganda tool leading up to the HMIS implementation. As a result, almost everybody was willing to share in making this project a success.

The major benefit of using Maximus was not its expertise in computer hardware or software but its transfer of information management knowledge. Understanding and managing the cultural effect of the system on end users was also a key service provided by Maximus. These results and the overall success of the project could not be achieved by a company or an institute alone. It needed the successful collaboration and interaction among all the partners involved in this project.

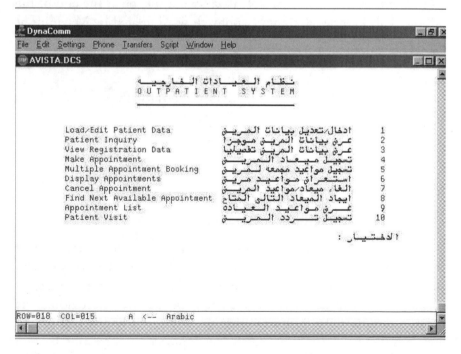

FIGURE 9-6 Copy of a VistA Outpatient Scheduling Screen Displaying Options in Arabic

Current Status

As of January 2005, at least two hospitals in Egypt were running components of the original VistA software installed by Maximus, but with lots of
help and support of Egyptian National Cancer Institute (NCI) programmers. NCI is upgrading all VistA system modules to the current versions
and are using CPRS. NCI also plans to use VistA Imaging.

Future Plans

NIH has plans to implement Picture Archiving and Communications
System (PACS) and other clinical-imaging capabilities. It also hopes to possibly implement the VA Computerized Patient Record System (CPRS)
module and integrate VistA with other existing activities and systems such as
Telemedicine, Cancer Registry, Quality Assurance, and Decision Support.

Mexico and VistA

In May 2004, representatives of the Instituto Mexicano del Seguro Social
(Mexican Government Social Security Healthcare System) visited the VA
Medical Center in Washington, D.C., to learn more about the U.S.
Department of Veterans Affairs comprehensive health information system
known as VistA. The Instituto Mexicano del Seguro Social (IMSS) was
interested in possibly installing VistA and the VA Computerized Patient
Record System (CPRS) in all of its hospitals. The IMSS operates a government chain of 40 large tertiary hospitals, 223 regional hospitals, and
more than 1200 clinics. They also have about 3,000 very small community clinics that provide care to some 10.5 million uninsured people. It is
worth noting that IMSS is a nonprofit state-owned organization and is
the main healthcare provider in the country. It serves a population of
more than 50 million insured people, making it the largest social insurance organization in Latin America. In terms of medical research, it has
67 research centers and more than 473 full-time researchers.

Representatives of the IMSS met with Veterans Health Administration
(VHA) senior IT staff three times during 2004 to be briefed on VistA and
see it in operation. During their meeting in mid-2004 with the chief health
information officer for the VHA, they raised a number of specific issues.
For example, they wanted to know how to go about gaining access to VistA
software, patches, training materials, and documentation. They also dis-

cussed how to collaborate on new software modules, exchange data in the border states where patients are treated in both countries, and many other issues. The director of the Health IT Sharing (HITS) program within the VHA Office of Information (OI) subsequently coordinated contacts between the agencies and helped them obtain copies of the VistA software, documentation, patches, and other information they have requested.

In July 2004, the VA was provided with an update by the VistA project manager for the IMSS on the status of their efforts to move forward with testing and implementing the VA VistA system. In brief, they had:

- Finished their preliminary evaluations of cost and performance.
- Installed and tested a number of VistA configurations successfully over the past months.
- Started loading in sample patient data on their test system.
- Started sizing the infrastructure required (PCs, servers, network, etc.) in order to operate the system across the IMSS.
- Begun concurrently modeling their business processes so they can attempt to reproduce and relate them to VistA to find any gap that might exist between their current model and the VA system.
- Begun doing some complexity assessments on changes that will need to be made to better tailor VistA to meet their needs.
- Developed plans to deploy VistA at a pilot site by September 2004.
- Developed plans to deploy the main modules of VistA in one of their hospitals and have it online by December 2004.
- Assigned approximately 15 full-time employees to the startup of the project.
- Received funding to proceed with the implementation of VistA over the next year at additional IMSS hospitals in Mexico.
- Requested additional information from the VA about VistA Imaging and VistA training opportunities.
- Began the translation of the VistA system and CPRS into Spanish.
- Made the preliminary decision to move forward with implementation of VistA in their IMSS hospitals by the end of FY 2006.

As of 2006, the VistA implementation project in Mexico was continuing to move forward at an aggressive pace. The IMSS reported having VistA installed in 20 hospitals with 11 more hospitals in the process of installing the system. The plan called for more than 40 tertiary hospitals to be running VistA by mid 2006. The goal was to bring up VistA in

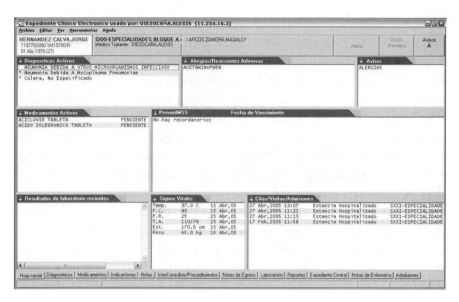

FIGURE 9-7 VistA/CPRS Cover Sheet Screen in Spanish

approximately 100 additional general hospitals by the end of 2006. Additional installations were planned for 2007.

In August 2005, a new VistA module was developed by the IMSS and released to support its emergency departments. It was embedded in CPRS and allows physicians to easily and quickly calculate and capture injury severity scores and revised trauma scores. The first version of a VistA Imaging module was also developed and released by the IMSS. It is a Java client-server application that allows physicians to view a digital copy of DICOM-compliant imaging studies from their computer workstations. The IMSS is also busy developing enhancements to the VistA Surgical and Nursing modules to better meet its needs.

This has been a highly successful international collaborative effort. In several years, Mexico may become the biggest user of the VistA system. Some of the new modules developed will prove beneficial to the VA and the global VistA community.

Germany and VistA

The German Heart Institute in Berlin opened in 1985. It is a hospital specializing in cardio-thoracic surgery and cardiology. It has more than

8,100 inpatient admissions each year and did 4,557 open heart procedures and 2,797 cath procedures in 2002.

In 1992, the German Heart Institute started adding software modules from the U.S. Department of Veterans Affairs (VA) VistA system to its existing system. The institute's hospital information system was already based on the "M" programming language that was also used in VistA. At the time, there was a need to address an application development backlog with its current system as well as hardware limitations, and VistA offered a low-cost alternative to purchasing a solution from established IT vendors in Germany at that time.

The VA Kernel was adopted and incorporated into the framework of the German Heart Institute's existing health IT systems. It gave the institute a set of software tools that allowed greater flexibility in new application development. In addition to the Kernel, the institute implemented a number of VistA applications such as Laboratory, parts of Blood Bank, Anatomic Pathology, and Record Tracking, in addition to other internally developed applications that were built using the VA FileMan and ScreenMan tools.

Marcus Werners, MD, reported on some of the problems encountered at the start of the project to introduce VistA software. Problems included:

- Convincing IT management and colleagues that applications written in the "M" language were not based on exotic or dying technology.
- Showing the functionality and speed of development, so it was much easier to convince users and hospital management.
- Gaining and keeping management support is an ongoing effort.

On the technology side, the natural language issues were the hardest to overcome. Fortunately the VA (i.e., the San Francisco OIFO) was very helpful in this respect. The VA FileMan and Kernel now contains code that allows different languages (prompts, date formats, date input) to coexist on the same machine.

In bringing up the Laboratory module, which meant automating the laboratory at the German Heart Institute for the first time, they were able to invite two people from the VA in San Francisco to help. Those two weeks made a tremendous difference. To train the institute's developers in FileMan, Greg Kreis (http://pioneerdatasys.com/home.html) came to Berlin to conduct two one-week training sessions.

The current VistA technical infrastructure in place at the German Heart Institute includes:

- **Servers**
  - ○ Database running on redundant HP Alpha servers.
  - ○ Applications also running on redundant HP Alpha.
  - ○ 26 Windows NT, 24 UNIX, and 1 Macintosh server.
  - ○ All servers also running True64 UNIX and Cache.
- **Clients**
  - ○ 600 PCs running Microsoft Windows.
  - ○ 135 SUN UNIX OS workstations.
  - ○ 15 Apple Macintosh computer workstations.
  - ○ Some ASCII terminals.
- **Network**
  - ○ ATM-Backbone, Gigabit and Fast-Ethernet.
- **IT Staff** 16 full-time employees.

Marcus Werner devoted many days of work in San Francisco and at home to helping the VA implement the multi-language capabilities found in the most recent versions of VA FileMan. Figure 9-9 is a screen shot of a local application they have developed with a graphical user interface.

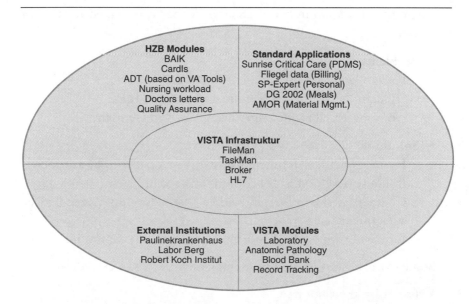

FIGURE 9-8 VistA Modules Implemented by the German Heart Institute

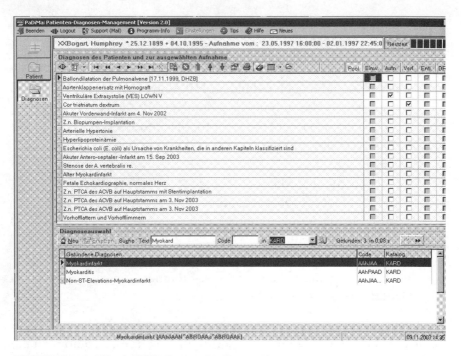

FIGURE 9-9 VistA GUI Screen in German

There have been a number of issues over the years related to support for VistA.

- **Problems**
  - Foreign language environment is weak.
  - Different healthcare regulations and business rules.
  - No commercial vendor supporting VistA in Germany.

- **Solutions**
  - Internationalization functionality in VistA needs to be enhanced.
  - In-house development of applications not in VistA.
  - Contacts with the VA and other VistA developers need to be strengthened.
  - Increased support for VistA by the open source community.

Some of the lessons learned from implementing VistA include:

- Free software is not free.
- You need more in-house IT capacity and support.

- IT management must bridge the gap between users and developers/administrators.
- You have to challenge conventional wisdom.
- Buying is better than making.
- Software from different sources can be integrated by just using standards.
- If you cannot pay a competitive salary for your IT professionals, job-satisfaction becomes an issue.

Despite the many challenges, the institute continues to use VistA, and its plans for the future include possibly implementing the complete Blood Bank, Radiology, Order Entry, Clinical Imaging, and other VistA software modules.

Finland and VistA

Introduction

The family of Finnish-made software applications packages, called MUSTI is one of the most important hospital information software systems in use in Finland. MUSTI is a VA Kernel and FileMan based hospital applications portfolio developed in the mid-1980s for deployment in Finland. By 1996, MUSTI information systems were installed in almost two-thirds of the hospitals in Finland. In the mid-1990s, a concerted effort began to redesign and significantly enhance the system. The MUSTI modernization effort and FixIT projects (Delphi-FixIT, Web-FixIT, Component-FixIT) have resulted in a stepwise migration path from terminal-based to Windows-based to browser-based component systems. The overall objective of the MUSTI modernization effort of developing technological solutions for gradually migrating from existing M-based departmental information systems toward systems that fit the requirements of the early 21st–century appear to be materializing in the Component-FixIT project.

Background

Finland installed its first system using the "M" programming language and operating system in 1978. Also in the late 1970s, Finland acquired and implemented the Costar health information system written in the "M" programming language and tailored it to meet Finland's needs, referring to the system as FINSTAR. The University of Kuopio Computing Centre played a key role in introducing the "M" and VA FileMan technologies into Finland.

The VA FileMan database management system was first installed in Finland at the Helsinki University Central Hospital (HUCH) in October 1981. During the 1982–1984 timeframe, HUCH installed the VA Kernel, MailMan, Patient Administration, and Laboratory software modules. In 1983, the MUSTI project was born, which was aimed at further developing and deploying VistA and other integrated software modules to other major university and public hospitals throughout Finland.

By 1985, selected VistA applications were in use at three university hospitals as well as several district hospitals. A number of additional FileMan-based applications that met the unique needs of Finland had also been developed, such as Library, Accounting, and Disease Registries. They also built an electronic data interface, called MUSTAR, which interfaced the FileMan-based systems with FINSTAR.

It was clear that the user interface and system architecture had become outdated by the late 1980s. In the early 1990s, the teaching hospitals set up a joint company to begin the process of completely replacing the core architecture and applications of their system. The MUSTI modernization project officially started in 1995 and consisted of one vendor, three hospitals, and the University of Kuopio Computing Centre. "M" technology and non-M alternatives were studied in 1995 and 1996. The VA FileMan database was found to be worth retaining. Non-M technologies were identified to be used on the client side of the new client-server architecture. When the VistA Broker was released, it was accepted as the tool to provide client-to-server linkage. Finland developed and began using the 16-bit Delphi-FixIT toolkit in 1996 and 1997. The 32-bit version was released in January 1998. Half a dozen applications were quickly developed by staff at the University of Kuopio using FixIT.

A research and development project was initiated in 1998 to further modernize MUSTI by developing a Web-FixIT toolkit. This multi-year project was funded by the National Technology Agency and consisted of a consortium of four vendors and three university hospitals.

Web-FixIT is based on the Java language and was designed to be used in producing browser-based user interfaces to the MUSTI hospital information system and departmental applications. It was tested on a small–scale in 1999 and was scheduled for initial release in January 2000.

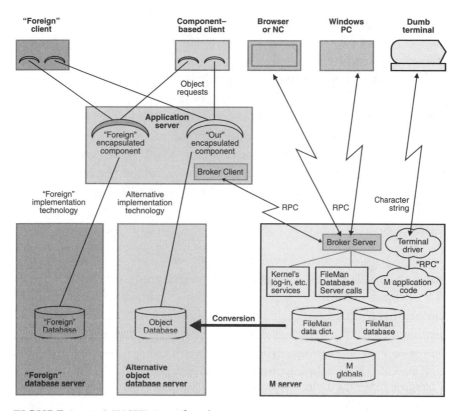

FIGURE 9-10 MUSTI Interfaced to VistA

One of the results of this highly successful project was the development of a plan for the next phase of the migration path, where the core functionality of the information systems will be encapsulated into business components, and a foundation laid for the application of alternative database management systems. Funding for this long-range Component-FixIT project for 2001 was granted by the National Technology Agency, TEKES. (http://www.uku.fi/tike/fixit/comp/english.html)

Current System

As of FY 2000, the MUSTI health information systems and the FixIT toolkit were deployed and in use at more than 30 major public hospitals in Finland. The system uses a variety of applications from a half dozen different vendors. Finland had successfully developed and deployed a comprehensive electronic health record (EHR) system that was tailored to fit the requirements for everyday use of the healthcare delivery system. The system continues to evolve.

The Kuopio Computing Centre continues to receive new versions of VistA software through the VA's Freedom of Information Act (FOIA) office and is in charge of translating FileMan and the VA Kernel to fit Finnish requirements. The centre also provides technical support to the various software houses in Finland using these products. Many small corrections and modifications proposed by the Finns over the years have been incorporated into new versions of the VA Kernel, FileMan, and MailMan.

Future Plans

In 2000, the Component-FixIT project was born. This new project received funding in 2001 from the National Technology Agency of Finland, TEKES. The project was further supported by the collaborative consortium of numerous software vendors and university hospitals in Finland participating in this project. The goal was to develop and test a platform-independent framework architecture and migration strategy looking toward the year 2005 and beyond. New solutions were to be sought with a focus on standards, interoperability, reusable distributed objects, and business components.

During the first phase of the project, toolkits are being developed to encapsulate existing MUSTI departmental systems' functionality to an applications server as business components, the interfaces of which will be used in composing clients. Component-based core applications and other "foreign" applications based on other technologies will be able to use FileMan-based components and vice versa.

Key Web Sites

MUSTI: http://neuro-www2.mgh.harvard.edu/PDF_Repository/
   MYKKANEN.PDF

MINPHIS: http://www.egov4dev.org/minphis.htm

VistA System: http://www.va.gov/cprsdemo
WorldVistA: http://www.worldvista.org

FixIT

Using the Windows-based Delphi-FixIT and the browser-based Web-FixIT toolkits, different parallel user interfaces can be developed to "M" or VistA FileMan-based applications in a stepwise manner, according to which type of a user interface is needed in which situation. The toolkits and their documentation are available as a commercial package localized to Finnish requirements and as freeware in English. Free support is available only through the Hardhats user community.

In the next phase, the ability to convert FileMan-based components to an alternative database technology internally is being sought, without having to make modifications in the user or software interfaces. One of the objectives is to also allow for the internal implementation of business components based on either FileMan or on an Object DBMS in 2005 or later.

Conclusion

The MUSTI modernization effort and FixIT projects (Delphi-FixIT, Web FixIT, Component FixIT) have resulted in a stepwise migration path from terminal-based to Windows-based to browser-based component systems. The overall objective of the MUSTI modernization effort of developing technological solutions for gradually migrating from existing M-based departmental information systems toward systems that fit the requirements of the early 21st–century appear to be materializing in the Component-FixIT project.

In addition, the establishment of collaborative international relations related to the further development of health IT systems and the internationalization of the FixIT toolkit succeeded far beyond expectations. Staff associated with the MUSTI modernization effort have been working with developers in the United States, Brazil, Nigeria, and other countries with some degree of success.

Nigeria and VistA

Introduction

The important role of information technology in Africa's development has recently been recognized by several international agencies, including the

United Nations, World Bank, USAID, and International Development Research Centre. Health care is one of the highest-priority areas where IT should be applied for public health benefits (Mandil, et al., 1993). However, appropriate off-the-shelf software packages for African hospitals and health centers cannot generally be found; they must be developed locally. There is one significant exception, the Made-in-Nigeria Primary Healthcare and Hospital Information System (MINPHIS) (http://minphis.4t.com/).

MINPHIS was developed as part of a joint research and development project by Nigeria and Finland on health informatics. The MINPHIS hospital information system has now been deployed in approximately eight teaching hospitals in Nigeria, is used to keep electronic patient records, and generates various reports for health management and research purposes. The system easily scales up or down in size to meet the needs of different types of healthcare facilities. It is very affordable and has been found to be a productive and efficient tool that opens up the path to more effective and higher quality of care over time. The system is based on free or open source software developed and used by the governments of Finland and the United States. Variations of these systems are being used by public and private healthcare institutions around the world. MINPHIS may prove to be of great interest to other countries across Africa that wish to acquire and implement a healthcare information system for their own use.

Background

Established in 1962, Obafemi Awolowo University (OAU) in Ife-Ife is one of the largest universities in Nigeria with approximately 20,000 students and 5,000 faculty and staff. OAU Teaching Hospital Complex consists of two hospitals (342 and 212 beds), two urban and one rural health center, a dental hospital, and schools including nursing and laboratory technology.

In 1987, initial contact between the OAU Teaching Hospital Complex and the University of Kuopio in Finland led to the creation of a joint research and development project on health informatics in Nigeria called the Ife Project. It was formally launched in 1989. The project partners jointly produced a rudimentary Hospital Information System in late 1989, using the public domain Admission/Discharge/Transfer (ADT) software module of the U.S. Department of Veterans Affairs (VA) VistA system. It also makes use of the VA Kernel, FileMan, and MailMan software modules, which are all written in the "M" programming language.

The software technology is the same as that deployed in the MUSTI systems deployed in most hospitals in Finland.

This computerized system for storing and reporting patient record data has been under operation and refinement in the Obafemi Awolowo University Teaching Hospital since 1991. Its use was expanded to the second OAU hospital in 1995.

Another proposal for continued Finnish–Nigerian collaboration on the system was approved by the Academy of Finland and funded for two more years in 1997. This new research project started January 1998.

Basic infrastructure improvements were made, followed by new systems development work on MINPHIS. In May 1999, an application to extend the project into 2000–2001 was submitted to the Academy of Finland.

The system was originally installed in 1991 on a PC server with three dumb terminals. The second generation of the system implemented in 1998 was based on more powerful servers running Microsoft NT, InterSystems Cache, the VA Kernel and FileMan, and the FixIT software developed in Finland for the MUSTI system. It was upgraded and enhanced for potential national use.

Current System

The MINPHIS application keeps patient records and generates various reports for health management and research purposes. The reports include the patient status, medical history, and admissions as well as indicators such as length of stay per patient, discharge summaries, mortality and morbidity data, and operations. The application can answer ad hoc queries from medical researchers (e.g., cases of cholera for a period per geographical location for specific age group or sex or both). It can also provide performance information relevant to particular healthcare professionals, such as the mortality rates for patients treated by a particular staff member. Such information can be used for self-appraisal by medical staff, or for formal appraisal by hospital managers. As of July 2005, there were eight teaching hospitals using MINPHIS in Nigeria.

Benefits

The system has helped to improve the quality of patient data, which, in turn, has been used through reporting to improve the quality of decision making. This should have helped in planning, for example to understand which disease categories are priorities for attention, or to understand the availability and requirements for particular drugs. It should help in research, for example to identify trends in patient health and care. It has also been used in resource management decisions, by improving the understanding of indicators such as the number of consultations per day handled by medical professionals, the number of patients per ward, the number of professionals who fail to write discharge summaries for their patients, and so on. The availability of such performance information should also help focus the minds of health professionals on their clinical performance.

Conclusions

The system easily scales up or down in size to meet the needs of different types of healthcare facilities. It is very affordable and has been found to be a productive and efficient tool that opens up the path to more effective and higher-quality care over time.

There have been two evaluations of the system, first in the 1990s and then more recently. The first evaluation found that MINPHIS was useful

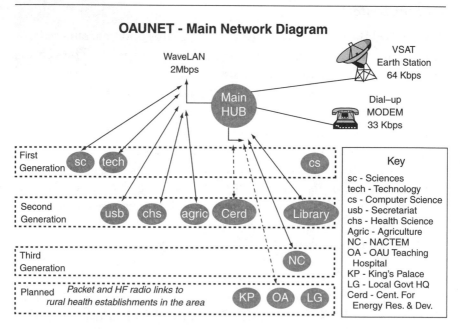

FIGURE 9-11 OAUNet in Nigeria: Main Network Diagram

Key Web Sites

Obafemi Awolowo University: http://www.oauife.edu.ng/

MINPHIS:

- http://minphis.4t.com/
- http://www.egov4dev.org/minphis.htm
- http://www.uku.fi/tike/indehela/Nig2004report.htm

MUSTI:
http://neuro-www2.mgh.harvard.edu/PDF_Repository/MYKKANEN.PDF

but should be expanded to give more clinical benefits. The second evaluation reported that MINPHIS was underutilized and was more like a "status symbol" at the hospital. It should therefore be categorized as a partial success and a partial failure. The MINPHIS package is now on the market.

A multidisciplinary Health Informatics Group gradually emerged in Ife-Ife, and it is currently the strongest research and development center in health informatics in sub-Saharan Africa, excluding South Africa. It will be interesting to observe the potential collaboration by Nigeria with other nations on the development and implementation of EHR systems in Africa.

Future Plans

MINPHIS v.2.0 is now available. The intention is to continue to extend the system to become a more comprehensive electronic health record (EHR) solution that can be deployed across the three tiers of the Nigerian healthcare system.

Conclusion

In conclusion, as the profiles in this chapter have clearly shown, VistA can be successfully implemented in a wide range of public and private sector healthcare organizations, from large hospital chains to stand–alone outpatient clinics and nursing homes anywhere in the world. It has demonstrated its ability to support the delivery of quality healthcare with low rates of medical errors and high patient satisfaction within the Veterans

Health Administration, Indian Health Service, and other organizations in the United State and around the world.

Healthcare organizations that do not investigate the VistA option as one of the choices when selecting a comprehensive health information system may end up paying higher costs with less favorable results. In this capital-constrained environment, being able to reduce the costs of licensing software is significant.

VistA has been backed, and will continue to be backed, by a huge investment from the U.S. government. Steps are being taken by the government (e.g., HHS, VA, CMS) to more closely collaborate with the private sector in supporting EHRs for everyone as part of a national health informatics infrastructure that can support nearly error-free care and quality. There is a rapidly growing private sector market available to support any healthcare organization seeking to evaluate and implement VistA to better serve patients and realize quality through EHRs, collaboration, innovation, and clinically focused health information technology systems.

CHAPTER 10

Profiles of Leading Open Solutions EHRs

". . . Given the huge increase in personal computer and Internet use, as well as the dramatic changes in other industries, most consumers assume that health care is highly electronic and computerized. The reality, however, is that 90 percent of the business of health care remains paper-based. Why? . . . Because health care (in the U.S.) is a trillion-dollar cottage industry!"

—*Rx 2000 Institute*

Introduction

Scans of key Free and Open Source Software (FOSS) Web sites including SourceForge.net and LinuxMedNews.com list more than 300 international open source collaborative software development initiatives in health care. The 2005 AMIA Annual Meeting paper "A Study of Clinically Related Open Source Software Projects" identified 179 clinically oriented FOSS efforts. More than 20 electronic health record (EHR) solutions are included in these numbers and were briefly described in Chapter 5. In addition, the previous chapter focused on the public domain VA VistA and the Computerized Patient Record Systems (CPRS), which have been successfully implemented in a number of large-scale healthcare provider organizations.

This chapter provides more detailed profiles on a small selection of the many other collaborative FOSS EHR solutions that are available. Many of these have been successfully implemented in small to mid-size health-care organizations and medical practices around the world. The VistA

Office–EHR initiative is not discussed here because details on that collaborative public–private sectors effort were presented in Chapter 6.

AMPATH Medical Record Systems (AMRS)

Introduction

The Academic Model for the Prevention and Treatment of HIV (AMPATH) is one of Kenya's most comprehensive initiatives to combat HIV. AMPATH is a working model of urban and rural HIV preventive and treatment services in the public sector. AMPATH cares for more than 17,000 HIV-infected adults and children, with nearly one-half of all patients on anti-retroviral drugs, and enrollment in the program is increasing by 800 to 1,000 patients per month. AMPATH demonstrates the power of U.S. and African academic medical centers united by common vision.

The AMPATH Medical Record Systems (AMRS) initiative is an international open source project that has built a scalable, flexible, electronic medical record (EMR) system based on open standards. It is a collaborative effort involving the Regenstrief Institute, the Indiana University School of Medicine, Moi University in Kenya, Columbia University, and Partners in Health (Boston, MA). AMRS was created as an EMR initially focused on supporting the IU-Kenya Program's project to target the prevention and treatment of HIV/AIDS in Kenya.

FIGURE 10-1 AMPATH/AMRS Patient Registration Screen

Functional Overview

The AMPATH Medical Record System (AMRS) is one of sub-Saharan Africa's first outpatient electronic medical record systems. AMRS is an important tool that will enable leaders of care to establish the best protocols for managing HIV/AIDS in resource-constrained environments and help establish guidelines for treatment that are specific to Kenya and similar developing countries. AMRS is used to identify patients who fail to keep appointments, to enable follow-up tracking, and to monitor the outcomes of care. It also provides summary data and computer-generated reminders to help guide care. Various standard reports are built into the system that are required by the Ministry of Health (e.g., immunizations, distribution of visits by clinic, and an activity report). Additional custom reports can be created at the request of a program's director.

AMRS has been used to register and track the care of all AMPATH patients since November 2001. It was initially implemented as an electronic medical record system in a rural Kenyan health center and was known as the Mosoriot Medical Record System (MMRS). The system was originally designed to exist on a single microcomputer run by the same clerk who had been responsible for check-in and check-out under the paper-based system. It used an MS Access database to capture patient data. As use of the system grew, it was redesigned by connecting a second computer to the original, host computer using a crossover cable between their network ports. A printer and zip drive were also included in the configuration.

By 2003, the productivity and vision of AMPATH had drawn the attention of the WHO, USAID, the Gates Foundation, and other international agencies. The initial two clinics had grown to eight different sites, and plans were in place to grow further; the patient load increased and so did the demands on the database. This led to some major enhancements to the original system.

Technical Overview

At the heart of the AMRS lies the data model. The structure of the data model dictates the scalability and flexibility of a system. The AMRS data model was redesigned using knowledge and experience gleaned from work with the Regenstrief Medical Records System. A useful open source tool, DBDesigner (www.fabforce.net), was used to build and manipulate the new data model. The data model was further enhanced by collaborating with colleagues from Partners in Health, who had been doing similar work with TB and HIV in Haiti and Peru.

The data model was implemented in MySQL (www.mysql.com) and used Plone (www.plone.org) to quickly create a Web interface from which to edit the dictionary. For increased security, all Plone content is served through Apache's Web server (www.apache.org). The system can run on either Windows or Linux platforms. The Plone portal provides out-of-the-box user authentication, session management, centralized documentation, file sharing, group announcements, and a convenient template-based site design. The system primarily used open source and freely available tools to build its database and the data entry tool.

To ensure sustainability and continued operation of the system, it has been provided with multiple backup systems:

- An uninterruptible power supply (UPS) battery
- A solar-powered system
- A gasoline-powered generator
- A paper backup system

They established redundant steps to assure data security and confidentiality:

- All accesses to the AMRS are password protected.
- Access to data for various users is limited to only those aspects of the AMRS for which they are responsible.
- Twice a day, the AMRS automatically backs up its entire database to a zip disk.
- At the end of the day when the AMRS computer is shut down, the entire database is again backed up onto a zip disk. The backup zip disk is taken home every night by the clinic program's matron (i.e., head nurse).
- Once a week, the AMRS's system administrator receives a copy of the entire database on a zip disk and places it on his own computer.

Findings

Benefits reported to date from using the system include the following:

- Patients spent substantially less time waiting, and their total time per visit to the program's clinic was marginally shorter after implementation of the system.

- Healthcare providers (nurses and clinical officers) also spent less time with patients and other staff and had substantially more time for personal activities.
- For healthcare providers, the AMRS also saved time, creating a resource that the managers of the HIV clinic could harness for additional activities (e.g., patient education).
- Clerks spent additional time registering patients but less time writing reports and interacting with other staff. For them, the MMRS was largely time-neutral for everyday tasks, although it was remarkably time-saving in terms of producing monthly reports for the Kenyan Ministry of Health.

Bottom line: AMRS is a simple, inexpensive, and effective electronic medical record system that can be established and work in a resource-poor, developing country.

The AMPATH project currently supports 11 clinic sites in western Kenya. The system was developed and maintained mostly by Kenyans—faculty and technicians.

See http://www.regenstrief.org/intranet/Regenstrief/medinformatics/amrs/ or http://openmrs.org/wiki/Main_Page.

Open Source Clinical Applications and Resources (OSCAR)

Introduction

OSCAR is an open source software, Web-based electronic patient record system for delivery of evidence resources at the point of care. The software was the brainchild of Dr. David Chan of the Department of Family Medicine at McMaster University in Hamilton, Ontario, Canada. The system has been deployed at several Canadian community health centers, and the Vancouver Coastal Health Authority is financially supporting the project.

Functionality Overview

OSCAR is available under the GNU Public License (GPL). Version 2.0 was released in June 2004 with the following features included:

- Appointment Scheduling; Billing; Referral; Secure Messaging

- Electronic Patient Record: Cumulative Patient Profile Encounter Record—free text, templates, and digital signature forms; three design modes—flat file, XML, or HTML clinical resource database, electronic document management
- Decision Support Tools: Evidence-based Antenatal Planner, Evidence-based Assessment Records for Long-Term Care, Link with Web search engines
- Support for both MySQL and PostgreSQL
- New prescription module based on Drugref (http://Drugref.org)
- Support for internationalization (currently only English and Portuguese)

Implementations and Current Status

According to the OSCAR Web site, the system was first installed in 2001 by two healthcare organizations in Ontario, Canada. The Maternity Center of Hamilton, which consists of ten doctors, installed the system in October 2001. The Joint PCN On-Call Group, also in Ontario, began implementing the system in December 2001. Their practice consists of 15 doctors and residents.

In 2002, they reported that OSCAR was installed at a number of other sites including:

- Ontario Nursing Home
- Stonechurch Family Health Centre
- McMaster Family Practice
- Obstetrics/gynecology specialist offices in Milton and Mississauga
- General practice offices in Grimsby, Miltoon, Mississauga, and Hamilton

In 2003–2005, OSCAR was installed at additional sites including:

- An eight-doctor clinic in Vancouver, November 2003
- A four-doctor office in Pemberton, March 2004
- A four-doctor office in Vancouver, October 2004
- A two-doctor office in Abbotsford, British Columbia, 2005
- A four-doctor office in Scarborough, Ontario, July 2005
- A nine-doctor teaching clinic, Kitchener, Ontario, August 2005

OSCAR has already become a major open source success story in Canada and may soon spread beyond that country's borders. For more details on OSCAR, visit http://oscarservice.com/index1.html.

OpenEMR

Introduction

OpenEMR is a modular, HIPAA compliant, open source, cross-platform EMR system developed by Synitech Incorporated (www.synitech.com). Thanks to the global efforts of physicians and developers, OpenEMR is claimed now to be the most widely distributed EMR system for small practices in the world. See http://sourceforge.net/projects/openemr/ and www.openemr.net.

Functional Overview

Automated patient-record journaling has been successfully integrated with third-party technologies including speech recognition, secure wireless access, touch-screen portables, and biometric authentication. Open EMR is based on widely used public standards and is available under the GPL. Features include:

- Appointment scheduling
- Patient registration
- Laboratory and ancillary tracking
- Online record of patient encounters
- Ability to enter CPT and ICD codes at the end of a patient encounter
- Advanced reporting capabilities with phpMyAdmin packaged with OpenEMR
- Prescription-writing capability with ability to e–mail or print prescriptions
- HL7 support to parse HL7 messages
- ANSI X12 support allowing clinics to send billing claims electronically to payers
- Support for two clearinghouses, ProxyMed and Zirmed
- HIPAA compliance
- Billing interface with printable daily/weekly/monthly billing summaries
- Includes a database of 19,000 ICD-9-CM codes

A new, self-installing version of OpenEMR 2.7.1 for Mandrake Linux is available for download. Mandrake Linux is a popular and user-friendly Linux operating system that can be found at www.Mandrakesoft.com.

Current Implementations

OpenEMR was implemented by CT NeuroCare in Wallingford, Connecticut. The company chose to utilize a central server with smart, NETion thin clients. NETions are embedded Linux machines with Mozilla browsers. Linux is run on a 64-bit Xeon Dell 2850 server. The server has 2GB of RAM, 300GB of RAID-5 SCSI disks, and dual-gigabit NICs (network interface controllers). Reportedly, the results have been excellent, and the simplicity of OpenEMR and the thin clients have improved worker productivity.

Medical billing companies in New York and Florida chose OpenEMR to enhance the services they offer their clients. These two companies host OpenEMR and maintain a secure environment for their outpatient clinic clients' medical records and billing information. These services free their clients from the maintenance of hardware, operating systems, and medical software. The clinics using OpenEMR from these medical billing companies are able to access their records from any desktop or laptop computer running Windows, Macintosh, or Linux operating systems. Each medical clinic client is provided a dedicated Web and IP address for a secure, private server.

In January 2005, Pennington Firm, LLC, began training and customization of OpenEMR with a Texas-based consulting company that specialized in implementing and maintaining WebMD's Medical Manager software. This Texas consulting company, in conjunction with several medical clinic clients, selected OpenEMR as a replacement for Medical Manager. Advantages of using OpenEMR include its numerous practice management and EMR features, the lack of licensing and user fees, the ability to integrate OpenEMR with other applications, and the ability to install OpenEMR on Windows, Linux, UNIX, or Macintosh OS X systems.

OpenEMR is also the choice one Ocala, Florida, family physician made when he opened his two-doctor family medicine group. According to the physician, it was an easy decision to make because the commercial EHR systems he had looked at cost $10,000 to $25,000 per physician, including annual support costs ranging from $3,000 to $5,000. By comparison, OpenEMR wound up costing $2,500 in implementation, training, and software-modification costs.

A number of physicians and staff in North Carolina and California are also improving care and administrative processes with OpenEMR.

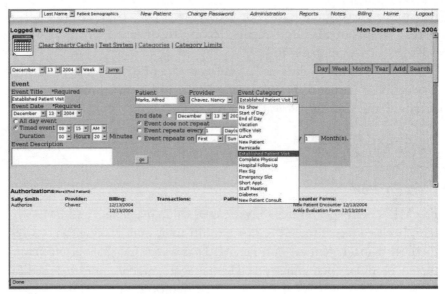

A

B

FIGURE 10-2 OpenEMR—Screenshot of Scheduling Module

According to Dr. Bowen in North Carolina, "We have already let go of three transcriptionists ($40,000 annually). Our paper and toner costs have dropped about 40%. Our filing is all caught up and "the chart hunt" has improved by about 95%. The staff were immediately impressed with the improved communication in the office. I have been printing office notes for our urgent care patients, letting them take a printed note to their primary care physician."

Finally, e-Health Solutions has tailored OpenEMR for use in Australia and New Zealand (http://www.e-health-solutions.com/). For more details, about OpenEMR visit www.openemr.net.

FreeMED

Introduction

FreeMED is an open source software medical management and EMR system, licensed under the GPL. It is a multi-user, multitasking, Web-based medical management system. FreeMED is a mature, six-year-old, completely modular open source practice management, computerized medical record, and billing system that has been deployed in the United States, Europe, and South America. FreeMED was developed by physicians for physicians and is designed to run a doctor's office or clinic.

Functional Overview

The FreeMED product is maintained and funded by the FreeMED Software Foundation. Some of its many features include:

- Fully customizable electronic medical record
- Modular, extensible setup means you only work with the portions of the medical record you need
- Resource-based calendaring and scheduling for multiple providers and facilities
- Integrates well with Dragon Naturally Speaking and other voice dictation systems
- Works on any machine with a Web browser
- Integrated document management
- "Episode of care" outcomes-management software
- Full internal messaging solution with time-delayed notifications
- REMITT for medical billing

For more information about FreeMED visit http://freemedsoftware. com/ and http://freemedsoftware.org/.

CHLCare

Introduction

CHLCare is an open source Web-based EMR and clinic management software system, originally developed for use by the Primary Care Coalition of Montgomery County in Maryland and its safety-net care providers who service the uninsured and underinsured residents of the county.

This Web-based EMR allows the clinics to collect and store information on the clients they serve using an application and database that is reliable, secure, and HIPAA compliant. At the patient's request, the clinics may share patient information with each other, thereby reducing the time spent collecting demographic data and basic medical information, while improving patient care.

It is licensed under the GPL, and the Primary Care Coalition plans to make the source code freely available to other organizations with similar needs.

Functional Overview

CHLCare tracks and displays:

- Patient demographic information
- Registration/enrollment history and status
- Encounter history with associated data fields including date, place, reason, outcome/diagnosis, laboratory results, prescriptions, and other vital information
- Immunizations, allergies, and medications
- Referrals
- Encounter-based notes authored by care providers during each visit
- Specific screening information, or information tied to specific grants or recommendations
- Screening and chronic illness protocols
- Charges and payments

For more details, about CHLCare visit http://SourceForge.net/ projects/chlcare and http://www.q-industries.com/services_software_ chlcareopensourceemr.php.

CottageMed

CottageMed is an open source electronic medical record (EMR) cross-platform system designed by practicing physicians that can be modified to fit specific needs. It was developed by Caring in Community, a nonprofit medical practice that produces this free and open source EMR using Filemaker technology. The developers report that it has been implemented and is being used by physicians in the United States and a number of developing nations.

Functional Overview

The latest version of CottageMed released in 2005 includes a simple and easy-to-use EMR system with the following features:

- Scalable to small- or medium-size physician offices
- Industrial strength security and flexibility
- Voice dictation for all notes
- Clinical photographs for any visit
- Advanced filing features and signature tracking
- Patient images, patient-held records, pediatric growth charts
- Practice statistics with powerful search functions for epidemiology and health maintenance studies
- Patient registration, appointments, records, and scripts
- Supports an appointment timer, semi-automatic receipting of Medclaims
- Open and industry-standard database format
- Wireless networking and PalmOS/PocketPC support
- Quick location of earliest appointment with Apple's iCal
- Versatile printer and fax control
- Point-and-click note writing for rapid entry of examination
- Custom medication lists, multiple-user customizable templates
- Macintosh, PC, and Linux platforms are supported

For more detail about CottageMed, visit http://mtdata.com/~drred/webpage.html.

PhoenixPM

PhoenixPM is a project of the Alliance for Rural Community Health (ARCH). PhoenixPM is funded by a one-year grant from the Community Clinics Initiative established by the Tides Foundation and the California Endowment.

The PhoenixPM project involves the development and deployment of a modern open source practice management software solution for use in a typical California Federally Qualified Health Center (FQHC), a type of safety-net clinic. As an open source solution, the new software will be available for download by any clinic at no charge. This collaborative project began in February 2004. The project includes the following four PhoenixPM project members located in Mendocino County, California: Anderson Valley Health Center, Boonville; Long Valley Health Center, Laytonville; Mendocino Coast Clinics, Fort Bragg; and Potter Valley Community Health Center, Potter Valley.

The plan calls for their open source software solution to be released to the public in 2006. For more detail about the PhoenixPM system, visit http://www.phoenixpm.org/ and http://www.ruralcommunityhealth.org/projects/phoenix.html.

"tkFP"

Introduction

"tkFP" is an open source software EMR suitable for solo or small-group physician offices for storing clinical information on patients and other functions needed to run a small medical practice. It is an open source Linux-based medical records solution functioning reliably to store patient office notes, demographics, and prescription information. Visit http://tkfp. SourceForge.net/.

> The idea of "tkFP" is to have everything the provider needs during the encounter directly at hand, from registering the patient, reading and writing progress notes, checking medications, writing and transmitting prescriptions, looking up information on medical questions, making referrals, and finally generating the bill and/or insurance claim, ready for transmission or printing, on the spot. The discovery we have made is that that physician can do most of the things him or herself that most offices currently hire a large number of ancillary staff to perform and gain very little or no increase in efficiency, but incur a great deal of expense.—*R. Jenkins and K. Broman, M.D.*

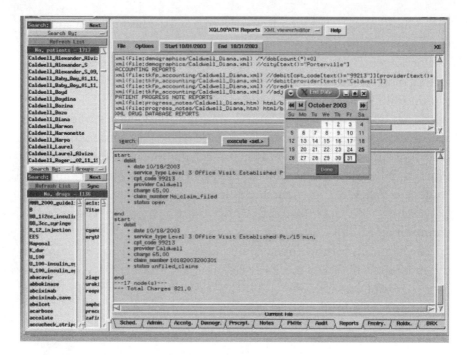

FIGURE 10-3 Screenshot: Reporting System Based on XML and XPATH Queries

Functional Overview

Modules include:

- System/User Administration
- Scheduling
- Patient Demographics and Insurance
- Accounting/Billing (paper and electronic claims)
- Prescription Management and Drug Database
- Laboratory Reports
- Progress Notes—Templates
- E and M Coding Helper
- Scanned Data
- Past Medical History—Problem List
- Medical Record export to Netscape, e–mail, fax, etc.
- Report Generation Using XPATH
- Expenses—Checkbook Ledger

- Rolodex—Referral Letters
- Secure Tclhttpd Web Server, SSL Enabled
- HtDig Search Engine
- Audit Trail

Implementation and Current Status

It is currently running in two separate dual-physician family practice medical offices in California and Iowa.

Author's Note: I put this system in the book because of the story told by Rebecca Jenkins and Katherine Broman about how they came to choose this open source solution and the trials and tribulations in their lives as they raised their families and worked to keep their small practice alive. Check out their remarkable story at http://tkfp.sourceforge.net/broman_jenkins/.

Conclusions

To conclude, many other EHR systems previously mentioned in Chapter 5 were not included here. The following is a list of some of the other Open Source Software EHR systems also worth reviewing:

- BHPC Electronic Medical Record Project: http://bphc.hrsa.gov/chc/CHCInitiatives/emr.htm
- Canada Health InfoWay: http://www.canadahealthinfoway.ca/home.php?lang=en
- Central Valley Health Network EMR Project: http://bphc.hrsa.gov/chc/CVHNinfo.htm
- Care2X: http://www.care2x.com
- GnuMed: http://www.gnumed.org/
- Michigan Electronic Medical Record Initiative (MEMRI): http://www.memri.us/home.html
- MirrorMed: http://www.mirrormed.org/
- Open Source EHR—AAFP & MedPlexus: http://www.aafp.org/x19365.xml
- Pacific HUI OpenVista: http://www.pacifichui.org/OpenVista/
- Open Source Health Record (xChart): http://www.openhealth.org/index.htm
- OpenEHR: http://www.openehr.org/

- The Medical Record (TMR): http://dmi-www.mc.duke.edu/dukemi/research/research.html
- SQL Clinic: http://www.sqlclinic.net/
- VistA Office EHR: http://www.vista-office.org/

The key point is that there are a number of high-quality open source EHR systems now available in the marketplace that have been successfully implemented in a wide range of facilities around the world. Any healthcare organization looking to acquire an EHR system should now consider open source alternatives in addition to the many other commercially available options.

Toolkit for Medical Informatics Excellence & Quality Improvement

"Less than a third of the nation's hospital emergency and outpatient departments use electronic medical records, and even fewer doctors' offices do."

Use of Computerized Clinical Support Systems in Medical Settings: United States, 2001–2003, March 15, 2005.

Section Overview: The Medical Informatics 20/20 model emphasizes the COSI strategies of Collaboration, Open Solutions, and Innovation. This section delivers in-depth knowledge on two key universal strategies: Collaboration and Innovation. Through detailed discussion and case studies this section reviews key tactics useful to healthcare organizations seeking to achieve operational and clinical improvements to reduce errors and realize quality.

Chapter 11, Universal Strategies and Tactics for Quality and Performance Excellence, discusses the universal strategies of Collaboration and Innovation within the Medical Informatics 2020 model. It takes a detailed look at six tactics within these strategies that are essential for performance excellence. The tactics that are examined are Open Collaboration and Leadership; Breakthrough, Distinctive, and Collaboration Innovation; LEAN Six Sigma—Process Improvement; Knowledge Management; Clinical Decision Support; and Business Intelligence.

Chapter 12, Case Studies in Collaboration and Innovation for Quality, features a series of case studies that highlight key strategies and tactics such as vision, leadership engagement, Six Sigma, knowledge transfer, and distinctive innovation that support organizational performance. Air Force Medical Services and Ascension Health Exchange highlight innovation acceleration and knowledge transfer while QualityFirst from Bon Secours Health System illustrates how Six Sigma process improvement and knowledge transfer can support healthcare transformation for quality. The Micromedex Infobutton case explores clinical decision support at the point of care. The role of collaboration and knowledge transfer across organizations is explored in the Institute for Healthcare Improvement, MedQic, and the eHealth Initiative case studies.

Chapter 13, Value Measurement and Return on Investment, provides knowledge on conducting return on investment (ROI), return on quality, and cost-benefit analyses of the various commercial off-the-shelf or Open Solutions health information technology implementation and use within an organization. Various tools and methodologies are presented along with benefit findings by healthcare provider organizations that have already implemented EHR systems.

Universal Strategies and Tactics for Quality and Performance Excellence

There is timing in everything.
Timing in strategy cannot be mastered without a great deal of practice.
This is the Way for those who want to learn my strategy:

1. Do not think dishonestly.
2. The Way is in training.
3. Become acquainted with every art.
4. Know the Ways of all professions.
5. Distinguish between gain and loss in worldly matters.
6. Develop intuitive judgment and understanding for everything.
7. Perceive those things which cannot be seen.
8. Pay attention even to trifles.
9. Do nothing which is of no use.

Miyamoto Musashi, *A Book of Five Rings—*
The Classic Guide to Strategy

Perspectives on Strategy, Openness, and Knowledge

Wisdom of the ages applies today in health care just as it did to Miyamoto Musashi, one of Japan's most renowned warriors, over 400 years ago. The context of life was different then, but the way to address the challenges for survival and prosperity holds relevance today. As we examine key aspects of the collaboration and innovation strategies necessary to the deployment of medical informatics technology, the lessons of leadership, learning and training, understanding processes "that cannot be seen," judgment, and focus on efficient execution and openness will be apparent in the strategies and tactics that are explored.

> **Information is data endowed with relevance and purpose. Converting data into information thus requires knowledge.**
>
> *Peter Drucker*

> **The productivity of knowledge and knowledge workers will not be the only competitive factor in the world economy. It is, however, likely to become the decisive factor, at least for most industries in the developed countries.**
>
> *Peter Drucker*

> **Open Source Everywhere: Software is just the beginning . . . open source is doing for mass innovation what the assembly line did for mass production. Get ready for the era when collaboration replaces the corporation.**
>
> *Thomas Goetz, Editor, Wired Magazine*

Taking Peter Drucker's observation one step further, his quote can be extended to include: *converting knowledge into action takes a dedicated team with the right skills and experience to create new more efficient processes.* Yes, open solutions and open source software are growing in numbers and importance and are clearly part of the Medical Informatics 20/20 mix. In the coming decade, it's seems highly likely we will see Collaboration, Open Solutions, and Innovation (COSI) live alongside existing corporate strategies, not replace them.

As we examine in detail the Medical Informatics 20/20 model and the strategies of collaboration and innovation in particular, each area will have a series of tactics. Also, within the tactics there are technologies, techniques, and methodologies to support smarter, better execution by health-

---

Six Aims for Improvement

Safe: avoiding injuries to patients from care that is intended to help them

Effective: providing services based on scientific knowledge

Patient-centered: providing care that is responsive to individual patient preferences, needs, and values, and assuring that patient values guide all clinical decisions

Timely: reducing waits and sometimes harmful delays for both those who receive care and those who give care

Efficient: avoiding waste, including waste of equipment, supplies, ideas, and energy

Equitable: providing care that does not vary in quality because of personal characteristics such as gender, ethnicity, geographic location, or socio-economic status

—Institute of Medicine

---

care providers and organizations. To guide thoughtful action, the Institute of Medicine's (IOM) six aims [See the Six Aims for Improvement above] provide very useful guidelines in the deployment of collaboration, open solutions, and innovation strategies.

Medical Informatics 20/20: A Focus on Collaboration and Innovation

This chapter examines in detail the Medical Informatics 20/20 model's key strategies of collaboration and innovation. Information on the tactics within the open solutions strategy was highlighted in Sections I and II, and extensive information on the concepts and deployment of open solutions in health care have been described throughout this book. The two strategies of collaboration and innovation, as well as their tactics, are essential support approaches to the effective deployment of either open source software or closed source software information technologies.

Chapter 11 is an expansion of the overview of the collaboration and innovation strategies and tactics discussed in Chapter 1. The Medical

Informatics 20/20 strategies and tactics offer an operational model for the application of medical and information technology to address the following challenges:

- *Poor vital health statistic performance* relative to other developed countries—despite the fact that the United States spends more money on health care
- *Not diagnosing and treating with the latest medical knowledge and evidence base at the point of care*
- *Epidemic of medical errors* due to system complexity, lack of applied clinical and medical information technology, insufficient process improvement capabilities, communication gaps, etc.
- *High failure rates in the implementation of health information technology solutions* because the of the lack of focus on processes improvement with technology
- *Partial, fragmented patient medical records* due to paper records at numerous sites of care and the inability to bring the most current evidence base to the point of care

This chapter will explore the broad tactical areas and specific tactics associated with the collaboration and innovation strategies. Five of the more important tactics are examined in even greater detail, with expanded descriptions and examples. These include:

- *Open Collaboration and Leadership:* leaders enabling the power of *sharing and focused execution*
- *Breakthrough, Distinctive, and Collaboration Innovation:* the *source* of invention and problem solving
- *LEAN and Six Sigma—Process Improvement Approaches:* the *way* to select and deploy the smarter approaches to making health care safe, cost effective, and patient centric
- *Knowledge Management:* the *method* for effective, rapid cycle knowledge, and best practice spread and optimizing the intellectual capital of a health care organization
- *@Clinical Decision Support:* the *systems* supporting efficient and timely delivery of medical knowledge at the point of care across multiple databases to improve diagnosis, treatment, and patient empowerment

- **Business Intelligence (BI):** a series of *processes and technologies* for collecting and analyzing business and clinical information to support the ongoing positioning, operations and success of an organization

In addition, Chapter 12 describes the highlights of four case studies on accelerating innovation advancement, applying knowledge management to support best practice diffusion, and delivering knowledge at the point of need through improved clinical decision support processes and technology.

The Medical Informatics 20/20 model shown in Figure 11-1 illustrates that the United States lags most other developed countries in vital health statistics, despite having medical expenditures consuming over 16% of the U.S. GNP (based on 2005 data), which is the highest level ever.

The Medical Informatics 20/20 model with its three strategies—Collaboration, Open Solutions, and Innovation (COSI)—is focused on supporting improvements in performance and quality of care by implementing medical informatics systems that include electronic health records (EHR), which can be used by providers and patients anywhere. As illustrated in Figures 11-2, 11-7, and 11-8 and described later in this chapter, each of the three key strategies—Collaboration, Open Solutions and Innovation—have driving tactics, technologies, and examples that support the intelligent application of the Medical Informatics 20/20 infrastructure needed for quality and EHRs. The tactics and technologies of the COSI strategies are critical for execution and optimization of quality and cost-effectiveness in health and medical care.

The authors are "advocates" for people when they are healthy seeking optimum health and when they are patients being treated for an identified acute or chronic disease. Our goal is to accelerate improvement in quality, support optimum proactive health, reduce medical errors, and enhance the cost-effectiveness of health care through the intelligent and appropriate use of Medical Informatics 20/20 strategies and tactics. The authors believe that there is a clear role for both open solutions and closed software technology applications. We are active in the strategy, development, deployment, and support of both open and closed health information systems. Nevertheless, it is our view that the Free and Open Source Software (FOSS) tactical area associated with the Open Solutions Strategy is a viable option to be considered by any healthcare organization seeking

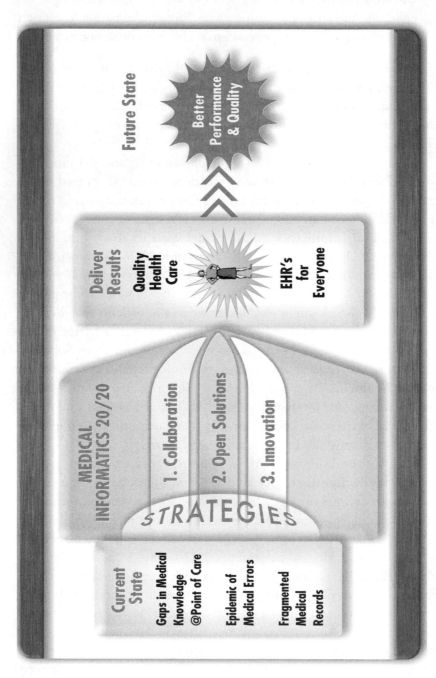

FIGURE 11-1 Medical Informatics 20/20 Model

to implement clinical informatics. The continued growth of FOSS in health care and other industries will add an invaluable dose of competition and choice that is essential in a market economy.

The Collaboration Strategy in Medical Informatics 20/20 Model

Highlights of Tactical Areas and Tactics

The collaboration strategy shown in Figure 11-2 has three major tactical areas, along with a series of tactics in each area, briefly highlighted below.

1. **Leadership and Open Collaboration**
   - *Executive and Clinical Leadership:* leaders engaging to solve the challenges of error reduction and quality care with knowledge, passion, a set of process improvement tools, and a dedicated team
   - *Collaborative Learning:* a series of cooperative, educational, and skill-building programs that are delivered through technology/communication tools; collaborative learning increases the capabilities of team members to contribute to positive healthcare transformation
   - *Empowered Development:* the support of a multidisciplinary team to research, plan, select, and deploy medical informatics solutions
2. **Public–Private Collaboration**
   - *Policy and Communication Forums:* meetings, conferences, and events that are policy- or education-based to provide a forum for knowledge sharing, dialogue, and participation
   - *Laws, Certifications, and Reforms:* federal, state, and local laws passed in an effort to improve public health and healthcare quality and safety
3. **Knowledge Management**
   - *Communities of Practice/Communities of Performance (CoP):* are interactive online spaces that enable collaboration, connect people and leverage human capital to achieve goals through learning, sharing, and problem solving using online communication and multimedia technology *to achieve targeted and measurable goals.*
   - *Facilitated Knowledge Transfer (FKT):* the use of dedicated human resources who specialize in identifying, profiling, and archiving emerging and best practices and all their associated tools and

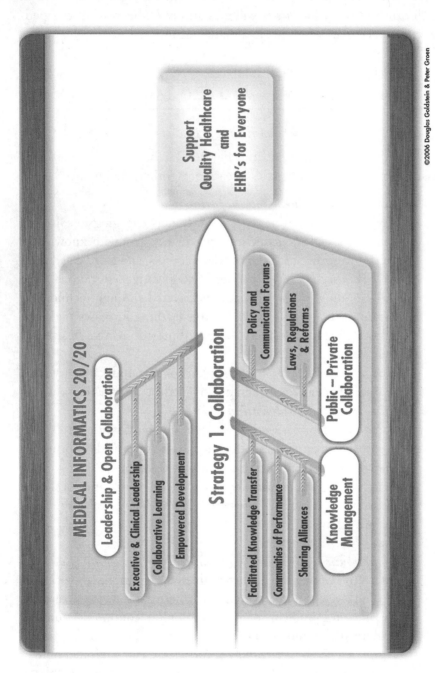

FIGURE 11-2   Tactics Supporting the Collaboration Strategy

resources; FKP often uses multimedia communications and information technologies, improvement methodologies, and educational techniques
- *Sharing Alliances:* formal or informal relationships that support the transfer of tacit and explicit knowledge within or across organizational boundaries

A Deep Dive into "Leadership and Open Collaboration" Tactical Area

With much of the American healthcare delivery system having a religious and/or not-for-profit orientation, collaboration is an extension of mission-driven hospitals and health care organizations across the country. This foundation in mission makes collaboration a natural extension of generations of cooperation and sharing in the healthcare sector. Collaboration can take many forms:

1. Inside an organization:
   - *By position:* Within large health systems, all chief operating officers could have an Intranet-based Community of Practice/Performance.
   - *By organizational goal:* A healthcare delivery organization involved in the Institute for Healthcare Improvement (IHI) 100k Lives reduction campaign could have Communities of Practice on its Intranet, targeting the five areas of improving performance—Rapid Response Teams, Preventing Adverse Drug Events, AMI Care, Preventing Surgical Site Infections, Preventing Central Line Infections, and Preventing Community Acquired Pneumonia.
   - *Formal:* A sanctioned network is supported by Internet, meetings, and communication technology and supplied with designated corporate resources.
   - *Informal:* Managers who share common needs can use existing corporate resources to share resources without special budget allocations.
2. Across organizational boundaries:
   - *Broad across the board:* Many members of an association such as the Catholic Health Association could agree to share best practices and resources through a facilitated Web service.

- *Narrow focus:* A number of the members of Health Tech, a technology research organization, could agree to share intellectual property and resources related to better, faster technology implementation through a central Web service exchange.

Collaboration, knowledge transfer, and resource sharing can be sponsored by and facilitated under either a not-for-profit or a for-profit arrangement. There are many possible dimensions and networks to link together if the focus is a measurable goal or common interest. Healthcare collaboration involves using open communications, online and offline learning, and applied problem-solving circles among diverse stakeholders for resolving problems. The principles of collaboration are also applied for accelerating commitments and maturation of open standards for the communication of clinical data and facilitating a collaborative incubator for innovation and enhanced processes. This is the beauty of today's new media communication and computing technology. It operates fast, in real time, and it is network-oriented, not hierarchical, in nature. The power of Web and new media technology is that it lowers the costs of sharing, publishing, communicating, and collaborating.

Open Solutions: The Power of Collaboration in an Amish Community

David and Annie Lapp had watched the roof topple into the blaze with a thunderous crash. Although their children and farm animals escaped unscathed, the couple's barn had burned to the ground. The Lapps' only comfort was knowing that their close-knit Amish community would help them build another one.

One morning the following week, the yard quickly filled with buggies as neighbors arrived. After a short discussion, the men rolled up their sleeves and got to work. The older, experienced men acted as supervisors. Young boys ran errands and helped in any way they could. The women and girls began preparing for a noontime feast. The youngest children played close by the house.

Soon the frame of the barn was in place. After the noon time meal, the group forged ahead with construction, and by sundown, the barn was nearly complete.

Collaboration is sharing. Just as the Amish are known for working together to build a barn better and faster, clinicians and managers in health care must come together within and across organizational and public–private boundaries to improve care processes. Enabled by appropriate and practical medical informatics technology, this is not just a possibility; it is an absolute necessity.

In the "Leadership and Open Collaboration" tactical area, making quality a first priority is the responsibility of senior leadership. Without the CEO and his or her team leading the way, it will not be possible to transform healthcare organizations into high-performance organizations. Leaders must engage with the support of team members who work to define the current state, then use appropriate technology to deliver the future state of care-delivery process. Executive dashboards need to put quality performance criteria first and compensation systems must change to reward quality on top of financial performance.

Open collaboration uses the principles of open communication and Web technologies that harness learning management systems to educate

Bon Secours Health System Focuses on "QualityFirst" and Enhancing Performance Excellence

When Richard Statuto came on board as BSHSI's CEO, he took a number of decisive actions. These included focusing on quality and mortality reduction, reducing debt, and setting out a three-year plan. Most importantly, Statuto walked the talk by being 100% supportive and involved in the CMS Pay for Performance demonstration project and the IHI 100k Lives campaign. He gave QualityFirst a prominent position in the Strategic Quality Plan (SQP) and revised the performance dashboard for the organization to include important quality indicators. As the largest system in the Premier, Inc.–CMS Pay for Performance demonstration project, BSHSI was accumulating extensive quality performance data. In revising the dashboard the priority placed on quality indicators such as the process measures and mortality was placed at the top of the agenda for all the senior management meetings. In addition, individual facility and overall system results were shared monthly on IRIS the organization's Intranet. Most recently, QualityFirst has evolved into CareConnect, a system wide, multi-year program to install clinical informatics and GHRs throughout the system. For additional information see the BSHSI case study on QualityFirst and Six Sigma in Chapter 12.

and expand skill sets of healthcare workers. Open collaboration focuses on critical goals using tools such as online Communities of Practice to create problem-solving networks in which all members can contribute their subject matter expertise and learn from other experts inside or outside the organization. Key tactics for "Leadership and Open Collaboration" as illustrated in Figure 11-2 are "Executive and Clinical Leadership," "Collaborative Learning," and "Empowered Development."

Leaders must lead by action and knowledge for transformation to occur. Clinical leaders must engage to solve the challenges of error reduction and quality care with knowledge, passion, a set of process improvement tools, and a dedicated team. The first question asked by CEOs in daily interactions and weekly executive meetings must be "How are we measuring up on quality indicators today?" By asking it first, the CEO

Quality Pays is Proven by CMS and Premier, Inc. Demonstration Project

Recent evidence overwhelmingly confirms that raising the quality of health care will, in turn, reduce costs. According to analysis from Premier, Inc., based on their Pay for Performance demonstration project with Centers for Medicare and Medicaid (CMS), if all pneumonia and heart bypass patients nationally had received most of a set of basic, widely accepted care measures in 2004, costs would have been as much as $1 billion lower. Other projected outcomes associated with this improved process delivery would have been 3,000 fewer deaths, 6,000 fewer complications, 6,000 fewer readmissions, and 500,000 fewer days in the hospital. The analysis utilized quality process indicators collected as part of Premier's HQID with CMS, the first national pay-for-performance project of its kind.

The analysis is an important one for hospital executives who must make decisions that affect both the cost and quality of care. Douglas Hawthorne, chairman of the Premier board of directors and president and CEO of Texas Health Resources, which has hospitals participating in the demonstration project stated "It makes intuitive sense that improving care delivery should eventually reduce costs, if only because of reduced complications and readmissions. Most of us in health care have taken that on faith. This is dramatic proof that hospitals can take relatively simple steps to significantly reduce costs without infringing on clinical decisions regarding patients' care."

expresses the main healing mission of the organization and an interest in patient welfare. Performance excellence starts with quality; profitability and cost-effectiveness follow. Clinical leaders must be empowered by executive leadership that understands, participates, and supports rapid cycle improvement in quality.

Building the skills and capabilities of all team members is an ongoing responsibility in our competitive and challenged world. The "Collaborative Learning" tactic is an approach being used by managers and clinical

---

A Collaboration on Collaboration

Doing research for this chapter led the authors to explore the term "collaboration" on Wikipedia.org, the world's largest collaborative, open solutions encyclopedia. A search resulted in a page on collaboration that provided very useful definitions, descriptions, etymology, history, barriers, and so on, all in one place.

The "collaboration" page and links were developed in conjunction with MetaCollab.net. A click on that link led to a definition: "Meta Collab is an open research, meta collaboration (a collaboration on collaboration) with the aim to explore the similarities and differences in the nature, methods, and motivations of collaboration across any and every field of human endeavor.

"Meta Collab's primary objectives are to:

- create a continuously developing repository of knowledge surrounding collaboration;
- develop a community of researchers and individuals interested in furthering an understanding of collaboration; and to
- work toward the development of a general theory of collaboration."

And within Meta Collab is a list of useful subtopics on Academia, Art, Business, Civil Society, Education, Government, Health Care, Industry, etc. A click on Health Care reveals some valuable information on the Cochrane Collaborative, but also provided an insight. There were gaps in collaboration on health care that could be filled by excerpts from this book and information that anyone on the planet could share to further the art and science of improving health care through collaboration.

Source: Wikipedia.org

professionals to reduce errors and improve quality. This cooperative learning approach uses the conferences, virtual networks, adult learning theory, and online and computer-based learning management systems to increase the medical informatics knowledge and know–how of care providers and managers in health care. Informal groups or formal alliances of participants work together to identify problems, conduct change tests, implement solutions, share results, and support accelerated improvement. "Share early, share often, and improve faster" is the approach. A good example of collaborative learning is the Institute for Healthcare Improvement (IHI), which conducts Breakthrough Series Collaboratives, a short-term cooperative learning system that brings together a large number of teams from hospitals or clinics to seek improvement in a focused topic area, such as the use of ICU cost reduction. Since 1995, IHI has sponsored more than 50 such collaborative projects on several dozen topics involving more than 2,000 teams from 1,000 healthcare organizations. The collaboratives combine face-to-face meetings with ongoing virtual communication and sharing through various Internet-based services. For more information, see the case study in Chapter 5.

In essence, these extended collaborations across organizational boundaries are a modern version of an Amish barn raising. Clinicians and administrators, federal agencies and pharmaceutical executives—all collaborate to solve chronic problems in health care that cause excessive errors or low quality by building a networked virtual support infrastructure that can support the needs of patients in the 21st century.

"Collaborative Learning" shares common roots and methods with an innovation methodology called "Collaborative Innovation" that is described later in the chapter.

The tactic of "Empowered Development" means establishing a multidisciplinary team to research, plan, select, and deploy medical informatics solutions. It involves fully engaging clinicians, medical informatics specialists, information technologists, managers, executives, and customer patients in the team. "Empowered Development" represents an enlightened and proactive clinical involvement in all states of planning, development, and deployment of medical informatics technologies. Institutions such as Johns Hopkins have actively engaged the patient voice through the Patient Safety Group (www.patientsafetygroup.org), which is an alliance between Johns Hopkins and the Josie King Foundation.

Early Warning of Pandemics Through Collaboration, Connections, and Clinical Data Standards

One vision for the interconnected Medical Informatics 20/20 grid is this: A patient presents in a Seattle emergency room with flu-like symptoms after arriving on a plane from Asia. The ER physician enters these symptoms into the ER's database and they are automatically transferred from the local, Seattle-area Regional Health Information Organization (RHIO) that is interconnected based on open standards to the national health information network—the next generation public health system. An alert is immediately sent back to the ER physician that the patient is the ninth person in the Seattle area to present with what could be the deadly Asian avian flu.

Possible? Not yet. To achieve this level of quality and interconnectivity in the American healthcare system we must strive to use collaboration, open solutions, and innovation in information technology, communications, and open interoperability standards. An electronic health record is only the beginning. The EHR must connect and interoperate on many levels. This is the challenge for Medical Informatics 20/20 in the 21st century.

What is needed:

- Leaders willing to support security data exchange based on open standards that supports patient health, public health, and national defense
- Privacy and security for the patient as disease data is analyzed for outbreaks
- Regional and national clinical data-exchange organizations collaborating with the same open clinical data standards

"Empowered Development" also involves increasing the technology literacy of all appropriate care-delivery associates in an organization. Improvement methodologies such as Six Sigma and LEAN (both of which are described in more detail later) offer a step-by-step methodology to guide transformation, thus creating an empowered and educated development process that uses valid data and analysis to determine and target the best interventions. If clinicians are not empowered and appropriately involved in all phases of development, the likelihood of deployment failure is very high.

A Quick Focus on Public–Private Collaboration: Disaster Preparedness

Successful public–private collaboration depends on federal and private sector leaders stepping forward to expand existing forums and foundations. The Consolidated Health Informatics (CHI) initiative that involves all federal government healthcare agencies has helped establish open standards for clinical data exchange across more than 20 different clinical data exchanges within the medical realm (http://www.hhs.gov/healthit/chi.html). Given that the federal sector directly pays for about 50% of all health care in the United States, the CHI initiative was an effort to move the private sector to accept the same set of open, interoperable clinical data standards. One of the most important federal efforts has been the establishment of an Office of the National Coordinator for Health Information Technology (ONCHIT) and the creation of the position of the health information technology and medical informatics czar. ONCHIT is taking the leading role in coordinating federal health information technology budgets, setting national priorities for action, developing metrics for EHR adoption, managing the allocation of demonstration grants for Regional Health Information Organizations (RHIO), and much more.

The key tactics previously discussed in this area were "Policy and Communication Forums" and "Laws, Certifications, and Reforms." Both seek to improve public health and healthcare quality and safety. Here are some examples that illustrate public-private collaborations and disaster preparedness across:

- *VistA and Veterans Health Administration Collaboration and Open Solutions: First to the Rescue after Katrina*—In the book's introduction, the case example "America's Veterans Were Prepared for Hurricane Katrina" demonstrates the Veterans Health Administration's leadership, foresight, and collaboration in the ability of VistA to deliver EHRs anywhere a veteran needs care.
- *Learning from Mistakes and Disaster Preparedness*—After Katrina, health plans, hospitals, and federal agencies were working to improve their electronic data and medical record systems. For example, in advance of Hurricane Rita, which followed Katrina by about three weeks, Blue Cross and Blue Shield of Texas (BCBSTX) created electronic patient clinical summaries for its evacuee mem-

bers. Because of what it learned from Katrina's aftermath, BCBSTX prospectively prepared treatment information that allowed evacuees to receive appropriate care after the storm. To achieve this, BCBSTX extracted member data relevant to its 830,000 members who lived in evacuated cities and delivered the data to MEDecision, a company that is a leader in collaborative care management. Within days, MEDecision was able to produce transportable, electronic records for healthcare providers across Texas. Included in the patient clinical summaries were historical and current medical data from doctors, labs, pharmacies, and other provider organizations.

- *National Coalition Focuses on Virginia Disaster Tracking*— ComCare Alliance (www.comcare.org), a national coalition and collaboration of public safety, medical, and industry executives that promotes interoperable standards for emergency communications, is working with Virginia hospitals to develop common standards for post-disaster patient-tracking IT systems. The systems would provide a central repository of information on patient evacuees that would specify where the patients were relocated, under whose supervision, in what condition, and what medicines and treatments had been provided to the patient under emergency conditions.[1]

These important collaborations are only a few examples of cooperative efforts that have evolved at a rapid pace since 2001. It is time for ongoing and expanded public–private collaborations that leverage collaboration, open solutions, and innovation to address this national and international challenge. It is time for continuous collaboration across multiple dimensions within the private sector. It is time for open and innovative collaboration within and across local, state, and federal government agencies. Only through committed leadership and continuity of multidimensional collaboration can we address the quality and EHR challenge of today and tomorrow.

The key underpinning of public–private collaboration is that both federal and private sector leadership must step forward to expand the forums and foundations in place and create new ones for gap areas. Within the federal government, the Consolidated Health Informatics efforts of all the federal agencies help establish standards for clinical data exchange. There

---

[1]A. Lipowicz, "Development Begins on Standards for Medical Resource Tracking," *Washington Technology,* 9/30/05.

are multiple areas of action within the federal government ranging from the Centers for Disease Control and Prevention's various initiatives to extensive activity with the U.S. Department of Health and Human Services (HHS). Within Congress there is a high level of bipartisan collaboration on legislation to expand medical informatics through the creation of standards and various incentives. Unfortunately, the budget situation in 2006 and 2007 limits the ability of the federal government to fund efforts. States are also taking action in creating statewide initiatives for EHRs to support better public health.

Over the intermediate term, payment reform and loosening of certain regulations will be essential. At the time of publication, HHS and Congress were working on exceptions to the Stark amendment so that physicians could rent access to hospital computer systems. This is just one method of helping physicians overcome the cost barrier that prevents them from investing in electronic medical records on their own.

A Deep Dive into Knowledge Management Tactical Area within Collaboration Strategy

"Knowledge Management" (KM) is a discipline that captures human and intellectual capital in the form of explicit and tacit information/resources/knowledge supported by technology tools to create, organize, and share knowledge efficiently and effectively. Truly effective KM supports behavior change in the form of innovation, process improvement, and the achievement of set goals. Traditional mentorship is a form of KM, but today KM is a discipline focused on liberating the power of human capital within an organization to support better service, quality, and achievement of goals. Human capital and the knowledge of employees is one of the most underutilized resources in organizations across many industries.

Wikipedia, a worldwide open solution resource, offers this definition of "Knowledge Management" and related concepts:

> "Knowledge Management" or open solution refers to a range of practices and techniques used by organizations to identify, represent, and distribute knowledge, know-how, expertise, intellectual capital, and other forms of knowledge for leverage, reuse, and transfer of knowledge and learning across an organization."
>
> Knowledge management today is frequently focused on personal and organizational change by accelerating the diffusion within and across organizations of proven practices, process improvements, and innovations

to achieve measurable organizational goals and objectives. This can involve both human and technological applications which help create, organize, or share knowledge.

- Knowledge Management: a process which transforms knowledge, know-how, and experience into intellectual capital that can be diffused, adapted, and applied in new settings
- Intellectual Capital: the intangible assets of a company which contribute to its valuation
- Chief Knowledge Officer (CKO): an executive responsible for maximizing the knowledge potential of an organization
- Knowledge: that which can be acted upon
- Personal Knowledge Management: the organization of an individual's thoughts and beliefs
- Enterprise Knowledge Management: the strategy, process, or technologies used to acquire, share, and reuse an enterprise's knowledge and understanding

TACIT Knowledge Management Examples

Web-based conference system for TACIT knowledge sharing: Connecting people so they can communicate and transfer tacit knowledge with each other. A Web-conferencing system with audio support, shared white board capabilities, online chat, and other functions is an example of a tacit knowledge transfer system.

Subject matter expert database: Identifying experts and capturing their expertise to make people and their knowledge more easily and broadly accessible to the organization. Expertise management is a class of processes/technologies that enable this functionality. Intelligence locating and Internet messaging systems support this connecting function.

Evidenced-based and community-based proven practices and innovation databases: Capturing tacit knowledge into highly insightful and explicit formats (e.g., richer content, such as proven practices, or richer formats, such as video, audio, or simulations). The term "capture" in this context is often interpreted as the production of a written document.

Storytelling and multimedia packaging for high impact: However, the most insightful representations of knowledge are often visual

(continues)

> (such as graphics or video) and/or audio recordings of people sharing what they know. Written documents are often effective when shared as a story or case study. Adults learn effectively through several methods, including storytelling (case study sharing) and practice.
>
> *Source:* Jeff Stolte, The Ascension Health Exchange: *Facilitated Knowledge Transfer White Paper 2005*

Wikipedia (www.wikipedia.org) is a perfect example of an open knowledge management resource, function, and application. Wikipedia is the largest encyclopedia in the world. Anyone on the planet can contribute to it. It functions as a commons and community for knowledge sourced from and maintained by volunteers contributing knowledge and information. The millions of articles represent the *collective wisdom of the community of users and contributors.* Wikipedia is aggregating, packaging, and presenting human knowledge to support learning and growth of individuals, enterprises, and government in an open, collaborative, and innovative manner.

Explicit vs. Tacit Knowledge

There are two primary types of knowledge: explicit and tacit. Explicit knowledge is formal and/or codified knowledge, while tacit knowledge is informal and/or uncodified.

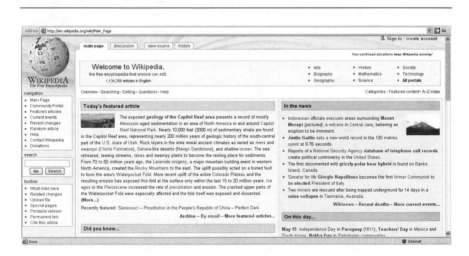

FIGURE 11-3 Wikipedia.org Home Page

Explicit knowledge takes the form of formal documents and materials such as books, documents, formulas, project reports, process diagrams, collected lessons learned, case studies, research reports, policy manuals, and so on. Tacit knowledge, on the other hand, is knowledge that can be shared and learned during interactions between employees, through methods such as enterprise storytelling, online Webcasts, conference calls, or other forms of communication.

Successful KM efforts must address three key elements or organizational development areas to support goal achievement. These are:

1. People, which includes leadership and dealing with the overall culture of an organization
2. Processes
3. Technology

As illustrated in Figure 11-4, a KM program for a healthcare organization has the following functions:

- ***KM Community Operations and Support,*** including training and community support for coordinators of Communities of Performance (CoP) within the KM effort. Increasingly organizations are recognizing that the strategy of initiating and supporting

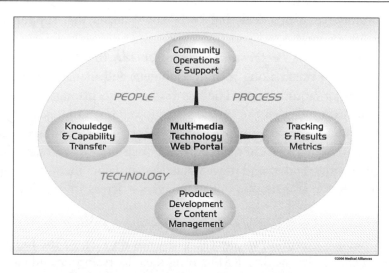

FIGURE 11-4 Knowledge Management—3 Core Competencies and five Program Components

Communities of Performance within an organization supports the achievement of goals better and faster. The authors prefer to use the term Community of Performance rather than Community of Practice because of the focus on achieving 'specific, measurable' results rather just 'practicing' sharing resources that may or may not be related to the mission of the organization and specific CoP.

- *Product Development and Content Management* supporting the delivery of fresh news, best practice, and innovation identification, review, packaging, presentation and promotion. Product development in this context means the resulting resource once organization–wide knowledge, documents, software, materials, etc. on a topic has been aggregated and made available for rapid spread through knowledge transfer tactics

- *Technology Infrastructure,* ensuring that the Internet and multi-media communication technology works and meets the business and clinical requirements of supporting technology so that members, coordinators, and leadership are able to effectively get work done through an online community that enables printed materials, audio, and video in a real-time environment.

- *Knowledge and Capability Transfer,* a dedicated subject matter expert team available to accelerate in the transfer and adaptation of tools and knowledge, implementation of best practices, proven community based practices, and know-how transfer that support goal achievement.

- *Tracking and Performance Measurement,* the definition of the metrics to track, along with development and management of the reporting requirements. The metrics have two primary categories: The first is whether the annual strategic and operating goals for the Community of Performance have been met. The second is a defined measure of activities of the online CoP such as views and downloads of resource toolkits and proven practices, and documented examples of diffusion and adoption of an innovation across an organization.

Operational execution effectiveness depends on each of the functions working effectively together. KM involves the understanding and harnessing of human and improvement processes and technologies for knowledge database development, organizing, searching, diffusing, or spreading, and

Making Online Communities of Performance Work

1. Identify measurable problems to solve by the team
2. Empower and train community leaders and members
3. Convert e-mail, fax, and mail processes to online transactions
4. Make sharing easy, fun, and part of the job
5. Structure formal and informal incentives for contributing
6. View online communities as an extension of meetings and activities of daily business
7. Use the online Community of Performance environment as the focus for Internet-based meetings
8. Provide ongoing facilitation for knowledge and capability transfer for rapid-cycle diffusion
9. Deliver robust enterprise search function that presents internal, licensed, and public results from knowledge bases
10. Establish metrics to measure, such as tracking the diffusion of innovations and proven practices across an organization
11. Demonstrate how Web collaboration delivers many advantages over always e-mailing
12. Deliver audio and video knowledge and know-how of proven practices to support rapid diffusion and understanding by members
13. Continuously track value and profile success stories monthly
14. Ensure senior leaders recognize and support the value of identifying, profiling, archiving, and diffusing intellectual capital to save time, money, and accelerate goals achievement.

Source: Medical Alliances Knowledge Base 2006

practical application of knowledge, resources, and human capital for the enterprise. KM is a vital cog in the rapid spread of demonstrated best practices, transference of explicit and tacit knowledge, and the framework for sharing and working better and smarter. Jonathan Schaffer, MD, and Nilmini Wickramasinghe have developed a model of a (Business) Intelligence Continuum which emphasises the need for continuous analysis of the current state of data and other socio-technical inputs by applying the tools and techniques of knowledge management and business intelligence (BI) to support developing valuable knowledge bases and improved performance. For additional information see the Business Intelligence discussion at the end of this Chapter.

Fully functioning KM programs realize that transferring knowledge and resource material (plans, financial models, guidelines, policies, software code, technology, and know-how) is often not enough. There is also a need to transfer capabilities, through human- and technology-enabled support systems. Getting an organization to adopt new ideas requires a process of reinvention—people need to own the result as their own idea. An Intranet interface supports the seamless delivery of multiple Web services, and the Enterprise Portal Framework used to support the Intranet used must be able to integrate other third-party Web applications effectively and seemlessly.

One of the prime objectives for an online KM solution is to create a central nexus that supports knowledge aggregation/packaging, diffusion/spread, capability transfer, and innovation advancement. This core team is frequently run from strategic planning and development function, but this team is focused on training, empowering leaders, and targed services delivery in the areas of innovation acceleration and process improvement. The core KM team is not a centralization of the function. The core team is responsible for training and skill building on how to innovate and how to share knowledge throughout the organization. It really is planting a seed that pushes down strong roots, while stimulating growth through the organization as it pushes up toward the sunlight.

Communities of Practice/Communities of Performance—The structure and operations of a Community of Performance (CoP) creates a nexus or so-called online town center that supports learning, sharing, and problem solving for associates who have common goals. Online CoPs frequently serve to extend connectivity for an affinity group at all times and make it easy to share ideas, exchange resources, create improved processes, and find solutions. Today, CoPs are usually supported with Internet and communication technologies that accelerate the diffusion of information, resources, and materials. The KM industry, in general, uses the term "Communities of Practice." In health care, the authors believe the term CoP should stand for "Communities of Performance" because healthcare organizations need to focus more on performance than simply practice.

CoPs connect people and leverage human capital to achieve goals. Inside a healthcare enterprise, CoPs frequently operate within an Intranet environment and provide a shared learning and working environment for people who have a common purpose: to deliver the tools needed to achieve business and clinical "Knowledge @ Point of Need."

Figure 11-5, "Community of Performance Functions Supported by a Six Sigma or LEAN Process Improvement Methodology," lists all the functions of a community of performance, which include: Search, Collaborate, Share, Innovate, Support, and Knowledge Transfer. In the background, an organization will embrace improvement methodology such as Six Sigma or LEAN to ensure a common language and approach to performance improvement. Knowledge transfer serves as the acceleration vehicle for the spread of a proven best practice through an organization or an alliance network of organizations working towards a common goal.

Facilitated Knowledge Transfer (FKT) is the use of dedicated human resources who specialize in identifying, profiling, and archiving emerging and best practices using multimedia communications and information technologies and techniques for rapid spread. FKT experts are innovation accelerators, storytellers, producers, and trainers of the organizational knowledge universe. Their mission is to identify and package in a compelling, complete, and interesting way a best practice so that it can rapidly be diffused and support rapid–cycle change. A FKT expert recognizes that sharing to support goal achievement in geographically disperse and complex organizations does not often happen naturally. FKT in health care works to train and support all clinicians and managers of an organization in sharing effectively to improve performance. FKT is focused on rapid

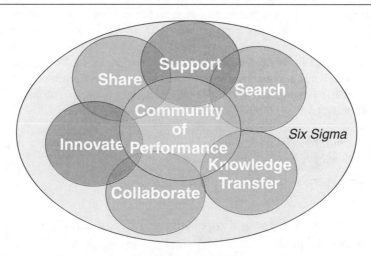

FIGURE 11-5 Community of Performance Functions Supported by a Six Sigma or LEAN Process Improvement Methodology

CMS Premier Pay-for-Performance Model Produces Remarkable Quality Improvements Among Nation's Hospitals

"Pay-for-performance" can increase clinical quality and save lives, according to the first year of official data from a national project involving more than 260 hospitals. The Centers for Medicare and Medicaid Services (CMS) will pay $8.85 million in incentives to the top-performing hospitals in the project, which is managed by Premier Inc.

Data from the first year of the CMS/Premier Hospital Quality Incentive Demonstration (HQID), validated by CMS and reported publicly today, demonstrate a significant improvement in the quality of care across five clinical focus areas as measured by 33 nationally standardized and widely accepted quality indicators. The average improvement across the clinical areas was 6.6%. These performance gains have outpaced those of hospitals involved in other national performance initiatives. Approximately 235 acute myocardial infarction (heart attack) patients were saved as a result of quality improvements in that related focus area alone.

"The ultimate goal of the HQID is to determine whether pay–for–performance impacts the quality of care in our nation's hospitals," said Richard Norling, president and chief executive officer of Premier, Inc. "Findings from the first year of this project clearly indicate that it does."

The pay-for-performance model demonstrated in the project includes financial incentives and public recognition for top-performing hospitals as well as financial penalties for hospitals that do not improve above a pre-defined quality measure threshold by the third year of the project. Additionally, Premier's relationship with participants enabled implementation of effective, collaborative knowledge transfer programs supporting identification and dissemination of best practices of top performers, a key component to the rapid pace of performance improvement.

For more information visit http://www.premierinc.com/informatics or http://www.premierinc.com/qualitydemo.

Source: Premier, Inc. Press Release, November 14, 2005

and targeted knowledge and capability transfer to achieve key strategic and operational goals.

A related concept to FKT is "Capability Transfer." The transfer of knowledge, community-based proven practice or an evidence-based best practices via an e–mail or sharing in a specific online Community of Performance doesn't necessarily mean that the receiver of knowledge will be able to implement that knowledge effectively. "Capability Transfer" refers to the application of human subject matter experts to assist other team members in deploying the knowledge and resources initially shared through an Intranet, meetings, or online Community of Performance.

The Premier, Inc. CMS Pay-for-Performance demonstration project is a great example of more than 200 hospitals working together to improve performance through collaboration and facilitated knowledge transfer. The success was supported by an online Web-portal service, rapid diffusion of performance data, support for inter- and intra-organizational sharing of best practices, and support from Premier clinical and professional consultants and management engineers. This effort also exemplifies the principles of a "Sharing Alliance" where hospitals come together to solve common problems and improve the quality of care.

"Sharing Alliances" are formal or informal relationships that support the transfer of tacit and explicit knowledge within or across organizational boundaries. A formal knowledge-sharing arrangement between two large, separate, multilocation healthcare systems would represent a "Sharing Alliance." Many times the term "network" is used to discuss various types of Sharing Alliances. As the previous discussions on collaborative learning and collaborative innovation indicate, networks and Sharing Alliances in their various forms are powerful tools in understanding how work gets done. Understanding how formal and informal networks perform in complex healthcare organizations can benefit significantly from the body of knowledge available in social network analysis and network theory. In the context of technology, the terms "social networking" and "collaborative software" refer to a category of Internet applications that help connect family members, friends, business colleagues, or other collaborators using a variety of tools for business and social purposes.

Social network theory discusses social relationships in terms of actors/ players who are viewed as nodes; the connections between them are frequently called connectors, ties or links. There can be many kinds of connectors/ties between the different types of actors/nodes. To understand the culture and determine the best way to collaborate within and across organizations it necessary to produce a map of the formal structure and an informal social map of all of the relevant ties between the actors being studied. Looking at both views, formal and informal maps will determine

Knowledge Continuum

- *Research-based:* explicit information and knowledge that is developed and packaged into useful reports and shared primarily through "publish and push" to customers
- *Resource-based or community-based:* explicit materials that have proven effective in one or more settings and are often shared documents in the form of business plans, financial models, benefit analysis, training material, etc.
- *Evidence-based:* explicit resources that have proven to be effective through a rigorous analysis process and are primarily shared through clinical protocols, order sets, alerts, business protocols, workflows, etc.
- *Experience-based:* tacit how-to knowledge that is primarily shared through lessons learned, debriefings, facilitated collaboration forums (online/offline), and connecting subject matter experts on demand, which may or may not be captured on audio and/or video
- *Implementation-based:* explicit how-to knowledge primarily shared through coaching, mentoring programs, and eLearning infrastructure; embedded in processes (e.g., IT systems, workflow redesign, observation, modeling, etc).
- *Innovation-based:* new kinds of knowledge/solutions that are developed by an intra- or interorganizational team to solve a healthcare clinical or business problem; the output can take the form of all types of explicit or tacit knowledge types

Source: Douglas Goldstein and Jeff Stolte, unpublished research, 2006.

the roles of individual actors and the relationship to node junctions. For instance, frequently employee/actors with the most connections are not the most important from a formal organizational chart perspective. Influential employees/ actors on the informal maps often have longevity in the organization, have invaluable knowledge, and know how to get things done. These relationships and concepts are often displayed in a social network diagram. An understanding of the relationships embedded in informal network maps are critical to determining how the work of alliances and Community of Practices/Performance can be optimized.

There are many rapidly evolving software applications designed to support robust organizational Intranets, which are often referred to as "Enterprise Portal" solutions and "Enterprise Content Management" systems. They are designed to enable knowledge management and smarter

FIGURE 11-6 Premier, Inc. Rapid Improvement Program

work flow and processes. Examples of Web services infrastructure and collaborative software to support Intranet-based communication and collaboration include Microsoft SharePoint Technologies and BEA's AquaLogic. For instance, the Bon Secours Health System Intranet called IRIS used the Enterprise Content Management system from BEA to support its communication efforts for 20,000 employee associates. In addition, advanced collaboration features support their organization-wide Six Sigma effort, which in turn is supporting their QualityFirst and Care Connect program. Chapter 12 has a case study on BSHSI QualityFirst and knowledge management efforts.

There are also a vast array of technology tools to support effective networking for entertainment, innovation, or work, including instant messaging, blogs, vlogs (video blogs), wikis, Internet forums, and discussion boards. There are numerous social- and business-networking Web services gaining popularity. For instance, MySpace.com, a social-networking Web site based on music and personal interests, is one of the top-ten most-visited Web sites. Linked-in (www.linkedin.com) is a professionally focused Web service designed to support better business through connecting and reconnecting colleagues and clients. YouTube.com delivers an ever expanding universe of online videos or vlogs on many topics and areas.

Network theory at the social and business levels has been used to assess how companies interact. By analyzing and mapping the informal versus formal connections linking executives and employees within a company, tremendous insight is gained about how to best structure knowledge transfer and organizational improvement using the latest technology, informatics tools, and quality improvement systems. Alliance-building theory frequently examines the role of trust in leading to successful alliances. Alliances and networks are critical tactics for organizations today seeking to deliver world-class service.

At the end of the day, it is "nice to share," and more and more healthcare professionals are realizing it "pays to share" through the leveraging and sharing of knowledge and resources inside organizations and across organizational boundaries. When it comes to "Knowledge Transfer," never underestimate the power of audio-visual based storytelling in robust multimedia fashion. This is clearly reflected in the rapid rise and success of YouTube.com which was bought by Google for $1.6 billion at the end of 2006. Throughout time, humans have relied on storytelling, and in large part, the power of television and movies is in storytelling. In "Knowledge Transfer," efforts to tell the stories behind best practices, along with discussion and associated resources, are key. Combining these resource elements will help people to stop reinventing the wheel, while they customize and adapt proven practices in a shorter period of time, while reducing investment costs.

We have taken a look at what "Knowledge Management" is as a discipline, and examined its core tactics. In Chapter 12 several case studies illustrate what an overall KM program looks like in health care, while also examining what problems are solved.

Highlights of the Open Solutions Strategy

The "Open Solutions Strategy" facilitates the ability to communicate and share information in a way that is completely interoperable and transportable across large-scale, macroeconomic, information technology systems. This strategy has a range of tactics to lower the implementation costs of health information technology deployment in healthcare delivery systems, today and tomorrow. Open Solutions are vital to realize a better healthcare system because:

- *Open Solutions in the form of Open Standards* will be essential to support interoperability and clinical data exchange. This is critical to the successful deployment of EHRs for all Americans and will ensure that medical records are accessible and readable across the healthcare system and wherever patients need access to care.

- ***Open Solutions in the form of Open Source Software*** will play a critical role in reducing the cost of health information technology in the near term by delivering competitive pressures to closed software solution vendors and offering a viable, no-license-fee options to organizations who otherwise could not afford closed source software solutions.
- ***Open Solutions in the form of Open Architecture*** is vital to interconnecting open and closed information technology systems for integrated and lower-cost operations that support better health.

"Open Solutions" are software applications, communications, or interoperability standards that are available on a free, no-cost license basis. The benefits of Open Solutions include lower costs, quality products (because they are constantly being improved by users), accelerated innovation and problem solving, and reduced cycle time. Often overlooked, yet integral to solving the problems that face today's healthcare industry, Open Solutions are the key to achieving higher-quality healthcare, lower implementation costs, and better disaster preparedness with affordable solutions and greater scalability.

Frequently, Open Solutions are seen as a "commons," much like a public park, where many but not all members of a community contribute and there are set of norms that govern the commons' maintenance and use.

As illustrated in Figure 11-7, the COSI strategy of Open Solutions has four major tactical areas: "Open Standards," "Free and Open Source Software (FOSS)," "Technology Transfer," and "Open Systems." Each tactical area contains specific tactics, initiatives, tools, and technologies to support the Open Solutions strategy that has been addressed throughout the book. Sections II and III focused on the assessment, deployment, and management of Open Solutions with a specific focus on FOSS in the various forms of VistA being implemented in healthcare organizations around the world. The dimensions of Open Solutions in health care are explored in detail throughout the majority of this book.

The Innovation Strategy in the Medical Informatics 20/20 Model

Innovation is the introduction of new ideas, goods, services, and practices that are intended to be useful. As healthcare executives, managers, and clinicians, we must commit to constantly learning how to use new tactics,

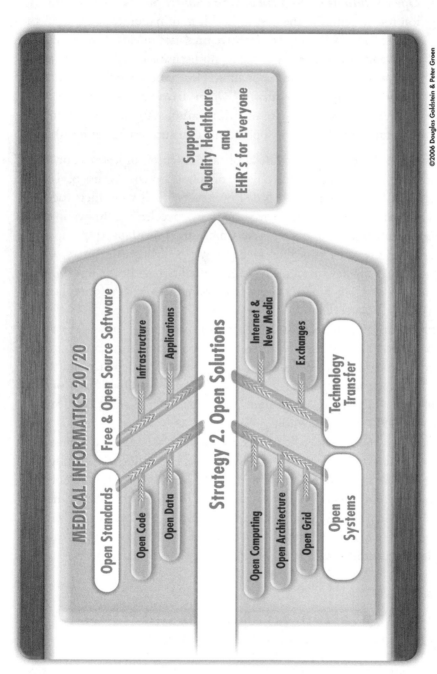

FIGURE 11-7 Tactics Supporting the Open Solutions Strategy

technologies, and tools that empower our teams to address the challenges before us.

Figure 11-8, "Tactics Supporting the Innovation Strategy," illustrates three major tactical areas with associated tactics:

1. *Process Improvement:* Six Sigma, LEAN, and Clinical Engagement
2. *Innovation Methodologies:* Breakthrough, Distinctive, and Collaborative
3. *Applied Knowledge:* Clinical Decision Support, Evidence-Based Medicine, and Knowledge on Demand

In each area there are specific tactics, technologies, and techniques that support the Innovation strategy.

Process Improvement: Exploring Six Sigma and LEAN

Six Sigma and LEAN are rapidly growing in popularity as preferred healthcare quality improvement methodologies. Organizations throughout the world and across many industries are embracing Six Sigma and LEAN as next-generation tactics to improve quality. Healthcare leaders realize that more rigorous and expansive methodologies are needed to map current state processes, assess problems using statistical and other tools, and develop solutions that are targeted at root causes so they have

---

Six Sigma Definition

Six Sigma is a rigorous and disciplined methodology that uses data and statistical analysis to measure and improve a company's operational performance by identifying and eliminating "defects" in manufacturing and service-related processes. Commonly defined as 3.4 defects per million opportunities, Six Sigma can be defined and understood at three distinct levels: metric, methodology, and philosophy. The methodology provides healthcare organizations with the tools to improve the capability of their business and clinical processes. This increase in performance and decrease in process variation leads to defect reduction and vast improvement in profits, employee morale, and quality of product.

Source: iSixSigma.com

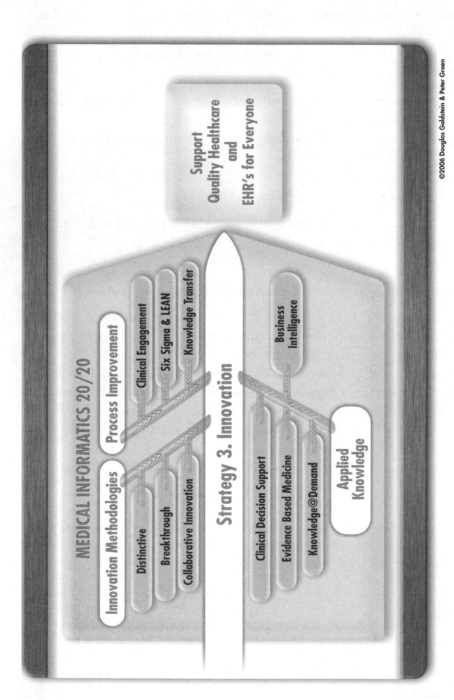

FIGURE 11-8 Tactic Supporting the Innovation Strategy

LEAN Definition

LEAN is a management and manufacturing approach "focusing on reduction of the seven wastes (Over-production, Waiting time, Transportation, Over-processing, Inventory, Motion, and Scrap) in manufactured products. By eliminating waste, quality is improved, production time is reduced, and cost is reduced. LEAN "tools" include constant process analysis (kaizen), "pull" production (by means of kanban), and mistake-proofing (poka yoke)."

Source: Wikipedia.org

the biggest impact on outcomes. Consequently, Six Sigma and LEAN have become vital tactics and tools in the hands of healthcare organizations seeking to significantly improve behavior and hold gains once improvement has been realized.

Six Sigma is a quality-management program that measures and improves the performance of an organization by identifying and correcting defects in an organization's processes and services. In healthcare, the focus of Six Sigma is to create a service that satisfies the customer and optimizes patient care and outcomes, in order to deliver higher quality cost-effectively. DMAIC is the acronym used to describe the methodology for improving existing processes:

- *Define* the goals of the design activity using various tools such as Quality Function Deployment (QFD) or Analytic Hierarchical Process to assure that the goals are consistent with customer demands and the organization's mission and strategies.
- *Measure* to define baseline measurements on current process for future comparison.
- *Analyze* to verify relationship and causality of factors and to determine which changes in process Y's will affect critical X's, which are the goals to realize.
- *Improve* to optimize the process based upon the results of your analysis.
- *Control* to continuously measure the process and institute control mechanisms to ensure that variances are corrected before they result in defects.

Bon Secours Health System and Six Sigma

"Achieving world-class clinical and operational excellence is a multiyear journey requiring system-wide cultural transformation. There is not a health system in America that can afford to fund the transformation from good to great without eliminating the cost of poor quality! The financial resources that are freed up will enable us to liberate the potential of people and redesign clinical care with advanced medical informatics technology."

Kathy Connerton and Douglas Sears
Bon Secour Health System Cost of Poor Quality Planning Process

Bon Secours Health System uses LEAN–Six Sigma throughout the enterprise to improve business and clinical processes. There is strong senior leadership support of the application of a LEAN–Six Sigma approach. Chapter 12 has a case study on BSHSI's QualityFirst and Six Sigma efforts.

Within each of these steps there are extensive quantity tools used to support the process of taking a practical problem, converting it into a statistical problem and determining which factors, from a statistical perspective, will have the desired solution. This statistical solution is then translated into a practical solution that can be delivered quickly and cost-effectively.

The LEAN management/manufacturing approach is focused on reducing the time from customer order to manufacture and delivery of a product or service by eliminating unnecessary production process steps. Despite its origins in manufacturing, LEAN is being applied to service industries, including health care. Many organizations are combining the best of Six Sigma and LEAN, using each where appropriate within health care.

Six Sigma and LEAN at Ascension Health—Ascension Health is the nation's largest Catholic and nonprofit health system, with more than 105,000 associates serving in 20 states and the District of Columbia. It has 64 general acute-care hospitals and more than 20 other healthcare facilities. Several hospitals within the Ascension Health system use LEAN and Six Sigma approaches to improve quality. Here are a few examples:

- *St. Agnes Hospital, Baltimore, Maryland*—Uses LEAN Transformation for Quality and Performance—The goal of the LEAN effort is to reduce waste, lower costs, and remove inefficiencies through the systematic application of LEAN management tactics for organizational transformation. The St. Agnes LEAN Transformation is a five day, results-oriented process emphasizing teamwork and continuous improvement. In the beginning, groups of about 25 managers mapped the processes in their assigned areas, identifying unnecessary steps, handoffs and waiting periods. Since that point St. Agnes has developed a 'central' function to coordinate LEAN Transformation activities across the organization. During the last year, the use of LEAN has expanded rapidly. St. Agnes is overhauling a significant number of processes in high value stream areas including: OR, ED, adult medicine, pharmacy, finance/coding, imaging, care management, home health and core measures. In 2006, it hosted an Ascension Health System-wide Lean workshop. Thirty-seven associates, representing 18 hospitals and the Ascension Health system office, attended. To date the overall benefits since March 2005 have been:

○ $600,000 in financial savings in what St. Agnes calls 'Green Dollars' areas (Actual).
○ Five million in estimated efficiencies in the 'Blue Dollars' areas (estimated) such as cutting down on waiting or unnecessary steps.
○ Since July, 300 associates have participated in 50 Rapid Improvement Events (RIEs).

A couple of examples of LEAN efforts include:

○ *Operating Room*—Created instrument "market" and moved 711 trays from OR to SP. Improved pre-op performance with 85% of patients ready on time—up from 34%. Room turnover was reduced from 30 minutes to 19 minutes.
○ *Emergency Department*—Discharge process realized a 40% improvement from 24 to 14 minutes, and from 16 steps to 8 steps. Registration process realized a 30% improvement. Reduced arrival to room time by 30%.
○ *Finance*—Month end close from 10 to 4 days. Average age of bad debt collection agency referral from 39 days to 7 days.

Those 300 of the 3,000 St. Agnes associates felt empowered after participating in a LEAN project. The entire organization realized that a significant impact on operations is being made that is enabled by people and process supported by technology.

(Source: Ascension Health Exchange Innovation and Best Practice Database, 2006 .)

- ***St. John Health in Michigan***—Some of the key commitments St. John Health has made in adopting Six Sigma include:
  - Pursuit of perfection in patient care delivery
  - Measuring everything that is done
  - Tying together cost, quality, and service—committing to all of these, every time
  - The customer (patient) dictates quality
  - Senior management is intimately involved in the quality of care and its improvement
  - Six Sigma permeates everything that is done, from one-on-one discussions with employees to building new facilities

"Our vision is to be the preferred healthcare provider in southeast Michigan by consistently providing the highest quality patient care experience in all that we do," said Elliot Joseph, president and CEO of St. John Health. "We are investing significant financial and human resources in Six Sigma to achieve our vision," he said. To that end, St. John Health is launching four projects at Providence Hospital and Medical Center and St. John Hospital and Medical Center to reduce average wait times and to decrease variation in wait times for the emergency department, operating room, and patient discharge. During the next fiscal year, the remaining St. John Health Hospitals will identify people trained as facilitators to lead process improvements. "Six Sigma will be the way we work at St. John Health, not an add-on to existing work," said Joseph.

(Source: St. John Health, Press Release, 2004, Providence Hospital: Southfield, St. John Health, St. John Hospital & Medical Center: Detroit. Monday, April 12, 2004.)

- ***Columbia St. Mary in Wisconsin***—Has implemented a "CSM Customer Value Improvement Process (CVIP)," which is a LEAN approach to continuous improvement that designs the safest, least-waste work processes. Standard work processes is created to assure that improvements are understood and sustained. By 2010, all CSM managers will use the CVIP to design and implement work process improvements, minimally every 90 days. The CVIP is based on the Toyota Production System or LEAN where customers value both the quality and price and process removes non-value-added steps as well as diligent removal of waste. It is based on respect for people and continuous improvement. During a presentation to the Ascension Health system group of chief operating officers, the Columbia St. Mary's experience and results using LEAN were described. With a "Rapid Improvement Event (RIE)," the following LEAN process was executed:

○ Seven-week cycle (three weeks of prep, RIE week, and three weeks of follow-up)
○ Focus on Columbia Medical Imaging orders
○ Main event: RIE, week four
○ Learn LEAN philosophy and tools Monday morning
○ Describe high-level process flow and observations Monday afternoon: current state
○ Tuesday morning use tools to improve understanding of flow; develop ideal and future state
○ Tuesday afternoon brainstorm ideas and identify solution to be implemented by 10 a.m. Thursday morning
○ Wednesday through Thursday 10 a.m. write procedures, trial new processes, and train staff
○ Thursday 10 a.m. live with new solution
○ Friday morning: present results to the organization

The system is realizing significant financial and operational benefits that outweigh the costs to develop and support the LEAN. Over time there is expected to be a 50% improvement in quality and a 15% improvement in productivity.

(Source: Columbia St. Mary Ascension Ministry Operating Executives Presentation, November 2005.)

Other health systems implementing Six Sigma and LEAN include:

• ***Virtua Health*** has been using General Electric's Six Sigma Master Black Belt development program, which is specifically for healthcare professionals. A single Six Sigma project at Virtua saved the organi-

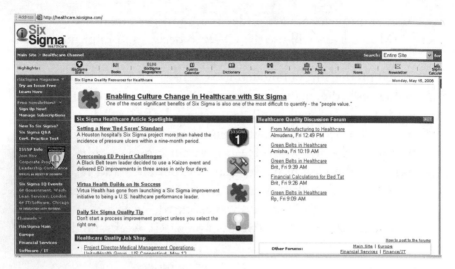

FIGURE 11-9 iSixSigma Web Site
Source: http://healthcare.isixsigma.com

zation more than $1 million a year by increasing insurance reim-
bursement for surgically implanted devices. Virtua has six process
improvement experts called Black Belts, and 29 managers have been
trained as Green Belt project leaders toward the objective of creating
150 Green Belt skilled change agents throughout the organization.

- **The Mayo Clinic** is using LEAN as a vital approach to servicing its
customers better and faster while also being able to improve quality
and reduce costs. In essence, the Mayo Clinic discovered that LEAN
is a way to do more with less. An interview about the Mayo Clinic's
LEAN approach can be found at http://www.leanadvisors.com/
Lean/ Healthcare/articles/lean_healthcare_interview.cfm.

LEAN was originally developed by Toyota as a methodology emphasizing
"getting it right" in the first place and "right" from a customer perspective. It
focuses on getting the right things to the right place, at the right time, the
first time, within a context of reducing waste, optimizing processes, and
embracing change that supports customers. In health care, it is a thought
process and a series of tools to evaluate an organization's processes and services in the delivery of care for patients. The key thought processes within
LEAN are identifying "waste" from the customer perspective and then determining how to eliminate it. The ten rules of LEAN can be summarized as:

1. Reduce and, if possible, eliminate waste
2. Minimize inventory
3. Maximize flow
4. Pull production from customer demand
5. Meet customer requirements
6. Do it right the first time
7. Energize and empower workers
8. Design for rapid change
9. Partner with suppliers
10. Create a culture of continuous improvement

Online Resources:

- *Introducing New Employees to Concepts of Six Sigma* A brief, well-organized presentation can be an effective method to introduce new employees to the concepts of Six Sigma, and at the same time stimulate interest and future participation in Six Sigma projects. (http://healthcare.isixsigma.com/library/content/c050216a.asp)

How Is Six Sigma Different?

Other Quality Programs
- Driven internally
- Looks at averages
- Focuses on outcomes
- Retrospective; fixes defects
- Focuses on quality
- Attentive to production
- Training is separate from management system

Six Sigma
- Driven by the customer
- Targets variation
- Focuses on processes
- Prospective; prevents defects
- Focuses on quality and ROI
- Attentive to total business
- Training is integral to management system

Source: http://www.psqh.com/janfeb05/sixsigma.html

- *One Piece of the Patient Safety Puzzle: Advantages of the Six Sigma Approach* provides an excellent summary of the differences between Six Sigma and other quality programs in the table below. In addition, it includes a summary of hospitals that have generated positive returns on investment (ROI) from Six Sigma programs, business case perspectives, and other useful information.
- *Coronary Artery Bypass Grafts (CABG): Healthcare Six Sigma Breakthrough Case Study* delivers a powerful case and very specific examples of Six Sigma's effectiveness in a CABG case study. It also links success in Six Sigma with the amount of commitment from senior leadership. (http://healthcare.isixsigma.com/library/content/c030311a.asp)

LEAN and Six Sigma will continue to grow in use throughout the healthcare industry over the next 20 years because they deliver a customer-first perspective along with tools and techniques that guide the transformation of healthcare processes to be safer, higher quality, and more customer satisfying.

A Deep Dive into Innovation Methodologies: Distinctive, Breakthrough, and Collaborative

Distinctive and Breakthrough Innovation

Who invented the light bulb? If you think it was Thomas Alva Edison, you are incorrect. In 1854, Henrich Globel, a German watchmaker, invented the first true light bulb. He used a carbonized bamboo filament placed inside a glass bulb. Henry Woodward and Matthew Evans patented Globel's invention in 1875. The creation of the first lightbulb was clearly a breakthrough innovation.

Edison bought the patent from Woodward and Evans and tinkered with the design until he invented a carbon filament that allowed the electric light bulb to burn for 40 hours. He then continued to improve his light bulb until 1880, at which point it could last for over 1200 hours, the first step toward widespread use.

Globel invented the light bulb, a "breakthrough innovation," but Edison provided the "Distinctive Innovation" that resulted in the light bulb becoming the ubiquitous lighting device around the world.

Now, not all of us can be a Thomas Edison, but we all know how to use, and improve upon, existing processes, tools, and technologies. And if we as healthcare leaders choose to be lifelong learners, we can commit to

©2006 Douglas Goldstein

constantly learning how to use new tools that empower our teams to address the challenges before us. And we can use the concept of *Distinctive Innovation*™ to achieve this.

Two or more things are "distinct" if the two of them are not the same thing. "Innovation" is the introduction of new ideas, goods, services, and practices that are intended to be useful. Distinctive Innovation is the process of using a rigorous methodology, such as Six Sigma, to improve something—a process, procedure, product, or invention—that results in a distinctly different outcome than the original.

Americans are used to having "problems" solved by the end of a 30-minute sitcom or after two minutes in the microwave, but Distinctive Innovation is not a quick fix. You can't fix the problem of infection rates that are higher than the national average, or a paper-intensive process for reimbursing physicians, in just a week. And the U.S. healthcare system is too complex to use gut instincts to make improvements. We need tools and methodologies such as Six Sigma to understand appropriate technologies. We need statistical quality-improvement techniques to help identify the critical issues through surveys and data analysis. Add this level of analysis to human ingenuity along with diffusion of the invention or improvement, and you have Distinctive Innovation.

Distinctive Innovation in health care means liberating the potential of people by giving them the tools and support to do their jobs better, which may mean redesigning broken processes that lead to so many errors. The result is better processes, fewer variations, and reduced errors due to training and empowering people. The fuel and tools to support Distinctive Innovation are knowledge, resources, and wisdom.

Innovation is being used throughout the healthcare system to move from a production-centered system to a consumer-directed system. Today, we pay lip service to a patient-centered healthcare system, but the truth is that health care is mired in a production- or provider-centric medical delivery system. The good news that the direction of change toward consumer empowerment is strongly in place.

Collaborative Innovation

According to Thomas W. Malone in the book *Future of Work,* "As managers, we need to shift our thinking from command and control to coordinate and cultivate—the best way to gain power is sometimes to give it away."

"Collaborative Innovation," a relatively new discipline, is a powerful trend in many industries. As documented throughout this book, it is quite evident in the technology, government, and service sectors. Growth of collaborative innovation in health care is just beginning to accelerate. Collaboration Innovation consists of working together with an extended network of colleagues who are allied in the problem solving necessary to improve health care. The key elements of Collaborative Innovation are:

- *Coordination:* A number of organizations challenged by the same problems agree through some mechanism to share information to reach a common goal(s).
- *Cooperation:* The members of these collaborating organization share a significant level of trust that is often based on shared mission, formal or informal agreements, common problems, and recognition that solving a problem can help "float all boats" in the interest of consumers and customers.
- *Collaboration:* All parties work together and build consensus to improve processes and services, which benefits all parties. There is a strong willingness to share ideas and develop them further together.
- *Creation:* Moving inventions to widespread innovation; involving acceptance by large number of organizations; always involves the ability to think, create, and apply.
- *Communication:* Participating parties use a wide range of multimedia communication and technology-enabled vehicles to support sharing and innovation. This includes live conferences and forums as well as all forms of electronic communication, including using advanced collaboration software applications that facilitate synchronous and asynchronous communication and sharing.

- **Competition:** This has been evident in the CMS Premier Pay-for-Performance program where the 280 participating hospitals have friendly competition to improve but also are actively sharing how each organization is improving.

Some powerful examples of Collaboration Innovation are gaining widespread visibility:

- **IBM's Openness strategy,** as mentioned earlier, is founded on the principles of Collaborative Innovation.
- **Wikipedia,** the world's largest online encyclopedia is an ongoing collaborative innovation effort of tens of thousands of people around the world.
- **Collaborative Innovation Network (COIN)** is defined in the free online book *Swarm Creativity: Competitive Advantage Through Collaborative Innovation Networks* by Peter A. Gloor. COIN is "a cyber-team of self-motivated people with a collective vision, enabled by technology to collaborate in achieving a common goal—an innovation—by sharing ideas, information, and work. Working this way is the key to successful innovation, and it is no exaggeration to state that COINs are the most productive engines of innovation ever."
- **Smart Mobs: The Next Social Revolution Transforming Cultures and Communities in the Age of Instant Access,** a book by Howard Rheingold, highlights how "Smart mobs emerge when communication and computing technologies amplify human talents for cooperation. The technologies that are beginning to make smart mobs possible are mobile communication devices and pervasive computing—inexpensive microprocessors embedded in everyday objects and environments."

Collaborative Innovation is closely related to and an extension of the Collaborative Learning tactic as discussed under the Collaborative strategy earlier in this chapter. It is a natural extension of the mission-driven nature of health care and the motivations of healthcare professionals to help others. This innovation methodology is an imperative for organizations to share tacit resources and explicit experience so that within and across organizations people can save time and money by not reinventing the wheel.

"Knowledge Transfer" is frequently being seen as the rocket fuel for the rapid diffusion of proven practices that are developed under a quality improvement program. A multiyear knowledge-transfer program with the active support of senior management and integrated with quality improvement efforts solves key healthcare organization challenges including:

- Identifies solutions that improve clinical outcomes by distributing best practices throughout the organization using a collaborative model.
- Incorporates an easy-to-use "Innovation Database" of leading/best practices already in place with proven results in medication error-reduction and other patient-safety improvements.
- Leverages the wisdom of the whole organization through the sharing of solutions, ideas, processes and key resources, and in doing so, saves time and money and rewards efficient and effective work performance.
- Energizes the implementation of new technologies through process transformation, enabled by the promotion and exchange of best practices. Identifies internal leaders and rapidly diffuses processes and systems in an efficient, cost-effective manner.
- Collects the organization's institutional knowledge, resources, and technology in a centralized knowledge resource database and provides an index map to innovations that are decentralized.
- Ties together an organization's network of Communities of Performance/Practice that support continuous change.

The Knowledge Transfer tactic under the Collaboration and Innovation strategies within the Medical Informatics 20/20 framework are one in the same.

Applied Knowledge

This tactical area in the Innovation Strategy within the Medical Informatics 20/20 model has four components: "Clinical Decision Support (CDS)," "Evidence-Based Medicine," "Knowledge@Demand," and "Business Intelligence."

Effective applications and services within these tactical areas meet an underserved and vital need as federal, state, and local governments are joining forces with private practice to implement electronic health records (EHRs) for every American within ten years as well as an interoperable National Health Information Network (NHIN). Having an EHR is one

National Clinical Guideline Resources

The National Guideline Clearinghouse™ (NGC) is a public resource for evidence-based clinical practice guidelines. NGC is an initiative of the Agency for Healthcare Research and Quality (www.ahrq.gov) and the U.S. Department of Health and Human Services. The NGC mission is to provide the healthcare industry with a very easy way to access clinical practice guidelines. The components are: 1) structured abstracts; 2) links to full-text guidelines; 3) Palm-based PDA Downloads; 4) a guideline comparison utility; and many other useful features where users can search for citations for publications and resources about guidelines.

thing, but being able to deliver appropriate and actionable medical knowledge to support optimum diagnosis and treatment is quite another.

According to a HIMSS survey published in February 2006, more than 80% of hospital and health systems in the United States indicate that they will be installing clinical informatics systems during the next five years. Some of the problems driving the need for significantly improved applied knowledge processes and technologies are:

- Fifty percent of the time, patients do not receive the best diagnosis, using the most current medical knowledge at the point of care.
- Clinical decision support systems with links to multiple clinical knowledge repositories and embedded order sets and alerts are an imperative, but since most healthcare organization do not have clinical informatics systems in place today, these clinical decision support tools are not available at the point of care.
- Many healthcare organizations license multiple databases, yet they are not effectively being integrated to deliver the knowledge that is needed at the point of care by doctors, nurses, and other clinicians.
- Significant variation in delivery of care is a key factor in medical errors and high costs of care.
- Medical knowledge is doubling every three years, but there is a substantial gap in making that information available and usable at the point of care.

As we get closer to the year 2020, increasingly sophisticated clinical decision support tools, technologies, and applications will become ubiquitous at the point of care and point of need. But there is a lot of work to be done to achieve this vision. EHRs plus CDS systems plus CPOE within a context of secure, private, and interoperable health information exchanges will lead to lower cost, fewer errors, and higher quality. This was the conclusion of the "Revolutionizing Health Care Through Information Technology" report to the president by President's Information Technology Advisory Committee in 2004 (http://www.nitrd.gov/pitac/reports/20040721_hit_report.pdf).

The following information in the Applied Knowledge section will provide a foundation for further discovery. For additional in-depth information on CDS, see dedicated resources such as the president's report and books such as *Improving Outcomes with Clinical Decision Support: An Implementer's Guide* (HIMSS 2005).

Clinical Decision Support

Clinical Decision Support (CDS) involves a variety of processes, technologies, and systems to support diagnosis and treatment of medical conditions using the most current medical knowledge. Traditionally, CDS involved the distribution of paper-based resources such as clinical practice guidelines.

From a systems perspective, Clinical Decision Support systems involve interactive computer/Internet information systems that directly assist physicians, researchers, and other health professionals with decision-making tasks related to patient care.

For medical diagnosis and research, there are various types of information inputs into a CDS that would help target and locate the appropriate information desired by a clinician or researcher in a timely fashion. This would include history, sex, weight, disease and medical conditions, physical examinations, laboratory test results, care location, and other factors. The basic components of a CDS include multiple medical knowledge bases; expert interface, usually a set of rules derived from the experts and evidence-based medicine; and a communication system and computer network made available in an easy-to-understand user interface.

Advanced computerized decision support tools can be divided into two types:

- *PULL:* when a user pulls from the various knowledge bases disease, drug, or other medical information that is needed relative to diagnosis or treatment.

- ***PUSH:*** when the system initiates outreach to a user with an alert or other knowledge to support clinical decision making. This could also include the push of a standard guideline or order set.

Figure 11-10, "Critical Elements for Clinical Decision Support Systems to Improve Outcomes," illustrates the key elements for execution of CDS. For CDS to work there must be an appropriate health information technology clinical infrastructure. It is important to note that some actions, such as the use of an information dashboard for reporting and process transformation, are ongoing activities that are operating throughout phases of testing. One of the most important success factors in a CDS is that these knowledge and decision support services must be embedded in a clinician's workflow, and they must also be accurate, easy to use, and fast.

Evidence-Based Medicine

Evidence-based medicine (EBM) is the application of the scientific method to medical practice. EBM has become an international discipline and movement in medicine to bring the latest medical information into clinical practice for patients. It recognizes that many engrained medical traditions and

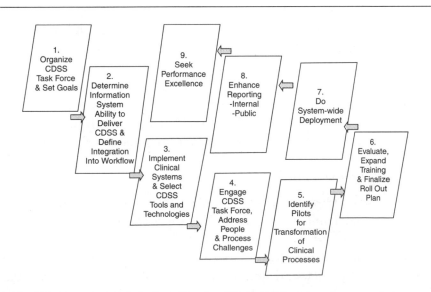

FIGURE 11-10 Critical Elements for Clinical Decision Support Systems to Improve Outcomes

Standardized Orders Sets, The Evidence, and More

Zynx Health is the leader in interactive online evidence-based health care. Its products and services address issues such as quality improvement, standardizing care, evidence-based medicine, patient safety, order set management, and clinical adoption of IT. Zynx's extensive team of professionals and experts rigorously review the latest peer-reviewed literature to develop clinical summaries and distill evidence-based best practices. Zynx empowers clinicians with "Web-based referential and integratable tools built upon the foundation of rigorous, systematic research." Evidence is made actionable in multiple forms including order sets, interdisciplinary plans of care, alerts, and reminders. Nearly a 1,000 hospitals in the United States and worldwide trust evidence-based decision support from Zynx Health to address regulatory initiatives, optimize pay-for-performance reimbursement, and measurably improve the quality and safety of patient care. See Figure 11-11, Zynx Health Web site, and visit www.zynx.com.

processes are not subjected to adequate scientific scrutiny. According to the Centre for Evidence-Based Medicine (http://www.cebm.net/), "Evidence-based medicine is the conscientious, explicit, and judicious use of current best evidence in making decisions about the care of a patient."

There are numerous clinical decision support knowledge and application service providers, and the number is growing rapidly as many public- and private-sector organizations seek to develop needed products and services. Chapter 12 includes a case study on Thomson Micromedex, which is extensively used by the Veterans Health Administration and thousands of healthcare professionals around the world to deliver vital health, medical, and pharmaceutical knowledge at the point of care for professionals and patients.

Knowledge on Demand

"Knowledge on Demand" has many aspects, but two critical concepts are: 1) Knowledge@Point of Care and 2) Knowledge@Point of Need. Knowledge on Demand, which the authors have also called "Open Knowledge," is a fast, intelligent, and efficient system of knowledge transfer using communication, Internet, and multimedia technologies to share evidenced-based best practices, community-based proven practices, knowledge, and innovations within one or more Communities of Performance and across

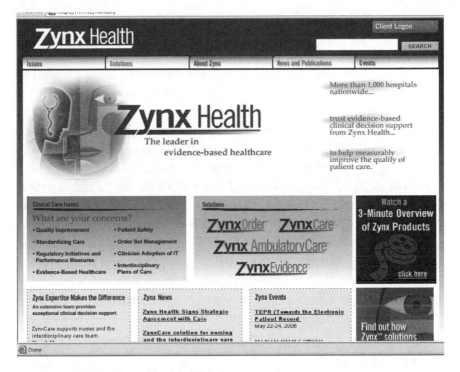

FIGURE 11-11 Zynx Health Web Site

organizational boundaries. Knowledge on Demand represents the organization of technology to enable information acquisition effectively to deliver knowledge and information at the point of need for a healthcare professional, knowledge professional, or customer. Google, Yahoo, and the more advanced search engine approaches such as Clusty (www.clusty.com), Live.com and Grokker (www.grokker.com) are Internet-based services for knowledge at the point of need.

- *Knowledge at the Point of Care* represents the field of clinical decision support systems that is focused on delivering knowledge to clinicians, researchers, pharmacists, or other professionals within the care delivery settings, quickly and accurately to improve medical diagnosis and treatment. In essence, this is a production orientation for the delivery of knowledge at the right place for the right patient at the right time.
- *Knowledge at the Point of Need* adds in the "patient-anywhere" dimension embedded in eHealth concepts. Patients want knowledge

about their health condition wherever they are. Delivery of the knowledge can be in the care setting, home, work, or anywhere in between. Knowledge at the point of need is the extension of the Medical Informatics 20/20 infrastructure out of the hospital or other patient care setting to wherever a patient or customer needs it. Inherent within this effort is the ability to know your patient customer. Knowing the customer depends on clinical and nonclinical healthcare professionals collaborating, sharing information, and using knowledge management tools and techniques.

- *Knowledge Before the Point of Need* With the right kind of patient medical history, claims history, lifestyle factor data, and intelligent decision support, it is possible to deliver valuable insights and preventive-care information to patients. The fast evolving field of preventive care will eventually evolve into preemptive care by taking the previous factors and adding genomic profiles and advances in personalized health care to predict and stop cancers and other illnesses before they become deadly and costly.

The real trick within health care is to increase sophistication and accuracy of earlier and earlier diagnosis and treatment based on the context of the situation. This requires access to patient demographics that include medical history, medical conditions, and care setting and, in the near future, real-time patient biometrics.

Business Intelligence (BI)

The use of internal and external information and market intelligence to improve decision making must include technology and the knowledge, insights, and strategies aggregated through established processes. With the rapid increases in health and medical knowledge on both the clinical and business side of care, extensive amounts of data are being generated. Various tools—data warehouses, data mining, enterprise application integration, neural networks, artificial intelligence, and other technologies and techniques—are used to achieve business intelligence (BI) goals and objectives. BI in the 21st century is a science and an art as large amounts of data are assessed, analyzed, and extracted against goals to realize actionable knowledge.

The wide range of BI tools listed and discussed in Figure 11-12 delivers an array of important tools from fuzzy logic and Bayesian Belief

Systems Dynamic Modeling	Fuzzy Logic	Rule-based Expert Systems	Other Systems
Statistics	Uncertainty Calculi	Probability	Decision Trees & Tables
Optimization	OLAP	AHP	Search Systems
Clustering	Self-Organizing Maps	Dempster-Schaffer Theory	Systems Dynamic Modeling
Delphi	Case-based Reasoning	Vector Analysis	Inexact Linear Modeling
Bayesian Belief Networks	Judgmental Bootstrapping	Evolutionary Programming	Artificial Neural Networks

FIGURE 11-12 Business Intelligence Tools. *Source:* Copyright 2006 Jonathan Schaffer and Nilmini Wickramasinghe

Networks to Search Systems and Artificial Neural Networks. According to Schaffer and Wickramasinghe—this set of BI tactics "is a collection of key tools, techniques, and processes of today's knowledge economy, that is, including but not limited to data mining, business intelligence/ business analysis and knowledge management" Recently, Wickramasinghe and Schaffer have captured this in their model of the Intelligence Continuum which emphasises the need for continuous analysis of the current state of data and other socio-technical inputs by applying the tools and techniques of the knowledge economy to develop prescriptions for the attainment of a superior future state and an enhanced extant knowledge base. Using the Intelligence Continuum to reengineer clinical processes will lead to safer, more efficient, and more effective clinical care. *(Source: Wickramasinghe, N. And J. Schaffer, 2006 Creating Knowledge Driven Healthcare Processes With The Intelligence Continuum, Intl. J. Electronic Healthcare (IJEH) vol 2, issue 2. pp.164–174)*

Applied Knowledge in all its current and future forms is a very exciting field within Medical Informatics 20/20 and promises to deliver vital and lifesaving knowledge to professionals and patients from the point of care to before the point of care as preventive care rapidly evolves into preemptive care.

Conclusion

Be "Open": Deliver Quality Through the Power of Medical Informatics 20/20

The three key strategies of Collaboration, Open Solutions, and Innovation are interlinked in concept and execution in the Medical Informatics 20/20 model. This chapter has explored several critical areas of the Collaboration and Innovation strategies. The various tactics that we have expanded on in Chapter 11 support efficient and effective execution of health information technology deployment in healthcare delivery systems today and tomorrow toward the goal of quality and performance excellence. Given the demands for a transformation to a patient-centered model, limited capital resources of many organizations, and the demand for quality, "open" strategies, tactics, tools, techniques, and technologies are indispensable for success.

The principle of "open" is a natural for the health and medical care mission given the desire of nearly all health and medical professionals to make a difference in the lives of patients. Additional forms of "open" specific to health care as defined by the authors include:

- *Open Health:* The extension of a consumer informatics subdomain that refers to a formal or informal digitally enabled network and collaborative of support where various open solutions are evolved and applied to improve patient health and wellness. It is where patients get online health and medical information and support from peers, knowledge bases and professionals.
- *Open Medical:* Focuses on open solutions on the business and clinical side of health care where multiple formal and informal networks that are collaborating throughout the healthcare industry to research, develop, promote, and facilitate open solutions application in the healthcare industry. Much of the efforts of these networks are focused on interoperability, open standards for clinical data exchange in the support of Regional Health Information Organiza-

tion (RHIO) development, and the overall National Health Information Network (NHIN).

The next chapter in Section IV, Toolkit for Quality Excellence, shares insights from several case studies about knowledge management, quality and outcomes management, and clinical decision support at the point of care. The last chapter in this section takes a look at value management and return on investment in the context of Medical Informatics.

CHAPTER 12

Case Studies in Collaboration and Innovation for Quality

"Most innovations fail. And companies that don't innovate die. In today's world, where the only constant is change, the task of managing innovation is vital for companies of every size in every industry."

Henry Chesbrough, *Open Innovation,*
The New Imperative for Creating and Profiting from Technology

"Sharing knowledge is not about giving people something, or getting something from them. That is only valid for information sharing. Sharing knowledge occurs when people are genuinely interested in helping one another develop new capacities for action; it is about creating learning processes."

Peter Senge

"Coming together is a beginning; keeping together is progress; working together is success."

Henry Ford

The National Academies, the nation's advisers on science, engineering, and medicine, released a report in 2003 strongly recommending that healthcare organizations adopt health IT systems capable of collecting and sharing information about patients and their care. In June 2005, the Advanced Medical Technology Association issued a report entitled "Health Information Technology: Improving Patient Safety and Quality of Care" (http://www.himanet.com/policy/hit/hitwhitepaper.pdf#search ='improved%20quality). It stated that approximately 31% of hospital emergency departments, 29% of outpatient departments, and 17% of doctors' offices have EHRs to support patient care. This shows that the use of electronic records in health care lags far behind other sectors of the economy.

By reducing duplicative care, lowering healthcare administration costs, and avoiding care errors, health information technology could save approximately $140 billion per year, according to the U.S. Department of Health and Human Services (HHS). That is close to 10% of total U.S. healthcare spending. Studies cited by HHS in its 2004 "Health I.T. Strategic Framework Report" suggested that the use of EHRs can reduce laboratory and radiology test ordering by 9% to 14%, lower ancillary test charges by up to 8%, reduce hospital admissions ($16,000 average cost) by 2%, and reduce excess medication usage by 11%. Two other studies have estimated that ambulatory EHRs have the potential to save all payers $78 billion to $112 billion annually.

While these measurable cost savings are impressive, our contention remains that the real return on investment comes from the many intangible benefits that we cannot yet accurately measure and translate into big dollar savings, such as better quality of care, improved patient safety, and increased patient satisfaction.

This chapter is devoted to a series of case studies that illustrates the Collaboration, Open Solutions, and Innovation strategies in action throughout the healthcare industry. Each case study demonstrates how the tactical areas and tactics within the three strategies are being used to support the realization of quality care. For instance, the Veterans Health Administration (VHA) case delivers a summary of the reviews on the high-quality care delivered by the VHA that has been supported by the VistA health information technology system. Other case studies such as Ascension Health Exchange, Air Force Medical Service, and Quality First–Bon Secours Health System show how collaboration, knowledge transfer, and Six Sigma within large geographically distributed healthcare organizations can save money and time. Case studies on MedQIC, the eHealth Initiative, and the Institute for Healthcare Improvement illustrate the power of cross-organizational sharing and collaboration to lower medical errors and improve quality. Medical Informatics 20/20 tactics and tools play an instrumental role in all the case studies explored in this chapter, which include:

- Veterans Health Administration—VistA and CPRS Quality Highlights
- Ascension Health Exchange
- Infobutton Medical Knowledge Access from Micromedex
- QualityFirst–Bon Secours Health System
- Connecting for Health and eHealth Initiative (eHI)
- MedQIC—Medicare Quality Improvement Community
- Institute for Healthcare Improvement (IHI)
- Air Force Medical Service—Knowledge Exchange

CASE STUDY 1
Veterans Health Administration—Quality and Patient Safety Through Leadership Supported by VistA and CPRS

Achieving Patient Satisfaction, Patient Safety, and Quality Through Medical Informatics

Problem: In the 1980s the U.S. Department of Veterans Affairs' (VA) healthcare system was focused on inpatient services, and the care delivery process was an inefficient paper-intensive process that couldn't be sustained over the long term.

Solution: Emphasize outpatient services and embrace the open development and deployment of health information technology and medical informatics with a central focus on patient-centered care.

Medical Informatics 20/20: The VA executed elements of all three strategies, Collaboration, Open Solutions, and Innovation, that have been explored throughout this book, as it moved forward and implemented the needed solutions. See Figures 1-3, 1-4, and 1-5 in Chapter 1 for more information.

"The Veterans Health Administration (VHA) is the largest healthcare system to have implemented an electronic medical record, routine performance monitoring, and other quality-related system changes, and we found that the VHA had substantially better quality of care than a national sample." **Comparison of Quality of Care for Patients in the Veterans Health Administration and Patients in a National Sample,** *Annals of Internal Medicine,* **2004; 141:938–945.**

"VHA's integrated health information system, including its framework for using performance measures to improve quality, is considered one of the best in the nation." **Institute of Medicine (IOM) Report, "Leadership by Example: Coordinating Government Roles in Improving Health Care."**

As documented in an article entitled "Comparison of Quality of Care for Patients in the Veterans Health Administration (VHA) and Patients in a National Sample" published in the *Annals of Internal Medicine* in 2004, "beginning in the early 1990s, VHA leadership instituted both a sophisticated electronic health record (EHR) system and a quality measurement approach directed at improving care." Other changes instituted included a system-wide commitment to quality improvement principles and a partnership between researchers and managers for quality improvement. The study concluded that "patients from the VHA received higher-quality care according to a broad measure. Differences were greatest in areas where the VHA has established performance measures and actively monitors performance." The study found that documentation practices coupled with other aspects of the VistA electronic health record (EHR) system, such as computerized reminders targeting performance measures and structured physician–patient interaction, may account for the differences between the VHA and other healthcare organizations.

Another journal article entitled "The Veterans Health Administration: Quality, Value, Accountability, and Information as Transforming Strategies for Patient-Centered Care," published in *The American Journal Of Managed Care* in November 2004, clearly shows that since 1996, improved outcomes have been achieved by the VHA in each of the following six value domains: technical quality of care, access to services, patient functional status, patient satisfaction, community health, and cost-effectiveness. These improved outcomes are attributed to the "active management of quality and value through performance measurement, timely data feedback, and *information systems* that increasingly support clinicians, managers, and patients in achieving the benefits of evidence-based practice . . ."

In the study, the VA identified several benefits that are hard to quantify, but are effective in improving healthcare delivery, quality of care, and patient safety. For example:

- Improvement in **patient safety**: reduction of pneumonia risk in high-risk patients by providing timely inoculations achieved with the use of VistA as EHR and appropriate clinical alerts based on rules
- **Reduction of variation** from evidence to practice by configuring templates to provide evidence-based practices at point of care
- Increase in **patient satisfaction**
- Improvement in **operational efficiency** by reducing turnaround time in order processing
- Optimal **patient outcomes**

Some specific examples of improved outcomes that were measured include the following:

- In 1995, the rate of pneumococcal vaccination in eligible VA patients was 29%. Today, it is 90%. Performance improvement and achievement have similarly occurred in the areas of disease treatment encompassed by more than 20 clinical practice guidelines such as coronary artery disease, heart failure, diabetes, and major depressive disorder.
- Veterans are increasingly satisfied by changes in the VA health system. On the American Customer Satisfaction Index, the VA bested the private sector's mean healthcare score of 68 on a 100-point scale, with scores of 80 for ambulatory care, 81 for inpatient care, and 83 for pharmacy services for the past three years.
- Since 1996, improved outcomes have been achieved in each of the six value domains, while simultaneously reducing the cost per patient by more than 25%.

Although information technologies such as computerized decision support and provider order entry that are part of the VA VistA and Computerized Patient Record Systems (CPRS) have been shown to improve quality and decrease adverse events in other environments, the article notes that more analysis of their specific impact on quality in the VA is needed. However, the study did recognize that some aspects of the contribution of the VistA system to improved care were self-evident. For example, patient records are available virtually 100% of the time today, in contrast to approximately 60% of the time back in 1996.

The following table extracted from the article is provided to show further VA performance scores related to selected quality indicators compared to non-VA scores. Again, while information technology has been shown to improve quality and decrease adverse events, more analysis of the specific impact of the VistA system on quality of care in the VA is still needed.

The Department of Veterans Affairs' (VA) clinical information system and EHR, known as VistA, has received wide recognition and numerous awards including:

- The prestigious "Innovations in American Government Award," the annual award, sponsored by Harvard University's Ash Institute

Clinical Indicator	VA 2003	Medicare Best 2003[16]	non-VA or Medicare
Advised tobacco cessation (VA *3, others *1)	75	63	68[17,†]
Beta-blocker after MI	98	93	94[17,†]
Breast cancer screening	84	74	75[17,†]
Cervical cancer screening	90	NA	81[17,†]
Cholesterol screening (all patients)	91	NA	73[18]
Cholesterol screening (post-MI)	94	80	79[17,†]
LDL-C < 130 mg/dL post-MI	78	67	61[17,†]
Colorectal cancer screening	67	50	49[18]
Diabetes HbA$_{1C}$ checked past year	94	88	83[17,†]
Diabetes HbA$_{1C}$ > 9.5% (lower is better)	15	NA	34[17,†]
Diabetes LDL-C measured	95	91	85[17,†]
Diabetes LDL-C, > 130 mg/dL	77	68	55[17,†]
Diabetes eye exam	75	65	52[17,†]
Diabetes kidney function	70	54	52[17,†]
Hypertension: BP ≤ 140/90	68	61	58[17,†]
Influenza immunization	76	74	68[18,‡]
Pneumococcal immunization	90	NA	63[18]
Mental health follow-up 30 days postdischarge	77	60	74[17,†]

*All measures are directly comparable, except for mental health follow-up, because the VA accepts telephonic followup.

All data are from 2002 and were published by the sources noted.

BP indicates blood pressure; HbA1C, glycosylated hemoglobin; LDL-C, low-density lipoprotein cholesterol; MI, myocardial infarction; NA, data not available; VA, Department of Veterans Affairs.

†Patients were of all ages and were in private managed care programs.

‡Rhode Island is the benchmark for influenza immunization.

FIGURE 12-1 VA, Medicare, and Best Measured non-VA, non-Medicare Performance for 18 Comparable Performance Quality Indicators (US benchmarks are bolded)*

for Democratic Governance and Innovation at the Kennedy School of Government

- VA hospitals scored higher than private facilities on the University of Michigan's American Customer Satisfaction Index, based on patient surveys on the quality of care received in 2005.
- The VA scored 83 out of 100; private institutions, 71. Males 65 years and older receiving VA care had about a 40% lower risk of death than those enrolled in Medicare Advantage, whose care is provided through private health plans or HMOs, according to a study published in the April 2006 edition of *Medical Care.*

The VA's complete adoption of electronic health records and performance measures have resulted in high-quality, low-cost health care coupled with high patient satisfaction. A recent RAND study found that VA outperforms all other sectors of American health care across a spectrum of 294 measures of quality in disease prevention and treatment. For six straight years, the VA has led private-sector health care in the independent American Customer Satisfaction Index.

According to an *Annals of Internal Medicine* editorial dated August 17, 2004: *"The 'culture of quality'* [at the VA] *depended on the successful implementation of several innovations: a uniform data collection system facilitated by nationwide implementation of an electronic medical record system, systematic application of quality standards, and externally monitored local area networks to monitor quality."*

The highly acclaimed VistA system is a public domain software system or Free and Open Source Software (FOSS) as described in this book. More information is available through VA's Web site at http://www.va.gov/vista_monograph/ and from other sources mentioned throughout the book.

CASE STUDY 2	Ascension Health Exchange— Knowledge Sharing and Innovation Acceleration Across Health Systems Save Time, Money, and Lives

Problem: Ascension Health needed a solution to support the acceleration of innovation and knowledge transfer to improve clinical and business per-

CASE STUDY 2   *continued*

formance. And it needed to implement this solution without a centralized Intranet.

Solution: Ascension Health Exchange—Elevating Quality and Service Through Knowledge Transfer and Innovation

Medical Informatics 20/20: Collaboration and Innovation tactics addressed are Knowledge Transfer, Communities of Performance (which are called Communities of Excellence), Executive/Clinical Leadership, Facilitated Knowledge Transfer, Collaborative Innovation, Knowledge @Demand, and Business Intelligence. See Figures 1-3 and 1-5 in Chapter 1.

Ascension Health is the largest Catholic, nonprofit health system in the United States, serving patients through a network of more than 75 hospitals and related health facilities that provide acute-care, long-term care, community health, psychiatric, rehabilitation, and residential-care services. It is an integrated delivery system that resulted when four leading Catholic health systems merged in 2001. Ascension Health is sponsored by four provinces, which include the Daughters of Charity, the Sisters of St. Joseph of Nazareth, and the Sisters of St. Joseph of Carondelet. The organization is committed to "caring for those who are most in need in the communities we serve."

With more than 100,000 associates in 20 states and the District of Columbia, Ascension Health has established a clear "Call to Action" that represents the conviction of every one of its local and national leaders to provide:

- Healthcare That Is Safe
- Healthcare That Works
- Healthcare That Leaves No One Behind

To achieve these goals, a series of foundation strategies have been put in place:

- Presence as Needed at Full Potential
- Knowledge on Demand as a Fully Connected Ministry
- Integrated Alliance Network of Values-Compatible Partners
- Model Community of Mission-Centered, Healthy Associates

These foundation strategies enable the realization of the Call to Action.

Access to Knowledge Provides Value

Based on recent surveys, members find the Exchange useful for the following reasons:

"[I like the] ability to put questions out to a community and to get answers and other types of information fed back in a relatively quick time frame without playing phone tag with many others for days."

"Excellent vehicle for sharing best practices."

"We might have spent months trying to brainstorm and create a program out of the blue."

"Provides me with an easy way to share best practice information with local mgmt."

"Didn't have to reinvent the wheel . . . strengthened our case for implementation."

Through a collaboration among Ascension Health's chief medical officer, chief information officer, and chief strategy officer, the organization created a multimedia effort called the Ascension Health Exchange, which had at its foundation a Web-based communication and collaboration portal that facilitates intra-organizational sharing across Health Ministries (Health Systems). The "Exchange," as it is known internally, is part of the health system's Knowledge Transfer Strategic Initiative—a multiyear, enterprise-wide program designed to facilitate knowledge sharing, stimulate innovation, and encourage collaboration within Ascension Health Ministries. The focus of the initiative is to create a sustainable culture of pervasive Innovation and Knowledge Transfer that helps achieve Ascension Health's Call to Action.

Research Yields Proven Practices, and the Exchange Is Born

In 2002, executives, clinicians, and leaders across the Ascension Health Ministries realized that the organization needed a way to communicate and collaborate with leaders in each of the facilities in the newly integrated health system. The initiative was led by Strategic Business Development and Innovation, a function under the chief strategy officer focused on diffusing knowledge across the system in conjunction with the chief information officer and chief medical officer. Ascension Health selected Medical Alliances Inc., a leader in innovation and knowledge management, to assist in the research, development, and operational support of the project.

A multidisciplinary team conducted extensive research on the needs of the organization's facilities, and simultaneously developed an inventory of proven practices and innovations based on what each ministry was willing to share. The research phase led to a series of business and technology requirements for what was to become the Ascension Health Exchange. With a multiyear business plan in place, the Medical Alliances team worked with Ascension Health leaders to evaluate technology tools that would allow knowledge to be shared and resources diffused rapidly and effectively across the system. The selected solutions included a variety of document repository, content management, site search, and communication features. In addition, a robust Innovation Database was integrated into the portal to allow associates to upload profiles of their innovations and effective practices, as well as attach reports, presentations, policies, tools, and photos.

Figure 12-2 shows the home page of the Ascension Health Exchange, the starting point for Ascension Health Exchange, which is a collection of more than 35 Communities of Excellence. The Exchange home page is updated regularly with system-wide resources and external news that supports strategic and tactical goals and objectives. The Share button, the Search window, and access to the Innovation Database are available on the top of every page within the Exchange and its ever-expanding number of Communities of Excellence.

Innovation Database Speeds Proven Practice Diffusion

The Innovation Database, a central and well-used feature of the Exchange, is a collection of shared resources from Health Ministry associates and National Office staff. It contains nearly 500 innovations and effective practices and thousands of presentations, reports, protocols, spreadsheets, data, and forms that can be downloaded and customized for use in a Health Ministry. Prominently accessible at the top of every page in the Exchange, the Innovation Database can be browsed by Health Ministry, department, Call to Action, or any number of other categories. It is also keyword searchable. To share an innovation, an associate simply clicks a "Share" button and completes a profile form. See Figure 12-3, which

FIGURE 12-2 Ascension Health Exchange Web Home Page

illustrates how members click the "Share" button at the top of every page in the Exchange to complete a profile and upload their innovations and effective practices into the Innovation Database. Ascension Health further encouraged sharing through its Integrated Scorecard management effort, which required that each facility contribute at least one innovation or effective practice to the database.

The Innovation Database has been instrumental in the rapid diffusion of knowledge across the hospitals and facilities. More than just a descrip-

A One-to-Many Communication and Collaboration Tool

E-mail Listserv has proven to be one of the most popular community tools in the Exchange, as it allows associates to quickly and easily query colleagues about pressing challenges. A senior VP/chief nurse executive from one ministry submitted three queries on the Chief Nursing Officers Listserv and received more than 50 responses for issues related to fetal monitoring and blood transfusion. The ministry implemented one of the suggestions from another ministry and saved an estimated $10,000 to $25,000 in development costs.

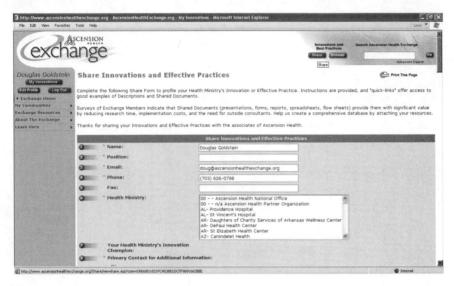

FIGURE 12-3 Easy to Use 'Share' Button and Innovation Knowledge and Know–How Upload Web Service

tion of a program or initiative, each database entry includes details about quantifiable benefits, implementation time lines, and ministries with which the innovation has been shared. More importantly, the ability for submitters to upload forms, policies, presentations, and spreadsheets allows associates in all ministries to rapidly adopt and integrate effective practices. For example, when the VP of Corporate Quality from a Connecticut ministry needed to help her hospitals reduce falls, she searched the Innovation Database and found the falls-reduction program of a ministry in Arizona. After downloading shared resources and talking with program directors at the Arizona ministry, the executive in Connecticut was able to implement the program in her facility quickly and cost-effectively. Likewise, a CNO in D.C. searched the Innovation Database and found an innovative way to conduct executive patient-safety rounds. After reviewing the innovation's accompanying documentation, she was able to convince her ministry's CFO to allocate resources for this important initiative.

The beauty of the Innovation Database is the ease with which it captures and maintains resources, innovations, and effective practices that can be downloaded and used by any Exchange member at no additional cost. In addition, custom-designed tracking features identify the person who submitted the innovation, along with the date and time an innovation or attachment in the database is viewed. This helps track diffusion of innovations across the system.

Communities of Excellence Support System Initiatives

Communities of Excellence (Communities) are specific workplaces within the Exchange that allow affinity groups to share resources, solve problems, collaborate on projects, and communicate ideas. "Community of Excellence" is another service on the Web site, which can help Ascension Health associates solve problems and share information among affinity groups. Each Community has a suite of tools that includes Alerts, Calendar, Online Survey, Listserv, Community Library, Links, News, and Discussion Board. Some Communities support the basic need for a group of individuals to communicate and share; others support the need to share resources and collaborate to solve a problem or rally around a strategic initiative. Although each Exchange Community has unique needs and content, all Communities are designed to:

1. Allow an affinity group to communicate and collaborate to solve problems across state lines and time zones
2. Create a system of knowledge-sharing across hospitals within the system
3. Provide an easy-to-access environment for associates to discuss daily challenges, provide honest feedback, and share ideas and resources
4. Facilitate new relationships among associates

Overseen and managed by volunteer "mayors" and "coordinators" and supported by the Exchange support team, Exchange Communities facilitate rapid knowledge/capability diffusion and quality improvement at Ascension Health. Each Community's suite of tools allows Community leaders to post information and communicate with members.

The mayor and coordinator receive technical training and knowledge-transfer assistance as needed, and can customize the Community home page if desired. They are automatically enrolled in the Nexus—a Community that provides knowledge and resources to meet the specific technical and sharing needs of Community leaders—and are able to participate in periodic "ShareShops" that facilitate knowledge transfer among the Community leadership.

Dedicated Exchange Team Facilitates Top Priority Knowledge Transfer

The central Exchange support team plays an important role in facilitating knowledge transfer in the high-priority areas. The team performs various roles in assisting Communities of Excellence work smarter and support performance excellence. Composed of consultants in business process transformation and experts in facilitated knowledge transfer, the Exchange team provides training and resources to Community leaders about how to optimize the Exchange for communication and collaboration. Exchange team members also work with Ascension Health executives to set annual goals and objectives for the growth of the Exchange. For instance, based on the needs of the Health Ministries, the team developed more than 100 knowledge bundles and developed in-depth "Knowledge Navigators" that provide easy access to a broad array of vital resources on topics such as Geriatric Services, Hospitalist Services, Emergency Services, and others. Figure 12-4 demonstrates the dashboard access to the Emergency Services Knowledge Navigator.

Leveraging Communities to Achieve the Call to Action

Ascension Health is committed to its three-pronged Call to Action, delivering "Healthcare That Is Safe," "Healthcare That Works," and "Health-

FIGURE 12-4 Knowledge Navigators on the Ascension Health Exchange

care That Leaves No One Behind." Exchange Communities move the organization toward the achievement of these strategic goals by providing centralized document repositories and communication tools that allow associates to collaborate and get work done.

For example, as part of "Healthcare That Is Safe," Ascension Health is working to improve patient safety and reduce preventable medical errors and deaths in all of its ministries. The goal of "Zero Preventable Deaths by 2009" has resulted in the creation of "Priorities for Action" to address issues such as falls and fall injuries, perinatal safety, and pressure ulcers. The Clinical Excellence Community provides easy access to Priorities for Call to Action "InfoCenters" through a customized Community home page designed for rapid diffusion of knowledge related to Priorities for Action and IHI initiatives. This home page, shown in Figure 12-5, illustrates how quick access to InfoCenters supports Ascension Health's Priorities for Action clinical initiatives. The Clinical Excellence Community is one of the largest on the Exchange, with more than 1,500 members in 20 states and the District of Columbia. Each InfoCenter helps diffuse leading practices from Health Ministries and connects members to background material, corporate documents, conference-call information, and event calendars. The Community also contains ten e–mail listservs that all members use to communicate about patient safety issues

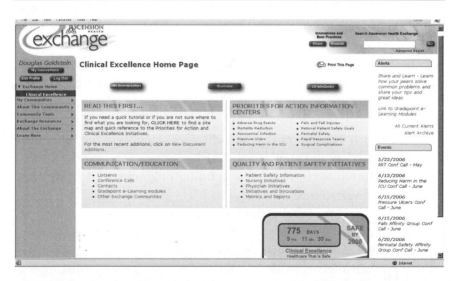

FIGURE 12-5 The Clinical Excellence Community Home Page

and the Priorities for Action, as well as links to multimedia presentations in the Ascension Health Learning Center.

To support "Healthcare That Works," the Departments of Associate Health, Workers' Compensation, and Disability save time, save money, and communicate better using the Associate Health and Safety Community. The Community home page provides work team materials, access to grant programs and RFPs, and "Tips from the Road," gleaned from ministry site visits. A Community Library has replaced the need to mail out CDs containing conference materials, and the e–mail listserv is used for queries, announcements, and event reminders.

Finally, to support "Healthcare That Leaves No One Behind," Ascension Health's Access Ministries built the Access Models Community on the foundation of Ascension Health's "5 Steps to 100% Access." The Community includes a section describing each of these steps, as well as a section for the Advocacy Staff in Washington, D.C., to upload information and request action when necessary. In addition, posted outcomes measure and Coalition Profiles provide easy access to important resources.

Program Results

The Exchange launched in April of 2003 with five Communities of Excellence: Chief Medical Officers, Chief Nursing Officers, Clinical Excellence Team, Ministry Operating Executives, and Healthcare Environments of the Future. In early 2006, nearly 4,000 members were visiting 32 Communities in the Exchange—from Clinical Excellence, Supply Chain Management, and Spirituality, to Associate Health and Safety, Access Models, and Finance. The Healthcare Advisory Board has called it a "Leading Innovations Web Portal," and key metrics indicated:

- More than 475 innovations and effective practices in the Innovation Database, with hundreds of attached resources that include business cases, spreadsheets, order sets, training programs, and many more know-how resources
- 12,404 reviews of innovations and resource downloads
- Many documented cases of diffusion and savings in time and money through sharing of knowledge and know-how resources
- Potentially millions of dollars in savings from the submitted innovations and through sharing and spread of proven practices and resources

- 100-plus knowledge bundles and "Knowledge Navigators" that provide easy access to vital resources
- Ten clinical excellence "Information Centers" that contain evidence-based and system-vetted proved practices, downloadable toolkits, policies, forms, and references. The Information Centers are used for targeted knowledge transfer, spread and adoption of key goals called "priorities for actions' all in an effort to achieve zero preventable errors and deaths by July 2008.

The Ascension Health Exchange has served as a powerful demonstration of the ability to support sharing across the organization. The Exchange team is evaluating the strengths, weaknesses, and opportunities based on the last three years of operations to develop a strategic and operating plan to guide the growth and expansion of the Exchange going forward.

CASE STUDY 3   Real-Time Clinical Decision Support at the Point of Care— InfoButton Access™ from Thomson Micromedex

Problem: Physicians and other healthcare providers have always had access to clinical information to help with diagnosing and treating patients. The problem is that clinical information is scattered, voluminous, and not always readily available when needed. In addition, wading through the vast databases of clinical support materials can take hours, if not days when the answers are needed in seconds. So how can providers get the patient-specific information they need when they need it fast, accurately, and in a way that empowers decision making?

Solution: Delivering Knowledge@Point of Care An important element in achieving the goals of patient care improvements and medical error reduction is clinical decision support: access to accurate and appropriate clinical knowledge at the point of care. Having the right information at the right time could mean the difference between life and death.

Medical Informatics 20/20: Innovation tactics addressed are Clinical Decision Support and Evidence-Based Medicine. See Figure 1-5 in Chapter 1.

The challenge with effective clinical decision support is the ability to deliver accurate information quickly when needed and in the proper context. Volumes and volumes of medical databases exist, but who has time to comb through them when a patient presents baffling life-threatening symptoms? What about allergic reactions to medications or contraindications with other prescribed medications? With only a few minutes or less to make a decision, physicians need proven medical counsel and they need it fast.

A key component of the Innovation strategy is the use of Applied Knowledge: The delivery of clinical decision support, evidence-based medicine, and knowledge@demand at the point of care. The objective is to deliver not only the knowledge, but the knowledge needed for that patient at that moment.

Imagine this scenario: The physician is preparing to discharge a patient and wants to prescribe a new medication. Will this medicine be appropriate for this patient's condition? What is the correct dosage and administration? Are adverse side effects present that must be considered? Will this medicine interfere with other medicines being taken? Is this medicine included on the patient's formulary? Obtaining answers to these questions takes time and access to the appropriate data. What is the likelihood that the physician has that information readily available?

InfoButton Access Delivers Knowledge@Point of Care

A new product called InfoButton Access™ from Thomson Micromedex shows tremendous promise in finally solving the "clinical decision support at the point of care" dilemma. Taking advantage of Micromedex's vast collection of clinical databases, which include drug and lab reference, disease state and management, and patient education information, InfoButton Access integrates this knowledge with patient-specific data to provide accurate clinical information when needed.

FIGURE 12-6 InfoButton Icon

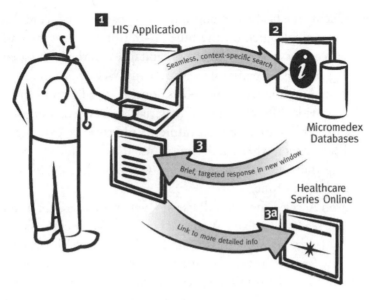

FIGURE 12-7 InfoButton Process Map

How does it work? The concept is amazingly simple:

1) The physician clicks the InfoButton Access button from within the desktop or handheld application.
2) InfoButton Access collects context-specific data from the patient's electronic medical record (EMR), computerized physician order entry (CPOE), or other health information system (HIS) application.
3) A request is sent to Micromedex, who then delivers upon return a detailed answer tailored to the patient's specific needs and medical condition—all within a matter of seconds—to the physician's handheld application.
4) Clinical data vocabularies from any EMR, CPOE, or other Health Information System are simply hyperlinked to online, context-specific reference materials if more information is needed.

Clinicians have ready access to detailed and specific health information with a single click. Access to information such as patient-specific treatment guidelines, dosages, and therapy recommendations are available immediately. Because it is a simple process to click on the blue InfoButton Access icon, clinicians are more likely to make time to use this feature, thereby reducing medical errors and improving patient care. And, because all it takes is a single click on the blue "i"-button, no lengthy end-user training is necessary. InfoButton Access capitalizes on the icon-based help methodology already recognizable within many Web applications.

InfoButton Access is also designed as context specific and can be customized to provide different types of materials and information to different types of applications. For example, a pharmacist can access the DRUGDEX® System, while a nurse might use the CareNotes™ System— guaranteeing that the right information will be delivered to the right clinician at the right time.

InfoButton Access is now in full use at Partners HealthCare in Boston, which comprises Brigham and Women's Hospital, Massachusetts General Hospital, and other hospitals associated with Harvard Medical School. Partners is the first institution to have the system fully operational.

According to Paul Szumita, PharmD, clinical pharmacy manager at Brigham and Women's Hospital, the InfoButton links, or Knowledge Links as Partners calls them, are available to clinicians through the pharmacy Web page, the physician order entry (POE) system, and the electronic medication administration record.[1] Statistics show that Partners HealthCare clinicians are answering clinical questions more frequently and more accurately with access to the right content, in the right format, at the right time. Current deployment reports demonstrate more than 400 look-ups occurring each day without any formal training.[2]

Both institutions have successfully implemented InfoButton Access with little or no end-user training. In a randomized group study, Partners HealthCare found the knowledge-based link affected the decision-management process of one in five clinicians. The product helped to answer 80% of the questions clinicians asked.[3] This ability to foster spur-of-the-moment fact checking is possible because of the product's intuitive design.

A major challenge in integrating InfoButton Access into health information systems is the widespread use of proprietary vocabulary. Not all institutions call clinical terms by the same name or terminology. Micromedex recognizes that challenge and has adapted the product to cross-talk

---

[1]US Pharmacist; June 2005; *Partners HealthCare Installs InfoButton Access™ US Pharm,* 2005, 6:82–86.

[2]An Approach for Improving Business and Clinical Performance; Jerome A. Osheroff, MD, Thomson Micromedex.

[3]*Healthcare IT News*; November 2004: Partners, Regenstrief will beta InfoButton.

different clinical data vocabularies. By expanding the product's data capabilities, users can perform more targeted queries. Information that is returned is hyperlinked to other reference sources so that more information is available if needed.

Micromedex is continuing to evolve the InfoButton Access solution, and is currently in HIS integration discussions with major healthcare IT providers. The company is working closely with its healthcare provider partners to define their clinical information needs and workflow and then integrate that knowledge into clinical information systems that will deliver knowledge at the point of care. Eventually, the goal is to seamlessly provide all clinicians with the targeted knowledge they seek when they need it. The focus is no longer on aggregating the most robust clinical information databases, but rather on using a detailed understanding of the clinician's workflow so that the clinical information can be integrated and disseminated appropriately.

Implications for Medical Informatics 20/20

Information technology leaders and suppliers must be more aggressive when it comes to delivering knowledge at the point of care. The technology already exists that allows fast access to clinical information across clinical databases. Health IT vendors need to look at ways that they can also access additional knowledge feeds such as evidence-based medicine and higher levels of clinical decision support such as artificial intelligence and other sophisticated diagnostic tools. The greatest challenge, however, is not just about access to data, but how to efficiently deliver the data with the right patient context when and where it's needed.

CASE STUDY 4   Bon Secours Health System Achieving "QualityFirst" Through Knowledge Transfer

Problem: Bon Secours Hospital System lacked a system to support proven practices spread and Six Sigma implementation, which were necessary to realize goals related to the Premier–CMS Pay-for-Performance demonstration project and the overall quality plan.

continues

CASE STUDY 4   *continued*

Solution: Develop a system-wide knowledge transfer and Six Sigma support service focused on people-process-technology to enable progressive realization of clinical and operational performance excellence goals.

Medical Informatics 20/20: Innovation tactics addressed are Knowledge Transfer, Communities of Practice, Executive/Clinical Leadership, Facilitated Knowledge Transfer, Collaborative Learning, Distinctive Innovation, Clinical Engagement, Six Sigma, and Business Intelligence. See Figures 1-3 and 1-5 in Chapter 1.

Bon Secours Health System (BSHSI) is an integrated delivery system based in Marriottsville, Maryland, made up of 20 acute-care hospitals, one psychiatric hospital, six nursing-care facilities, numerous ambulatory sites, six assisted-living facilities, and home health and hospice services. BSHSI has long been committed to quality and was the largest health system in the CMS Pay-for-Performance demonstration project being facilitated by Premier, Inc. In 2003, BSHSI's Board Quality Committee adopted the following vision statement on quality:

- As part of the healing ministry of the Catholic Church, Bon Secours Health System and all of its caregivers strive to bring people and communities to health and wholeness.
- When health and wholeness cannot be achieved, all caregivers will assure palliative and end-of-life care that is compassionate and brings comfort.
- This mission commits to excellence in providing health care within a collaborative learning culture, which continuously strives to improve.
- Success is reflected in all patients and residents by care that is holistic, demonstrably safe, effective, timely, efficient, and equitable, and measured by clinical outcome as well as patient/resident satisfaction.

Phase 1: Targeted Knowledge Transfer (TKT) Plan and Implementation

Execution of BSHSI's vision statement and its Strategic Quality Plan was based on the following guiding principle:

The BSHSI "Knowledge Transfer for Performance Improvement" is a strategic imperative that optimizes the integration of human resources, processes, and technology to liberate the potential of our people.

Therefore, the first phase of development focused on BSHSI's need to identify proven practices and accelerate the diffusion of these practices through a Targeted Knowledge Transfer effort to support cost reductions and improve quality. Targeted areas included Revenue Enhancement, Expense Management (i.e., Productivity Management, Nursing Agency Reduction, Workers' Compensation, Supply Management), and Physician Alignment Strategies, as well as the CMS Pay-for-Performance demonstration project.

BSHSI enlisted the aid of Medical Alliances, Inc., a leader in knowledge transfer, innovation acceleration, and Communities of Performance solutions to assist them with the planning, development, and operations of the targeted knowledge transfer effort. Within 45 days, the Medical Alliances team had deployed a no-license-fee open source software Web portal content management system (www.BSHSIShare.org) at low cost and initiated Web-based knowledge transfer, online performance reporting, search, online data collection, knowledge library for approved franchise practices, resource topics aligned with the CMS clinical conditions where members can share on a real-time basis with other members, and a more efficient and lower-cost method of holding virtual meetings.

Medical Alliances associates evolved into an operational support role as the Targeted Knowledge Transfer Support Team (TKT Team), which acted as an integrated member of BSHSI's quality team supporting continuous process improvement, the CMS Pay-for-Performance demonstration project, and ongoing operational support of the Phase 1 knowledge transfer efforts.

Figure 12-8 describes the five major program components of a Targeted Knowledge Transfer Program, which are:

- *Community Operations and Support:* the dedicated team focused on effective transfer of top priorities
- *Knowledge and Capability Transfer:* links in an extended network of subject matter support from within and outside the organization to support execution of proven practices
- *Multimedia Technology Portal:* the Internet-based content management system, Web portal, and other technologies (video

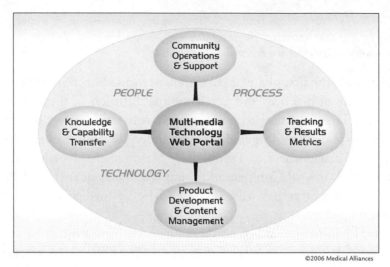

©2006 Medical Alliances

FIGURE 12-8 Knowledge Management—Three Core Competencies and Five Program Components

conferencing, instant messaging, etc.) that support rapid–cycle learning and knowledge exchange

- ***Product Development and Content Management:*** the packaging of proven practices into knowledge bundles that includes all the know-how, including business plans, training programs, financial models, audio interviews, and other documents and resources that help reduce the replication time in other environments
- ***Tracking and Results Metrics:*** the methodologies and systems that allow the tracking of proven practice diffusion

"People," "Technology," and "Process" represent the three fundamentals that must be addressed through every Targeted Knowledge Transfer program component. The first-generation Targeted Knowledge Transfer Web site, BSHSIShare.org, is shown in Figure 12-9.

Some of the services provided by the TKT Team included the following:

- ***Incentive Campaigns to Stimulate Resource Sharing***—The BSHSI Quality Leadership and TKT Team organized an incentive campaign to encourage sharing of resource documents, guidelines, materials, and so on by members. This campaign actively encouraged members to submit resources to the resource topics (organized by Pay-for-Performance conditions and procedures being tracked) area on

FIGURE 12-9 Bon Secours Health System—Targeted Knowledge Transfer for Performance Excellence Plan Framework

BSHSIShare.org. The organization whose members contributed the most received $10,000 in capital to apply to a program or service, and the member who contributed the most resources won a trip to attend the annual IHI Premier Breakthroughs Conference. The TKT Team encouraged resource submissions primarily through eAlerts that featured recent submissions (with direct links back to submissions) and encouraged more people to share. More than 200 order sets, training programs, protocols, processes, and so on were shared within 45 days.

- *AMI Expert Panel—Best Practices Rating Process and Criteria—* The TKT Team formed an AMI Expert Panel to evaluate AMI resources posted on BSHSIShare.org and to develop guidelines and criteria to rate resources shared via the Web portal in an effort to improve AMI scores across the system. The rating system uses a four-point scale from "Discouraged Practice" to "Franchise Practice" to be implemented system-wide. The expert panel met monthly and was made up of representatives from the TKT Team, as well as CM leaders and other clinicians throughout BSHSI. Figure 12-10 shows one example of the work

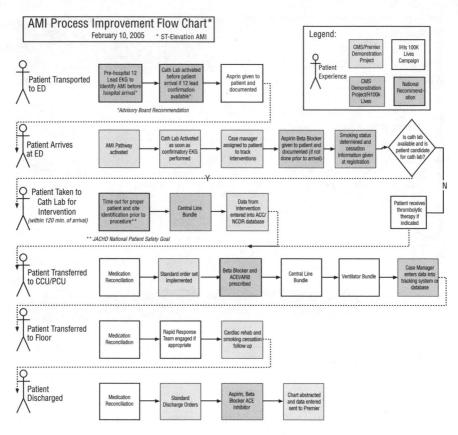

FIGURE 12-10 AMI Process Improvement Flow Chart

produced by TKT Team members. This AMI Process Improvement Flow Chart described the optimal treatment course for AMI patients and incorporated recommendations from the IHI 100k Lives campaign.

- *Web-Based Clinical Data Reporting and Collection for Rapid–Cycle Diffusion*—The TKT Team worked aggressively with the BSHSI management engineering team to move from CDs and FedEx shipments to real-time eServices that gathered and disseminated critical performance data as soon as it was received from CMS and Premier. Complex Excel workbook files with extensive filtered and pivot tables were Web-enabled for direct viewing and printing and efficient downloading. TKT Team members have supported the quality effort through process flow-charting and providing subject matter expertise in key areas of innovation, knowledge transfer, physician relations,

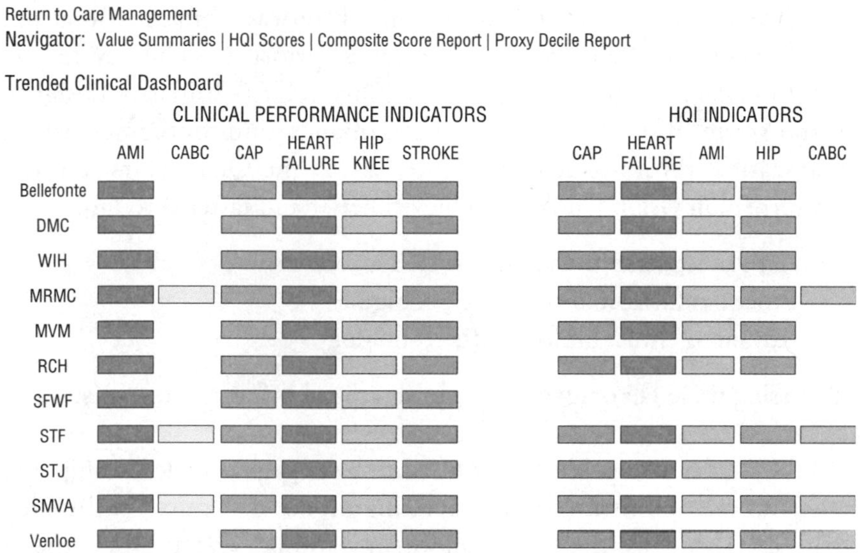

Return to Care Management
Navigator: Value Summaries | HQI Scores | Composite Score Report | Proxy Decile Report

Trended Clinical Dashboard

FIGURE 12-11 Rapid–Cycle Online Clinical Dashboard

clinical informatics, etc. Figure 12-11 illustrates the BSHSIShare.org Rapid–Cycle Online Clinical Trended Dashboard Reporting, which provided quick access to performance scores for each facility.

- *AMI Webinar—Lower Cost Than WebEx and No Problems Accessing*—The AMI expert panel conducted "Webinars" online at BSHSIShare.org. The TKT Team initiated the planning, organized the technology, hosted the meeting, and then supported rapid dissemination of the documents and audio files of the Webinar. For example, one Webinar featured presentations from cardiologists from two BSHSI facilities illustrating AMI initiatives from each of their facilities, followed by discussion and Q&A. The presentations were posted online at BSHSIShare.org along with the agenda and discussion guide. The TKT Team captured the audio portion of the event and posted it online for future reference to enhance member learning based on the vast amount of detail that is spoken and never written into a document or PowerPoint presentation.

Phase 2. QualityFirst and Six Sigma Expansion

In 2005, under the leadership of a new CEO, BSHSI focused on improving performance across critical dimensions of quality and financial performance. A streamlined Strategic Quality Plan was established that put quality as one of the organization's highest priorities. The key implementation component to this was the "QualityFirst" initiative designed to transform BSHSI to a high-performance and outcomes-driven organization. As illustrated in Figure 12-12, the QualityFirst clinical transformation vision would be achieved better and faster through:

- Activist leadership and empowered associates
- Process transformation using Six Sigma
- Advanced clinical informatics technology

Addressing these factors would establish critical infrastructure to support goal achievement.

BSHSI set out to achieve performance by engaging its leadership and associates to committing to an operating model that puts QualityFirst with Six Sigma as the common organizational system for process improvement. A comprehensive clinical transformation plan was developed to execute the QualityFirst strategy, which involved creating a unified clinical collaborative of physicians, nurses, and care management that focused on outcomes management. The four key strategies are shown in Figure 12-13.

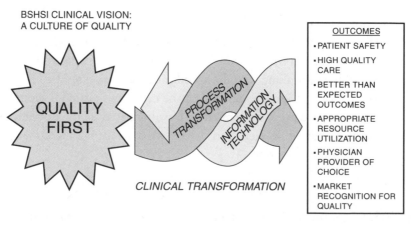

FIGURE 12-12 "Quality First" Transformation Model

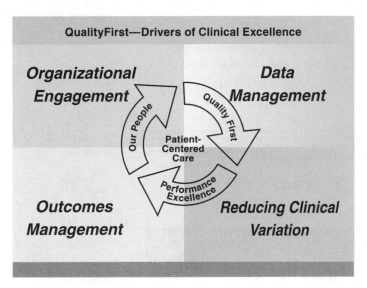

FIGURE 12-13 Drivers of Clinical Excellence

Within each of the four areas there were a series of tactics such as executive huddles, Medicare LOS analysis and reduction, and real-time data review. These strategies and their tactics were integrated with the proven rapid–cycle techniques such as Six Sigma process improvement and Targeted Knowledge Transfer for rapid diffusion of proven practices.

Six Sigma is a way of thinking that builds on the continual development of individuals, processes, local systems, and the system itself. Six Sigma within BSHSI involved the systematic, data-driven design and redesign of services and processes of work so that they met and exceeded the needs and expectations of the people served, while achieving clinical and operating excellence. Six Sigma Green Belt training was offered to all leaders throughout BSHSI as a foundation for performance excellence. Black Belt training, a more advanced and intensive statistical approach for continuous performance improvement, was offered to certain selected system leaders.

In September 2005, BSHSI launched its new enterprise-wide Intranet, IRIS. The TKT Team worked closely with BSHSI to migrate the features and functions from BSHSIShare.org to the IRIS platform. In addition, the team worked closely with various groups within BSHSI to help develop and support their IRIS communities such as Palliative Care, Medication Safety, Six Sigma, Risk and Insurance, Nursing Collaborative, and others.

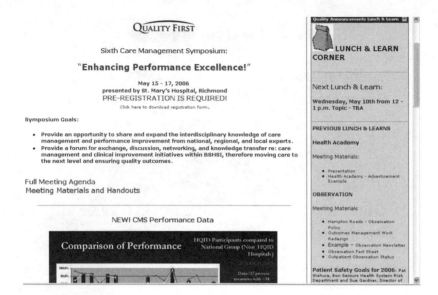

FIGURE 12-14 Quality Community home page in IRIS

Figure 12-14 shows the Quality Community home page on IRIS. Other specialized functions that were developed by the TKT Team included:

- ***Expert Locator—Connecting Experts Within the Organization***—A Six Sigma Expert Locator was developed to facilitate communication among BSHSI's Green Belt and Black Belt communities. As illustrated in Figure 12-15, BSHSI associates can easily search for others throughout the system who have the expertise and knowledge they seek. In addition to the Six Sigma community within IRIS, the TKT Team is also working with the BSHSI Palliative Care, Risk, and Quality communities to customize a version of the application for their IRIS community.
- ***Lunch & Learn Series—A Weekly Forum for Sharing Knowledge and Communicating Results***—BSHSI was looking for a way to rapidly spread results and support the testing of change throughout its system. Along with the support of the TKT team they began conducting weekly a "Lunch & Learn" via teleconference and their new Intranet, IRIS. E–mail announcements are sent weekly to lists of quality care management, corporate compliance, finance, HIMS, nursing, and medical staff across the system, and all meeting materi-

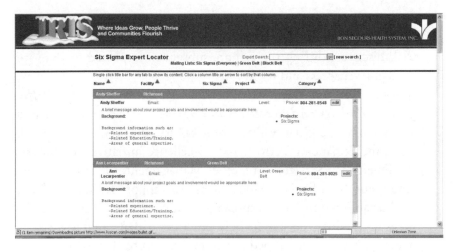

FIGURE 12-15 Six Sigma Expert Locator

als and dial-in information are posted on IRIS, as shown in Figure 12-16. The calls revolve around discussions highlighting local system (peer–to–peer) success stories with measurements of success and brainstorming. The calls are recorded and the audio transcript is

FIGURE 12-16 Lunch & Learn Corner on IRIS

posted to IRIS for those who could not make the call; they can then listen and follow the PowerPoint presentation at a later time. Materials discussed during the call are subsequently posted to IRIS for system-level access and use.

- ***Easy to Navigate Knowledge Dashboard that Accelerates Diffusion of Toolkits and Resources to Improve Performance***—As part of the 'Strategic Quality Plan' for 2007 to 2009 BSHSI has developed the Enhancing Performance Excellence initiative that focuses on Emergency Services, Outcomes Management, Operating Room and a number of other critical areas. To support rapid knowledge and capability transfer and spread of community-based proven practices and evidenced–based best practices a dedicated IRIS EPE Community was developed with rapid access to 'Knowledge Centers' on the priorty areas and a series of Action buttons were created enabling online reporting, asking questions to experts or team members, and sharing resources.

BSHSI continues to strive toward its goal of achieving an operating model that puts quality first. Always on the forefront of delivering quality care and excellence, BSHSI has truly recognized and capitalized on its strength in liberating existing human resources to support the progressive achievement of the organization's Strategic Quality Plan and meet the needs of their patients throughout their system.

Initial Results (24 months of BSHSI Share)

- Launched and Supported Quality-Care Management, Supply Chain, and Nursing Collaborative
- 225 Resources Shared
- 41,000 Page Views
- 400+ Members
- Best Practices Rating Program Developed
- Online Clinical Performance Dashboard
- Online Executive Dashboard
- Overall Improvement in CMS Decile Scores
- Successful Migration to Enterprise Intranet
- Launched and Operated Next-Generation Quality Community Supporting QualityFirst Initiative
- Continuous Lunch & Learn Series Operated

CASE STUDY 5 eHealth Initiative (eHI) and
Connecting for Health

Public–Private Collaboration for the Rapid Diffusion of Health Information Technology

Problem: As the 21st century arrived there was no nexus for public–private collaboration around the application of eHealth and Health Information Technology to support quality health care.

Solution: The not-for-profit eHealth Initiative and Connecting for Health initiatives were formed through a collaboration of leading healthcare technology companies, healthcare providers, and clinical leaders.

Medical Informatics 20/20: Collaboration tactics addressed are Knowledge Transfer, Sharing Alliances, Policy and Communication Forums, Collaborative Learning, and Executive/Clinical Leadership. See Figure 1-3 in Chapter 1.

Healthcare leaders and politicians realize that the healthcare industry must transform itself into a more efficient, more patient-centered entity or run the risk of being unable to keep pace with medical science advancements or safely meet the needs of the public. A report released on October 12, 2005, by the Technology CEO Council, a coalition of technology company executives, states that the healthcare industry is lagging behind in electronic record keeping.[4] (http://www.techceocouncil.org/) Almost every other industry is transforming itself through new IT-enabled processes, such as direct-to-consumer connectivity, real-time online access to critical information, and aggregation and analysis of detailed data. The report found that electronic medical records (EMRs) and other IT could help reduce medical errors by 40% to 60% over the next 5 to 10 years. It is estimated that a fully standardized health information exchange and interoperability (HIEI) system could yield a net value of $77.8 billion per year once fully implemented. The U.S. healthcare industry needs to appreciate the urgency and move quickly toward an information system that addresses critical public needs. Several commonly cited statistics include:

---

[4]"A Healthy System: How Improved Information Management Can Transform the Quality, Efficiency, and Value of Americans' Health Care"; Technology CEO Council; October 2005.

- Annual needless deaths of more than 57,000 Americans, because they did not receive appropriate care[5]
- Clinical errors that are estimated to kill approximately 100,000 patients per year[6]
- Higher healthcare spending, with an overall lower quality compared with other industrialized countries
- Insufficient care, as U.S. adults receive barely half of the recommended care[7]
- Duplicative or ineffective tests and procedures amounting to one-third of the $1.6 trillion spent on health care each year, due to poor information flow between hospitals, labs, doctors' offices, and pharmacies[8]

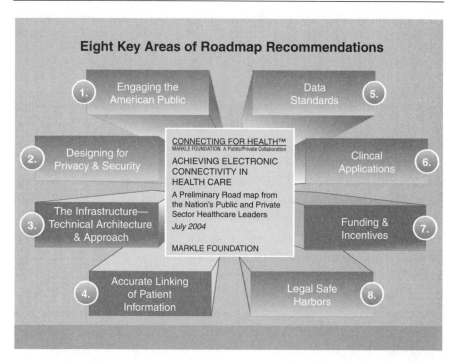

FIGURE 12-17 Eight Key Areas of Connecting for Health Roadmap Recommendation

---

[5]NCQA

[6]Building a Better Delivery System: A New Engineering/HealthCare partnership, IOM; July 2005.

[7]McGlynn, et al.

[8]CECS at Dartmouth.

Two efforts are underway that use open solutions and collaboration to work toward an interoperable infrastructure for the U.S. healthcare system: Connecting for Health and the eHealth Initiative (eHI). Both programs understand the importance of uniting public and private healthcare organizations to accelerate the development and implementation of an interconnected, electronic National Health Information Infrastructure.

Connecting for Health

Connecting for Health began its work in September 2002 with a clear understanding of the importance of information exchange to healthcare safety and quality *and* the political support and endorsement for change. It was established by the Markle Foundation and received additional funding and support from the Robert Wood Johnson Foundation. Connecting for Health involves a collaboration between public and private entities from across the entire healthcare spectrum, including more than 100 participants including physicians, hospitals, patient and consumer groups, payers, accreditors, government agencies, researchers, and IT systems manufacturers. Their main focus is to address legal, technical, and political barriers to establishing an interconnected health information infrastructure and accelerate its adoption and implementation. Once this is accomplished, they believe quality of care will be improved, medical errors will be reduced, costs will be lowered, and patients will be empowered.

During the last three years, Connecting for Health has achieved a number of goals related to addressing barriers and encouraging adoption:

- Established widely adopted initial data standards for interconnection and interoperability between the public and private sector
- Developed case studies on privacy and security
- Defined the key characteristics and benefits of the electronic personal health record (PHR)
- Developed an incremental road map called "Achieving Electronic Connectivity in Healthcare" that lays out future actions for achieving electronic connectivity; it was based on four design principles focused on open solutions and collaboration:
  - Build on existing systems ("incremental") and create early value for doctors/patients

- ○ Design to safeguard privacy—impose the requirements and then design the solution
- ○ Include an interoperable, open standards–based "network of networks" built on the Internet
- ○ Leverage both "bottom-up" and "top-down" strategies

Connecting for Health also focuses on two elements that will make adoption of an interconnected electronic health infrastructure possible: Element 1: "A Common Framework" that includes the:

- Adoption of critical tools, including open technical standards for exchanging clinical information
- Explicit policies on handling information
- Uniform methods for linking information accurately and securely

Element 2: A Standards and Policies Function for a decentralized environment that requires:

- Basic standards and policies for sharing health information
- Uniform adoption and public and private sector participation
- Transparency, accountability, and the ability to operate in the public interest

In 2005, the secretary of Health and Human Services and the administration integrated many of these road map recommendations, as well as recommendations from a request for information for nationwide electronic health information exchange. These recommendations include the creation of a national common framework of policies and standards to achieve interoperability in health care; the use of the Internet to create health information sharing; open and nonproprietary standards; full patient control of electronic medical information; strong common policies to protect privacy and maintain security of patient information; rejection of the creation of a centralized, national databank for medical information; and a commitment to not erecting barriers to innovators entering the field of healthcare IT.

eHealth Initiative (eHI)

The eHI programming is managed by eHealth Initiative staff and guided by the Foundation for eHealth, both of which are nonprofit, independent organizations focused on improving the quality, safety, and efficiency of health care through health information technology. They strive to unite hospitals and other healthcare organizations, clinician groups, employers and purchasers, health plans, healthcare information technology organizations, manufacturers, public health agencies, academic and research institutions, and public sector stakeholders through collaboration on interoperable information technology. eHI focuses on gathering funding and support for an interoperable information exchange while also providing the Connecting Communities for Better Health resource bank.

The Connecting Communities for Better Health (CCBH) program promotes community demonstration projects and related evaluation and dissemination activities that are targeted to improve the quality, safety, and efficiency of health care. To accomplish this, the Foundation for eHealth Initiative in cooperation with Health Resources and Services Administration (HRSA) Office for the Advancement of Telehealth (OAT) focuses on eight key strategies:

- Creating "learning laboratories" through the provision of seed funding for communities that wish to implement electronic health information exchange and IT tools, and by evaluating and widely disseminating lessons learned
- Gaining critical input from experts, "on-the-ground" implementers, and other key stakeholders on each of the following key areas relevant to electronic health information exchange: organization and governance, funding and sustainable business models, clinician adoption and clinical process change, technical architecture and applications, assuring privacy and security, and engagement of patients
- Through the Community Learning Network and Resource Center and meetings such as the Connecting Communities Learning Forum and Resource Exhibition, providing both a community network and a resource to enable communities and healthcare stakeholders to learn from national experts and each other, strategies for addressing the challenges related to implementation of IT and a health information infrastructure
- Collaborating and aligning with related activities within both the public and private sectors
- Creating and widely publicizing a pool of "electronic health information exchange-ready" communities to facilitate interest and public and private sector investment in such initiatives

- Building national awareness among policymakers, healthcare industry leaders, and other drivers of change, regarding the feasibility and value of health information exchange for every stakeholder in health care, the key barriers that need to be overcome to achieve these goals, and the strategies and policies that must be deployed to overcome those barriers and support wider diffusion of electronic data exchange tools and practices

In 2006, the eHealth Initiative released the Connecting Communities Toolkit, which is a series of modules designed to support the rapid development of Regional Health Information Organizations (RHIOs). There are seven modules, which include online documents, resources, community experiences, and a series of tools. The development of this free and open set of solutions was made possible through funding from the Health Resources and Services Administration Office of the Advancement of Teleheath.

Conclusion

Connecting for Better Health and eHI are valuable examples of how improving information management through collaboration and knowledge sharing will result in a healthcare system that does not fail patients or healthcare providers. As they strive toward their goal of a national interoperable EHR system, they are relying on open solutions and public–private collaborations. By having vital patient information quickly and reliably available, healthcare providers are enabled to make the best medical decisions. By collecting information on quality and outcomes, providers have access to the best available data about the results of medications and treatments.

It is conservatively estimated that there are nearly 100,000 preventable deaths per year, that a half-trillion dollars are wasted annually through inefficiency, that healthcare costs are rising at roughly three times the rate of inflation, and that about 43 million people are uninsured.[9] These preventable deaths are caused in some part by the use of outdated procedures. Although medical science has rapidly progressed in the last decade in the

---

[9]Building a Better Delivery System: A New Engineering/HealthCare Partnership, IOM; July 2005.

form of nanotechnology, robotics, genomes and genomic biorepositories, and wearable health information computers, studies released by the Institute of Medicine (IOM) and other organizations conclude that the gap between knowledge and practice has resulted in a deterioration of what was once considered by many as the best health system in the world. In other words, the United States is failing to consistently deliver to *all* patients the six quality aims envisioned by the IOM in Crossing the Quality Chasm: safe, effective, timely, patient-centered, efficient, and equitable care. In particular, rural communities, representing nearly 20% of the population, do not have access to high-quality health services.[10] To enhance health and health care over the coming decade, we need better systems and processes, faster dissemination of proven approaches, and an investment in an information and communications technology infrastructure.

CASE STUDY 6 — MedQIC—Medicare Quality Improvement Community

A National Knowledge Forum Collaborative to Accelerate Improvement in Health Care

Problem: The need to improve quality in United States healthcare organizations and the growth of CMS Pay-for-Performance demonstration projects created a need for a better mechanism to support rapid–cycle process improvement with and without health information technology.

Solution: The Centers for Medicare and Medicaid developed a comprehensive online Web service with quality improvement strategies, tools, and stories in success that is available to all healthcare professionals at www.MedQic.org

Medical Informatics 20/20: Collaboration tactics addressed are: Knowledge Transfer, Collaborative Learning, Communities of Practice, and Public–Private Collaboration. See Figure 1-3 in Chapter 1.

Medicare Quality Improvement Community or MedQIC (pronounced med-quick),[11] developed by the Centers for Medicare and Medicaid Services (CMS) and its 53 Quality Improvement Organizations

---

[10]Building a 21st Century Community Health Care System in Rural America. IOM; Nov 2004.

[11]MedQIC: http://www.medqic.org

(QIO), demonstrates how communities are attempting to advance the quality and efficacy of health care by improving their goals, changing their strategies, and providing "the right care for every patient every time." Launched in 2003 and redesigned in 2004 and 2005, it is a national network of information and resources that supports high-level transformational change across all healthcare settings and facilitates. The MedQIC Web site home is illustrated in Figure 12-18. MedQIC fosters a community-based, open approach to quality improvement. Its goal is to improve quality of care for Medicare beneficiaries in home health agencies, hospitals, nursing homes, and physician offices. They do this through a no-fee Web-based Improvement Support Center section that provides healthcare workers, institutions, improvement support organizations, purchasers, and regulators with procedural, structural, and behavioral strategies, tools, literature, and success stories. Contributions to MedQIC, in the form of success stories and improvement stories, are

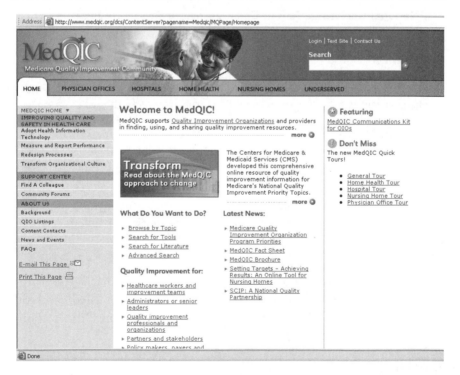

FIGURE 12-18 MedQIC Web Services Home Page

encouraged and reviewed by one of the seven Quality Improvement Organization Support Centers (QIOSC). For instance, in the Tools section of the Physician Offices center under "Redesign Processes—Tools: Standardize Care Processes Using Evidence-Based Guidelines and Care Pathways," there are number of tools such as:

- Diabetes Care Flowsheet
- Diabetes Foot Exam Chart Sticker
- Diabetes Management Chart Sticker
- Diabetic Eye Exam Referral Form
- Standing Orders for Administering Pneumococcal Vaccine

MedQIC offers an open solutions, powerful knowledge base to improve care for physician offices, hospitals, home health, nursing homes, and the underserved.

Through MedQIC, registered participants access CMS's Health Care Quality Improvement Program (HCQIP), which guides quality improvements for Medicare beneficiaries. Strategies include:

- Measure and report performance to identify opportunities for improvement, track progress, and create comparative data for use in quality improvement, public reporting, pay-for-performance, and accreditation with appropriate provider consents
- Adopt health information technology that supports health-care providers in their processes and decision making (e.g., EHR, e-prescribing, CPOE)
- Redesign processes and implement changes in care management, patient self-management, flow, and scheduling
- Transform organizational culture to one that is more patient-centered through open communication and teamwork

MedQIC's Open Solutions provide Pay-for-Performance participants access to quality initiatives already developed by CMS in collaboration with public and private organizations. Pay-for-Performance programs are currently available for hospitals, physicians, and physician groups, and plans are underway to develop programs for nursing-home care, home health, and dialysis providers. Several of these programs are outlined below with an emphasis on Premier, Inc.'s Hospital Demonstration Project.

Hospitals

Hospital Quality Initiative, part of HHS's broader National Quality Initiative, focuses on ten quality measures by linking reporting of those measures to payment at discharge. Hospitals receive the full pay-ment update to their Medicare DRG payments upon submission of the required data. Approximately 98% of the hospitals eligible to participate in this program are complying with the requirements of the provision.

Premier, Inc.'s Medicare Pay-for-Performance Demonstration Project tracks hospital performance on 34 widely accepted measures of processes and outcomes of care for five common clinical conditions. An initial analysis of the 270-plus participating hospitals during the project's first year shows improvement in all five clinical areas being tracked, with median quality scores for hospitals improved for patients with:

- *Acute myocardial infarction:* from 90% to 93%
- *Coronary artery bypass graft:* from 86% to 90%
- *Heart failure:* from 64% to 76%
- *Hip and knee replacement:* from 85% to 91%
- *Pneumonia:* from 70% to 80%

Overall, these conditions make up a substantial portion of Medicare costs, which, if improved, could result in better quality of life for the patient and less costly follow-up care. Bonuses are paid based on how well hospitals meet the quality measures for each condition (e.g., hospitals in the top 10% for a given condition will receive a 2% bonus on their Medicare payments for that condition; a 1% bonus for hospitals in the second 10%; and only recognition for hospitals in the remainder of the top 50%). Bonuses for high-performers during the three-year life of the demonstration project, which began in October 2003, are expected to total $7 million per year; poorly performing hospitals may face penalties in the third year.

At the end of the first year, baselines will be set for the bottom 10% and 20% levels. These levels remain static, and CMS and Premier expect that all hospitals will be above the baselines by the final year of the demonstration. If any hospitals are below the 10% baseline in the third year of the demonstration, they will get a 2% reduction in Medicare payments for the clinical area involved, and those between 20% and 10% will get a 1% reduction. Incentive payments will be paid annually.

In June 2006, Premier, Inc. published results of groundbreaking analysis of several years of data from the CMS Pay–for–Performance demonstration project that demonstrated that "improving patient care can reduce costs, save lives."[12] The study concluded that process improvement in the treatment of pneumonia and heart bypass patients could reduce hospital costs $1 billion while leading to 3,000 few deaths, 6,000 fewer complications, 6,000 fewer readmissions and 500,000 fewer hospital days. The analysis is based on data from Premier's Pay-for-Performance demonstration project with the CMS where participating hospitals reported to Premier results in collecting quarterly data on 33 quality indicators from more than 250 hospitals across the country. Premier researchers then extrapolated the results from participating hospitals to overall national levels using statistical methods.

Physicians and Physician Groups

Physician Group Practice Demonstration rewards physicians for improving the quality and efficiency of healthcare services delivered to Medicare fee-for-service beneficiaries. Ten large group practices (200-plus physicians) across the country will earn performance-based payments after achieving savings in comparison to a control group. This demonstration is the first Pay-for-Performance initiative for physicians under the Medicare program.

Medicare Care Management Performance Demonstration rewards physicians in small and medium-sized practices who adopt and use health IT to manage the care of eligible Medicare beneficiaries. Physicians who meet or exceed performance standards established by CMS in clinical delivery systems and patient outcomes will receive bonus payments. This three-year Pay-for-Performance demonstration, modeled on the "Bridges to Excellence" program, focuses on improving the quality of care for chronically ill patients. It will be implemented in four states: Arkansas, California, Massachusetts, and Utah, with the support of the Quality Improvement Organizations in those states.

Medicare Health Care Quality Demonstration is a five-year program that strives to enhance quality of care through a variety of projects that improve patient safety; reduce variations in utilization by appropriate use of evidence-based care and best practice guidelines; encourage shared decision

---

[12]Data from http://www.cms.hhs.gov/media/press/release.asp?Counter=1441

making; and use culturally and ethnically appropriate care. Physician groups, integrated health systems, and regional coalitions are eligible to participate.

Disease Management/Chronic Care Improvement

Chronic Care Improvement Program is a pilot program that will test a population-based model of disease management. Disease management vendors and large organizations (e.g., insurance companies) are paid a monthly per-beneficiary fee for managing a population of chronically ill beneficiaries with advanced congestive heart failure and/or complex diabetes. These organizations guarantee CMS a savings of at least 5% plus the cost of the monthly fees compared to a similar population of beneficiaries, if they perform satisfactorily on quality measures, and satisfy both beneficiaries and providers. Nine sites have been selected for the pilot phase: Humana in South and Central Florida, XLHealth in Tennessee, Aetna in Illinois, LifeMasters in Oklahoma, McKesson in Mississippi, CIGNA in Georgia, Health Dialog in Pennsylvania, American Healthways in Washington, D.C. and Maryland, and Visiting Nurse Service of New York and United Healthcare in Queens and Brooklyn, New York. If this pilot program is successful after two years, it may be expanded.

ESRD Disease Management Demonstration involves a fully case-mix adjusted payment system for an expanded bundle of end stage renal disease (ESRD) services and is expected to be operational in 2006. This three-year demonstration will link ESRD-related quality measures to a portion of the payments. An advisory board for the demonstration is required by the legislation.

Disease Management Demonstration for Severely Chronically Ill Medicare Beneficiaries began enrollment in February 2004. Organizations receive a monthly payment for every beneficiary they enroll to provide disease management services and a comprehensive drug benefit, and must guarantee that there will be a net reduction in Medicare expenditures as a result of their services. It is designed to test whether applying disease management and prescription drug coverage in a fee-for-service environment for beneficiaries with illnesses such as congestive heart failure, diabetes, or coronary artery disease can improve health outcomes and reduce costs. Quality is determined by mandatory data submission on several relevant clinical measures. Participating organizations include XLHealth in Texas, CorSolutions in Louisiana, and HeartPartners in California and Arizona.

Conclusion

MedQIC is an excellent example of the emerging health IT and knowledge sharing collaboration trend targeted at improving quality of care and patient safety. Healthcare entities need partnerships and collaboration to be successful, and quality indicators can help measure a program's success. They can also measure progress in disease prevention, recognition, and treatment and help to close the gap between what is known and what is practiced in hospitals, physicians' offices, and homes. And quality indicators for one disease can serve as a model to devise similar indicators for other diseases. MedQIC offers providers and healthcare organizations a way to achieve measurable quality improvement and come closer to providing the right care for every patient every time and achieving the IOM's aims and standards.

CASE STUDY 7 — Institute for Healthcare Improvement (IHI)

Clinical Collaboration to Save Lives and Realize Clinical Quality Excellence

Problem: For many years the healthcare industry did not have a focus on quality. Then the Institute of Medicine, through a series of studies, identified an epidemic of medical errors and a chronic lack of use of information technology to support better care processes.

Solution: The Institute for Healthcare Improvement (IHI), a not-for-profit organization, was organized to promote safety, effectiveness, patient-centeredness, timeliness, efficiency, and equity in health care. Since the early 1990s, IHI has been a leader and advocate of safe quality care for all people.

Medical Informatics 20/20: Collaboration tactics addressed are: Executive and Clinical Leadership, Facilitated Knowledge Transfer, Collaborative Learning, Communities of Practice, and Policy/Education and Communication Forums. Innovation tactics addressed are: Collaborative Innovation, Six Sigma/LEAN, Clinical Decision Support, and Clinical Engagement. See Figures 1-3 and 1-5 in Chapter 1.

The Institute for Healthcare Improvement (IHI) is an example of a multidimensional advocate, facilitator, and educator that promotes collaboration and information sharing as a means for accelerating positive change in health care, in the areas of patient safety, effectiveness, patient-centeredness, timeliness, efficiency, equity, and clinical quality. Founded in 1991 and based in Cambridge, Massachusetts, IHI is a not-for-profit organization that offers online and offline products and services to improve the quality and value of health care for patients and the overall job satisfaction of healthcare workers. The ultimate goal is to provide a convenient, efficient, fast way for providers and organizations worldwide to share improvement knowledge, ideas, and practices with world-class experts across the healthcare field.

IHI has several high-profile activities:

- IHI 100K Lives Campaign
- IMPACT Network
- Offline and Online Educational Programming

IHI's 100K Lives Campaign has enrolled thousands of hospitals across the country that are committing to implementing changes in care that have been proven to prevent avoidable deaths by initially focusing on six proven interventions. The campaign is targeting to save 100,000 human

---

122,300 Lives Saved Through IHI 100K Campaign

IHI President and CEO Donald Berwick announced on June 14, 2006 that hospitals in the 100,000 Lives Campaign have saved an estimated 122,300 lives, exceeding the original goal. (Read the June 14 press release for more information.)

A campaign to reduce lethal errors and unnecessary deaths in U.S. hospitals has saved an estimated 122,300 lives in the last 18 months, the campaign's leader said, Wednesday.

"I think this campaign signals no less than a new standard of health care in America," said Dr. Donald Berwick, campaign leader.

About 3,100 hospitals participated in the project, carrying out study-tested procedures that prevent infections and mistakes. Experts say the cooperative effort was unusual for a competitive industry that doesn't like to publicly focus on patient-killing problems.

Source: IHI Press Release, June 14, 2006.

lives that would have been lost to medical errors by June 14, 2006, using the slogan "Some Is Not a Number. Soon Is Not a Time."

This slogan drives home the point that over the past decades healthcare executives paid lip service to reducing medical errors and it was high time that someone outlined specific measurable goals and targets to reduce medical errors.

IMPACT is a fee-based collaborative network designed to help organizations improve together. IMPACT is IHI's membership network of organizations founded on the belief that it is "easier to improve together than it is alone." More than 190 healthcare organizations belong to IMPACT, mostly U.S. organizations, with three from Canada and one from the United Kingdom. Membership provides an opportunity for collaborative learning among IMPACT members and IHI's staff to achieve, sustain, and spread breakthrough improvements. Fees for membership range from $30,000 (annual base fee) for single operating entities such as a hospital or medical practice, to $15,000 for system-level membership (annual base fee) plus $20,000 for each participating sub-entity. There are additional costs for other services, such as frontline improvement projects, the national forum, International Summits, Calls to Action audio conference series, the Breakthrough Series College, and education/training programs.

Members can:

- Download or use interactive tools
- Participate in discussion groups with peers and expert hosts
- Use the Find a Colleague Directory to search for and connect with peers/experts with common interests
- Use Improvement Tracker to document improvement projects, collect performance data, and track changes
- Share improvement reports, tools, resources, and tips for improvement

IMPACT members have proven that breakthrough improvement is possible through a strong leadership community that is focused on a specialized "Frontline" projects. For example:

- St. Joseph Hospital, a 446-bed hospital in Lexington, Kentucky, reduced the number of adverse events per ICU day from 8.4 to consistently below 3.0.
- Baptist Memorial Hospital–DeSoto in Southaven, Mississippi, reduced its rate of ventilator-associated pneumonia by 46% in one year.

- The Everett Clinic in Washington State offers the third next available appointment (a standard measure of appointment access) within 24 hours of a patient's call.

IHI Educational Programming

Offline and Online Educational Programming includes an Annual National Forum on Quality Improvement in Health Care and an extensive extranet network of healthcare clinicians and managers who participate in various efforts to improve care.

The Annual National Forum on Quality Improvement in Health Care offers continuing education credits for healthcare leaders from around the world in person or via satellite. It is designed for people committed to the mission of improving health care.

The IHI Extranet network offers a Web-based learning series for members. Programs scheduled for 2006 focus on helping hospitals improve patient flow and improving patient safety. Examples of continuing education opportunities include:

- *Improving Patient Flow: Queuing for Clinicians* teaches queuing theory principles and how to apply the principles to improve hospital waits and delays without expending more resources.
- *Managing Hospital Operations* is an intensive six-month program developed by IHI for healthcare executives, managers, and clinicians that teaches effective operational management to improve flow in hospitals.
- *Improving Patient Flow: Streamlining Discharges* teaches synchronization and discharge "slots" to streamline the discharge process, maximize the capacity of inpatient beds, and improve patient flow.
- *Patient Safety Officer Executive Development Program* is an eight-day program that covers topics that will prepare patient safety officers to oversee the organization's strategy to meet patient safety needs.

The IHI offers a number of educational products available in book, audio, or white-paper form, many of which were developed through a partnership between the Robert Wood Johnson Foundation and IHI. Examples include:

- A seven-part video series called Pursing Perfection in Health Care, which includes themes such as shared care plans, composite measures, leverage points for senior leaders, and multidisciplinary rounds. It strives to raise the bar on healthcare performance, improving safety, mortality, and costs. It was produced by award-winning filmmakers Frank Christopher and Mathew Eisen.
- An initiative that is currently being piloted in 13 hospitals, called Transforming Care at the Bedside (TCAB). It strives to create a framework for change on medical/surgical units by improving four main categories:
  - Safe and reliable care
  - Vitality and teamwork
  - Patient-centered care
  - Value-added care processes

IHI Knowledge Transfer Program

The Knowledge Transfer Program is based on the premise that people who need the knowledge will actively seek it out, and then build a reciprocal relationship with those who have the experience. Basically, you get some knowledge, develop your own, and share it with those from whom you got the knowledge.

An Example of IHI Progress in Safety

OSF HealthCare, with six hospitals in Illinois and Michigan, has replaced medication carts with an automated medication-dispensing system that accurately dispenses the medication and enters automatically data into the patient's electronic medical record. Through another automated system, pharmacists double-check all physician-ordered medications and make changes to medications that would affect renal function. This change has reduced ADEs (adverse drug events) by 50% and significantly dropped mortality rates. OSF, an IHI IMPACT member, used the four-level approach recommended by the IHI: transform the culture to embrace "systems thinking," improve medication reconciliation, focus on safe handling of high-risk medications, and streamline dispensing mechanisms to reduce errors.

IMPACT Learning and Innovation Communities are groups of organizations that work on projects with the IHI to develop new solutions to improve care where best practices do not currently exist. Projects last approximately ten months and are open to IMPACT member organizations only. During the first year of this community, teams worked on the five diagnoses that make up the Premier–Centers for Medicare and Medicaid Services Hospital Quality Incentive Demonstration Project.

The IHI makes this knowledge for improvement free and available to all in the Topics area of the Web site. Each Topic area has a section on how to improve, measure improvement, make changes, access tools (all free and downloadable), find resources and literature, and share improvement stories. Topics range from leadership system improvements, chronic conditions, critical care, developing countries, health professions education, medical-surgical care, office practices, and patient safety, to name a few.

Members can submit "Improvement Stories" that describe their improvement projects or the changes they implemented and the results they achieved that can then be used by other organizations as lessons learned. These stories are continuously updated. The following examples cut across six different interventions:

- *Deploy Rapid Response Teams (RRTs)*
  - Austin Hospital in Heidelberg, Victoria, Australia, achieved a 65% drop in cardiac arrests and a 37% reduction in mortality after introducing RRTs.
  - Baptist Memorial Hospital, Memphis, Tennessee, has experienced a 28% drop in codes. In addition, a higher percentage of all codes now occur in the ICU. Floor nurses report that they are now more confident in their ability "to rescue patients before they get into serious trouble."
- *Deliver Reliable, Evidence-Based Care for Acute Myocardial Infarction (AMI)*
  - By implementing a discharge medication program including key AMI measures, Utah, was able to achieve greater than 90% compliance with aspirin and beta-blocker guidelines among AMI patients.
  - Through its Cardiac Service Line, Hackensack University Medical Center, Hackensack, New Jersey, developed standardized processes for AMI care, resulting in an increase in the composite AMI score as calculated by CMS (aggregate of the key measures). The

composite score increased from an average of 72% in the first quarter of 2003 to an average of 91% by the fourth quarter of 2003, resulting in a decrease in AMI inpatient mortality from 7% to 5.2% in the same time period.

  ○ By developing protocols based on the evidence, McLeod Regional Medical Center, Florence, North Carolina, increased the percentage of patients who received "perfect care" (all AMI key measures) from 80% in January 2001 to 100% by November 2003. This has reduced average inpatient mortality rate for AMI to 4% for the past year, below the CMS reported average of 7% in 2003.

- *Prevent Adverse Drug Events (ADEs)*
  ○ Luther Midelfort, Mayo Health System, Eau Claire, Wisconsin, eliminated virtually all ADEs in the Telemetry/Intermediate Care Unit by implementing a medication reconciliation system.

- *Prevent Central Line Infections*
  ○ Baptist Memorial Hospital–Memphis, Memphis, Tennessee, has reduced CR-BSIs and ICU length of stay by implementing the central line bundle and other measures to improve care in ICUs.
  ○ Allegheny General Hospital, part of the Pittsburgh Regional Healthcare Initiative, Pittsburgh, Pennsylvania, has virtually eliminated catheter-related bloodstream infections by implementing measures included in the central line bundle.

- *Prevent Surgical Site Infections (SSIs)*
  ○ OSF St. Joseph's Medical Center, Bloomington, Ilinois, has significantly reduced SSIs by implementing the SSI bundle and other measures to reduce infection.
  ○ Mercy Health Center, Oklahoma City, Oklahoma, reduced SSIs by 78% in one year using evidence-based strategies, including the SSI bundle.

- *Prevent Ventilator-Associated Pneumonia (VAP)*
  ○ Baptist Memorial Hospital–Memphis, Memphis, Tennessee, implemented several "best practices" in the ICU, including the ventilator bundle. They achieved a reduction in the incidence of VAP and a decline in ICU length of stay.

As testimony to its overall success, IHI offers the following statistics:

- Approximately 4,000 healthcare leaders from around the world attended IHI's National Forum on Quality Improvement in Health

Care in December 2004, with another 6,000 expected to join via satellite broadcast.

* More than 2,800 hospitals have joined the 100K Lives Campaign with the goal of saving 100,000 patient lives that would have been lost to medical errors by June 14, 2006.
* 2,800 people joined a single phone call on November 12, 2004, to mark the fifth anniversary of the IOM's "To Err Is Human" report.
* 35,000 people have subscribed to IHI's monthly electronic newsletter.
* More than 2 million visits were logged on IHI's Web site in 2004.
* 190 organizations have joined IHI's IMPACT network.
* 700 people have graduated from IHI's Breakthrough Series College.
* People from more than 50 countries on six continents are involved in IHI's work.

Although the IHI charges for many of its services, it is a not-for-profit organization. Even without membership there is a wealth of information and knowledge available at www.IHI.org. The IHI is a great example of how healthcare organizations can use improvement knowledge aggressively to achieve better healthcare results by improving system-level performance and rapidly deploying major changes that produce breakthrough results which spread throughout an organization or community. IHI is an excellent example of how structured collaboration learning and facilitated knowledge transfer can help many, many healthcare delivery organizations improve the quality of their care and reduce medical errors.

CASE STUDY 8 — Air Force Medical Service Knowledge Exchange— Connecting for Better Care

Problem: Accelerate the delivery of medical knowledge and improve the sharing of knowledge that can improve the quality of medical care across the world.

Solution: The Knowledge Exchange is the Air Force Surgeon General's Intranet site that delivers knowledge and resources to Air Force Medical Services (AFMS) at the point of need.

continues

CASE STUDY 8 *continued*

Medical Informatics 20/20: Collaboration and Innovation tactics addressed are: Knowledge Transfer, Communities of Practice, Executive/Clinical Leadership, Facilitated Knowledge Transfer, Collaborative Innovation, Knowledge@Demand, and Business Intelligence. See Figures 1-3 and 1-5 in Chapter 1.

The Knowledge Exchange is the Air Force Medical Service (AFMS) Intranet and knowledge management application. Figure 12-19 shows the AFMS Knowledge Exchange Home Page that provides a launching pad for news, document repositories, advanced search, and collaboration tools for the AFMS. The Knowledge Exchange supports 40,000 AFMS personnel in providing the best medical care to Air Force patients by allowing all staff to share, store, and exchange knowledge across 75 hospitals and clinics worldwide.

The Knowledge Exchange leverages both explicit and tacit knowledge via more than 300 microsites called Knowledge Junctions. Each of these Communities of Practice offers a suite of Web-based tools that include

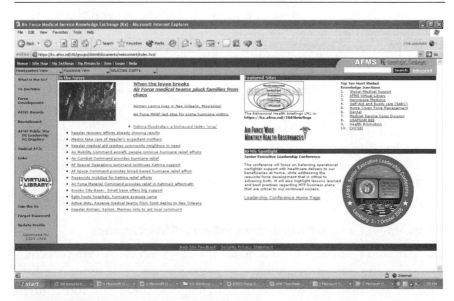

FIGURE 12-19 The AFMS Knowledge Exchange Home Page

document management, Web content management, robust search, discussion forums, expertise location, and a collaborative project tool. The platform is a highly customized version of Stellent's enterprise content management suite and was launched in January 2004.

Ninety-five percent of content on the Knowledge Exchange can be accessed without a log-in (from any "dot-mil" domain), which makes it easy for AFMS personnel to find information they need to do their jobs. As of March 2006, the Knowledge Exchange had more than 14,000 active members. (Membership enables access from a "dot-com" domain and the ability to contribute documents and participate in discussion forums.)

Functionality

Key features of the Knowledge Exchange include:

1. *Home Page:* access to the *Surgeon General's News Wire* (news stories), featured sites, and featured content within the Knowledge Exchange
2. *Organizational Hierarchy, Functional Hierarchy, and Site Map:* fast navigation and an easy way to locate resources
3. *Search Tool:* a robust engine for locating relevant Knowledge Junctions, documents, and discussion threads
4. *Document Repository:* storage and retrieval of documents; any member can "check in" a document, and the system contains version control and an automatic expiration notification feature
5. *Virtual Library:* a wealth of knowledge that includes content from licensed databases and gives physicians, nurses, and other healthcare providers in the AFMS access to online medical library resources such as OVID, Micromedex, MD Consult, Stat!Ref, UpToDate, and others
6. *My Projects:* a private area for teams to share knowledge and documents
7. *My Settings:* allows users to configure personal settings

Knowledge/Content Management and Maintenance

Every major organization and functional area within the AFMS is encouraged to create a Knowledge Junction microsite, which is supported by a sponsor and managed by a content manager. More than 300 content managers manage individual Knowledge Junctions using a Microsoft

Word–based content management system that can be mastered in just two hours of training.

There is no training required for members to "check in" documents to the Knowledge Exchange, making it easy for members to share best practices or manage documents as part of a project. Each document uploaded to the Knowledge Exchange is converted to PDF format, but can also be accessed in its native format. Clicking on the name of the person who checked in a document links to a page with the author's POC information. Icons indicate whether a document was reviewed and approved by a subject matter expert (SME). The Knowledge Exchange contains more than 25,000 documents that are kept up to date by an automated expiration system. When the expiration date of a document approaches, an e–mail prompts the document owner to renew or archive the document. Within the Knowledge Exchange there are robust search capabilities that allow AFMS personnel to quickly search and find relevant documents that ultimately improve the quality of patient care. Abstracts provide a quick overview of each document's content, and icons allow users to access the native document, access a PDF copy of the document, access metadata about the document, discuss a document, or generate an e–mail with links to the document.

Evolution and Enhancements

AFMS is currently piloting state-of-the-art Concept Search technology. This toolset will allow members of the Knowledge Exchange to efficiently find the "right" document, Web page, or discussion, because the technology finds concepts, not just text, in the searched content. The system conducts a federated search, searching indexed external Web sites, documents on an enterprise Web site, and documents on local network drives. The tool allows bulk loading of documents into automatically classified enterprise taxonomies, which in turn allows AFMS personnel to rapidly collect, index, and classify unstructured information into a taxonomy relevant to organizational needs. The system uses clinical, operational, and organizational taxonomies that include more than 40,000 "class clues" used to classify the documents.

Success Factors and Metrics

According to J.D. Whitlock, LtCol, USAF, MSC, CPHIMS, and Chief, Knowledge Management of the Office of the Surgeon General, the three primary reasons for the success of the AMFS Knowledge Exchange are:

1. *Easy, flexible Web content management system*—Because the system is MS Word–based, everyone can quickly learn to use it. Also, content managers can do whatever they want with their screen real estate—AFMS doesn't enforce a common look and feel for the microsites beyond the existing top and left navigation that is common for all. Says Whitlock, "If you don't do 'easy' and 'flexible' together, then you're not serious about winning the Web content management battle."

2. *"Warm body" help is always available*—"If you're seriously expecting subject matter experts instead of webmasters to do Web content management, then you must have solid help desk support," advises Whitlock. "Not just answer-your-technical-question support, but how-can-I-help-you-make-your-microsite-more-effective support." AFMS employs two full-time employees to support 300 content managers and 14,000 registered users, which works well

---

Concept Search in Action

In 2004, nine officers from nine different career fields were tasked to review 208 after-action reports from Operations Enduring Freedom and Iraqi Freedom. The purpose was to identify issues that arose in military operations, good or bad, and task those issues to an appropriate authority for action. Because the nine officers had many other duties, this work took four months, during which many reports, each with different formats, were either inappropriately tasked to a wrong location or incompletely tasked due to lack of subject matter expertise of a particular reviewer. Using an "objective" taxonomy that included 22,000 classes and more than 63,000 clues, Concept Search classified the 208 documents in 28 seconds. Instead of creating a folder/file structure and drag and dropping copies of the same document to many folders based on an individual's limited perspective, Concept Search rapidly classified each of the after-action reports into the appropriate area for action. Frequently, one report would touch on three to four subject areas. Each time that report would be linked to its respective multiple folders, ensuring that the information was reaching its appropriate destination for action.

and is an efficient use of resources. These same people handle non-system-administrator and developer duties for tasks that still require webmasters.

3. ***Document ownership and expiration are taken seriously—*** "Content managers get sick of reviewing documents that are about to expire, and they complain about it," Whitlock laments. "But if you don't insist on removal of outdated resources, your Web-based document management system turns into the same tangled mess of outdated junk that everyone has on their network drives."

As of March 2006, the Knowledge Exchange contained about 28,000 documents and had 14,000 registered users. In terms of volume, AFMS measures page views—a viewed Web page or a viewed document each count as one page view. In March 2006, the Knowledge Exchange was seeing about 10,000 page views a day, which Whitlock anticipated would increase once the site's new discussion forums, launched in early 2006, take off. For an online overview and description of the AFMS Knowledge Exchange visit https://kx.afms.mil/demo.

CHAPTER 13

Value Measurement and Return on Investment

> "The paper-based medical record is woefully inadequate
> for meeting the needs of modern medicine."
>
> E.H. Shortcliffe, MD, Ph.D, *Academic Medicine,*
> 1999–74(4):414–419.

Healthcare provider institutions today are faced with many new challenges, including the need to implement Health Information Technology (HIT) solutions, especially electronic health record (EHR) systems. However, these institutions are also faced with a demand for capital investments outpacing their available funds. This means HIT or EHR projects must compete against other capital investment requests for scarce funds. Senior management teams will need to build the business and quality case that justify the return on investment (ROI) and return on quality (ROQ) before significant financial commitments for HIT are made.

Healthcare CEOs, in a 2003 HIMSS survey, identified the following as the top business issues facing health care:

- Cost pressures
- Medicare cutbacks
- Availability and retention of staff
- Increasing patient safety
- HIPAA compliance
- Improving operational efficiency
- Consumerism/satisfying consumers
- Obtaining capital

Until recent years, significant investments in the acquisition and implementation of HIT and EHR systems have not been that common in many healthcare provider organizations. Yet the investment in HIT systems plays a key role in overcoming some of the top issues facing healthcare executives. Some of the significant barriers to date hampering the acquisition and implementation of HIT systems include insufficient capital, lack of expertise, inefficient business practices, nonstandard clinical processes, lack of common clinical data standards, and the daunting challenges of clinical process transformation.

Now the tide has turned and there is widespread acceptance that health information systems are essential in improving clinical and business practices and enhancing the quality of care provided to patients. This is reflected in recent surveys. In the Medical Records Institute's *Seventh Annual Survey of Electronic Health Record Trends and Usage for 2005,* less than 25% of respondents said "Difficulty in building a strong business case (ROI)" was a major barrier to plans for implementing an EHR system. The 2006 HIMSS survey indicated that more than 80% of hospital and health systems in the United States plan on installing clinical information systems over the next five years.

Significant improvements in clinical care, reductions in medication errors, and sharing "best practices," cannot be fully realized without the use of clinically focused health information systems. This has been demonstrated by the Institute for Healthcare Improvement (IHI) 100K Lives campaign and thousands of other efforts by healthcare organizations around the globe. The Institutes of Medicine and many other authorities recognize that significant gains in cost-effectiveness and quality of care will require the deployment of clinical health information systems throughout the entire healthcare delivery system. The use and access to EHRs is needed across the continuum of care, by patients from their homes, to clinicians in hospitals, outpatient clinics, and long-term care facilities.

A number of projects over the past years have specifically focused on measuring the value of health IT and have documented these results. There is a growing body of information from vendors and healthcare professionals now about how to measure the ROI and justify the investment in medical informatics and EHR systems. (See HIPAAlert, April 20, 2004, by Randa Upham, principal, Phoenix Health Systems: http://www.hipaadvisory.com/alert/vol5/number3.htm)

Also, a recent article by Mark Winchester entitled "Wanted: New Partners" states, "Despite the concerns of CEOs, more and more physicians and caregivers are ready to embrace the EHR. By talking with their colleagues and reading about real-life ROI, these healthcare professionals realize the tremendous benefits this technology can bring, from cost savings and speed, to increased accuracy of reporting and improvements in patient safety and quality of care." (See http://www.healthmgttech.com/archives/0804/0804thought.htm)

Many healthcare organizations are achieving tangible and intangible benefits by adopting health information technology with clinically focused EHR systems. They include:

- Increased revenue
- Cost reductions
- Improved productivity
- Improved patient datisfaction
- Reduced length of stay
- Improved quality of care
- Improved medication safety
- Enhanced compliance efforts
- Utilization of community-based and evidence-based best practices

Even though the literature and many case studies clearly demonstrate these benefits, the healthcare executives still want to see the quantifiable numbers and demonstrated qualitative benefits for their organization. Historically, there has not been a clear linkage between quality of care and use of information technology. However, this is changing. Many Pay-for-Performance programs now link quality of care delivery and use of information technology, resulting in improved reimbursement in all sectors of health care. For example:

- *Pay-for-Performance:* CMS programs and health plans are now offering additional reimbursement to hospitals when they show improvement in clinical performance. The current pilot focuses on five clinical conditions. A similar program is being piloted for physicians as well. Health systems with clinical health information technology systems are finding that there is significant cost-efficiency in reporting on clinical process and outcome measures rather than relying on manual, paper-driven process that nonautomated health systems in these projects are forced to employ. In June 2006 Premier

Inc. released groundbreaking evidence that improving patient care can reduce costs and save lives. Initial finds from the CMS Pay-for-Performance demonstration project indicated that process improvement in treatment of pneumonia and heart bypass patients could reduce hospital costs by $1 billion.

- **Bridges to Excellence:** (http://www.ncqa.org/Programs/bridgesto excellence/) offers incentive payment for physicians when they can show technology use to improve quality of care.
- **eValue8:** (http://www.evalue8.org) makes IT adoption a critical factor in selection of health plans for employers.
- **Clinical Transformation:** Health systems such as Bon Secours Health System, Ascension Health, and others realize that medical informatics and health information technology deployment are intertwined with process transformation. Moving from inefficient, error-prone processes to high-quality and lower error-rate systems requires clinical transformation deployed using the strategies and tactics of the Medical Informatics 20/20 model.

Value-based Reimbursement is becoming more common, making healthcare organizations think of revenue cycle management beyond billing and collection. Basically, adoption of EHR systems is coming down to the bottom line. Future reimbursement strategies will increasingly be based on clinical outcomes, which can only be reliably measured with accurate clinical information, captured as a direct by-product of patient care delivery, which leads back to the implementation and use of EHR systems.

Return on Investment (ROI) has traditionally been measured by organizations in terms of costs and savings and quantifiable benefits.

FIGURE 13-1 Connecting Quality of Care with Health Information Technology

Their approach toward IT has been to follow the same philosophy used to justify typical capital investment projects. They tended to focus on payback period and total cost of ownership. Unfortunately, measuring actual ROI and financial bottom lines can be difficult, especially in a field such as medicine where it may be hard to put a price tag on such intangibles as enhanced patient safety, improved quality of care, patient trust, and physician recruitment and retention.

As healthcare organizations begin to evaluate the benefits, value, and/or ROI in health IT, they need to remember a few important things:

- Organizations may need to think "out of the box" when it comes to looking at the acquisition and implementation of health IT systems, and EHR systems in particular.
- Organizations should look at technology as a "business solution" and not simply as a new tool.
- Measuring the ROI for health IT investment projects must include not only cost and quantifiable benefits, but also intangible or value-based benefits that organizations can derive from such projects.
- Some technology investments need to be considered as a cost of doing business. Organizations would not operate an office without electricity or water. Similarly, they should not operate an office without IT systems in this day and age.
- Implementing a health IT system may not reduce cost but will improve outcomes; for example, a surgical information system may or may not reduce operational costs, but it will result in better patient care outcomes.
- Some technology investments are necessary for compliance with HIPAA and JCAHO regulations, accreditation processes, and other state and federal requirements.
- Organizations should also assess the cost of not investing in health IT. For example, if appropriate tools are not implemented to support a patient billing office, it could result in additional staffing, an increase in accounts receivable, and lower patient satisfaction.
- Organizations should look at a longer-term vision and strategy when considering the acquisition of an EHR system. Use of the planned National Health Information Network (NHIN) and Regional Health Information Organizations (RHIO) will necessitate the use of an EHR system in order to exchange data with others.

- Measuring of benefits should focus on all components; calculating ROI should be a team assessment that should include everyone that would benefit from the project: clinicians, administrators, technicians, clerical, and other staff.
- Finally, while it is important to calculate the *expected* benefits, it is equally important to measure realization of *actual* benefits a year or so after the system has been implemented.

Return on Investment (ROI), Return on Quality (ROQ), and Value Measurement

Healthcare executives have to prioritize their capital projects for funding. They are now looking at both ROI and Value Measurement as means to help them decide which project should be funded and what benefits should be expected. The historical approach for standard ROI analyses did not take into consideration the *value* of the project such as realizing clinical quality goals such reducing medical errors, achieving zero preventable deaths, competitive leadership, and staying up to date in the ever-changing marketplace. This is changing as new important value oriented measures are developed.

Value, ROQ, and ROI analyses should be conducted at four levels:

- ***Level 1—Return on Quality:*** Healthcare organizations in the United States and around the world are focusing on delivering high-quality, safe health care. For many this has become the number-one

FIGURE 13-2 ROI and Value Analysis

challenge. Spurred on by projects such as the Institute for Healthcare Improvement (IHI) 100K Lives campaign to reduce medical errors and the CMS–Premier, Pay-for-Performance demonstration project, there is a new focus on quality. Lessons learned and results databases from these efforts has created a wealth of data and information regarding the case for quality. The areas of focus are medical error reduction, zero preventable mortality, figuring out how to hold the improvement gains, length of stay effectiveness, and clinical transformation. In Chapter 12, the case on the quality gains at Veterans Health Administration from its use of extensive medical and clinical informatics and a drive for quality is a great example of the knowledge gained that supports the return on quality (ROQ) case.

- *Level 2—Reasonability Check:* In the early stage of the project when it is just a concept, each project should be validated against the following five factors to determine whether it should move forward:
  - *Breadth:* How many people within the organization will be affected by this project; for example, if it is a payroll system upgrade, it will affect almost everyone in the organization rather than just one department?
  - *Usability:* How often will this project/system be used within the organization: daily, weekly, and/or monthly?
  - *Cost:* How costly the project will be; make sure all cost components are included; for example, if additional staff will be required during the implementation to support operations while existing staff works on the new system, that cost for temporary help should be included in the overall cost of the project?
  - *Collaboration and Knowledge Sharing:* Will this project allow staff to collaborate and share knowledge working toward improving performance of the entire organization?
  - *Business Imperative:* Will this project address key business problem or imperative? For example, a healthcare organization is starting to offer a new program for senior citizens, and without new software, it cannot adequately track the service, patients, or performance.
- *Level 3—Relevance to Institutional Goals:* If the project passes the Level 1 analysis and it is determined that the project has merit, the project sponsor should validate the project against key components of institutional strategy. The authors have developed a tool that is a

questionnaire that needs to be completed by the project sponsor and focuses on key components of the institution's strategy, such as:

- **Mission and Strategic Goals:** Is the project directly related to institution's mission, strategy, and business goals? Is the project going to contribute to the external image of the organization? Will the project meet today's needs as well as future needs? What will be the organizational impact of not doing this project?
- **Process Efficiency and Operations:** Will this project resolve a key problem? How many manual steps will be eliminated by this project? Will it reduce unit cost of the function? Improve overall performance? Will it help improve turnaround time for customer service? Increase patient satisfaction?
- **Knowledge Management:** Will this project generate useful information versus data? Will it result in providing data faster? Will it help improve internal knowledge?
- **Project Management:** Has this project been clearly defined between business process owners and IT? Have adequate resources been assigned to this project?
- **Risk:** Do business process owners understand the impact of this project on operations and how committed are they to moving forward? Does the solution offered by this project have a successful track record?
- **Patient Safety and Clinical Outcomes:** Will this project help the organization improve its clinical outcomes and patient safety? If this project is not done, how will these goals be achieved?
- **Compliance, HIPAA, Business Continuity:** Will this project help with the compliance effort? Is this HIPAA compliant? What plans will need to be in place for business continuity?
- **Infrastructure Replacement:** Is this project a replacement of an outdated system or infrastructure? Will the organization be at risk if this replacement is not completed?
- **Growth; Market Share Improvement:** Will this project provide organization a competitive advantage? Will it offer better services to the community and attract them to the organization?
- **Physician Partnership:** Will this project help physicians in their daily operations and create a positive impression? Will it offer more/better services to physicians?
- **Financial Responsibility; Cost Savings:** Will this project offer benefits to commensurate its cost? Will it help reduce cost?

- *Level 4—ROI Analysis:* Once the project is categorized in its relevance to the institution's strategic goals and it is determined that the project should move forward, the project sponsor can complete ROI calculations to support the business case. Typically, five measures are calculated as part of the ROI calculations:
  - ○ Return on Investment (ROI)
  - ○ Payback Period
  - ○ Net Present Value (NPV)
  - ○ Internal Rate of Return (IRR)
  - ○ Total Cost of Ownership (TCO)

The *Value and ROI Analysi*s involves several key components:

- *Cost Components:* These should include only the items that are required for the system; without these items, the system cannot be implemented. Major cost components include:
  - ○ *Software*—This includes application software, operating system software specifically related to the system, and any third-party software specifically related to this system. Any operating or third-party software that is not specifically required for the project, such as Microsoft Windows, should not be included in this cost.
  - ○ *Hardware*—This includes servers, clients, and any other technology components necessary to implement the system. Some organizations include purchase of desktops and laptops in the project cost even though the computers may be needed for general technology support, whereas some organizations include them as common technology infrastructure and do not include them in a specific project budget. Whether or not you include technology components is often a decision made based upon your general guidelines and economic impact.
  - ○ *Personnel*—This includes external personnel as well as internal personnel. Most often, external personnel include a vendor implementation team and third-party teams helping with the implementation. Internal personnel costs, typically, include loaded costs (salary plus benefits). Internal costs should also include any cost related to temporary staff hired to support operations while employees work on the new system implementation project.
  - ○ *Training and/or travel*—This includes costs of training and travel related to training. Most often, organizations only include the training fees paid to the vendor or third parties and do not

include their staff time in training or any temporary back-fill staff while employees are being trained.

- ○ *Other*—This would include other areas, such as costs incurred if an organization had to set up a project team office and had to spend on setting up office space.
- • *Benefits Components:* Benefits fall into two major categories. It is important to make sure that you identify benefits that are directly related to the project, are a manageable number, and can be measured. If the benefits cannot be attributable to the project, they will not be believable. Also, setting up too many parameters will create an overlap between multiple measures and they will become difficult to measure, which may result in an organization losing its commitment. Major benefits components are:
  - ○ *Direct Benefits* can be easily quantified, such as cost reduction in the system maintenance of the old system when it is being replaced or reduction in paper cost by automating manual processes.
  - ○ *Indirect Benefits* include two categories:
    - –*Quantifiable benefits* are benefits such as efficiency in staff time, reduction in administrative time, etc.
    - –*Value-based benefits* are the ones that cannot be quantified but will bring value to IT and/or institution. These benefits can be demonstrated on a scale of 1 to 5.

ROI Methodologies and Tools

Figure 13-3 shows that when looking at the value of technology, one should look at the value of an IT portfolio and not just a single project at a time. One project may not show positive benefits, but all together, they deliver value.

- • *Value Measurement and ROI Toolkit*
  - ○ Once you adopt ROI measurement as a normal process in your organization's project evaluation, you can select a tool that can help project sponsors and executives conduct the ROI study.
  - ○ There are several tools available in the market, such as Nucleus Research, where the tool offers a checklist of items in cost and benefits categories and provides ROI analysis including total cost

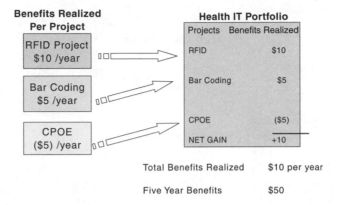

FIGURE 13-3 Health Information Technology value measurement portfolio analysis example

of ownership. Some other tools offer similar categories and analysis. *The authors customized this tool to include value-based benefits categories where the analysis included ROI and other quantifiable parameters along with rating of value-based parameters.*

○ Some organizations develop tools specific to their process. Most often, software vendors develop tools that include parameters specific to their product.

○ It is important that organizations integrate the ROI and value measurement tools with their capital and/or project budgeting process to instill the needed discipline. Integration of the capital request form into the ROI tool could provide a more comprehensive report for decision makers.

○ It is also important to integrate the value measure parameters into the system while it is being implemented. This way, the measurement of benefits can become a normal by-product of the system's use.

○ Organizations should assess the value of their IT portfolio every year and measure the benefits realized by each project within their portfolio. Most of the tools today assess individual projects and provide results. However, you may have to create your own consolidated report of all projects. It is important to measure benefits of your IT portfolio as opposed to measuring an individual project.

○ A key step in the ROI/Value analysis is to create a database of *all* projects in order to better evaluate the value of *all* IT investments and track their performance over a period of time.

ROI Calculators

ROI Calculator
http://www.acgroup.org/pages/396843/

ROI Notes Calculator
http://www.medinotes.com/roi.htm

GEMMS EHR ROI Calculator
http://www.gemmsnet.com/ROI/ROIOVERVIEW.HTM

AAFP EMR Cost/Benefit Tools
http://www.aafp.org/x20091.xml#f

○ An ongoing, multiyear analysis will provide organizations with a more comprehensive value assessment.

Value and ROI Findings to Date

The major issues for our healthcare industry today are affordability, quality, access, and effectiveness. There is increasing agreement that deployment of health information technology within a Medical Informatics 20/20 framework can help address these challenges. However, technology alone cannot deliver the desired result or improve operational excellence. Results are achieved by collaborating and integrating technology, processes, and people.

To date, benefits of health information technology have been quantified and documented in selected areas, EHR is among one of them. These benefits have been estimated at a global level as well, as there are some documented case studies that show benefits achieved by specific organizations. The following points highlight some global-level benefits:

- *Health Information Exchange and Interoperability*
  - ○ Reduction in redundant tests, reduction in delays and costs associated with paper-based ordering and reporting would result in $31.8 billion in benefits per year
  - ○ Savings from avoided tests and improved efficiencies—$26.2 billion in benefits per year

- ○ Medium-size hospitals would accrue $1.3 million in benefits per year with improved efficiency in transactions with providers, ancillaries, payers, and pharmacies
- *Benefits of Health Information Technology*
  A recent GAO study showed:
  - ○ Forty percent decrease in radiology tests resulting in $1 million in savings among the pilot group
  - ○ Reduction in staff with automation of manual processes resulting in savings of over $700,000
  - ○ Savings of $4 million in automated claims processing without manual intervention

The actual benefits can be summarized as follows:

- *EHR Systems*
  - ○ It is estimated that over five years, EHR benefits will be $86,400 per provider and the benefits will be accrued by several stakeholders such as physician practices, ancillary services, pharmacies, and, most importantly, patients.
  - ○ Ohio State University Health System reduced the time for getting medication to patients by 65% from 5.28 hours to 1.51 hours. They also reduced radiology turnaround from 7.37 hours to 4.21 hours.
  - ○ Maimonides Medical Center reported a 30.4% reduction in average length of stay from 7.26 to 5.05 days. It also realized organizational efficiencies by preventing duplicate ancillary tests.
  - ○ Heritage Behavioral Health experienced a 70% reduction in costs of clinical documentation with Electronic Health Records.
  - ○ University of Illinois at Chicago Medical Center gained significant benefits in reallocation of nursing time from manual documentation to direct care, estimated to be $1.2 million with an EHR system.
- *Clinical Decision Support Systems and Tools*
  - ○ Medical Informatics 20/20 can help improve quality of care through tools for chronic care and disease management where continuous interaction between doctor and patient is critical.
  - ○ Clinical decision support tools can help bring up-to-date information to the care provider, offer best practices at the point of care, and many more benefits.

- ○ Bridges to Excellence program offers incentives to leverage technology in disease management and best practices. Endocrinologists and primary care providers following these guidelines reduced costs by an average of $350 per patient per year. For patients with diabetes, these savings are estimated at $600 per year.
- *e-Prescriptions*
  - ○ Many errors occur because of handwritten prescriptions that can be easily misunderstood and can result in adverse drug events or complications. More than 3 billion prescriptions are written annually, and according to an eHI report, medication errors account for 1 out of 131 ambulatory care deaths, and many deaths in acute care are also attributed to medication error.
  - ○ Studies indicate that the national savings from universal adoption could be as high as $27 billion annually.
- *Computerized Provider Order Entry (CPOE)*
  - ○ The Center for Information Technology Leadership (CITL) estimates that implementing advanced ambulatory CPOE systems would eliminate more than 2 million drug events per year; avoid nearly 13 million physician visits, 190,000 admissions, and more than 130,000 life-threatening adverse drug events per year and save $44 billion per year.
  - ○ Brigham and Women's Hospital in Boston reported a 55% reduction in serious medication errors and a 17% reduction in preventable adverse drug events (ADEs). The average cost of an ADE was $2,595, resulting in projected savings of $480,000 per year. It estimated net savings of $5 million to $10 million per year.
  - ○ Maimonides Medical Center in New York realized a 55% decrease in medication discrepancies and a 58% reduction in problem medication orders. It also eliminated pharmacy transcription errors.
  - ○ Children's Hospital of Pittsburgh eradicated handwriting transcription errors completely and cut harmful medication errors by 75%.

Other Value and ROI Examples: EHR and Group Practices

The following are some brief excerpts from an article entitled "ROI Analysis Critical for Clinics," written by Bill Briggs and published by *Health Data Management* in October 2005. This excellent article contains story after story of ROIs done by clinics or small practices that have been substantiated. The article states, "Physician decision-makers in small group practices or clinics often rely on hard ROI analysis to determine whether they will come out financially ahead or behind with technology investments." Clinics are often are more cautious than large facilities when making investments that they cannot directly link with their practice. They tend to have "more skin in the game." The biggest difference between small group practices and large hospitals is that "physicians are writing personal checks to buy the technology."

See http://www.healthdatamanagement.com/html/current/Current IssueStory.cfm?PostID=20339. Dr. Kenneth Adler, in his article "Why It's Time to Purchase an Electronic Health Record System" (see http://www. aafp.org/fpm/FPMprinter/20041100/43whyi.html), mentions that with the speed of current computers, broadband connections, and improved scanning technology, information can typically be filed and retrieved electronically faster than it can be manually. Patient note creation speed has improved dramatically with point-and-click technology, more sophisticated templates, and integration of dictation with templates. He claims that savings from implementing an EHR system include the following:

- *Reduced transcription costs*—If you currently dictate your notes, you're probably spending $3,600 to $12,000 per year on transcription. Using an EHR typically cuts these costs by 50% to 100%.
- *Savings in paper-chart-related costs*—Consider how much of your budget for staffing, supplies, copying, printing, and storage is devoted to the care and management of charts.
- *Improved staff efficiency*—With an EHR, staff time currently devoted to searching for charts, entering charges manually, and so on can be devoted to value-added activities or eliminated, thereby reducing overtime charges.

Adler also states that revenue enhancements include increased income through improved coding, improved charge-entry accuracy, and improved provider productivity:

- *Coding*—EHRs now typically incorporate an automated coding adviser. This feature alone may pay for the system.

- *Charge capture*—Automated charge entry eliminates missed or overlooked charges.
- *Productivity*—With an EHR, provider productivity increases as a result of improved office efficiency. If you eliminate half an hour of paperwork, that's two more patients you could see per day or 30 more minutes you could spend with your family.

The American College of Physicians (ACP) has put its might behind creating a paperless office for doctors. In April 2004, it released a discussion paper entitled "The Paperless Medical Office: Digital Technology's Potential for the Internist." The paper points out the multiple benefits of automating patient records. "The universal use of EHRs will create a quantum leap in the quality of patient care," Dr. Munsey Wheby, ACP president, stated in the paper. See "American College of Physicians Backs EHR Efforts" by Bernie Monegain, *Healthcare IT News,* April 26, 2004, for additional insights. Some other documented case studies show the benefits achieved by physician practice offices. For example:

- *Texas-based Omega OB/GYN Associates,* a five-physician practice with three locations, achieved a $30,000 reduction in office supply expenses, including labels and file folders, six months after implementing EHR. Gail Burdine, practice administrator, said that "comparing the first six months of this year versus last year, our production and collections are up 15%."
- *Central Utah Clinic based in Provo,* a subspecialty group employing 75 physicians in ten locations throughout the state, saved $1 million in the first year. It also reduced staff and eliminated transcription costs. Those results basically paid for the system.
- *North Valley Family Medicine in Glendale, Arizona,* a two-physician practice, was able to save up to 500 square feet and allocate it to patient care by omitting the need for paper chart storage space. The practice saved about $18,000.
- *Mid Carolina Cardiology in Charlotte, North Carolina,* is a group practice with 45 cardiologists in five locations. After 12 months, returns came flowing in, says CEO Stephen A. McAdams, M.D. The clinic saved $3,000 per physician by cutting out transcription expenses. It reduced postage by $20,000, medical records staff salaries by $105,000, and paper chart costs by $30,000. There were many other unexpected benefits as well.

History Repeats Itself

History is repeating itself. People are asking how much time will it save the doctor or nurse to use an EHR system. Will it be more efficient? How many keystrokes will be saved by using the system? Will the pharmacy or laboratory operate more efficiently and process more Rx or lab tests at lower costs? While it seems intuitively obvious to some of us who have already implemented EHR systems, most organizations are going to continue to jump through the bureaucratic hoop of conducting detailed cost-benefit or return-on-investment (ROI) studies for a few more years before these exercises fall by the wayside.

This is reminiscent of the days back in the 1970s when we were asked to justify the acquisition of word processing systems. We weren't allowed to buy a single machine without a detailed cost-benefit study that took into account the number of words typed, the number of errors in typed documents, time saved related to retyping documents, and lots of other detailed measurements. It seemed ludicrous, given that once you used a word processing system for a day or two it was intuitively obvious that this was the way to go. But organizations had to jump through the hoops for four to five years before the need for the detailed justifications for word processing technology went away. It appears the need to justify EHR systems is following the same path.

At first blush, the request for a cost-benefit study does make sense. It's a good management practice. In fact, when you first implement an EHR system, you will find many people questioning the value of the system. When you first begin implementing automated health information systems, it may initially take longer to do many tasks using the new systems. The pharmacy service will report that it takes just as long to process an Rx using the automated system as it did using the manual system. The same will hold true for the laboratory service, radiology, nursing, and other services within your healthcare organization. Doctors will report that placing orders in an EHR or filling out discharge or progress notes is too time-consuming. The benefits of the system will not be immediately obvious to each of the parties implementing their portion of a comprehensive EHR system.

It's when you step back and look at the whole system several months after it has been implemented that the lights start to go off. It will take a while before you begin to see the overwhelming benefits of the new system and resistance starts to crumble. When the ward clerks and nurses see a timely

(continues)

and accurate list of patients to be admitted to their floor, when lengths of stay in the hospital by patients start declining, when building management staff know what patients are being discharged so they can clean the patient room in a timely manner so the next patient can be admitted, when clinic clerks and nurses know what patients are scheduled in their clinics so they can pull the medical records in time, when the number of clinic appointment no-shows declines, when everyone sees clear and accurate orders and reports—that's when the benefits of the health information systems are noticed.

When the doctors and nurses are able to pull up clear and accurate patient prescription profiles from anywhere in the facility, when they can see the list of lab tests ordered and get timely results, when radiology reports are also readily available, the benefits become real obvious. When doctors have complete medical records at their fingertips, no charts are being lost, drug-to-drug interactions are being flagged, clinical guidelines are being displayed, clinical reminders are popping up, JCAHO scores are improving, quality of care by any measure is increasing, in retrospect it will then seem hardly worth questioning the cost benefits of the new systems.

It really comes down to this: if you aren't using an EHR system and are still questioning the value of the system, you are practicing bad medicine. You are not keeping up with best practices, you are operating in a less-than-efficient manner across your organization, and you are harming your patients. Cost-benefit studies and reports on improvements in quality of care resulting from using EHRs abound. It is time to stop questioning the value of the investment. It is time to move on and start acquiring and implementing your EHR system.

Peter Groen
Director, Shepherd University Research Corporation

According to an article entitled "Physicians Buy In, IT Pays Off" by Lance Helgeson and published by *Health Data Management* (http://www.healthdatamanagement.com), executives at Columbia Basin Health Association decided to convert their five-clinic, rural healthcare organization to an electronic medical records system. Columbia Basin's switch to electronic records is beginning to show clear signs of payoff: "They report that physicians now see an average of 25 patients per day, seven more than when the organization's care staff relied on paper records. Patient wait times have been cut from nearly 30 minutes down to 11 minutes." In addition, the electronic medical records system "enables faster links to Columbia Basin's lab and pharmacy, which in turn can provide lab results and prescription orders more quickly to patients."

These types of case studies are emerging every day. Automating physician practice office and implementation of EHR systems in practice offices is not a choice anymore; it is a necessity to stay in business and continue to provide quality care.

Quality of Care, Patient Safety, and EHR Systems

While the potential for measurable cost savings are impressive, the real return on investment comes from the many intangible benefits that we cannot yet accurately measure and translate into dollar savings, for example, better quality of care, improved patient safety, and increased patient satisfaction.

For example, the Institute of Medicine estimates that 44,000 to 98,000 deaths each year result from preventable medical errors in hospitals, and other estimates indicate that the number could be closer to 300,000. Each year, hundreds of thousands of preventable adverse drug events also occur. This has not yet been translated that into dollar savings. Functions commonly found in EHR systems today include allergy checking, drug-interaction checking, medical alerts, access to additional patient data maintained by other healthcare organizations, and many other features paper-based patient records are not capable of providing. It is these features of EHR systems that significantly contribute to patient safety and better quality of care that provide the real justification for acquiring and implementing these systems.

Other Examples of EHR Systems and Quality of Care

In June 2005, the Advanced Medical Technology Association issued a report entitled "Health Information Technology: Improving Patient Safety and Quality of Care." It stated that approximately 31% of hospital emergency departments, 29% of outpatient departments, and 17% of doctors' offices have EHRs to support patient care. These numbers indicate that the use of electronic records in health care lags far behind other sectors of the economy.

Many errors occur because of handwritten prescriptions that can be easily misunderstood and can result in adverse drug events or complications. More than 3 billion prescriptions are written annually, and according to an eHI report, medication errors account for 1 out 131 ambulatory care deaths; many deaths in acute care are also attributed to medication error.

Today's medical field is replete with illustrations of how Medical Informatics 20/20 is improving the quality of care for American patients. Quality-of-care enhancers include remote patient monitoring, cardiac and implantable device monitoring, CPOE, expanding telemedicine possibilities, and decision support software. The results are more accurate, lifesaving diagnoses; less invasive surgery; fewer visits to emergency rooms; fewer hospital and nursing home admissions; and more convenient, higher-standard care.

- *The American Health Quality Association (AHQA)* has a Web page that links to a whole series of presentations by physicians' on quality improvements from use of an EHR. See Health Care Quality Improvement at http://www.ahqa.org/pub/education/224_1034_4895.CFM.
- *Brigham and Women's Hospital* in Boston reported a 55% reduction in serious medication errors and a 17% reduction in preventable adverse drug Events (ADEs).
- *Evanston Northwestern Healthcare (ENH)* recently successfully implemented a $30 million EHR system, and according to its CEO, Mark Neaman, the benefits have been impressive. He has said, "Not only is the system enhancing financial performance, it is substantially enhancing patient care. The turnaround time, for example, in obtaining test results has fallen significantly. Entire categories of medication errors and potential errors have been eliminated. In addition, delayed administration of patient medications has decreased 70%, while omitted administration of medication has dropped 20% across the organization."

To conclude, many executives have said that health IT is a key solution that is helping them deal with the major challenges facing them. While healthcare executives are investing more in health IT solutions, they are still being very cautious. They look to their chief information officers and chief medical officers to build the business case and show the return on investment and return on quality justifying the acquisition and implementation of new health information systems. The methodology and tools presented in this chapter should prove helpful in developing the justification for investments in these new systems.

Medical Informatics 2020—Inventing the Future

Section Overview: The future is in our hands and is created from our collective foresight, values, and actions. Our strategies and tactics today and tomorrow will invent our future. The choices we make will transform health care from a production-centered system to one focused on enabling and supporting optimum health and quality medical care for all people. Information technology and medical informatics are essential tools to support this vision for 2020. Focused execution and intelligent application of the COSI strategies—Collaboration, Open Solutions, and Innovation—are vital.

As we close out this book, let us paint a picture of the future and shed light on ways we can get there. In Chapters 15 and 16 each subsection highlights an emergency department in health care by describing:

- **DIRECTION OF CHANGE:** what we expect to see in Medical Informatics by the year 2020
- **CURRENT STATE:** a review of current technologies and those on the horizon
- **STEPS TO TOMORROW:** sharing thoughts on the steps to take on the journey into our future

Chapter 14, Healthcare 2020, describes global driving forces and delivers several approaches to aid in understanding the transitions that health care is experiencing today and forward to the year 2020 and beyond. It gives a snapshot for the future by illustrating health-care paradigm shifts and examining several scenarios on health and medical technology time lines. It reiterates the focus of this book on the execution and intelligent application of the COSI strategies: Collaboration, Open Solutions, and Innovation.

Chapter 15, eHealth—Emerging and Electronic Innovative Solutions, takes a systems approach to evolving technologies and disciplines in support of EHR adoption and quality. The chapter also explores the meanings of the "e" in eHealth as representing both *electronic and emerging* technologies that are being researched, developed, and deployed. The Medical Informatics 20/20 model is a discipline and delivery system that harnesses the power of the universal strategies of Collaboration, Open Solutions, and Innovation (COSI) to bring solutions to healthcare organizations seeking to transform services to meet the needs of people and the communities they serve. The COSI strategies are universal in that they can be applied to the advancement of any technology, from solar energy, robotics, nanotechnology, conservation medicine, and the next-generation Internet to health care.

Chapter 16, Health@Everywhere—From Inpatient and Outpatient to Everywhere, starts with a look at the person-centered health world of 2020 that takes integrative medicine to the next level. Then it discusses health IT and medical informatics systems as they evolve from being focused on inpatient and outpatient services to anywhere a person may be: work, home, or play. It delivers predictions about the next decade, especially with regards to telemedicine, electronic health records, personal health records, health information exchange solutions, and other specialized systems, especially those focused on patient-centered care.

Fast Forward >> Better . . . Smarter . . . Wiser, The year 2020 will be here before we can blink, so let's fast-forward by taking action to achieve quality care using the power of our hearts, minds, better processes, and technology tools.

Healthcare 2020

"Information technology in health care is the means to
the transformation, not the end goal."

Harvey Robbins and Michael Finley:
"Why Change Doesn't Work?"

21st Century Driving Forces and Observations to Aid Understanding

Health and medical care operate within a world undergoing rapid change, in which driving societal customer and political forces have significant impact on health care. Understanding the driving forces behind the trends has significant implications for using the strategies and tactics described in the Medical Informatics 20/20 model to transform health care. In preparation for the information discussed in Chapters 14 and 15, there are several frameworks that will be helpful in assessing the rate of change and the implications of medical and technological advances that are highlighted in the remaining chapters.

Our strategies and tactics today and tomorrow will invent our future. The choices we make can transform health care from a production-centered system to one focused on enabling and supporting optimum health and quality medical care for all people. Information technology and medical informatics are essential tools to support this vision for 2020. Focused execution and intelligent application of the COSI strategies— Collaboration, Open Solutions, and Innovation—are vital. In Chapters 1 and 11, we examined the COSI strategies within the Medical Informatics 20/20 model in some detail.

Our purpose in sharing these perspectives is not to predict the future, which is becoming increasingly impossible given the rapid increases in the expansion of knowledge and technology and diverse driving forces. The goal is to empower decision-makers with knowledge about the direction and pace of change by sharing probabilities, possibilities, and reasonable extensions of current developments into the coming decade. It was only 12 years ago that the World Wide Web burst onto the scene. Today, access to it is nearly universal for most developed countries. Our mission is to support us all in *the intelligent and wise creation of the future,* guided by consideration of the whole person, his or her family, and the community.

Thomas Friedman, in his best-selling book *The World Is Flat,* synthesizes and illuminates ten vital trends that are reshaping and "flattening" our world. Flattening represents the compression of distance and time through the Internet and communications to real-time. There are significant implications and insights for leaders around the world across all business sectors, including health care. The ten "Flattening Trends," along with some observations for health care, are:

1. ***11-9-89:*** *When the Walls Came Down and the "Windows" Came Up*— The fall of the Berlin Wall freed the captive societies of Europe and symbolized the power shift toward democratic, free-market-oriented governance and away from centralized autocratic rule. The "Windows" in the tagline refers to the growth of Windows as the dominant operating system and the rise of the Internet.
   - ***Observation:*** *This shift is also reflected in movement within organizations to virtual and network models of governance and flexible teams connected by communication, computer, and collaboration technologies and techniques.*
2. ***8-9-95:*** *When Netscape Went Public*—This represents the breakout of the Internet in public awareness and the beginning of the migration from a PC-based computing platform to an interconnected Internet-based platform and the rapid movement from paper to the digitization of content.
   - ***Observation:*** *Knowledge, information, and performance results now can be rapidly disseminated to anyone in real—time for accelerated business and clinical process change or for evaluation of the quality of care. Consumers and professionals now have unprecedented access to a vast amount of health and medical knowledge.*

Outcomes and quality ratings will become transparent and public to anyone with the time and ability to find it.

3. **Workflow Software:** *Let's Do Lunch: Have Your Application Talk to My Application*—There is an interconnected global network in place to support the production of products and services from production of animated children's movies to just-in-time production of iPods. This chain of value creation is collaborative and international.
   - **Observation:** *People and knowledge are very transportable, and the rise of medical tourism is an example. Get your bypass or plastic surgery in Thailand at a first-class facility at a fraction of the cost, plus get a two-week vacation as a bonus.*

The first three flattening forces laid the foundation for the next six.

4. **Open Sourcing:** *Self-Organizing Collaboration Communities*—Marc Andreessen, inventor of the first Web browser, stated, "Open-source is nothing more than peer-reviewed science. Sometimes people contribute to these things because they make science, and they discover things, and the reward is reputation. Sometimes you can build a business out of it, sometimes they just increase the store of knowledge in the world."
   - **Observation:** *Sharing and collaborating is the way to address many of the EHR needs and quality challenges we face. This can happen on a software level and on a business process level so that technology is deployed faster and more intelligently.*
5. **Outsourcing:** *Y2K*—This is the rise of India and its engineers. To fix the Y2K issues, the world turned to India and the realization that PCs + Internet + Collaboration could lead to tremendous value creation.
   - **Observation:** *In many ways, IHI's campaign to Save 100K Lives tapped a human capital resource of clinicians across the country who, through their collaborative efforts and the campaign, could achieve improvements in quality that they were not able to achieve before they were sharing with others outside of their organizations. This equation is Campaign Goal + Internet + Computers + Sharing = Saved Lives. The sharing principle is represented by the phase 'all share, all learn.'*
6. **Offshoring:** *Running with Gazelles, Eating with Lions*—China has joined the WTO and this gave a significant boost to offshoring,

which is a form of collaboration that moves whole factories from one country, such as the United States, to another country, in this case China. Similarly, outsourcing is the movement of one function from a local region, such as call center operations for an airline, to another country.

- *Observation: In the medical field this will be evident when a worldwide medical brand, such as the Mayo Clinic or the Cleveland Clinic or an emerging-brand healthcare organization, establishes its model of medical care in a desirable vacation spot outside of the United States to take advantage of the growth in the medical tourism business. Don't be surprised if such a venture is launched with a major insurance partner committed to cover the cost of care and vacation for its members.*

7. **Supply Chaining:** *Eating Sushi in Arkansas*—This 24/365 just-in-time organization of the supply chain process of delivery-sorting-packing-distributing-buying was pioneered by Wal-Mart.

- *Observation: This efficiency in the supply chain in health care offers the opportunity for lower costs. However, there is a risk, due to the fact that health care is a public health service. In the case of a major natural or terrorist disaster, there could be severe shortages of vital supplies and materials where they are needed most. Just-in-time health care could become just-too-late.*

8. **Insourcing:** *What the Guys in Funny Brown Shorts Are Really Doing*—UPS and FedEx are doing much more than delivering packages. They are in the logistics business and are partnering with companies large and small to create a new value chain. For instance, UPS runs a computer-repair facility next to its transit hub that repairs Toshiba laptops, thus saving shipping to a third party, cutting costs, and shortening the return time to the customer.

- *Observation: The logistics, service, and delivery platforms and infrastructure of companies like UPS put such companies in a position to partner with a leading healthcare brand to deliver interactive, eHealth services via communication channels and support them with rapid medical supplies when needed.*

9. **Informing:** *Google, Yahoo!, MSN Web Search*—"Just 'Google' or 'Yahoo' it!" is the catch phrase of the times. If you need to know something now, just surf the Web and you are likely to discover what you need when you need it.

- *Observation: Information and quality ratings in health care are transparent. The federal government, the states, the insurers, and many others are publishing performance data. Be honest, work smarter, and deliver your best, because your customer—the patient-consumer-person—wants to know.*

10. *The Steroids: Digital, Mobile, Personal, and Virtual*—Wireless and "going mobile" started with cell phones. Now you can get your video on demand anywhere, too. Many parts of the world, such as Japan, Korea, Singapore, and the Scandinavian countries, are more mobile than the United States. So, for the United States, it's time to accelerate.

    - *Observations: People with chronic disease will be the first adopters and will also have the greatest benefits as preemptive health and disease management services are delivered anywhere via small mobile devices and virtual eHealth coach/avatars powered by the next generation of intelligent agent software.*

In reviewing the extensive material presented about the Medical Informatics 20/20 model and examples throughout the book, the conclusion can be made that the knowledge and how-to information shared here is in harmony with the current trends just discussed.

Healthcare 2020 Change Categories and Paradigm Shifts

Kevin Fickenscher, MD, Executive Vice President of Healthcare Transformation for Perot Systems, has developed an excellent summary of the "Eight Categories of Change Impacting Healthcare." These eight categories and a brief description follow:

- *Standardization*—Quality and patient safety require the reduction of variation in order sets, guidelines, and other knowledge through evidence and collaboration.
- *Digitization*—The digitization of content in the form of EHRs, radiological images, and all forms of health and medical information is already well underway and accelerating.
- *Nanotization*—Very, very small devices or "nanobots" will revolutionize the diagnosis and treatment of many different diseases.

- *De-tethered Networks*—Health care is going mobile. Doctors, nurses, and patients move around to treat and be treated. They are not chained to desktops or workstations. Finally, technology and connectivity systems have evolved to support this mobile work environment.
- *Peripheral Intelligence*—The development and distribution of biosensors is being done in a noninvasive manner throughout the environment.
- *Integrated Biogenomics*—According to Fickenscher, there are "over 1,000 biotechnology medicines, targeting more than 200 diseases, in the pipeline. These medicines are using, recreating, or improving upon proteins and other substances produced by the human body to counter diseases."
- *Noninvasive Modalities*—More and more treatments or preventive approaches are becoming minimally or noninvasive.
- *Robotics*—The growth of robotics in the surgery suite or in the patient's home is accelerating and will play a major role in addressing the human power shortage in health care we face today and tomorrow.

These eight categories provide an excellent framework for monitoring the rate of technological change in health and medical care.

There also are numerous dimensions of change where a dominant way of doing things in health care is going to shift radically by the year 2020. Table 14-1 is a summary of these movements and shifts. The material earlier in the book and in the final two chapters will further illuminate these paradigm shifts.

The paradigms of 2020 are clearly visible today. The big difference is that today you will only find scattered pockets of organizations living the future, but by 2020 the future state will be widespread and the dominant mode of health and medical services.

- *Organizational Structures*—These structures will be more flexible and virtual. Organizational development will focus much more energy on understanding the informal structures and collaborative environments inside and outside organizations, rather than the formal structures depicted in organizational charts. Understanding the informal networks that exist identifies critical human connectors that facilitate work getting done. Often these connectors don't have powerful positions on the formal organization chart.

Table 14-1 Healthcare Paradigm Shifts

Paradigm	Current State	Future State 2020
Technology	Information Technology (IT)	Intelligent Information Technology (I^2T)
Medical Records	–Retrospective Paper and Electronic Health Records –Provider Entered Data	–Real-time eHealth Advisor/ Avatar (Virtual Doctor) –Doctor and Patient Entered Data
Software Model	Closed Source Software	Open Source Software
Innovation Type	Internal Innovation	Collaborative Innovation
Decision Support	Order Sets and Alerts	Medical Informatics Artificial Intelligence
Care Model	Acute and Chronic Care	Preemptive Care
Reimbursement Model	Fee for Service	Pay–for–Performance
Team	Internal Teams—Multi-disciplinary	Collaborative—Both Internal and External
Economy	Information Age Economy	Conceptual Age and Knowledge Economy
Reporting	Outcomes Data Not Available to the Public	Outcomes Data Available to Everyone
Knowledge Management	Knowledge on Demand	Recommendations on Demand
Online Communities	Communities of Practice	Communities of Performance
Search	General Results Based on Popularity	Specialized Results Based on Rules Engine and User Preferences
Organizational Structure	Hierarchical and Matrix	3D Virtual Network Organization

- *Search*—The sophistication and specialization of the search capability will be rapid and powerful. General search engines such as Yahoo and Google will be forced to build or buy powerful, tailored search engines to meet the specific needs of business and clinical audiences through artificial intelligence and advanced programming.
- *Knowledge Management*—This field will evolve from a focus on how to deliver Knowledge@Demand of structured and unstructured data to the delivery of recommendations that are tailored to personal preferences and will evolve from simple information to specific next-step recommendations.
- *Communities of Performance*—Networks of professionals within and between health organizations are using advanced Web–based collaboration tools to share evidence-based and community-based proven practices to improve the quality of health care. Communities

of Performance differ from online Communities of Practice in that they are focused on achieving measurable results and goals.

- *Reporting*—Public reporting of health and medical care performance is here to stay. Communicating about quality of care and medical error reduction rates, along with services available, will provide a competitive advantage.
- *Economy Type*—The industrial and information age is quickly giving way to a "knowledge age" when individuals and organizations will excel based on a strong foundation of math, science, and technology. The ability to create and conceptualize will play a key role in solving problems and realizing a competitive edge for organizations and countries.
- *Team*—In the past, we looked to augment internal teams with select outside consulting experts. Today and in the future, internal teams will be leveraged significantly through outside public or subscription-based networks that deliver value at a lower cost structure than the traditional consulting model.
- *Reimbursement Model*—Efforts in the past have used approaches such as capitation to transition from fee for service, but pay-for-performance in one form will be a component of the reimbursement system going forward.
- *Care Model*—Preemptive care is the next generation of prevention, and major companies are already branding it. GE calls it "Early Health"; Intel calls it "Proactive Health."

Early Health

You'll learn things in kindergarten your parents didn't know in college. You might take your first road trip in a car that runs on water. And you'll experience what we call Early Health—a completely new way of looking at health care that focuses on early detection instead of late diagnosis to help identify disease when it is easier to treat. It's healthcare reimagined.

www.gehealthcare.com

Source: GE Healthcare's seven-page advertisement in the *Wall Street Journal*, 2/14/06

Quicken Helps Manage Medical Expenses and History

Not only does the latest version of Quicken help manage medical expenses and insurance coverage, but it also organizes a person's medical history.

- *Decision Support*—Over the next five years, standardization of clinical care will gain significant momentum as more and more healthcare organizations implement medical informatics systems. But as order sets and guidelines become mainstream, quality will demand new tools in the form of artificial intelligence embedded in clinical decision support systems.
- *Innovation Type*—Over the next ten years, healthcare organizations will gain an appreciation of the power of Collaborative Innovation. IHI's 100K Lives campaign, and the availability of VistA and other open EHRs and medical information solutions in various forms without license fees, will demonstrate the power of Collaborative Innovation.

PinnacleCare Services

This firm is a "comprehensive health advocacy" firm that navigates the health and medical system for patients and families. Some of its services are:

- Counseling on the latest treatment options including traditional and alternative
- Accelerating access to the best doctors and treatments
- Aggregating a comprehensive medical record from multiple providers
- Informing you of the latest research and clinical trials
- Offering a 24-hour nurse help desk that works for you, not a health plan
- Scheduling appointments and handling paperwork

The PinnacleCare professional staff of humans offers services tailored to your situation and needs as long as you subscribe to its Platinum, Gold, or Silver membership levels. More information is available at www.pinnaclecare.com.

- *Software*—In 2020, the dominant model of software development will involve shared or open source code. The cost structure of maintaining traditional closed source software will become a bigger and bigger disadvantage.
- *Medical Records*—When the industry completes the current challenge of digitizing and standardizing medical information in the EHR, there will be realization that the concurrent embedding of intelligence within these systems will have led to the development of "virtual doctors." The huge paradigm shift is the transition from a medical record in which only doctors/nurses enter data, to a record in which the patient enters information on a real-time basis, perhaps via wireless implanted biosensors.
- *Technology*—Information Technology (IT) will be perceived as "*so 20th century*," because if it isn't Intelligent Information Technology (I^2T) then it will not be able to compete in the 21st century.

Future Health: A 20/20 View of PHRs in 2020

Over the next 10 years, healthcare organizations large and small will have full-scale Medical Informatics systems that include EHRs that are used effectively. During this time period, leading systems will have added enhanced services and features that meet the needs of their customers. At the same time, many people, particularly those with chronic and acute conditions that warrant close monitoring and support, will have adopted the use of a Personal Health Record (PHR). The evolution from a patient's perspective could go something like this:

- *2007 Crawling*—A PHR on a personal computer, linked to application like MS Word and Quicken, kept on a portable hard drive or smart card, containing most of a person's medical information.
- *2010 Walking*—My PHR embedded in my mobile phone, PDA, or iPod, with full-time connection to the Internet, capable of scanning for needed health and medical information programmed into the personal support system.

- **2015 Jogging**—The PHR has evolved into the complete medical record, plus basic digital eHealth nurse software that continually seeks "health and medical information I want" and processes real-time biometric information from implanted biosensors.
- **2020 and Beyond . . . Running Fast**—*eHealth Advisor Live,* a secure interactive Internet-connected service, combined with a portable virtual doctor with artificial intelligence, that provides full access to medical history and all necessary real-time biometric information being collected via intelligent clothing and implanted biosensors. The virtual doctor has arrived for people with the specific medical needs that require such services.

The information above has provided a brief snapshot of the possible evolution of the Personal Health Record (PHR). Our effort is not to predict the future, but to point in a direction of what is possible and share knowledge to help healthcare professionals make judgments about the pace of change. Relative to EHRs and PHRs, there are a number of "Wild Card" events that are highlighted in the Future Health and Technology Timeline (Table 14-2) that could accelerate or decelerate adoption. If a major healthcare organization had a breach in security and thousands of medical histories got posted publicly on the Web, this would reinforce current public concerns about privacy and security of eHealth and decelerate the process. Accelerating the adoption, however, could be effected by events similar to Hurricane Katrina or a major bioterrorism event. It is safe to conclude that most Americans, and many people throughout the world, will eventually have EHRs and PHRs—the only question is when. Even without the "Wild Card" events, there are numerous factors that can slow or speed up EHR adoption: complexity, lack of interoperability, high cost of installation, and significant change in delivery processes in medical practices and other healthcare settings, among them. Also, there is the fundamental fact that people are used to balancing their checkbooks and financial histories, but not used to managing their own medical records or histories in a formal way.

More information and speculative views on how a PHR will evolve are explored in Chapter 15. As EHRs and PHRs evolve, there are two models that will need to be supported when clinical data standards are universally in place. These are the person as "nexus" and as "network aggregator":

Table 14-2 Future Health and Technology Timeline

	2010	2015	2020
Health and Medicine	–Smart skin for intelligent clothing –Handheld scanner to detect tumors using tissue resonance interferometer –Diabetes cure via stem-cell research	–Drugs delivered in carbon buckyballs and opened by laser light –Individual's own tissue is used to grow replacement organs –Genetic links of 90% of all diseases identified –Genome is part of a person's EHR –Use of stem cells in brain after stokes and accidents	–Fully functioning artificial eyes –Synthetic immune system –Genetic, chemical, and physiological bases of human behavior understood
Computing & Communications	–60% of Internet access is from mobile devices –Personal memory sticks replace hard drives for files –Voice synthesis quality is up to human standards –Virtual friends –AI used for classroom assistants	–Computer link to biological sensory organs –Bacterial supercomputer –Computer agents seen as colleagues instead of tools –AI teachers practical and AI students outperform students of human teachers	–Thought recognition is a major input and interface to computing devices
Wild Cards	–100,000 EHRs including several Senators become public after security breach. People reject personal health records and eHealth for security and privacy reasons –Katrina and new biological terrorist attack continue acceleration toward EHRs for public health and national defense	–Fetal Sex Selection is the Norm –Computers and robots think like humans	–Hybrid Nanotech-organic creatures –Global epidemic kills 100M people as a result of high population density and global travel

Source: Adapted from *The Futurist*, "A Timeline for Technology to the Year 2030 and Beyond," Ian Pearson and Ian Neild, March–April 2006.

- *Personal Nexus:* A person's designated eHealth support Web service consolidates and maintains all medical and health information regardless of the source: doctor, hospital, alternative care professional, personal bio-monitor, and so on.
- *Network Aggregator:* Just as a credit reporting agency can assemble a financial profile, a designated and trusted entity will be identified to aggregate and support secure diffusion whenever a patient or care professional requires the information.

Perhaps the future of health care will see the emergence of one or more "chaordic" organizations that will be able to provide a secure trustworthy EHR solution for people across the country and around the world. It is quite possible and entirely feasible for an organization similar to VISA and its credit card and financial solution to emerge and evolve to meet the healthcare information needs of patients and healthcare providers. VISA actually delivers both a vision and model for health care to emulate. There

VISA: Unique Collaborative/Competitive Alliance

VISA's 22% per year growth over the past 25 years is an amazing track record. As a $1.25 trillion enterprise that is jointly owned by more than 20,000 financial institutions, its success lies within the success of its strategy of "localization," which is supported by a highly decentralized organization. VISA is not a traditional multinational corporation, because it lives by rules that govern cooperation and competition. Dee Hock, the founder of VISA, called it a Chaordic organization, which is a combination of the word chaos and order. According to Dee Hock, "*chaord* means any self-organizing, self-governing, adaptive, nonlinear, complex organism, organization, community, or system, whether physical, biological, or social, the behavior of which harmoniously blends characteristics of both chaos and order." Visa also has a formal alliance program, which leads to global strategic alliances and investments with key emerging technology companies. VISA, with its alliance partners, is defining and developing the future of electronic payments, including standards, security, systems, and functionality, to meet the needs of member financial institutions, merchants, and cardholders. Perhaps one day, they will bring their success to the healthcare EHR market.
http://www.corporate.visa.com/av/alliances_proposal.jsp
http://www.chaordic.org/

is a critical need to create a trusted EHR system and health information exchange solution that will be an enabler for healthcare provider organizations, third-party payers, and patients.

Another potential collaboration that could deliver the necessary foundation is the continued growth of the Free and Open Source Software (FOSS) health information systems and health information exchange solutions we have reviewed extensively throughout this book—systems like VistA and the Federal Health Information Exchange (FHIE). These and other collaborative open solutions could be used to create the trusted and secure infrastructure and environment needed in health care. Today, VistA and FHIE are supporting millions of retired and active duty military personnel, allowing secure access to their medical information by authorized users on a real-time basis anywhere on the planet. This collaborative, open source solution is based on proven clinical data standards and has a huge foundation of users and an infrastructure already in place. With the rapidly expanding international ecosystem of developers and enterprises supporting VistA, FHIE, and similar open solutions, the possibility of having a system like VISA serving the healthcare sector could become a reality within the next decade.

The Medical Informatics 20/20 model represents the infrastructure and the processes necessary to effectively and efficiently transform the current state medical records environment from paper to electronic digital knowledge and intelligence. Table 14-2 shares a view of what will be delivered by Medical Informatics systems in 2010, 2015, and 2020 in health and medicine as well as communications and computing.

A Focus on Heart Care: Today and Tomorrow

Examine Table 14-3 to consider various examples of how a person with heart disease can be helped and healed, today and tomorrow. Today, a number of traditional, digital, and interactive tools are available to help manage heart disease. Tomorrow, these choices will grow and become more digital, intelligent, and noninvasive as we approach 2020. From gluco-watches and Web-enabled life shirts to bio-bypasses in a pill and a

Table 14-3 Treatment of Heart Disease Today to 2020

	Today	2015	2020
Disease Monitoring Becomes Automatic	Home monitoring devices allow patients to take and transmit their vial signs and blood pressure data to the doctor. Doctors e–mail or call when there is trouble.	Implantable devices such as pacemakers and defibrillators automatically capture and transmit data to doctors over the Internet; patients do not have to do a thing.	Implantable devices gather data and automatically send it to doctors, who remotely administer treatment and medication using wireless and Internet technology.
Medication Reminders Become No-Brainers	Wristwatch medication reminders tell patients when to take their pills.	Drug-coated stents and other devices are implanted into the artery around the heart, and release anti-clogging medication to keep arteries clear.	Implanted chips monitor arrhythmia, blood pressure, and other vital signs, and release medication based on need—all automatically while the patient goes about his or her day.
Designer Drugs and Foods Fit the Genome	Scientists identify the gene marker for cardiovascular disease.	Genetic testing is widely available for adults who want to know the probability that they will get heart disease. Pharmaceuticals tailored to their genotype help prevent the onset of the disease.	Genetically modified foods cure heart disease–think cholesterol lowering French fries.
Nano-Machines Work from the Inside Out	Nanotechnologists develop internal medication delivery systems that can deliver anti-clogging and other heart medicines directly where they are needed.	Implanted chips or nano-membranes attached to the myocardium allow continuous time release of anti-clogging drugs that keep arteries clear of plaque.	Heart disease patients are injected with "mini machines" that filter through the circulatory system and scrub plaque from clogged arteries.
Care Becomes Interactively Remote	Patients suffering from a stroke are given clot busting medicine while being monitored remotely, using telemedicine.	Surgery is routinely performed from remote locations; surgeons use telemedicine and robotics to facilitate the operation.	Routine doctor visits are done on an interactive television or other interactive device in the home. Patients transmit vital sign data using devices connected to the Internet.

(continues)

Table 14-3 *continued*

	Today	2015	2020
Prevention Goes Genetic	MRI and CT scans screen for heart disease by viewing blood vessels in the heart without the use of injections, dyes, or needles. Images show calcium build-up in the coronary arteries, an indication of arteriosclerosis.	Adults are routinely given genetic tests to screen for their propensity toward heart disease. Preventive measures are taken. Pre-implantation genetic diagnosis is common. Eggs are evaluated for genetic mutations; those with them are discarded and those without them are fertilized and implanted in a woman's uterus.	Infants receive a vaccination against heart disease.
Surgery Morphs Into Custom-Made Organs	Surgeons perform heart bypass surgery through a small hole and without opening the patient's chest.	An artificial heart replaces diseased hearts, extending life for many that would have otherwise died of heart disease.	Cells are taken from a patient with heart disease; a biological "custom made" heart is grown and implanted. "BioBy-passes" replace surgery; vascular endothelial growth factor is injected and forms new blood vessels.

nano-pancreas, medical advances and technology are enabling doctors and patients to work together to manage, conquer, and cure diseases.

This chapter has delivered an overview of the global forces of change that are flattening the world and creating many opportunities for innovation and value creation. The healthcare categories of change, paradigm shifts, and snapshots of what health and medical care will look in the future, all taken together, have laid a context to examine specific research and development at both system and individual professional levels that support the medical informatics vision focused on the whole person articulated throughout the book.

eHealth—Emerging and Electronic Innovative Solutions

"The future's already here; it's just not very evenly distributed."

William Gibson, science fiction author who coined the term "cyberspace" in 1984.

"Trends, like horses, are easier to ride in the direction in which they are going."

John Nasibett

The "e" in eHealth represents not only *electronic* tools but also *emerging* technologies being researched, developed, and deployed in support of electronic health record (EHR) adoption and improving quality care. At end of the day, the ultimate outcome is quality. EHRs, and their electronic medical record (EMR) and personal health record (PHR) brothers and sisters, create a vital set of tools within the Medical Informatics 20/20 black bag of people, processes, and technologies in support of quality improvement.

In Medical Informatics 20/20, the COSI model is a discipline and delivery system that harnesses the power of universal strategies of Collaboration, Open Solutions, and Innovation to bring solutions to healthcare

---

Health Record Formats

Electronic Health Records (EHRs)

Electronic Medical Records (EMRs)

Personal Health Records (PHRs)

"e" Personal Health Records (ePHRs)

---

organizations seeking to transform services to meet the needs of people and the communities they serve. The COSI strategies within the model are "universal" in that they can be applied to the advancement of any technology from solar energy, robotics, nanotechnology, conservation medicine, and the next-generation Internet to the field of health care.

William Gibson is right—the future has arrived for some:

- Patients in clinical trials are offered a sampling of future treatment today.
- Sophisticated cancer treatment is available, but only from a few organizations that offer the future to people who are smart and lucky enough to find these clinical services and match them to their conditions.

The rapid diffusion of knowledge and know-how necessary to allow more people to participate depends on understanding which technologies, analytical methods, and tools are in the pipeline, so that leaders and managers can make the right decisions about when and how to invest. Follow the dollar. It is estimated to take between 15 to 20 years to move a technology or clinical breakthrough from bench to bedside. This is largely due to the amount of time it takes for Medicare, Medicaid, and the insurance companies to decide what is to be reimbursable. eHealthcare in the form of telemedicine is great example. Despite all the benefits to patients, the lower cost of technology, and the demonstrated results, Medicare as of 2005 spends only a few million dollars for the provision of telemedicine services, and most of this is for demonstration projects. The reimbursement system rewards and pays for the traditional care approach, even with alternatives available. Many organizations, from HHS's Agency for Healthcare Research and Quality (www.ahrq.gov) to Health Tech (www.healthtech.org) and many others, are seeking to compress this timeframe. Health Tech recently set up a series of knowledge transfer collaboratives to assist member organizations in implementing technology better and faster, thus saving time and money.

Yes, acceleration of diffusion depends on reimbursement, but the rationale for payment depends on proven solutions. This is the role of the Medical Informatics 20/20 model strategies of:

Collaboration+Open Solution+Innovation =
Better, Smarter, Efficient Deployment.

These strategies and tactics are the critical fuel-injection system for accelerating the development and diffusion of technologies and systems critical to quality.

This chapter includes a brief review of major trends and highlights of several approaches for organizing and thinking about the changes in technology, processes, and systems that will affect EHR deployment and the realization of quality. Each section explores electronic and emerging technologies and systems that will have an impact on healthcare organizations as they reach for performance excellence. First, the future stage is set by the fact that information technology (IT) is fast evolving into I²T (intelligent information technology). Subsequent sections describe emerging and electronic technologies and disciplines by highlighting the "Direction of Change," "Current State," and "Steps to Tomorrow" in the following areas:

- Health Information Exchange (HIE) and Regional Health Information Organizations (RHIO)
- Trusted EHR and HIE Management Solutions and Systems
- Public Health Systems, Disease Registries, and the NHIN Grid
- Mobile@Anywhere
- Next-Generation Internet
- Nanomedicine and EHRs
- Robotics and EHR Systems
- Hybrid Solar-Powered Health IT Systems
- Conservation Medicine
- Emerging Technologies Impacting Quality and EHRs

Toward Intelligent Information Technology I²T

The information technology of today is fast on its way to becoming the intelligent information technology (I²T) of 2020. The goal for I²T is to improve information technology through the progressive realization of practical levels of intelligence in a way that is sustainable, safe, and cost-effective for the users. In health care, I^2T must also be supportive of the optimization of health and medical care for individuals and populations. Features of I^2T will:

- Be aware, adaptive, and responsive to the environment
- Monitor, collect, and transmit relevant data to and from intelligent nodes
- Interact with responsible human or artificial intelligence systems
- Deliver automated responses that are practical and safe for users

The examples highlighted in the next two chapters, from smart shirts that can splint broken bones or monitor heart health to nanobot medical devices that know when to release their pharmaceutical intervention, illustrate the evolving logic and intelligence embedded into medical devices. Health and medical care is a knowledge business, and profession-als will operate surrounded with "ubiquitous computing" options from stand–alone sensing and computing devices to embedded intelligence in the hardware and software of PDAs, eyeglasses, walls, and so on. The Internet cloud will be available anywhere, anytime as long as a mobile multipurpose phone or PDA device is with a person.

Health Information Exchange (HIE) Systems and Regional Health Information Organizations (RHIOs)

Direction

The movement toward mutual collaboration is beneficial to organiza-tional health IT initiatives, and continues to strengthen in terms of the number and type of collaborative ventures. By the next decade, most healthcare organizations will find themselves collaborating with other organizations on a wide variety of ventures in areas such as software devel-opment, joint operations, information exchange, standards, knowledge sharing, technology transfer, and innovation. We predict that by 2020, thousands of community-level health information exchanges (HIE) will

> ### Tools for Organizing Health Information Exchanges
>
> The eHealth Initiative has developed a step-by-step guide and series of tools and resources to help state, regional, and community collaboratives plan, develop, and operate HIE networks. The toolkit includes a set of key principles, road maps, sample community experiences, and a module of resources to equip states, regions, and communities with the information and expertise to begin or advance HIE initiatives and RHIOs to improve healthcare quality and efficiency. The toolkit is available online at **http://toolkit. ehealthinitiative.org/**.

exist and will be interconnected to form a National Health Information Network (NHIN) across the United States.

Current State

Regional Health Information Organization (RHIO) or HIE initiatives are designed to support interoperability and facilitate access to and retrieval of clinical data, privately and securely, and to provide safer, more timely, efficient, effective, equitable, patient-centered care. They allow for the secure movement of healthcare information electronically among different organizations and disparate information systems within a region or community. Getting to an interoperable HIE network is a complex and costly endeavor. Implementation of HIE requires a significant degree of collaboration among diverse stakeholder groups and the creation of new organizational and governance models to facilitate common agreement on the technical aspects and policies for information sharing. There are also several architectural approaches to consider, given the players and the level of information exchange that will take place.

According to the "Second Annual Survey of State, Regional, and Community-Based Health Information Exchange Initiatives and Organizations" by the eHealth Initiative Foundation in 2005, there were only 40 HIEs in the implementation phase and 25 in operation in the United States. The growth of HIEs and/or RHIOs is accelerating, however, and by early 2006, there were more than 200 RHIOs that were members of Connecting for Health (http://www.ehealthinitiative.org/

coalition/). Despite increasing public concern about the privacy and security associated with RHIOs, the growth will continue as the driving forces of quality, error reduction, and national security push forward. As privacy and security issues are addressed and the benefits communicated to the public, accelerated growth will be realized. It is envisioned that by 2020, there may be tens of thousands of community-based RHIOs or HIEs that will be interconnected to form a NHIN across the United States. The key characteristics of these HIEs are:

- Standards based
- Secure and protect patient privacy
- Trusted networks
- Regional HIE networks
- Used to interconnect EHRs and PHRs

The bottom line is that HIE capabilities and the development of a NHIN are dependent on the widespread implementation and use of EHR systems. If the source of medical information at the point of care is not electronic, then the effectiveness of the NHIN and associated HIEs is much diminished.

A number of high-profile alliances and coalitions have emerged around mutually beneficial collaborative opportunities in the health IT market. These include collaborative efforts surrounding the development of open source EHR software, establishment of RHIO systems, the establishment and acceptance of health IT standards, and the sharing of knowledge to make the NHIN a reality. Some specific examples of successful health information exchange collaborations include:

- ***Consolidated Health Informatics (CHI) eGov Initiative*** is an initiative of 22 federal agencies in the United States to adopt a portfolio of existing health information interoperability standards (e.g., health vocabulary and messaging) enabling all agencies in the federal health enterprise to "speak the same language" based on common enterprise-wide business and information technology architectures.
- ***Federal Health Information Exchange (FHIE) Project*** is supporting clinical data transfer between the Department of Defense (DoD) and the Department of Veterans Affairs (VA). The newly enhanced version of the system is known as the Bidirectional Health Information Exchange (BHIE). See Chapter 7 for more detailed information on BHIE.

Steps to Tomorrow

It is imperative for healthcare organizations today to tune into the HIE and RHIO activity in their state and region. Specific recommendations include:

- *Build a RHIO Inventory:* Work with others to compile an inventory of the planned, developing, and functioning RHIOs in your organization's market. Ensure that senior management is apprised of the developments on a regular basis.
- *Evaluate RHIO Participation and Implications for an Organization's Strategic Information Technology Plan:* The key question to answer is whether an organization's IT plan and systems will be compatible with national and international clinical data standards. This means that clinical data standards compatibility needs to be a requirement for any medical informatics project. Key components to evaluate in any health information system are its use of open architecture and open standards and its interoperability, measured against current and future clinical data exchange standards.
- *Identify Your Medical Informatics-Savvy Stakeholders— Doctors, Patients, and Board Members:* Form a diverse task force to provide guidance and oversight over a multiyear period. There are significant implications for the clinical informatics component of the IT plan that need to be vetted and reviewed with a diverse team.
- *Initiate Regional Medical Informatics Coalitions:* If there is a low level of RHIO activity going on in your community, step forward and provide a nexus for action. Commit to lead in interoperability and connecting for quality. Identify several other leaders and ask them to form a steering committee and lend some analytical and managerial resources to jump start the effort to build a plan.

Public Health, Disease Registries, and the Future NHIN Grid

Direction

By 2020, public health information systems such as disease registries will be integrated into the National Health Information Network (NHIN) grid, which will run on the next-generation Internet, referred to as Internet2.

(Internet2 is discussed in greater detail later in this chapter.) Early versions of the NHIN operated on the existing Internet, but for security, privacy, and speed purposes, the entire network was recast on the second-generation Internet. The necessary additional fees that support participation in Internet2 will actually be less than the costs of all of the layers of security and anti-virus/anti-spam related to the original Internet, or Internet 1.

Current State

Both federal and state health departments in the United States gather public health information on births and deaths, immunization and vaccines, environmental and occupational health, and have established a number of disease registries. Many states also have some form of automated biosurveillance systems in development, related to the national Public Health Information Network (PHIN) and the National Electronic Disease Surveillance System (NEDSS). These functions serve as key mechanisms for improving chronic disease care, when the data is made available through health information technology to provide timely information to clinicians (and patients) to ensure that appropriate care is provided and received. EHR adoption throughout the United States and world will support increasingly computerized disease registries systems used to capture and track chronic conditions. Many states use automated systems to collect, store, or process public health information. At the local level, there appear to be numerous opportunities for improved data sharing between private healthcare organizations and the state public health departments. At the state level, there appear to be many opportunities for health information technology sharing opportunities among the states that have already developed automated clinical systems and those that have not yet done so. At the national level, there are many opportunities to better share knowledge and public health information between federal, state, and local governments.

Steps to Tomorrow

Specific recommendations that support the transition for healthcare organizations to tomorrow include:

- ***Organize Statewide Health Informatics Collaborations:*** State health departments should consider establishing statewide health informatics collaboration working groups to address such areas as:
  - Clinical data standards

- ○ Electronic health records (EHRs)
- ○ Personal health records (PHRs)
- ○ Health information exchange (HIEs)
- ○ Public health information systems and databases
- **Establish the Office and Position of State Health Collaboration Czar:** Create a state health IT sharing liaison position to serve as the focal point for coordinating and facilitating communications on all health IT collaborative projects in which the state is involved. This would be modeled on the Office of the National Coordinator for Health Information Technology at the federal level. Some of the functions of the state level office would be to:
  - ○ *Develop Health Information System Databases:* State health departments should consider establishing a database to track information on health information systems used by all provider organizations in the state, key contacts, and other relevant information.
  - ○ *Create a Collaborative Project List:* This list can be based on input from public and private sector participants of the health informatics collaboration working groups. Funding and staffing for statewide collaborative projects should then be made a part of the state public health programs and their IT budgets.
  - ○ *Identify Connectivity:* The status of all the connections that are being made between electronic health information systems and disease registries.
  - ○ *Spur Advocacy:* Be an advocate for connectivity of clinical data exchanges in a way that protects patients' privacy and addresses problems on the individual and community levels related to public health and population health management.
  - ○ *Seed Funding:* Work with state government to obtain seed funding for the integration of disease registries, statewide EHRs, clinical data standards, and connectivity between providers at all levels.

Free and Open Source Software (FOSS) in Health Care

Direction

FOSS in health care is growing in three key dimensions: 1) infrastructure and network; 2) tools and utilities; and 3) application software (specific function: stand alone and enterprise). By the year 2020, FOSS software will have achieved greater than 50% market share in most classes of software across enterprise and in homes in the United States. In countries such as China, India, and many others in the developing world, FOSS will be the dominant software used across all IT classifications.

- *Infrastructure and Network Direction:* The movement toward the development and use of FOSS in health care continues to grow, and the number and type of FOSS products available are steadily increasing. By the next decade, most healthcare organizations seeking to acquire and implement an EHR system will examine FOSS solutions as part of the evaluation process, while also considering closed source commercially available alternatives. 'Open Solutions' in health care will probably grow fastest in the area of HIE infrastructure.
- *Utilities and Tools Direction:* By the next decade, most healthcare organizations will have integrated FOSS products into their portfolio of standard IT utilities and tools.
- *Application—Stand alone and Enterprise Direction:* In the short and medium term, the question is not whether to use FOSS, but where it can be used best.

Perot Systems Builds an Open Source Software Solution

PÉRADIGM Healthcare Technologies has established a modified open source model that delivers a state-of-the-art software solution for business and clinical processes, advanced middleware solutions for integration, communication, and interoperability, along with infrastructure applications that enhance network security, connectivity, accuracy, and reliability—all without up-front license fees.

Members of the PÉRADIGM community can benefit from software enhancements contributed by other community members and from new applications as they are added to the library of open source software model components. PÉRADIGM is a modified open source model in that it is not open to everyone, only to healthcare organizations that are Perot outsourcing clients, but it nevertheless builds on many of the sharing and community principles of open solutions. See Chapter 4 for more knowledge.

Organizations will also be faced with needs that require support by leadership and participation in the development of new FOSS solutions as well the use of FOSS in various enterprises.

Current State

As described in detail earlier in Chapters 2 and 3, over the last five years, there has been a continued explosion in the amount and quality of Free and Open Source Software (FOSS) being developed and deployed around the world in virtually every industry, including health care. Specific examples of FOSS being used in health care include:

Applications

- *OSCAR* is an open source Web-based electronic patient record system developed at McMaster University in Hamilton, Ontario, Canada. It was first implemented in 2001 and is now used by a growing number of healthcare organizations in Canada.
- *OpenEMR* is claimed now to be the most widely distributed open source EMR system in the world.
- *Ampath EHR* promises a very simple, yet powerful EHR system geared to developing countries internationally.

Utilities and Tools

Some specific examples of FOSS tools that can be used in the healthcare setting include:

- *Linux:* An alternative operating systems to Windows
- *Apache:* The world's leading Web site server software
- *mySQL:* An open database software application
- *OpenOffice:* A complete suite of business applications, comparable to Microsoft Office
- *SugarCRM:* An enterprise customer relationship management software application
- *Open Infrastructure for Outcomes:* A shared FOSS infrastructure that supports the creation of Web-forms as plug-and-play modules for medical information systems with integrated statistical reports generation

- *BLOX:* A FOSS project sponsored by Kennedy Krieger Institute and Johns Hopkins University, which is focused on developing a quantitative medical imaging and visualization program for use on brain MR, DTI, and MRS data

Applications—Enterprise

- *VistA* (http://www.va.gov/vista_monograph) is the U.S. Department of Veterans Affairs' comprehensive healthcare information system. It is in the public domain and readily made available through the Freedom of Information Act (FOIA). VistA–Office EHR, Hui OpenVista, and RPMS are leading variants of the VistA system that are also available.

All of the above examples were explored in greater detail in Chapters 2 and 3.

Steps to Tomorrow

Healthcare organizations seeking to lead into the future should take the following steps:

- *Inventory FOSS Already in Use:* Compile an inventory of the use of FOSS products across your organization. This will provide a current landscape of FOSS adoption in your organization and a baseline to measure future progress.
- *Evaluate FOSS Offerings as Part of Any Healthcare Information Technology Deployment:* Lowering the cost of technology, while maintaining functionality, is an imperative. All forms of open solutions, open source software in particular, can support quality and EHR adoption effectively.
- *Perform an Open Solutions Assessment of Any Closed Source Healthcare Information Technology Solution:* Evaluate the closed source software offering for its use of open architecture, open standards, and interoperability against current and future clinical data exchange standards.
- *Identify Your Tech Savvy Stakeholders, from Doctor Allies to Patients:* Involving key stakeholders in the process is critical to success. Many doctors active in computing and clinical informatics are experienced and knowledgeable about open solutions.

- *Selecting Open Source Licensing Option:* Further investigate licensing options related to the acquisition or release of open source software that fits the needs of your organization.
- *Release Software Modules as FOSS:* Consider releasing health information software modules you may have developed as FOSS products. This effort would offer an opportunity for some "lessons learned" about working with the FOSS community.
- *Test One or More FOSS Modules Developed by Other Organizations:* Consider pilot testing the implementation and use of one or more FOSS healthcare products. This pilot effort can offer an opportunity to learn about the implications of introducing FOSS solutions.
- *Investigate Potential FOSS Partnerships:* Establish criteria for identifying and possibly pursuing mutually beneficial collaborative relationships with other organizations in the FOSS community.

Online Resources

- *Enterprise OpenSource Magazine:* http://opensource.sys.con.com
- *NewsForge:* http://www.newsforge.com/search.pl?query=medical
- *eWeek Online Magazine:* http://www.eweek.com/category2/0,1738,1237915,00.asp

Next-Generation Internet—Internet2

Direction

By 2020, organizations and individuals will have the luxury of surfing with speed and style on the 21st century, next-generation Internet2 (NG2). Operating on test beds that are 100 to 1,000 times faster end-to-

> The Net's basic flaws cost firms billions, impede innovation, and threaten national security. It's time for a clean-slate approach. David D. Clark, Past Internet Chief Architect

end than today's Internet, the NG2 will vastly improve the ability to deliver telemedicine, access medical libraries, share medical records, and move clinical images.

Current State

The current Internet is lacking in its ability to truly deliver speed and services. It is overloaded with spam, viruses, and traffic. Its architecture and security protocols were never designed to support the level and type of traffic that is being generated.

A study by IBM in 2005 found that "virus-laden e-mails and criminal-driven security attacks" increased 50% in the first six month of 2005. Another study by the Pew Internet and American Life Project showed that 43% of U.S. Internet users reported having spyware or adware on their computers, thanks merely to visiting Web sites. Increasingly, Internet users must spend more time and money protecting themselves from harm.

David D. Clark, once the Internet chief architect, has identified four areas to address in future Internets:

- *Security:* The Internet should authenticate people and computers to address ever more problematic spam and virus issues.
- *Protocols:* There is a need for better Internet traffic routing agreements between Internet service providers.
- *Mobility:* Future Internet systems should assign Internet Protocol addresses to mobile computing devices to allow for secure connection.
- *Instrumentation:* Intelligence should be embedded in the network to detect and report problems.

There is good news on the horizon. The National Science Foundation and its managers are developing a multiyear plan using $200 million to $300 million in research funding to develop clean-slate architectures that provide security, accommodate new technologies, and are easier to manage. In addition, Internet2 (http://www.internet2.edu/) is a consortium, led by 207 universities, that is working in partnership with industry, government, and international communities to develop and deploy advanced network applications and technologies, accelerating the creation of tomorrow's Internet. Internet2 is enabling a new generation of Internet applications that recreate leading-edge research and development network capability for the national research community and ensure the transfer of

Next Generation Internet and Internet2

Internet2 is being led by the university community in close partnership with industry and the Federal government. The Federal government has its own advanced Internet initiative, called the *Next Generation Internet* (NGI) Initiative (http://government.internet2.edu/ngi.html). Many government agencies taking part in the NGI Initiative are also collaborating with Internet2.

technology and experience to the global production Internet. There are more than 60 corporate members, more than 40 affiliate members, and more than 30 international partners involved in Internet2.

Committing the U.S. healthcare industry to creating a fully functional Next-Generation Internet (NGI) represents a major step forward in the greater revolution to transform Web-based communication and realize a nationwide interoperable 'Medical Internet.' Internet2 can be a testing ground for the development of advanced multimedia Internet solutions in health care, such as 3-D simulated virtual surgical training, 3-D brain mapping, and virtual reality visualizations. Development and deployment of the NGI infrastructure is necessary to support the nation's future electronic health information systems.

Some health and medical examples of Internet2 initiatives include:

- *Virtual Surgery:* Stanford University and the Commonwealth Scientific and Industrial Research Organization (CSIRO) are involved in the Virtual Surgery Master Class (http://health.internet2.edu/ news/archive.html). Advanced networking will enable a surgical instructor to lead a student, who is immersed in a 3-D view of the abdominal organs, through a live simulated surgical procedure. Both participants can simultaneously "grasp" pliable body organs, cut tissue, and at the same time feel the actions and forces provided by each other. This is particularly valuable in regions/countries where the population is small and unevenly distributed, and where access to specialized surgical expertise for training can be difficult.

- *3-D Brain Mapping:* The University of Pittsburgh Supercomputing Center, Carnegie Mellon University, and the University of Pittsburgh Medical Center are collaborating on the 3-D Brain

Mapping project (http://www.psc.edu/science/Goddard/goddard.html). Using high-speed networks to link an MRI scanner with a Cray T3E supercomputer to view the brain at work, they are able to convert scan data almost instantaneously into an animated 3-D image showing what parts of the brain "light up" during mental activity. What previously took a day or more to complete has now been cut down to seconds. This real-time capability will aid neurosurgeons in precision surgical planning, and can be used to test and diagnose cognitive dysfunctions. With high-speech networking, healthcare providers at locations distant from the MRI scanner can actively consult in patient testing.

- **Real-Time Virtual Laboratories:** The University of North Carolina at Chapel Hill and the Center for Computer Integrated Systems for Microscopy and Manipulation are collaborating on the Distributed NanoManipulator project (http://www.cs.unc.edu/Research/nano/cismm/nm/). They are using virtual laboratories to offer real-time access to remote instruments.

- **Medical Informatics Education:** Oregon Health and Science University and the University of Pittsburgh are involved in a distributed medical informatics education project (http://www.ohsu.edu/biccinformatics/ and http://www.ohsu.edu/dmice/), which covers a broad range of fields including electronic medical records and information retrieval. Distance learning provides students with access to faculty, expertise, and other students.

- **Human Embryology Digital Library:** George Mason University, Oregon Health Sciences University, and the National Library of Medicine are collaborating on the Human Embryology Digital Library and Collaboratory Support Tools project (http://www.nac.gmu.edu/visembryo.htm). They are using an Internet2 network of medical collaboration workstations, operating at data rates of more than 100 Megabits/second (compared to 3 to 15 Megabits/second for a cable modem in the United States in 2006), to provide a way for medical professionals to communicate detailed information about human embryo development in a visual form. Healthcare providers will be able to remotely visualize and manipulate real-time high-resolution 3-D image data collaboratively for diagnoses, clinical case management, and medical education. It will also provide animations of embryo system development for students.

- ***Virtual Pelvics Tele-Immersion:*** The University of Illinois at Chicago is involved in the Virtual Pelvic Floor, A Tele-Immersive Educational Environment project (http://www.sbhis.uic.edu/vrm/Research/PelvicFloor/PelvicFloor.htm). They are using tele-immersive applications, combined with teleconferencing, telepresence, shared virtual reality, and Internet2 networking capabilities to allow surgeons, teachers, and students to share and interact with 3-D complex anatomical structures, even in geographically remote locations. Participants use ImmersaDesk™ systems to interact with 3-D anatomical models.

- ***Virtual Aneurysm:*** The University of California at Los Angeles is involved in the Virtual Aneurysm project (http://www.radsci.ucla.edu:8000/vra/index.html), which is a simulation and virtual reality visualization of brain blood flow. Using Internet2 high-performance networking and advanced capabilities, researchers and healthcare providers are able to examine critical flow patterns and evaluate simulated surgical interventions.

- ***Rural Health and GIS:*** The University of Wyoming and the Wyoming Department of Health are involved in the Surveyor project, which uses a Web-based research environment to integrate rural health data with GIS technology (http://www.internet2.edu/presentations/20040224-Health-Kratz_files/slide0507.htm). High-level Internet2 applications quickly locate and transmit large volumes of reliable data on healthcare issues, providing support for rural healthcare providers in underserved areas. This project also supports continuing education through Internet resources and telecommunication.

- ***Very Fast, Secure, Real-Time Video Conferencing:*** The National Library of Medicine is providing a test bed environment that demonstrates the use of MPEG-2 video conferencing and NTSC quality video over Internet2 networks and the NGI for use in telemedicine/consultation and distance-learning programs. The test-bed environment allows point-to-point and multi-point videoconferencing (via multicast) between and among collaborating sites, and also allows transmission of a range of medical content from varied sources, including data from instruments. This effort is part of the NLM Collaboratory for High Performance Computing and Communications that focuses imaging and collaboration research. In addition, it is a venue for communicating electronically with others over advanced networks using a complement of collaboration technologies (http://collab.nlm.nih.gov/).

Steps to Tomorrow

Healthcare organizations interested in collaborating on Internet2 or NGI medical informatics initiatives should:

- *Develop a business case* focused on quality and customer service for collaborating in the healthcare initiatives of Internet2 or NGI.
- *Identify potential partners* for actively joining in Internet2 workgroup committees that focus on health care and related initiatives.
- *Review and prioritize Internet2* or NGI projects for potential participation within organizations' key clinical departments.
- *Assess implications of IPv6 on medical informatics deployments:* Examine closely implications of current and anticipated technologies and the transition into the use of the next-generation Internet Protocol version 6 (IPv6).
- *Conduct a detailed feasibility analysis* for collaborating on selected projects.

Online Resources

- *Health Sciences Advisory Group:* http://health.internet2.edu/about/advisory_group.html
- *Internet2 Health Sciences Cardiology Special Interest Group (SIG):* http://health.internet2.edu/WorkingGroups/Cardio.html
- *Internet2 Radiology Special Interest Group (SIG):* http://health.internet2.edu/WorkingGroups/Radiology.html
- *Internet2 Health Sciences Security Special Interest Group (SIG):* http://health.internet2.edu/WorkingGroups/Security.html
- *Internet2 Orthopaedic Surgery Working Group:* http://health.internet2.edu/WorkingGroups/OrthopaedicSurgery.html

- *Internet 2 and RHIOs:* http://www.internet2.edu/presentations/ spring05/20050503-Health-Anderson.ppt

Nanomedicine

Direction

Nanotechnology will revolutionize almost every industry, including health care, pharmaceuticals, communications, computers, manufacturing, materials, energy, and security. In the coming decades, cheaper and high-performance nanotechnology solutions, combined with convenience and greater functionality, will change the daily business practices of healthcare organizations and how they provide a person's care when they are a patient. In general, nanotechnology refers to the field of developing, engineering, and creating devices that range from 1 to 100 nanometers (nm) in one, two, and three dimensions. A nanometer is one billionth of a meter.

Current State

Biologists, physicists, chemists, materials scientists, computational scientists, and mechanical and electronic engineers are all collaborating to share knowledge of tools and techniques and information on the physics of atomic and molecular interactions. The following are just a few examples—the nano-tip of the iceberg, so to speak—of nanotechnology initiatives in the healthcare arena:

- *Better Artificial Joints and Nanotube Brain Surgery:* Researchers at Purdue University, the University of Alberta, and Canada's National Institute for Nanotechnology have discovered that bone cells called osteoblasts attach better to nanotube-coated titanium than they do to the conventional titanium used to make artificial joints. Purdue University researchers have shown that extremely thin carbon fibers called nanotubes might be used to create brain probes and implants to study and treat neurological damage and disorders. These nanotubes not only caused less scar tissue but also stimulated neurons to grow 60% more finger–like extensions, called neurites, which are needed to regenerate brain activity in damaged regions (*Purdue News,* January 2004, at http://news.uns.purdue.edu/ html4ever/2004/040107.Webster.neural.html).

- *NanoDrug Delivery:* A chemical engineer and professor at MIT was awarded the Albany (NY) Medical Center Prize in Medicine and Biomedical Research, America's top tribute in medicine, for his research on polymer-based drug-delivery systems that allow clinicians to control the release of large molecules in a steady, controlled manner through surgically implanted plastic devices. His work has spawned revolutionary advances in cancer treatment (*Modern Physician,* May 3, 2005, at http://www.modernphysician.com/news.cms?newsId=3488).
- *NanoBioMarkers:* Northwestern University developed the "Bio-Barcode Assay," a highly sensitive diagnostic test that could revolutionize the detection of disease. The technique involves nanotechnology and the use of magnets, gold, DNA, and antibodies. Experts are already exploring ways of using it to spot early markers of Alzheimer's disease, and in the future, it could be used to diagnose the earliest signs of cancer, HIV infection, or the human form of mad cow disease (news.scotsman.com, November 2004, at http://news.scotsman.com/latest.cfm?id=3746912).

Nanotechnology will lead to new generations of prosthetic and medical implants designed to interact with the body, fundamentally altering the management of illnesses, patient-doctor relationships, and medical culture in general. Three major areas in which nanotechnology applications will be valuable to healthcare organizations include:[1]

- *Implants and prosthetics:* "With the advent of new materials, and the synergy of nanotechnologies and biotechnologies, it could be possible to create artificial organs and implants that are more akin to the original, through cell growth on artificial scaffolds or biosynthetic coatings that increase biocompatibility and reduce rejection. These could include retinal, cochlear, and neural implants, repair of damaged nerve cells, and replacements of damaged skin, tissue, or bone."
- *Diagnostics:* "Within microelectromechanical (MEMS), laboratory-on-a-chip technology for quicker diagnosis, which requires less of the sample, is being developed in conjunction with microfluidics. In the medium term, it could be expected that general personal

---

[1]The Royal Society and The Royal Academy of Engineering Nanoscience and Nanotechnologies, July 2004, http://www.nanotec.org.uk/report/chapter2.pdf.

health monitors may be available. Developments in both genomics and nanotechnology are likely to enable sensors that can determine genetic make-up quickly and precisely, enhancing knowledge of people's predisposition to genetic-related diseases." MEMS is related to nanotechnology because both deal with very small microminiaturized materials/devices, but MEMS deals with devices that are measured in micrometers or one millionth of a meter.

- *Drug delivery:* "With nanoparticles, it is possible that drugs may be given better solubility, leading to better absorption. Also, drugs may be contained within a molecular carrier, either to protect them from stomach acids or to control the release of the drug to a specific targeted area, reducing the likelihood of side effects. The ultimate combination of the laboratory-on-a-chip and advanced drug delivery technologies would be a device that was implantable in the body, which would continuously monitor the level of various biochemicals in the bloodstream and in response would release appropriate drugs. For example, an insulin-dependent diabetic could use such a device to continuously monitor and adjust insulin levels autonomously."

A quick listing of some areas that are converging on the field of nanomedicine includes: Biotechnology, Genomics, Genetic Engineering, Cell Biology, Stem Cells, Cloning, Prosthetics, Cybernetics, Neural Medicine, Dentistry, Cryonics, Veterinary Medicine, Biosensors, Biological Warfare, Cellular Reprogramming, Diagnostics, Drug Delivery, Gene Therapy, and Clinical Imaging. Looking forward to the next decade, the linkage of these nanotechnology diagnostic, drug delivery, or implant devices to a patient care information system and personal health record become very real possibilities.

Steps to Tomorrow

Next steps for large healthcare organizations to take include:

- *Establish Nanotech Monitoring as Part of Technology Early Warning Systems:* Obtain lessons learned from existing nanotechnology projects, especially as they relate to health care and IT systems.
- *Investigate Research and Development Opportunities:* If your healthcare organization has a clinical research and development function, assess the opportunities in research and development

efforts in nanotechnology that relate to the delivery of patient-centered health care and health information systems.

- ***Identify Potential Nanotechnology Pilot Projects*** involving healthcare-related product development and implementation that may benefit your patients in the future (e.g., drug delivery, gene therapy, and diagnostics).
- ***Investigate Changes in Clinical Practices*** and business processes that your organization may need to make in anticipation of implementing nanotechnology applications/devices.
- ***Conduct a Cost-Benefit Analysis and Return on Investment*** for this type of initiative for your organization.

Online Resources

- ***A Nanotech Cure for Cancer:*** http://www.wired.com/news/technology/0,69206-0.html
- ***National Cancer Institute:*** http://nano.cancer.gov/resource_center/video_journey.asp
- ***Nanotubes Blast Cancer Cells:*** http://www.wired.com/news/technology/0,69406-0.html
- ***How Gamers Can Help Cure Cancer:*** http://www.wired.com/news/technology/0,67835-0.html

Solar- and Other Renewable Energy–Powered IT Systems and Facilities

Direction

By 2020, a significant number of healthcare organizations around the world will have begun to acquire and deploy "hybrid" energy systems that tap into renewable solar and wind energy sources along traditional electrical energy sources to support their IT infrastructure and overall facility energy needs. Realizing that lower emissions stand to improve air quality and therefore reduce incidences of health conditions such as asthma and other respiratory ailments, healthcare organizations will actively seek energy from renewable resources. In addition to reducing pollution and global-warming impacts, alternative energy sources such as wind and solar will allow health care to power the delivery of care in rural and hard-to-reach areas around the globe.

Current State

In the last 35 years, the message has been clear but ignored by most people, organizational leadership, and policy makers. Much of the world, including the United States, is being held over a barrel—an oil barrel—when it comes to energy. The public and private sectors need to collaborate and take the initiative to lead the way into our diversified energy future where the centerpieces of our strategy are conservation and increased usage of solar power and renewable energy sources across all sectors of the economy internationally.

The times have changed. More efficient solar energy systems, now being produced at lower costs, are becoming attractive alternatives as the price of oil climbs ever higher. The number of examples where commercial off-the-shelf (COTS) solar energy components are being used to power computer systems has increased dramatically, including installations by healthcare facilities in various locations around the world.

In the healthcare industry, there are compelling reasons to acquire and implement hybrid energy systems that include solar power. These include providing continuity of care during major natural and man–made disasters, as well as providing power for health IT systems in remote locations where traditional electrical services cannot be reliably provided to support these systems. Healthcare organizations will need to modify their corporate visions to include having more and more of their IT infrastructure, Web sites, and computers powered by a "hybrid" energy system that taps into solar, wind, and traditional electrical energy sources.

Solar-Powered Health Facilities and Clinical Computer Systems

Lack of electricity has a substantially negative impact on the health of millions of rural villagers in developing countries, severely affecting many women and young children. Indoor air quality, water quality, and fire safety in rural homes and health clinics all depend on reliable electricity. For many of the nearly two billion people in developing countries who still live without electrical power, solar energy offers a cost-effective, reliable, and earth-friendly solution. When Hurricane Katrina hit the Gulf Coast of the United States in 2005, large parts of the region quickly found themselves operating in third-world-like environments.

HHS Solar Energy Project Enhances CDC Healthcare Facility in Kenya—The Centers for Disease Control and Prevention (CDC) Health Initiative facility in Homa Bay, Kenya, benefits from a solar energy power system that delivers reliable power and reduces losses of vital medicine and laboratory test samples. The facility houses an on-site laboratory that supports a project to reduce diarrheal diseases using a simple household-based method to improve water quality. In the past, the facility and program has experienced frequent power outages that required excessive use of an emergency diesel-powered generator. This has added excessive costs, due to the simple facts that: 1) there is no maintenance available, 2) the cost of fuel is so high, and 3) the generator has to be replaced every five years. To reduce the site's power disruptions, CDC teamed up with the U.S. Department of Health and Human Services (HHS) to install a photovoltaic module for the laboratory. The program to install a solar energy system at the Homa Bay laboratory was a culmination of the dedication of personnel in many different offices such as the CDC, the HHS Energy Program, and the Department of Energy. As a result, the CDC Homa Bay laboratory now has a more reliable energy source that will allow the staff to address the real needs of improving the health of the Kenyans.

WiFi on Wheels and Solar-Powered Computers in Cambodia—An article by Amanda Thomas, "Doctors here link up with patients in remote Cambodia via innovative system" (*Boston Globe,* December 12, 2004), reported on a cart pulled by two oxen that was used to transport computers for use in remote rural areas of Cambodia. The article states, "Ratanakiri province is gradually emerging from the shadows due in part to technology developed by First Mile Solutions, a Cambridge-based company founded by two MIT graduate students, Rich Fletcher, 38, and Amir Hasson, 28, which in turn has enabled a telemedicine link with Massachusetts General Hospital to be forged. Their wireless system, which Hasson calls 'wi-fi on wheels,' uses a combination of wireless technology and motorcycles to bring the Internet to places like Ratanakiri. The system relies on an Internet access hub in the provincial capital, Ban Lung, wireless-equipped solar-powered computers in Ratanakiri, and five motorcycles, each with a storage device, a wireless transmitter card, and an antenna fitted to the back." (http://www.boston.com/news/local/articles/2004/12/12/long_distance_house_calls?pg=full)

Solar-Powered Hospital in Uganda—In a USAID news release, it was reported that youth volunteers from the United States traveled to rural areas of East Africa to work with "Solar Light for Africa," a faith-based nongovernmental organization, in providing power to clinics, orphanages, schools, and churches. With USAID assistance, the organization electrified the Kakuuto Hospital in Uganda's Rakai District using solar energy, which has improved the health of patients and enabled staff to treat them more effectively. This includes solar power for computers. (http://www.usaid.gov/stories/uganda/fp_uganda_solar.pdf#search='solar%20powered%20hospital%20computers')

Solar Energy Supports Safe Vaccines in Latin America—The Cold Chain is a World Health Organization and Pan American Health Organization support effort that uses reliable refrigeration to conserve vaccines from manufacture to distribution to point of use. Solar electricity is used in nonelectrified communities to maintain a safe supply of vaccines and to freeze icepacks for transport to the most remote populations. Vaccine refrigeration, lighting, safe water supply, communications, and medical appliances are powered by solar electricity at rural healthcare facilities throughout Latin America.

CubaSolar Powers 300 Rural Clinics—CubaSolar is a nongovernmental organization promoting the use of renewable energy and energy consciousness in Cuba. The organization has worked to install photovoltaic panels in 300 medical clinics in the remote mountain regions of the country, which have proven to increase quality of life and decrease infant mortality rates in these areas. Initially, all of the systems included lights, a vaccine refrigerator, and other medical equipment such as electrocardiographs and X-ray machines. Because each clinic has a live-in doctor, the systems included a TV and radio for the physician as well. After CubaSolar employees noticed that many children in the communities they served were crowding around the TV in the physicians' homes at night, they evolved their installations to include a photovoltaic panel on the community center for TV and other social functions.

FEMA and Solar Power—When energy efficiency, passive solar, and daylight are combined with solar systems to generate electricity and hot water, partial or even full operation can be maintained when traditional utility services fail. National Renewable Energy Laboratory (NREL) is working with the Federal Emergency Management Administration (FEMA) to educate staff and field personnel on the use of portable photovoltaic systems. There are currently two systems traveling to several FEMA training centers to educate emergency response teams. The National Center for Photovoltaics (an NREL center of excellence), the National Association of Independent Insurers, and the U.S. Department of Energy are working together to promote a new tool for disaster recovery using solar technology. Unfortunately, this work has been chronically underfunded for years. Otherwise, solar energy could have been part of the solution in responding to Hurricane Katrina. For more information, visit http://www.nrel.gov/.

The following are some key points to keep in mind about the future:

- Conservation of all energy forms should be elevated in the daily priorities of all people and organizations worldwide.
- Costs of traditional nonrenewable, fossil fuel energy sources are escalating.
- Commercial off-the-shelf (COTS) solar energy solutions are becoming readily available.
- Solar energy can be part of a hybrid solution that uses solar, wind, and traditional electrical energy sources, all working together to reduce dependence on nonrenewable energy sources.
- Solar energy meets nanotechnology: Research into nanoparticles of gallium selenide for solar energy conversion holds the promise of increasing the efficiency of solar energy capture while reducing the cost of equipment production.
- This should be a first-world solution, not just a third-world solution.

Worldwatch Institute reports that solar energy has surpassed wind power generation to become the world's fastest-growing energy source. World solar markets are growing at ten times the rate of the oil industry. Worldwatch predicts that "solar energy may join computers and telecommunications as one of the leading growth industries in the 21st century."

One final observation: Solar power and open solutions (including open source software and open standards) are intriguing many progressive-minded people. The underlying philosophy is very similar. Both appeal to the ideas of:

- Independence
- Freedom
- Thriftiness
- National Security
- Improved Health Status
- Creativity and Innovation
- Being Good Stewards of Resources

Steps to Tomorrow

There are a number of recommendations and next steps for healthcare organizations relating to conservation, solar and other renewable energy sources:

- ***Conduct a Conservation and Renewable Energy Feasibility Analysis:*** Commission a detailed systems requirements analysis and cost-benefit study on the potential uses of hybrid solar energy systems in current and future facility design.
- ***Consider New Facility Design and Existing Facility Renovation That Includes Conservation and Renewable Energy:*** Encourage healthcare facility and technology designers and architects to integrate solar and renewable energy into their next-generation designs.
- ***Initiate Solar Energy Pilot and Demonstration Programs:*** Conduct a pilot test of solar-powered computer systems and incorporate renewable energy considerations in all future healthcare buildings. Or, implement a solar–powered demonstration project for a Web site, rural health clinic, or telemedicine program.
- ***Advocate for Solar:*** Support political action to encourage much higher levels of government funding of solar and renewable energy as well as tax cuts/incentives for healthcare facilities and health information computing systems that install solar.
- ***Document the Benefits:*** Use of solar-powered systems will expand over time, as the benefits are documented. Be sure to quantify how the system reduces pollution and lowers costs.
- ***Seek Resources:*** Take a solar and renewable energy position and seek out funding sources that will support this next generation of community and economic development.

Robotics and EHR Systems

Direction

In 2020, the use of robots will become a routine part of health care and an important component of EHR systems. Up to 30% of all minimally invasive surgery will be performed robotically. In this next decade, we will see a wide array of more sophisticated robotic devices being used to collect and feed clinical data into the EHR, including nanobots injected or embedded in patients. There will also be a growing range of robotic devices used at the back end of an EHR system to package and dispense prescriptions, and also to deliver prescriptions, supplies, and other items directly to the nursing station or to a specific patient's room.

Current State

The 1980s saw the emergence of some of the first uses of robots in the healthcare setting. These were primarily restricted to robotic carts used to move mail, medical records, prescriptions, and laboratory specimens around a medical center. There was also an increasing commitment to research and development of stationary robotic devices used for specialized purposes, for example, packaging drugs.

The 1990s saw the production and deployment of a limited array of stationary robotic devices, used to package and dispense drugs. The decade also witnessed the emergence of the first robotic surgical devices used by surgeons to perform selected procedures either on–site or via telesurgery at very remote locations, for example, RoboDoc, Aesop 1000, Neuromate, da Vinci, and the Zeus surgical systems.

This first decade of the 21st century is seeing more widespread deployment of robotic surgical systems for use in a growing range of surgical

---

Health Tech Predicts Robotics Impact

Health Tech (www.healthtech.org) is a nonbiased, member-supported network of leading healthcare organizations that produces accurate research reports on all forms of technology. In addition, Health Tech supports rapid knowledge and capability transfer and how-to information to assist members in rapid and effective technology adoption.

procedures. Robotic surgical assistants are now being used in a number of operating rooms. In addition, robotic devices used to package and dispense drugs are becoming more sophisticated and are now being interfaced to EHR systems. Prototype robotic systems are being tested as robotic health aides, for remote bedside teleconsultations, as personal care assistants for the elderly, and for many other purposes.

Robots in Healthcare Facilities and Programs

OTELO European Project: OTELO (mObile Tele-Echography using an ultra-Light rObot) offers an alternative to medical centers that lack ultrasound specialists. It is a portable ultrasound probe holder robotic system, associated with state of the art communications technologies that reproduces the expert's hand movements to perform at a distance an ultrasound examination. Although being held by a nonspecialized paramedic on the remote site, the robotic system brings, in real–time, good ultrasound image quality back to the expert site. (http://www.hoise.com/vmw/04/articles/vmw/LV-VM-04-04-8.html)

In an article in *Virtual Medical Worlds* in June 2005, it was reported that a new surgical assistant at the University of North Carolina (UNC) Hospitals had arrived. It sports three arms, a computerized brain, and a glowing track record in helping to repair heart valves, remove cancerous prostates, bypass blocked coronary arteries, and perform gastric bypass operations for morbid obesity. The new arrival is a robotic machine, the da Vinci Surgical System, manufactured by Intuitive Surgical. UNC currently is the only gynecological oncology program in the Southeast that is using it. (http://www.hoise.com/vmw/05/articles/vmw/LV-VM-08-05-8.html)

Robotic Delivery System: According to an article in the *Washington Post* by Susan Okie on the use of robots by the VA, whenever a new patient is admitted to the VA Medical Center in Durham, North Carolina, a four-foot eight-inch talking robot rolls up to the nurses' station nearest to the patient's room, bringing doses of whatever drugs the doctor has ordered. TOBOR, the robot, is a delivery "droid" that glides along the corridors day and night, ferrying medicines from the hospital's central pharmacy to its wards. Pyxis Corp., the company that manufactures HelpMate robots such as TOBOR, has placed almost 100 of its robots in U.S. hospitals, including 11 in seven VA medical centers.

Robotic Packaging and Dispensing Systems: OptiFill, AutoScript III Robotics, and Robot-Rx are some examples of robotic Rx packaging and dispensing systems deployed at VA medical Centers across the country. The McKesson Robot-Rx is used to fill unit dose inpatient medication orders for the Hines VA Medical Center in Chicago.

These are just a few of the many applications of robotics in the field of healthcare. See www.hoise.com/vmw/05/articles/vmw/LV-VM-11-05-19.html for more detail.

Steps to Tomorrow

We recommend that advanced healthcare organizations seeking to acquire, develop, and deploy robotics technology take the following steps:

- *Assemble an Interdisciplinary Team:* This team would identify functional requirements and/or potential uses of robotic systems designed for use by physicians and for the care of patients.
- *Research Existing Options:* Conduct a detailed literature search on a regular basis and learn lessons from robotics projects underway at other institutions.
- *Seek Collaborators:* Identify potential organizations to collaborate with on the research, development, testing, and use of robots in health care, for example, medical schools and vendors.
- *Conduct a Feasibility Study:* Conduct a feasibility study into the use of robotics and select potential pilot projects. Investigate changes in clinical practices and business processes that may need to be made in anticipation of utilizing robot technology.
- *Select and Fund Pilot Projects:* Use the outcome of these projects to choose the most cost-beneficial robotic systems for organization-wide deployment.

Mobile@Anywhere

Direction

For the foreseeable future, wireless technology will complement wired computing in enterprise organizational environments. Even new buildings will continue to incorporate wired LAN because wired networking remains less expensive than wireless, even though wireless has lower support costs. In addition, wired networks offer greater bandwidth, allowing for future applications that may be beyond the capability of today's wireless systems. By the year 2020, due to technological advances and the demands of a very mobile workforce, wireless will be the dominant connectivity infrastructure.

Current State

Wireless communication is currently one of the fastest growing technologies in the information technology industry. The use of wireless modalities in settings such as hospitals, clinics, long-term care facilities, and home care is becoming well established, as indicated by the proliferation of software applications and use of mobile computing devices in such settings. The wireless landscape is finding a secure place within major healthcare organizations.

Many companies have already chosen to move forward and are using wireless networks to connect portable computing devices to enterprise applications. These are the companies that have examined the business

---

VA Program Wins Mobile and Wireless Security Award

The Department of Veterans Affairs (VA), in support of its healthcare facilities nationwide, has already taken initial steps to support medical services at the point of care through the use of wireless technology and the adoption of appropriate mobile computing devices and applications. Staff from the Veterans Health Administration (VHA) Office of Information's national Bar Code Medication Administration (BCMA) Joint Program Office were recently selected by the Security of Mobile and Wireless Business Applications in Government II Conference Awards Committee to receive the award for Outstanding Accomplishment in the category of Enterprise-wide Applications of Mobile and Wireless Security. The award was given for their work on deploying VHA's BCMA software over secure wireless data networks throughout VHA medical facilities. The system ensures that VHA's network and patient information are secure from unauthorized access and meet HIPAA privacy guidelines for the healthcare industry.

processes of their customer-facing employees and identified areas where today's technology can improve those business processes. Possible business process improvements exist in the following areas:

- *Cost reduction:* Activities and resources can be removed from existing processes.
- *Cycle time reduction:* Sales, service, expense, and billing cycles can be reduced.
- *Increased revenue:* Wireless networks can introduce revenue-generating activities that would not otherwise be possible.
- *Optimal use of time:* At points in a business process where workers must wait, wireless can support them in the performance of other useful tasks.
- *Increased customer satisfaction:* The quality of the service to the customer is maximized.
- *Increased employee satisfaction:* Mobile solutions can reduce tedium, unnecessary trips to the office, and paperwork.

Physicians today can acquire a mobile practice companion, or PDA device, that offers immediate and secure access to critical clinical information, no matter where or when they need it to help them provide patient care. One of the biggest challenges for mobile computing vendors is to provide deeper and broader functionality. Expect mobile computing vendors to continue to expand functional capability, from tasks such as prescription writing and charge capture to actual clinical documentation, in the coming years—especially as these companies merge with or acquire other mobile computing application vendors. The complexity of mobile and wireless applications, combined with a lack of standards, will continue to make mobile and wireless an area of overdue innovation. The lack of sufficiently useful and usable applications will be the biggest barrier to "always-on" consumer acceptance in the near term.

The real question about the future of the wireless enterprise network is not whether it is here to stay, but rather the extent to which we have the foresight to fully exploit it while preserving the privacy and security of the individual's health information.

Health care is reimagining its workplace and the provision of care and using wireless information technology to achieve many of its business objectives. Optimal to its success is the priority of securing the infrastructure and data stream. Any wireless strategy must understand how every

---

Wireless Solutions Inventory

- Wireless Phone Switch (PBX)
  - Pagers
  - Phones
- Wireless Data Networks
  - Wireless LANs (WLAN)
- Wireless Internet/Intranet
  - Wireless Web-based Reference Sites
- Wireless/Mobile Enterprise Computing Devices
  - Cellular Phones
  - Handheld Personal Digital Assistants (PDA)
  - Laptop Portable PC
  - 'Wearable' Computing Systems
- Wireless/Mobile Enterprise Healthcare Applications
  - Clinical Documentation
  - Alert Messaging
  - Electronic Health Records (EHRs)
  - Bar Code Medication Administration (BCMA)

---

decision affects the security of the enterprise and yet implement devices and applications that provide great value. In general, wireless technology will complement wired computing in enterprise environments through the next decade.

Steps to Tomorrow

Here are recommended next steps in exploiting wireless technologies in health care:

- ***Operate a Multidisciplinary Work Group:*** Establish an enterprise wireless working group to develop a long-range strategy and plan
- ***Agree on Infrastructure, Device, and Application Standards:*** Standardize on a single mobile infrastructure platform and a single application solution whenever possible
- ***Set High Security Standards:*** Maintain a comprehensive security protocol, and conduct ongoing monitoring of advances in security threats and responses

- *Establish the Connectivity Imperative:* Enable connectivity with your Intranet and legacy systems
- *Rethink Processes Based on Mobile Technology:* Use innovation and quality improvement tools such as Six Sigma and LEAN to transform, streamline, and improve business and clinical processes throughout the healthcare organization
- *Identify and Conduct Pilots:* Build the organization's wireless knowledge, skills, and capabilities sooner with pilot deployments in selected facilities and departments; achieve some wins and expand the program to additional locations
- *Be Wireless:* Deploy wireless systems management tools from the outset

Conservation Medicine

Direction

"Conservation medicine" is an emerging, interdisciplinary field that studies the relationship between human/animal health and environmental conditions. By leveraging technology such as an international, open database of genetic information about animals and viruses, the discipline of conservation medicine will be focused on early identification, vaccine development, and isolation of epidemics and pandemics. Due to the world's ever-faster globalization, conservation medicine will play a critical role in the coming decades in detecting human-to-animal health interactions such as a virulent strain of swine flu making its way from Hong Kong to the United States.

Current State

Humans have always been part of their environment. Environmental conditions have affected the growth and development of humans throughout our species' history. Conservation medicine, also called "ecological medicine," champions the integration of multiple techniques and the partnering of scientists from diverse disciplines. The field has begun to evolve rapidly as a result of human-induced environmental degradation that has resulted in more than 30 new diseases that have moved from wildlife to human populations since the 1970s, including AIDS, ebola, Lyme disease, and SARS.

Conservation medicine evolved out of a crisis: unprecedented levels of disease and ill health in many species, driven by the increasing burden of environmental change. Climate change, chemical pollution, global trade, domestic animals, encroachment into wilderness areas, and the overuse of antibiotics are some of the primary mechanisms through which humans are rapidly transforming ecosystems worldwide.

Conservation medicine represents a significant paradigm shift in the environmental movement and in medicine. The basic principle is that all things are related. An example is when large tracts of the rainforest are burned for agriculture, driving wild animal species into contact with livestock, often transferring diseases to domesticated animals, which then enter the human food chain and in turn create a new human disease problem. According to the *Newsweek* article referenced below, "The destruction of the Peruvian rain forest, for example, has led to an explosion of malaria-bearing mosquitoes that thrive in sunlit ponds created by logging operations. Even a 1% increase in deforestation leads to an 8% increase in mosquitoes," according to Jonathan Patz at the University of Wisconsin. The interaction of humans and environmental causes of health problems are complex, global, and just now starting to be understood. Conservation medicine brings together multidisciplinary teams of microbiologists, pathologists, marine biologists, toxicologists, epidemiologists, climate biologists, anthropologists, economists, and medical doctors to solve problems and develop solutions.

Another branch of conservation medicine is focused on creating healthcare systems that are compatible and sustainable from an ecological perspective. One group leading this effort is Health Care Without Harm, an international coalition of hospitals and healthcare systems, medical professionals, community groups, health-affected constituencies, labor unions, environmental health organizations, and religious groups. Its mission is "to transform the healthcare industry worldwide, without compromising patient safety or care, so that it is ecologically sustainable and no longer a source of harm to public health and the environment." Several of its key goals are:

1. Create markets and policies for safer products, materials, and chemicals in health care. Promote safer substitutes, including prod-

ucts that avoid mercury, polyvinyl chloride (PVC) plastic, and brominated flame retardants.

2. Eliminate incineration of medical waste, minimize the amount and toxicity of all waste generated, and promote safer waste-treatment practices.

3. Transform the design, construction, and operations of healthcare facilities to minimize environmental impacts and foster healthy, healing environments.

More information on how to gain a better understanding of this new and vital field of medicine is available below in the Online Resources section.

Steps to Tomorrow

- *Raise Awareness:* Take the time to research and understand the scope of the environmental issues that interact with health care. Recognize that ecological principles can help in designing the next-generation healthcare systems for the year 2020.
- *Recognize the Connection:* The Hippocratic oath states, "I will prescribe regimens for the good of my patients according to my ability and my judgment and never do harm to anyone." This can be extended to the design of the business and medical informatics systems that support the operation of healthcare services anywhere a patient might be.
- *Participate:* Consider supporting the various organizations that are working to expand the understanding and effectiveness of conservation medicine.

Online Resources

- *Healthcare Without Harm* is a global coalition of 443 organizations in 52 counties working to protect health by reducing pollution in the healthcare industry. (www.noharm.org)
- *The Consortium for Conservation Medicine* is a unique collaborative institution that strives to understand the link between anthropogenic environmental change, the health of all species, and the conservation of biodiversity. (http://www.conservation medicine.org/)

- *The Conservation Center of Chicago (CMCC)* is a collaboration among the Chicago Zoological Society and universities including Loyola and the University of Illinois that links a unique team of physicians, veterinarians, researchers, and clinicians in many disciplines. (http://www.luhs.org/depts/cmcc/)
- *"Conservation Medicine: Combining the Best of All Worlds"* by Bob Weinhold describes the field and how the interdisciplinary teams are finding solutions for the environmental problems that are affecting the health of ecosystems and the species inhabiting the world. (http://ehp.niehs.nih.gov/docs/2003/111-10/focus-abs.html)
- *"Tracking Disease,"* an online article from *Newsweek*, discusses how the changing environment influences the way viruses evolve and spread and how this knowledge can prevent future outbreaks. (http://www.msnbc.msn.com/id/9936993/site/newsweek/)

Emerging Technologies for Quality and EHR Adoption

Direction

There are numerous technologies currently being researched, tested, and deployed that will affect the quality of healthcare services and the speed of EHR adoption around the world. Many of these technology tools and systems will allow for radical change in the business and clinical processes of health and medical care. The Medical Informatics 20/20 model, previously discussed in Chapters 1 and 11 in detail, delivers the methodology for the integration of these technologies as they become practical and proven to save time and money and improve quality.

Curent State

- *Radio Frequency Identification Device (RFID)* is an automatic identification method that stores and remotely retrieves data stored on a small-device RFID tag attached to or inserted into a product, animal, or person. Each RFID tag has a small silicon chip that provides the ability to receive and respond to radio-based queries from an RFID transceiver. There are two kinds of tags: passive tags, which require no internal power source, and active tags, which do. RFID use is growing in health care and is typically used to track the location of equipment, patients, and the timing of the administration of medicine.

- *Ubiquitous Computing* is a term that references computing elements embedded in surrounding objects such as walls, desks, chairs, and just about anything else. "Pervasive computing" is another term for this approach, which evolves computers from distinct objects to being incorporated into clothing and surrounding objects. There are various goals of ubiquitous computing, such as the ability to sense changes in the environment then automatically adapt and act on these changes based on user needs and preferences. Embedded, hockey-puck-sized gait home-monitoring sensors are being used to identify early stage walking abnormalities in the elderly. This early detection allows for interventions such as home redesign or assistance devices before the abnormality leads to a serious fall.

- *Grid Computing* describes the use of many networked computers to create a virtual computing architecture that provides the ability to perform higher throughput computing. This virtual network of computers distributes process executions across a parallel infrastructure. Success of this approach depends on data communication standards and interoperability. Grids use this Internet-networked computer power to solve large-scale computation problems. Grids also provide the ability to perform computations on large data sets, by breaking them into many smaller steps that can be executed during low use time of a personal or business computer.

  ○ *The Cancer Research Project* is one of several distributed computing projects that have been operated on the grid.org Web site by United Devices. This project began in 2001 and uses distributed computing power to find drugs for the treatment of cancer. Nearly 300,000 people and their computers participate in this effort, which is also supported by an alliance of organizations such as the National Foundation for Cancer Research and the University of Oxford Department of Chemistry. In the past, Intel and Microsoft participated.

  ○ *Folding@Home* creates a system that studies how proteins "fold." One of the basic processes of biology is the folding of proteins.

When proteins fold incorrectly, they can cause disorders such as cancer or Parkinson's disease. There are 100,000 computers networked through the grid working on this problem. Imagine if 100 million X-Box and PlayStation 2 systems were unleashed and integrated into a distributed network computing grid to help solve complex problems.

- *Security Biometrics* is the study of automated methods for uniquely recognizing humans based upon one or more physical or behavioral traits. Biometric authentication refers to technologies that profile and assess human physical and behavioral characteristics for purposes of validating the identity of an individual. Fingerprints, eye retinas and irises, facial patterns, and hand measurements are examples of physical characteristics. Gait, signature, and typing patterns are examples of behavioral factors. Voice is considered a mix of both physical and behavioral characteristics. In information technology, biometrics is used to provide access to computers or levels of access within computer systems. Various forms of encryption such as PKI (Public Key Infrastructure) and other evolving technologies can be used to identify the identity of individuals and to validate rights for access to levels of security within a medical informatics system.

In Support of Better Medical Care

To conclude, this chapter has delivered many highlights of electronic and emerging technologies that will affect quality and EHR adoption over the next 20 years. The Medical Informatics 20/20 model is the delivery system to aid in the transport of new technologies and techniques to the point of care and point of need. Within the Medical Informatics 2020 model, the anchor strategies of Collaboration, Open Solutions, and Innovation are essential to accelerating the development and rapid diffusion of proven technologies to radically improve the quality of health and medical services and care.

Health@Everywhere— From Inpatient and Outpatient to Everywhere

"I will prescribe regimens for the good of my patients according to my ability and my judgment and never do harm to anyone."

Hippocratic Oath

"Previous generations assumed that we would always rely on nonrenewable fossil fuels to meet our energy needs. They regarded environmental pollution as an inevitable by–product of economic development. And they assumed that we would always rely on medical professionals to supply all the health care we needed. They were wrong on all counts. But while we are now actively protecting our environment and developing sustainable energy resources, we are just beginning to understand that our present healthcare system is also becoming unsustainable."

Thomas Ferguson, MD

Health@Everywhere starts with a look at the person-centered healthcare world of 2020 that takes integrative medicine to the next level. It discusses eHealthcare information technology systems and Medical

Informatics 20/20 solutions as they evolve from their existing focus on inpatient and outpatient services to anywhere a person may be: at work, home, or play. Health@Everywhere delivers an overview of critical developments needed to navigate effectively through the next several decades. This chapter concludes with a snapshot of the next-generation preventive care called "preemptive medicine" and a final fast forward view into the future. The following key areas are highlighted in this chapter:

- *Person-Centered Health Care:* powered by self-care and eHealth Advisor Live
- *Cutting-Edge Medical Sciences:* "-omics" (genomics, glycomics genomics, proteomics, lipidomics, metabolomics, etc.), regenerative medicine, psychoneuroimmonology
- *Complementary & Alternative Medicine (CAM) and EHRs*
- *eHealthcare—TeleMedicine and More*
- *Wearable Intelligence Technology Systems (WITS)*
- *Smart eHealth Record Systems for People and Providers*
- *Genetic Information Systems and Biorepositories*

Forces Driving the Need for Innovation and Collaboration

Meeting the needs of people in health care is becoming an ever-more challenging proposition as costs rise, reimbursement goes down, quality accountability goes up, and demands for new cures increase. Professionals, politicians, and patients are realizing that the current healthcare system, despite all its strengths, is broken and must be transformed.

Simply put, the current system must evolve from a doctor-centered production system to a person-centered, holistic, integrated system, supported by advanced health and medical informatics. The fact of the matter is that each of us is the primary healthcare provider for ourselves. In many ways, people are becoming their own "ConsumerMD," supported by the information systems, technologies, and techniques that enable the self-care we have previously highlighted in this book. Over time, with the growth of eHealth and new forms of preemptive care, individual accountability for our health will grow beyond the role of the doctor.

From the perspective of the PERSON (or Person Centric Continuum of Care, as described in Figure 16-1), the leading challenges and drivers of change are:

- *Explosion of Medical Science Knowledge and Technologies:* Medical knowledge doubles every couple of years. Add to that the belief that technology can solve most of our problems and that technology development is an unstoppable force. This force is tempered by the current 15 to 20 years it may take to move a medical invention or technology from bench to bedside or anywhere a person might be.
- *Human-Made Epidemic of Medical Errors:* The rise of medical errors as a result of system complexity and other factors
- *Threats of Disasters and Epidemics:* Threat of natural or terrorist-driven disaster, outbreaks of avian flu or CA-MRSA, and other communicable diseases
- *Rising Cost of Health Care:* The ever-increasing costs of health care as percentage of United States GNP, in part due to global warming and dependency on nonrenewable energy sources for our lifestyle
- *Live Long and Prosper:* The fundamental demand that people be properly treated, cured, and live as long as possible
- *Unlimited Demand, Finite Resources:* The seldom articulated fact that health care is a periodic, unwanted purchase for which there are unlimited demands and finite resources
- *The Internet and the Rise of Sophisticated Consumers:* The Internet has delivered medical knowledge to the fingertips of any person connected. Online health and medical information is making people more aware and more empowered because they now have access to the brains
- *Person-Directed Care:* The shift of responsibility for healthcare costs onto the consumer within a complex medical care market, using the theory that people who are able to access more information will make better decisions
- *No Access to Care:* The reality that billions of people across the planet have no access to even the most basic of healthcare services
- *No Access to Affordable Insurance:* The fact that because 40 million or more Americans have no health insurance, many conditions are not addressed until it is more costly or too late

- *Outdated and Uninformed Care:* The fact that 50% of patients' treatment or diagnosis is not based on the most current medical evidence, and 20% to 30% of patients receive improper care
- *Care for the Aging Population:* A future cornerstone of many acute and chronic disease states for the baby boomers of the United States and other developed countries. Plus, given this group's view that they are ever-young, there will be a robust market for prevention and health maintenance products and services.
- *Self-Care or "My Care":* Self-care is and has been the largest provider of health care since the beginning of time. Only in the industrial age of medicine did the myth that "doctors knows best" become widespread. In the information age of medicine, the empowered person seeks help from appropriate professionals who act as coaches, facilitators, detectives, and healers.
- *Here Come the Baby Boomers:* One of the most important multi-faceted driving forces is the aging of the societies of developed countries. In the United States, this is illustrated by the aging baby boomers, a generation that has radically shifted and altered history by their needs, choices, and preferences for the last 60 years. The first baby boomers turned 60 in 2006 and the last will be turning 60 around 2020. Yes, this age cohort is healthier but their needs for better health and quality medical care will define the next generation of healthcare services. The baby-boom generation is the first that realized that the establishment or the doctor doesn't always know best. This generation also realizes that maintaining health and overcoming illness requires an integrated, holistic approach.

Predicting the future is impossible, but these final chapters of the book highlight important technologies that will help empower people and allow them to become much more of their own primary healthcare provider. Wearable systems, nanotechnologies, embedded sensors, personal health records, and virtual eHealth Advisors will all contribute to this vision. Many of these Medical Informatics 20/20 inventions are in development and early diffusion, which in turn supports the increasing deployment of EHR systems leading to the realization of quality healthcare. The intent of this chapter is to enlighten you to possibilities and potentials. When we are enlightened, inspired, and informed, we can properly prepare ourselves and our organizations for the future.

Transforming into a Person-Centered Healthcare System

During the next 15 years, the consumer-directed movement of the early 21st century will evolve and fully recognize that in health care, people do more than consume a product. The healthcare industry will realize that people are not simply patients to be defined by their disease or condition. The healthcare industry will fully realize that healing and supporting optimum health depends on a person-centered philosophy that recognizes that people, not physicians, are their own true primary healthcare providers. There will also be a recognition that the whole person must be treated: mind, body, and spirit. Hopefully, we will finally create a sustainable healthcare system that delivers access to all and is in sync with a more healthy environmentally sustainable world.

As we continue to move forward and attempt to transform the system, we must remember that health care is a very personal "knowledge-based" service. Unfortunately, at this point in time, people and clinicians are finding that they are drowning in information. People and clinicians do not have the intelligent interfaces that deliver the information they really need when they need it. Over the next decade, the number and kind of healthcare coaches or "infomediaries" will expand rapidly. A current example of this is PinnacleCare (www.pinnaclecare.com), where a human health coach is supported by leading medical experts and online information resources, such as extensive knowledge databases, that can support a person undergoing complex medical care. This human coach helps a person navigate a complex medical field and also seek out and analyze the most advanced treatment options available that may be appropriate for an individual. (See the PinnacleCare example in Chapter 13.)

At the beginning of the 21st century, the field of health coaching and advocacy started to grow with humans being aided by computers, knowledge bases, and the Internet. The field of health coaching seeks to support people in finding and managing a complex system to get better care. Initially, health coaching was only available to people that could afford the membership fees, but advances in medical informatics, artificial intelligence, and mobile-anywhere services will ultimately allow anyone in need of these services to access them. In fact, the next decade will see health services, that in the past were provided only by human professionals, converted into easy-to-access, cost-effective, artificial intelligence programs that are embedded in a PDA, iPod, Zune or some other mobile device in essence creating virtual eHealth advisors/nurses and support entities.

Over time, public health officials and doctors operating in this virtual world will become more sophisticated as they monitor people's health through data-mining of EHRs and monitoring of real-time physiological changes reported by wearable and embedded sensors. Using the knowledge gained from these sensors, a virtual health counselor (eHealth Advisor Live) will diagnose, treat, and recommend preventive measures. Automating the processes using thinking "mindware" (advanced anticipatory/predictive software)—and the continual ability of technology advancement to exponentially reduce the cost of hardware devices—will drive the costs of the virtual smart health counselor services down to affordability.

Over the next several decades, the direction of change will lead to the vision of the "Person-Centric Continuum of Support—Health@ Everywhere 2020" illustrated in Figure 16-1. At the center is the person who seeks optimum health and effective treatment of acute or chronic conditions. This figure represents the evolution from the ConsumerMD described in Chapter 1. We anticipate that by 2020, a person (if they desire and their conditions demand it) will be surrounded by virtual and

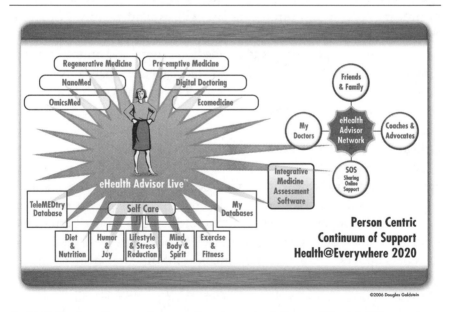

FIGURE 16-1 Person Centric Continuum of Care—"Health@Everywhere 2020"

real-time, around-the-clock health and medical assistance through various wearable, mobile, and implanted systems.

In Figure 16-1, the surrounding sunburst represents points of connection with eHealth Advisor Live™, an intelligent software virtual agent designed to support optimum health and acute/chronic treatment through multiple communication and connection methods. The elements of a person's health connections as represented by the sunburst are described below.

Person–Centered—In health care, people are more than just consumers or patients. A person must take responsibility for his or her own health and leverage all the knowledge and resources available. In the first chapter, we discussed the concept of ConsumerMD, whereby people are their own primary caregivers. Person-centered care is the next evolution, whereby healing and health are part of a multidisciplinary approach that addresses the mind, body, and spirit holistically. In the future, the person with acute and chronic conditions will access the best care and quality through the integration and communication of multiple systems that leverage intelligent software agents that have artificial intelligence, networks of care professionals, and multiple medicine modalities. Person-centered health care is powered by a person's knowledge and know-how, along with online support by what we are calling the virtual eHealth Advisor and eHealth Advisor Network.

Self-Care—Self-care has been and will continue to be the largest provider of healthcare services. The difference in the 21st century is that the medical professional has started to realize the healing power of the mind, body, and spirit. A person's state of health results from a complex interplay of biology and environment, and the medical mainstream now recognizes that health and healing is enabled by various elements including support by friends and family, right diet and nutrition, humor and joy, lifestyle, and mind–body–spirit connection. The solution is not always a pill. Self-care harnesses the power of preventing illness, curing disease, maintaining optimum health, applying the best medical modalities, and using the next generation of wearable, go-anywhere medical services. Later in the chapter, the status and evolution of wearable intelligent technology systems (WITS) and other technologies are highlighted. Medical science, technology, and personal empowerment will come together in the next 20 years to create a service that we call eHAL or the eHealth Advisor Live.™

eHealth Advisor Live™ (eHAL)

eHAL will serve a person's every medical need with the following services:

- Access wireless real-time connection to Internet2 and public and private health and medical knowledge bases
- Access your electronic personal health record (ePHR) anywhere, for review or an emergency
- Have your ePHR updated real-time from wearable or embedded biometric sensors
- Get answers (not just a listing of thousands of Web pages) to health and medical questions
- Get decision support based on billions of bits of medical evidence reviewed and assessed against your medical history and genetic profiles
- Interact with others who have similar interests
- Have a smart, personal, digital advisor, who knows your needs and preferences, manage information for you
- Query a network of care professionals via subscription services or through an alternative access mode
- Buy health- and medical-related products
- Maintain eRx services that manage and monitor the appropriate use of personalized prescriptions and over-the-counter products, from drugs to nutraceuticals
- Schedule live, in-person appointments, if needed
- Monitor and record food and drink consumption, exercise, and other desired activities from sensors in the home or on/in the body
- Get preferred services from health system and doctor partners
- Access an array of additional services tailored to a health or chronic medical condition
- Be a virtual coach and support to the person

eHealth Advisor Live™ (eHAL)—An always-connected virtual health advisor that is more than software and more than hardware. It is a virtual nurse–doctor who knows your needs and is on-call 24/365 to guide and support your health and medical journey. The first HAL was the ubiquitous computer that guided the mission and maintained the life-support systems in the movie *2001: A Space Odyessy*. The eHealth Advisor Live, or eHAL, is a series of health and medical programs and services embedded in a mobile-anywhere device that is always connected to the Internet2 grid (see Chapter 14 for more information about Internet2).

Think of eHAL as a highly evolved, digital assistant with exponentially more computing power than today's personal computer, but available in a mobile device the size of a video iPod or smaller. This eHealth Advisor artificial intelligence service and system could be worn, held in a pocket, put on a belt, or even attached to sunglasses, with a visual display on the lenses and an audio feed in the frame. It is an advanced thinking software system, tailored to the health and medical needs of the specific person. It is a knowledge source, a decision support advisor, health coach, and much more. It represents significant evolution from the mobile multipurpose device described in Chapter 1.

The Institute for Alternative Futures report, "The 2029 Project: Achieving an Ethical Future for Biomedical R&D" (http://www.altfu tures.com/2029/The2029Report.pdf), which outlines significant health and medical advances that are likely to occur, refers to a similar concept called a "Health Coach Avatar."

The eHealth Advisor Live is the gateway, filter, intelligent search engine, and coach that knows the second-by-second status of medical conditions as fed in real-time to TeleMEDtry and medical history databases that include genetic profiles. The eHealth Advisor Live™ will be the synthesis of the information and health developments underway that involve intelligent computer-embedded clothing, self-generating software programs, and artificial intelligence health agents. Depending on a person's condition, electronic circuitry can be connected wirelessly or even hard-wired to nerves and tissues.

My Doctors—A person's network of medical professionals who maintain medical records about the patient as a result of past in-person interactions. This network will likely include a primary care professional, which could be an advanced practice nurse, primary care physician, board-certified holistic practitioner, or other qualified professional. In-person diagnostic and treatment services would be linked with the provider who actively supports eHealth Advisor Live™ with software/ knowledge updates and online help from humans when needed, under monthly subscription arrangements.

Integrative Medicine Assessment Software (IMAS)—Imagine the beauty of having the world's latest and greatest medical evidence base across conventional western, alternative, complementary, Chinese, Native American, and Ayurvedic medicine available upon voice request from your eHAL. IMAS is an example of a comprehensive "multi-medical modality

Health care in 2020 will be dominated by Human User Interfaces (HUI) that allow people to regularly interact with virtual agents that exist only in the programming of a sophisticated artificial intelligence program. For a sample of a virtual agent, visit Ray Kurzweil's Web site and explore the future as the speed of innovation and technology change accelerates. Be sure to visit with Ramona, a virtual agent prepared to answer your questions.

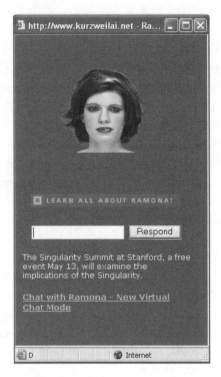

FIGURE 16-2 From GUI to HUI—Human User Interfaces
Source: http://www.kurzweilai.net/index.html?flash=1

search-synthesize-tailor to a person's specific health needs" program that would be assessed when needed by eHealth Advisor Live. When there was a new diagnosis of prostate cancer, eHAL would take the person's information provided through medical and genetic profiles, along with electronic feeds from doctors' medical records, include updated information from all provider-based medical records, and combine it with up-to-date TeleMEDtry (see description that follows). Remember, in 2020, clinical data standards and seamless interoperability have been solidly in place for five years. And the dominant interface to computer/Internet services will have evolved from keyboard/graphic interfaces to voice/virtual agent interactions with neuro-interface in advanced trial and experimental phase.

TeleMEDtry—Medical telemetry is the process of monitoring health and medical vital signs, biomarkers, environmental factors, and other physiological processes within and surrounding a human being. TeleMEDtry in 2020 will use all modes of data and information transfer from wired to wireless, and the source devices will include wearable devices, nanotech bots implanted and circulating within the human body, or embedded sensors in a person's home. The data from these sensors will enter the eHAL database for processing, archiving, and analysis.

My Databases—A person's health and medical history in 2020 will far exceed the 20th century paper form that lists little more than conditions and allergies. It will consolidate medical information from every type of care professional from primary care physician, specialist, and hospital to nutritionist, chiropractor, and mental health therapist. The database will also compile real-time physiological information from wearable, implanted, embedded bio-sensors. In addition, the complete genetic, proteomic, glyccomic, and other "-omic" profiles will also be available for the personalization and targeting of NanoMed and MEMSMed to treat and cure diseases.

Search, Screen, and Recommend—With the rapid increase in medical and business knowledge comes the need for better search technology and interfaces that deliver the medical knowledge and recommendations needed by people and professionals. This means better decision support tools that offer ongoing analysis and synthesis of medical evidence for those who subscribe.

eHealth Advisor Live™—Network—eHAL will be augmented by a psycho-social support network to help deal with issues associated with the many chronic and acute conditions encountered through a 100-plus-year life span.

- *SOS (Sharing Online Support):* A pick-and-choose set of online support groups that are screened and recommended based on the quality of the interactions and nature of the condition
- *Friends and Family:* A private network of selected friends and family who can be available in synchronous or asynchronous mode depending on the preference of a participant

Advanced Medical and Health Science @ Point of Need—The delivery of the latest and greatest health and medical knowledge appropriate for an individual, based on profile and conditions. Additional information about biological sciences, technology, and other disciplines is provided throughout Chapters 14 and 15.

Preemptive Medicine—The current revolution in preventive medicine of leads to the next-generation approach called "preemptive medicine," which will zap cancers and other conditions based on the genetic and environmental warning signals before they even become a disease. Since the field has not yet been invented, and due to limited space in this book, a complete description of this new medical and health discipline will be available at www.medicalinformatics2020.com.

This section has outlined what is possible and probable based on the direction of change and driving forces. Of course, every individual will not use all of these eHealth support options at the same time. Each person will determine which of these services to use at a particular time, and there will be phases of high use—such as a period of time when cancer is being treated—versus times of use that purely focus on exercise and fitness training. Our purpose in building this personal profile of "surround medicine" is to describe what could easily be available in 2020. The views of the future are based on the current technologies and services in development, testing, and initial stages of diffusion throughout healthcare systems in countries around the world.

eHealth Advisor Live™

Is the embodiment of Medical Informatics 2020 as it represents the evolved technology, social science, clinical decision support, and so on that extends and supports people wherever they are. In the future, people will not have to find a computer with an Internet connection and then spend hours searching, assessing, and just getting more and more confused. In 2020, an individual will have the same access to knowledge as professionals. Empowered self-care that is supported by the virtual eHealth Advisor Live (eHAL) will become steadily more important.

The healthcare system exists to serve people when they are in need as patients. *"Quality and People First!"* Tomorrow, emerging technologies can transform this system into one that really focuses on individual and population health optimization. To achieve this future by using the health and medical innovations described in this chapter requires guiding principles and a foundation such as the IOM Ten Rules for Redesigning Health Care, which can be a great foundation. Table 16-1 lists these rules and

Table 16-1 Ten IOM Rules for Redesigning Health Care and Medical Informatics 20/20 View

IOM's Ten Simple New Rules for 21st Century Healthcare System	The Medical Informatics 20/20 View
1. Care based on continuous healing relationships	. . . real-time eHealthcare anywhere, based on a person's acute or chronic conditions
2. Care is customized according to patient needs and values	. . . recognizing the interrelationship of mind, body, and spirit in health and disease treatment
3. The patient as the source of control	. . . with a focus on the person first, and his or her right to participate in the treatment process
4. Knowledge is shared and information flows freely	. . . which empowers people to make wise decisions
5. Decision making is evidence-based	. . . and delivered effectively at the point of care
6. Safety is a system property	. . . at the highest possible levels of quality
7. Transparency is necessary	. . . including safety, evidence-based treatment, proven community-based treatment and the delivery of knowledge to clinicians and people at the point of need
8. Needs are anticipated	. . . through preemptive care using data from interoperable electronic health records that are accessed by patients and care providers
9. Waste is continuously decreased	. . . and the health system is sustainable and ecologically sound
10. Cooperation among clinicians is a priority	. . . as are partnerships among clinicians, patients, and their families
IOM Rules + Two Medical Infomatics 20/20 Rules	
11. Quality and appropriate care delivery anywhere is reimbursed	. . . which means the reimbursement system must reward quality care for professionals and support appropriate care regardless of location
12. Spread the risk through population-based risk pools	. . . and reward positive health behaviors of individuals

provides a Medical Informatics 20/20 perspective to guide us in creating the future.

The column on the right of the table adds perspectives representing the Medical Informatics 20/20 view regarding the ten simple rules. Rows 11 and 12 represent gap areas in the IOM rules that are needed for the year 2020. A well-known phrase states that if you want to understand and change behavior then "follow the money." None of the IOM ten rules addresses reimbursement and spreading the risk issues. Transformation of health care depends on changing the reimbursement to reward quality and accountability within the context of broad risk pools that spread risks and costs.

The following highlights reflect driving medical and technology forces and include a discussion of the direction of change, current state, and thoughts on steps for tomorrow that leaders, managers, and healthcare organizations can take as they create the future.

Cutting-Edge Medical Sciences and Technologies

Direction

Medical science—biomedical, "-omics," pharmaceutical, nanomed, regenerative medicine, and all areas of specialty research and development— will revolutionize the preemption, diagnosis, treatment, and care of acute and chronic conditions. Unfortunately, the reimbursement for medical advances will not evolve as fast, so the time it takes a medical advance to move from research to bedside and from bedside to anywhere will not be significantly compressed.

Current State

This section highlights several very exciting frontiers in medical science that are moving from research phase to testing, and some cases widespread use, in the battle against disease and epidemic and in support of optimum health by 2020. Highlighted here are the fields of medical biology and regenerative medicine. Other emerging medtech areas such as nanomedicine and ecological medicine were reviewed in Chapter 14.

Genetics is the science of genes, heredity, and the variation of organisms. In research today, genetics is the science for the research and analysis of gene function and interactions. Within organisms, genetic information generally is carried in chromosomes, where it is represented in the chemical structure of particular DNA molecules. Genes encode the information necessary for synthesizing the amino-acid sequences in proteins, which in turn play a large role in determining the final phenotype of the organism. Genetics determine much (but not all) of the appearance of organisms, including humans, and possibly how they act. Several medical genetic breakthroughs are:

- **Breast Cancer Research:** The BP1, a gene discovered by Dr. Patricia E. Berg, is activated in 80% of breast cancer tumors and a majority of acute myeloid leukemias, and shows similar activity in other cancers. Recent data show that BP1 is associated with the progression of normal cells to cancerous breast tumors, and research is underway regarding the development of a gene suppressor and a blood test for diagnosis and monitoring therapy, and confirming the impact of BP1 on other cancers. Additional research by Berg has shown unusually high numbers of BP1 positives in the breast tumors of African American women. This knowledge could prove very useful in discovering answers to racial disparities in rates of breast cancer.

- **Genetic Breakthroughs in the Cause of Crohn's Disease:** Researchers have discovered the first gene that confers susceptibility to Crohn's disease, which affects more than 500,000 Americans and millions worldwide by inflicting a debilitating form of inflammatory bowel disease. Through a multidisciplinary collaboration, scientists across the spectrum of various fields identified a mutated form of a gene called NOD2 that significantly increases a person's risk for developing Crohn's disease. This discovery is built upon research into how genetic and environmental factors combine to initiate an aberrant immune response, which cascades into a destructive inflammation of the digestive system. Crohn's disease, because it involves two or more genes, is genetically complex, and thus the search for the specific genes is much more difficult. Researchers believe that discoveries such as these, indicating the genetic and environmental causes of Crohn's disease, will lead to new therapies and new methods for identifying individuals at risk for developing the disease, and eventually result in better treatments.

"-Omics" is the suffix reference to rapidly specializing fields within biology and biomedical research and development. It evolved from the use of the "-omes" suffix. For instance, prote*omics* is the accepted term for the study of the prote*ome*. Other uses of "-omics" include:

- **Genomics:** The study of an organism's genome and the use of genes at the system level toward the development of useful therapies and other applications

- ***Glycomics:*** The area of investigation relating the function, interaction, and structure of chains of sugar. Glycome is the entire carbohydrate component of an organism.
- ***Lipidomics:*** The field of study of lipids (non-water-soluble metabolites) and their interactions
- ***Metabolomics:*** The investigation of chemical traces/evidence that cellular processes generate

Regenerative medicine is the field of applied tissue engineering, which has the tremendous and realistic promise of regenerating damaged tissues in vivo (in the living body) and externally creating "tissues for life" available for implantation. Through research and products developed from this field, previously untreatable diseases will become easily and routinely cured. Regenerative medicine will become a major component of health care in the next 20 years. This field refers to the use of stem cells, xenotransplantation, tissue engineering, induced regeneration, and modulation of the aging process. Regenerative medicine applies medical science and technology to restore the structure and function of damaged tissues and organs. This new field encompasses many novel approaches to treatment of disease and restoration of biological function through therapies that stimulate the body to regenerate damaged tissues and the use of tissue engineered implants to encourage regeneration. The promise of regenera-

FIGURE 16-3 HHS Regenerative Medicine Web Site
Source: http://www.hhs.gov/reference/newfuture.shtml

tive medicine is that there will a higher quality of life for people suffering from advanced stages of diseases such as Parkinson's, and it will also lead to extended healthy life spans for others, based on the ability to repair damage that results from aging.

Psychoneuroimmunology is a field of research that studies the connection between the brain, or mental states, and the immunal and hormonal systems of the human body. For instance, the placebo effect and psychosomatic disease are part of this subject. One source of information on this field is the Psychoneuroimmunology Research Society (PNIRS) an international organization for researchers in such scientific and medical disciplines as neuroscience, psychology, immunology, pharmacology, psychiatry, behavioral medicine, infectious diseases, endocrinology, and rheumatology. This organization supports the interchange of research and knowledge among researchers and clinicians studying the interactions between the nervous system and the immune system, and the relationship between behavior and health. Some of the research areas identified on the PNIRS Web site (www.pnirs.org) are:

- Neurochemical and hormonal mechanisms that convey messages to and from the immune system and brain
- Stress and immunity, including the role of stress-related hormones and neurotransmitters on the immune system and brain
- Actions of cytokines and growth factors on neuronal and glial cells to regulate behavior, cognition, and neuroendocrine function
- Roles of hormones, growth factors, and cytokines in the immune and central nervous systems
- Inflammation, neuroscience, and behavior
- Neuroimmunopharmacology and the immunomodulating effects of psychotropic drugs and drugs of abuse
- Sleep, exercise, immunity, and health
- Roles of cytokines, hormones, and neurotransmitters in the aging immune system and brain
- Cancer, brain, and immunity
- Regulation of nerve injury and repair by the immune system
- Psychosocial, behavioral, and neuroendocrine influences on immunity and on the development and progression of immunologically mediated disease processes
- Genomics of behavior and immunity

Genetic markers, personalized medicine, shift from disease to health potential, regenerative medicine, "-omics," psychoneuroimmunology, and much more are coming our way. The health and medical industry of the next 25-plus years will be dominated by the need to cater to and serve the aging baby boomers. In the United States, folks over 65 in 2030 will represent 20% of the population. Collaboration, Open Solution, and Innovation (COSI) approaches to the care and support of this population will be vital.

Steps to Tomorrow

- *Monitor Developments and Gain Understanding:* Organizations should establish regular communication channels for monitoring medical developments and their implications for clinical informatics. This can be done through various Web-based tools and through subscription relationships with research and news organizations.
- *Brainstorm About Application to Products and Services:* Environmental and medical technology analysis and opportunities need to be compared against current and future customer services. With the most attractive opportunities to expand services or improve the quality of care, business cases should be developed.
- *Establish Knowledge Networks by Area of Interest or Medical Breakthrough:* Within every organization team, members have specific interests in different aspects of the medical industry. Profile people's expertise and skills and embed them in a knowledge database where it is searchable. With this foundation in place, it would be possible to set up knowledge networks on topics such as proteomics, regenerative medicine, or any number of other options to involve a broad network of participants, which in turn will help keep the organization up to date on developments that are under the radar screen. Human intelligence linked in a collaborative community can deliver a distinctive advantage through ideas, news, advice, and insights, if properly managed.

Online Resources

- *Health Technology Center:* http://www.healthtech.org
- *SG2:* http://www.sg2.com

- *The Advisory Board Company:* http://www.advisory.com
- *Healthcare Intelligence Network:* http://www.hin.com
- *Knowledge Scan:* http://www.kxnowledge.com
- *Medical Breakthroughs:* http://www.ivanhoe.com/
- *NewsRx:* http://www.newsrx.com/

Complementary and Alternative Medicine (CAM) and EHR Systems

Direction

In the year 2020, increasing numbers of people will understand that health is both the absence of disease and the realization of the optimum health status. Over the next decade, look for automated complementary and alternative medicine (CAM) software modules to emerge that will be integrated into the central electronic health record (EHR), personal health record (PHR), and eHealth Advisor Live™ systems of the future.

Current State

The goal of CAM is to support the health and welfare of an individual or population by encouraging healthier lifestyles, stimulating the natural healing abilities of the body, and discovering natural methods of disease treatment and care.

CAM is a group of diverse medical and healthcare systems, practices, and products that are not currently considered to be part of conventional medicine. Patients are increasingly turning to CAM to enhance their health and well-being. CAM includes acupuncture, chiropractic medicine, osteopathic medicine, the use of herbal remedies, and other practices as augmentations to more conventional medical treatments. The marketplace reflects this growing acceptance of complementary medicine by many patients and a small, but growing number of healthcare providers.

By gathering and integrating healthcare information associated with the application of CAM procedures into a patient's EHR, more accurate measurements of outcomes can be generated. Best practices can then emerge showing which complementary medical practices are most effective when coupled with conventional medical treatments of specific disorders.

> ## The Goal of CAM
>
> The goal of CAM is to support the health and welfare of an individual or a population by encouraging healthier lifestyles, stimulating the natural healing properties of the body, and discovering natural methods of disease treatment and care.

Definitions

CAM includes a broad domain of healing resources that encompasses all health systems, modalities, and practices and their accompanying theories and beliefs, other than those intrinsic to the dominant health system of a particular society.

CAM therapies are termed "complementary" when used in addition to conventional treatments. They are termed "alternative" when they are used instead of conventional treatment. Integrative medicine, as defined by the National Center for Complementary and Alternative Medicine (NCCAM), combines mainstream medical therapies and CAM therapies for which high-quality scientific evidence of safety and effectiveness exist.

Many other traditions of medicine and health care are still widely practiced throughout the world, most of which are still considered to be separate and distinct from conventional Western medicine. The most highly developed systems of medicine outside of Western medicine are traditional Chinese medicine, the Ayurvedic traditions of India, and other forms of indigenous or "native" medicine such as those practiced by Amazonian rainforest, African, and North American tribes.

CAM Categories

NCCAM classifies CAM therapies into five categories, or domains:

1. *Alternative Medical Systems*—Alternative medical systems are built upon complete systems of theory and practice. Often, these systems have evolved apart from and earlier than the conventional medical approach used in the United States. Examples of alternative medical systems that have developed in Western cultures include homeopathic medicine and naturopathic medicine. Examples of systems that have developed in non-Western cultures

include traditional Chinese medicine, Ayurveda, and Native American medicine. (See NIH's Web site at http://nccam.nih.gov/health/whatiscam/ for more information.)

2. *Mind–Body Interventions*—Mind–body medicine uses a variety of techniques designed to enhance the mind's capacity to affect bodily function and symptoms. Some techniques that were considered CAM in the past have become mainstream techniques (for example, patient support groups and cognitive-behavioral therapy). Other mind–body techniques are still considered CAM, including meditation, prayer, mental healing, and therapies that use creative outlets such as art, music, or dance.

3. *Biologically-Based Therapies*—Biologically based therapies in CAM use substances found in nature such as herbs, foods, and vitamins. Some examples include dietary supplements, herbal products, and the use of other so-called natural, but as yet scientifically unproven, therapies (for example, using shark cartilage to treat cancer).

4. *Manipulative and Body-Based Methods*—Manipulative and body-based methods in CAM are based on manipulation and/or movement of one or more parts of the body. Some examples include chiropractic or osteopathic manipulation and massage therapy.

5. *Energy Therapies*—Energy therapies involve the use of energy fields. They are of two types:
   - *Biofield therapies* are intended to affect energy fields that purportedly surround and penetrate the human body. Some forms of energy therapy manipulate biofields by applying pressure and/or manipulating the body by placing the hands in, or through, these fields. Examples include Qi Gong, Reiki, and Therapeutic Touch.
   - *Bioelectromagnetic-based therapies* involve the unconventional use of electromagnetic fields, such as pulsed fields, magnetic fields, or alternating-current or direct-current fields.

The following are the ten most commonly used CAM therapies in the United States during 2002 (see CDC Advance Data Report #343 at http://en.wikipedia.org/wiki/Complementary_and_alternative_medicine#The_top_ten_CAM_therapies), when use of prayer is excluded:

1. Herbalism (18.9%)
2. Breathing Meditation (11.6%)

3. Meditation (7.6%)
4. Chiropractic Medicine (7.5%)
5. Yoga (5.1%)
6. Body Work (5.0%)
7. Diet-Based Therapy (3.5%)
8. Progressive Relaxation (3.0%)
9. Mega-Vitamin Therapy (2.8%)
10. Visualization (2.1%)

Major CAM Organizations

The National Center for Complementary and Alternative Medicine (NCCAM) is the federal government's lead agency for scientific research on CAM. NCCAM is dedicated to exploring complementary and alternative healing practices in the context of rigorous science, training CAM researchers, and disseminating authoritative information to the public and professionals.

The Office of Cancer Complementary and Alternative Medicine (OCCAM), established in October 1998, coordinates and enhances the activities of the National Cancer Institute (NCI) in the arena of CAM (http://www.cancer.gov/cam/). There are many other links to CAM associations and organizations. (http://www.pitt.edu/~cbw/assoc.html)

Native American Indian Health Care

Increasingly, traditional Native American healing practices are being requested by Native Americans and nonnatives alike. Recent years have shown a surge of interest in the therapies of traditional cultures, in patients' use of alternative medicine, and in the desire for mind–body therapies and for spiritual treatment, as well as for behavioral medicine treatments for chronic medical illness. Some hospitals have included traditional Native American healers as part of their staff. One of the spiritual practices that patients may request (especially in the American Southwest) is Native American healing (NAH) to complement their conventional medical treatment. Some patients even voice a preference for exclusive NAH. (http://www.healing-arts.org/mehl-madrona/mmtraditionalpaper.htm)

The Market

In a recent report on CAM in the United States (2005), the Board on Health Promotion and Disease Prevention states that the total visits to CAM providers exceed total visits to all primary care physicians. Out-of-pocket costs for CAM are estimated to exceed $27 billion, which shows that CAM is now big business. That does not include those therapies or treatments covered by insurance. Hospitals, managed care plans, and conventional practitioners are now incorporating CAM therapies into their practices. Medical schools, nursing schools, and schools of pharmacy are teaching their students about CAM.

It is hard to get an exact handle on the market for CAM; however, according to a recent article published on the Investors.com Web site, consumers snapped up about $54 billion worth of CAM services and dietary supplements in 2003. Of that figure, they claim that $34 billion went to all types of alternative services such as chiropractic, naturopathy, osteopathy, and massage therapy, up from $25.5 billion in 1999. The U.S. market for dietary supplements is not far behind, generating sales of $19.8 billion in 2003, up from $16.5 billion in 1999.

In 2004, NCCAM reported results based on survey data collected in partnership with the Centers for Disease Control and Prevention from more than 31,000 Americans. The data revealed that 62% of survey respondents used CAM in 2002. Another NCCAM report states that approximately 14% of Americans use herbal supplements to prevent disease, maintain wellness, or treat illness or pain.

The *New England Journal of Medicine* estimates that by 2010 the per capita supply of alternative medicine clinicians will grow by 88%, meeting the needs of an increasingly CAM friendly public. Bottom line, there is a huge amount of money tied to the CAM marketplace.

Challenges to Integrating CAM into Conventional EHR and PHR Systems

Most modern EHR, PHR, and other health informatics solutions to date have been developed to meet the requirements of conventional Western medical practitioners. These systems embody many of the implicit assumptions of researchers, doctors, administrators, and other stakeholders associated with these conventional Western healthcare provider organizations. To develop a more effective tool that includes support for CAM practitioners, additional studies further exploring the major differences between CAM and conventional Western medical practices and systems must be conducted.

The major differences in the two forms of medicine are rooted in the patient–practitioner relationship, the larger worldview and system beyond the specific practice, and the core definition of health in each system. While it is outside the scope of this book to explore these differences in depth, additional studies and more detailed analyses will greatly contribute to the design of health informatics systems that will be useful in taking steps to integrate CAM modules within future releases of EHR and PHR systems.

To gain greater acceptance for CAM, there is a need to utilize the power of advanced computational systems to introduce more rigor in capturing and analyzing data related to complementary and alternative medicine practices. By gathering and integrating healthcare information associated with the application of CAM procedures into a patient's EHR, more accurate measurements of outcomes can be generated. Best practices can then emerge, showing which complementary medical practices are most effective when coupled with conventional medical treatments of specific disorders.

At present, there appear to be a number of companies marketing CAM software modules. There are also a number of open source solutions available. However, none appear to have taken any major steps forward to integrate their products and data with PHR or EHR systems. There also seems to be little coordinated activity related to standardizing data elements within the major CAM domains.

Steps to Tomorrow

There are a number of recommendations and next steps for healthcare organizations to take with regard to the development of CAM software modules to be integrated within their EHR systems:

- *Engage Customers* in research to fully understand how your customer segments are viewing and using CAM.
- *Expand Research:* Conduct more detailed research into CAM information systems. Identify and prioritize CAM software modules to be developed, based on the needs of high-priority customers.

- *Participate in Open Source CAM Networks and Projects:* Initiate a collaborative, open source initiative to develop the CAM modules. Initiate efforts to identify and standardize data elements for each CAM domain.
- *Conceptualize and Roll Out Pilots:* Develop a prototype and begin pilot tests of high-priority CAM modules
- *Focus on Enhancing EHRs and PHRs to Leverage CAM for the Patient:* This would include developing and releasing production versions of CAM modules, and eventually integrating CAM software modules with selected PHR or EHR systems. Also, put in place mechanisms needed to refine and further enhance CAM modules.
- *Analysis and Improvement:* Encourage efforts to analyze and evaluate the outcomes of CAM using data collected by CAM modules in PHRs

Online Resources

- *National Center for Complementary and Alternative Medicine:* http://nccam.nih.gov/
- *MedLine:* http://www.nlm.nih.gov/medlineplus/alternativemedicine. html
- *White House Report on CAM:* http://www.whccamp.hhs.gov/ finalreport.html
- *British Register of Complementary Practitioners:* http://www. i-c-m.org.uk/brcp/default.htm
- *Commercial Site:* http://www.alternativemedicine.com
- *Resources/Links:* http://www.pitt.edu/~cbw/hospital.html
- *Databases Resources/Links:* http://www.pitt.edu/~cbw/database. html
- *Evidence-Based CAM Journal Databases:* http://ecam.oxford journals.org/
- *Journal of Alternative and Complementary Medicine:* http:// www.liebertpub.com/publication.aspx?pub_id=26
- *Other Web Sites:*
  - http://www.alternative-medicine-software.com/
  - http://www.alternativelink.com/ali/press/PRMitchell6-01.asp
  - http://www.999alternatives.com/

- http://www.biopulse.org/software.html
- http://www.vadino.com/wellness.html

eHealthcare—TeleMedicine and More

Direction

eHealthcare will become the overarching term that describes multimedia health and medical management using technology, Internet, mobile media, and emerging technogies. The "e" in eHealthcare stands for electronic and emerging technologies that support better care and quality medical care for people and societies. The dual meaning for "e" better represents that the fact that emerging technologies in areas of artificial intelligence, self-generating software programs, and other human–computer interface sciences will play significant roles in the tailored and personalized delivery of these services in the year 2020.

Current State

Today's telecommunications and televideo technologies have enabled great strides forward in telemedicine over the past decade, for example, TeleRadiology, TeleDermatology, and TeleConsultations. Early in the 21st century, the technology moved rapidly into the arena of TeleMedicine at home or anywhere. At home or anywhere health management is based on those developments, innovations, services, and technologies of governments, associations, corporations, and collaborative alliances that are focused on shifting the care paradigm from inpatient and outpatient to anywhere a patient might be—at work, at home, or at play.

The goals of TeleMedicine are to improve care, reduce the number of visits to actual doctors and providers, and allow patients to be seen and treated at locations of their own choosing, thus lowering the per unit cost of care while delivering high-quality care conveniently. At present, patients with chronic diseases are normally required to visit outpatient facilities for periodic monitoring and treatment management. In many cases, however, the preferred place of monitoring and care would be the patient's home.

Analysis by the Veterans Health Administration has shown that providing home-based service improves outcomes of care for these patients, increases levels of patient satisfaction, and provides cost efficiencies. The role of patients is to interact with the home device and transmit vital signs and other data to the clinical systems used by the healthcare provider. The major role of home TeleMedicine vendors is to furnish recording and transmission devices for the home setting and to process and store data for access by healthcare providers and their clinical systems. TeleMedicine initiatives parallel the broader societal trend in health care whereby providers are seeking ways of offering more cost-effective, high-quality care in the home or at a mobile location rather than in an institutional environment.

Online Resources

- *International Society for Telemedicine and eHealth (ISfTeH):* http://www.isft.net/cms/index.php?id=1
- *American Telemedicine Association:* http://www.americantelemed.org/index.asp, http://tie.telemed.org/
- *Viteron TeleHealthcare, a Bayer-Panasonic company:* http://www.viterion.com/
- *Intel Proactive Health Innovation Center:* http://www.intel.com/research/prohealth/
- *Body Media:* http://www.bodymedia.com

Steps to Tomorrow

eHealthcare projects lay the foundation for both providing quality care to patients with complex chronic conditions—such as diabetes, congestive heart failure, mental health disease, spinal cord injury, wound care, and infectious disease—and making the home the preferred place of care.

- *Create eHealthcare Infrastructure and Collaborations* to secure a national TeleMedicine IT infrastructure including architecture, standards, and so on.
- *Expand eHealthcare Integration into EHRs and PHRs* in order to integrate TeleMedicine data into EHR systems and PHR solutions.

Wearable Intelligent Technology Systems (WITS)

Direction

Wearable information technology devices are rapidly evolving to 'Wearable Intelligent Technology Systems' (WITS). Current and emerging developments in wireless communications, integrated with developments in pervasive computing and wearable technologies, will have a radical impact on future healthcare delivery systems. It is anticipated that wearable computing will become a routine part of healthcare delivery and patient self-management in the coming decades.

Current State

The 1980s were dominated by the use of personal computers (PCs). The 1990s saw the widespread acquisition and use of laptop computers. This decade is seeing the acceptance and use of personal digital assistants (PDA) by many people. The next decade will be dominated by the production and use of wearable IT systems where information technology has evolved into intelligent technology systems. Wristwatches, pagers, cell phones, pocket calculators, PDAs, and Blackberries are all examples of simple wearable information systems that are already in widespread use.

With ever-accelerating innovations and technology and advances in artificial intelligence, it is clear that building blocks are in place that will profoundly affect wearable computing-based intelligent technology:

- *New fibers* called Aracon, made of super-strong Kevlar, can conduct electricity and be woven into ordinary-looking clothes.
- *Chip packaging* allows wearable computers to be washed and dry-cleaned. The electronics are insulated and directly woven into clothing and other textiles.
- *Flexible video screens* made of optical fiber can be woven into clothing and display static and animated graphics downloaded from the Internet, a desktop computer, or a mobile terminal.
- *Head-mounted displays on visors or glasses* allow users to focus on a task while at the same time check information on a computer.

- ***On-body and off-body enabling technologies*** are becoming more sophisticated and include VPNs, PANs, ISM, DECT, GSM, and Bluetooth wireless.
- ***Nanotechnology*** is playing a significant role, making computing and communications systems microscopic in size and more conducive to on-body usage.

Wearable Healthcare Intelligent Technology Systems

Although wearable computers have started to enter healthcare delivery environments, wearable systems for both physicians and patients will more fully emerge over the next decade. Wearable computers for physicians will allow them to treat patients and complete their rounds, while connected via wireless networks to computerized patient records. Wearable computers are already allowing physicians to remotely observe patients' vital signs and monitor progress of surgery, from outside of the operating room, using handheld devices.

Medical sensors are now available for use by patients and range from conventional sensors (based on piezoelectrical materials for pressure measurements) to infrared sensors for body temperature estimation to optoelectronic sensors that monitor blood oxygen, heart rate, heart recovery ventilation, and blood pressure. Other health-monitoring devices, such as the vestibular-ocular test apparatus, the glucose counter, and the insulin delivery system, can also be hooked up to a wearable computer without wiring the patient's body. The following are some examples of WITS:

Setting Broken Arms with Smart Material Instant Splints: The U.S. Army Institute of Soldier Nanotechnologies, a research unit devoted to developing military applications for nanotechnology, is working with MIT to incorporate wound detection and treatment systems within uniforms made of "smart" materials, such as a responsive system that provides an instant splint for a broken bone. (http://web.mit.edu/isn/newsandevents/index.html)

Monitoring Vital Signs with a Ring Sensor is an ambulatory, telemetric, continuous health monitoring device developed by d'Arbeloff Laboratory for Information Systems and Technology at MIT. It combines basic photo plethysmographic techniques with low-power telemetry.

Worn by the patient as a finger ring, it is capable of monitoring vital signs related to cardiovascular health. Remote monitoring is possible via a wireless link transmitting patient's vital signs to a cellular phone or computer. Clinical trials have been done in conjunction with Massachusetts General Hospital's emergency room, and researchers are now working on commercialization of the ring-sized device (Technology Review magazine, April 2004). (http://darbelofflab.mit.edu/ring_sensor/ring_sensor.htm)

"SmartShirt" or the Sensate Liner for Combat Casualty Care was first developed by researchers at the Georgia Institute of Technology under the auspices of the U.S. military's 21st Century Land Warrior Program and the Defense Advance Research Projects Agency (DARPA). The "SmartShirt" is a fiber-optic-laden garment with a built-in patented conductive fiber/sensor system that relays a soldier's vital signs in real-time, his location, and the exact time of injury. This technology can also be woven into children's sleepwear, possibly preventing sudden infant death syndrome (SIDS) by alerting parents (via PDA or wristwatch) the moment a baby stops breathing. (http://www.gtwm.gatech.edu/images/wear.html and http://www.gatech.edu/news-room/archive/news_releases/sensatex.html)

X-Ray "Vigilance" Vision for patient safety is being used by anesthesiologists at Vanderbilt University Medical Center (VUMC) to see an object right in front of them or in a distant operating room. A portable computer and high-tech eyepiece allow them to simultaneously monitor multiple operating rooms from one location. Vigilance integrates information from multiple preexisting sources: the operating room's anesthesia machine, heart monitor, and video cameras are connected to Vanderbilt's secure data network, and surgical teams use in-room workstations to document care and vital signs. The physical package was assembled from off-the-shelf components, but its software was developed at Vanderbilt. (http://tennessean.com/business/archives/04/05/51946027.shtml?Element_ID=51946027 and http://www.healthcare-informatics.com/issues/2005/01_05/cover.htm)

As If You Were There: The Vocera Wearable Communication System is being used at the Providence Portland Medical Center. This wireless system provides hands-free, voice-activated communications within networked buildings/campuses. Aimed at mobile workers in hospitals, retail operations, and other industries, the system allows users to wear a device that weighs less than two ounces to interact with each other instantly and make decisions quickly with simple voice commands. (http://www.vocera.com/products/products.aspx)

Wireless Patient Monitoring: BodyKom is a new system being tested by Kiwok (a Swedish technology company), TeliaSonera AB, and Hewlett-Packard that connects wirelessly to sensors on the patient. If changes are detected in the patient's body, the hospital/healthcare services are automatically alerted over a secure mobile network connection. It could be used to monitor heart rate, diabetes, asthma, and other diseases that require timely intervention. (http://www.usatoday.com/tech/news/2005-03-30-wireless-monitoring_x.htm)

Helping Me Lose Weight Anywhere: BodyMedia, a Pittsburgh company, is a leader in wearable body monitoring. Its affordable watches, bands, and other devices collect, process, and present information about an individual's health and behaviors. The company makes a special "smart band" that is worn on the upper arm and collects data on the wearer's physical state, such as the way the body releases heat. These devices support weight management, fitness, disease management, and research. BodyMedia has developed special bands for monitoring the well-being of infants and the elderly. (www.bodymedia.com)

Alert: Fireman's Body Temperature Is Critical. The LifeShirt System, developed several years ago by VivoMetrics of Ventura, California, is being used in several top medical schools. The garment, which collects and analyzes its wearer's respiration flow, heart rate, and other key metrics, demonstrates in real-time whether a new treatment is working. There will also be a shirt for emergency-services workers, such as firefighters, that will wirelessly alert commanders when a firefighter's core body temperature or stress levels reach critical levels. VivoMetrics expects to introduce a shirt in 2006 that will allow parents to monitor asthmatic children. (http://www.vivometrics.com/site/system.html)

Finally, it is hypothesized that as sensor and computing technologies continue to evolve, their integration into wearable medical devices for monitoring, diagnosis, and treatment of illnesses will become commonplace. A personalized health management device would allow a person to be more interactive and more conscious of his or her own condition in order to adopt a healthier lifestyle and obtain personalized therapy. These devices could also help healthcare providers monitor patients during rehabilitation, thereby decreasing hospitalization time.

Steps to Tomorrow

The following are a set of recommendations for technologically advanced healthcare organizations to take:

- *Establish a Multidisciplinary Workgroup* to identify functional requirements and/or potential uses of wearable health IT systems for physicians and patients.
- *Identify Partners and Funding Sources* to collaborate on the development of wearable health IT systems and determine each organization's roles (e.g., research, development, pilot testing). Identify possible funding sources such as foundations that might support the use of wearable health IT products/services in under-served populations.
- *Conduct Research and Feasibility Studies,* including a detailed literature search, to obtain lessons learned from existing projects in this field. Complete a feasibility study and cost-benefit analysis for the potential initiative. Investigate changes in clinical practices and business processes that may need to be made in anticipation of utilizing wearable health IT products/services.
- *Initiate Pilot Projects* to acquire, develop, and test wearable technology that could eventually be incorporated into the healthcare organization.

Smart eHealth Record Systems for Providers and People

Direction

By 2020, more than 80% of people in developed countries, including the United States, will use an ePHR that is connected to a mobile device and EHR system with various levels of intelligence embedded in its software application. In addition, primary care physician and consulting physicians will have access to an integrated comprehensive EMR that includes both textual data and medical images from across specialties and facilities based on an interoperable network.

Current State

As of 2007, it appears that less than 20% of healthcare provider organizations have acquired and implemented an electronic health record (EHR) system. By 2020, however, we predict that the situation and numbers will be reversed. It is anticipated that more than 80% of healthcare provider organizations, large and small, will have acquired and implemented EHRs. The EHRs in use will be interoperable and standards-based, and many will be open solutions that are supported by an international network of companies and community of users and developers.

As of 2007, the development and implementation of personal health records (PHR) are still in the very early stages. However, by 2020, we predict that more than 80% of the people in the United States will have begun using PHRs in one form or another. These Web-based, encrypted applications will provide people with online educational materials, interactive tools for physician communication and wellness, and storage banks for personal health data that includes genomic information and clinical images.

Many healthcare provider organizations have already started to deploy and use EHR systems and have begun to acquire and use a variety of electronic clinical imaging systems. However, these systems have not typically been integrated into a single, comprehensive EHR system. Providing clinicians with online access to these more complete, multimedia medical records, whenever or wherever they might need them, will result in increased clinician productivity, facilitate medical decision making, and improve quality of care.

- A truly effective EHR system should have the capability to capture clinical images, scanned documents, electrocardiogram (EKG) waveforms, and other nontextual data files, and make them part of the patient's electronic medical record.
- Both image and text data should be provided in an integrated manner that facilitates the clinician's task of correlating the data and making patient care decisions in a timely and accurate manner.
- Computer workstations used by clinicians, wherever they might be, should be able to display the high-resolution clinical images stored in the EHR.
- Imaging systems should be able to use the Digital Imaging and Communications in Medicine (DICOM) standard to obtain images

directly from image-acquisition modalities like CT, MRI, ultra-sound, and digital X-ray.

- All captured clinical images should be associated with the text report of the procedure or the related progress note within the EHR.
- The EHR system of 2020 should serve as a tool to aid communication and consultation among physicians, whether in the same department, in different medical services, or at different sites.

Steps to Tomorrow

The level of national awareness for the adoption of healthcare IT as an enabler of change has never been so high. One of the highest priorities today is the reduction in medical errors and preventable deaths, which is much more achievable using Medical Informatics 20/20 and the EHR tactic. The following is a set of recommendations for healthcare organizations to take in digitizing the medical record:

- *Understand the Role of Collaboration–Open Solutions–Innovation* in supporting efficient and effective implementation.
- *Establish an Interdisciplinary Workgroup* to identify functional requirements and/or potential uses of wearable health IT systems for physicians and patients.
- *Educate and Engage Customers:* Develop several groups of patients/customers with different medical conditions and situations, and educate them about the benefits of PHRs. These groups can also become the first test markets for your next-generation EHR with a PHR view for patients.
- *Identify Partners* to collaborate on the development of EHRs and the patient-view PHR, and determine each partner's roles (e.g., research, development, pilot testing).
- *Conduct a Feasibility Study* and cost-benefit analysis for this initiative.
- *Establish a Pilot Project* to acquire, develop, and test EHR and PHR technology for the healthcare organization.
- *Profile Clinical and Business Processes Changes and the Paradigm Shift* that happens when patients take control of their medical records through electronic PHRs. The opportunities for supporting health expand dramatically when patients can add

information, vital signs, and other physiological data into a PHR for monitoring and support.

Genomic Information Systems and Biorepositories

Direction

By 2020, the first generation of genomic information systems will have been deployed. Genomic software applications and biorepositories will become a standard component of any sophisticated and increasingly smart EHR system by the end of the coming decade, which was described earlier in this chapter as the virtual eHealth Advisor Live (eHAL).

Current State

It is clear that genomic information will become a standard component of a person's health and medical record in the coming years. Much of the work being done in this area involves collaboration between public and private sector organizations with a heavy emphasis on standards and open source solutions. By integrating computerized electronic patient records with genomic biorepositories, bioinformaticists will be able to begin development of sophisticated applications that will truly transform healthcare delivery in the 21st century. These applications will use advanced statistical and computational analytic techniques and will combine human genome research with the identification of proteins within chromosomes that cause inherited diseases and predispositions toward diseases that might be triggered by environmental, dietary, and other catalysts. These advances could usher in a new era of individualized preventive medicine.

The creation of biorepositories is closely linked with the development of genomic information systems. Several institutional-level biorepositories have arisen over the past few years. Already, governmental systems have been established at the National Institutes of Health (NIH), the Centers for Disease Control and Prevention (CDC), and within the Department of Defense (DoD). Several universities have also created such a resource. In industry, there are about a half dozen companies that are attempting to create similar resources.

Over the next two decades, a goal for genomics will be to transform knowledge about the human genome into improvements in clinical practice, moving it from bench to bedside to beside a patient anywhere. Many of the government agencies and private clinical research enterprises engaged in developing genomic information systems are embracing collaborative ventures and open source solutions. Collaboration within this community of genetic researchers, biomedical drug developers, and clinicians is essential if substantial progress is to be made over the near term.

Steps to Tomorrow

Genomic information and applied knowledge will routinely become part of a person's virtual eHealth Advisor Live™ (smart medical record system and network) in the coming decade. Organizations should take the following next steps:

- *Initiate an EHR Genetic Council:* Establish a council addressing the integration of the organization's clinical record systems with genomic information systems into a unified electronic health record system of the future.
- *Research the State of Development:* Review existing genomic and bioinformatics systems for emerging languages, standards, and open source solutions that may be used or easily adapted to meet organizational needs. Implications for current clinical data repository/EHR projects should be assessed.
- *Identify Pilot Projects:* Do a pilot project to acquire and/or build the genomic information system that will eventually be incorporated into the EHR. This project could be designed to align with service line priorities and populations in need with a genetic component such as women's health and breast cancer.
- *Form Collaborations:* Collaborate further with other organizations on the collection of genomic data that could potentially be shared for the mutual benefit of everyone involved.
- *Track Clinical Development and Practices:* Investigate changes in clinical practices and business processes that the organization will need, in anticipation of using genomic information in the future.

In Support of Better Health Care

Throughout the book, we have highlighted and built the case that Collaboration, Open Solutions, and Innovation do play a vital role in achieving quality care and supporting EHRs for all people. Chapter 16 has described a number of examples of electronic and emerging technologies that are and will affect personal health and medical care over the next 20 years. The Medical Informatics 20/20 model is the delivery system to aid in the transport of new tools to support a quality of life and extension of health care to wherever a person may be and at the point of need and eventually on a preemptive basis.

Medical Informatics Superhighway

Medical Informatics 20/20 is the vital infrastructure delivery system for the diffusion of proven medical breakthroughs to be delivered to people before or at the point of care. It's the knowledge superhighway to better health.

Fast Forward >>
Better . . . Smarter . . .
Wiser . . .

"The future belongs to the unreasonable ones, the ones who look forward not backward, who are certain only of uncertainty, and who have the ability and the confidence to think completely differently."

Bernard Shaw

"Dreams are the seedlings of realities."

James Allen

"After assessing your bio-signs, symptoms, and the latest evidence from all medical modalities worldwide, the best approach for care is . . ."

eHealth Advisor Live™—The Virtual Doctor
Recovered from a time capsule from the future

"Make it so . . ."

Captain Jean-Luc Picard, *Star Trek: The Next Generation*

Dreaming and Visioning

The future will arrive before we know it. It is impossible to predict the future, yet it is quite possible to dream, vision, and act to create the future. Storytellers of all kinds—movie directors, science fiction writers, and our own imaginations have created many pictures of tomorrow. *Star Trek* and *Star Wars* helped several generations create a visual images of health care's future that include diagnostic "wands," sick-bay beds with magical sensors, needle-free injections, virtual doctors, robot nurses, and much more. Gene Roddenberry created the original *Star Trek* more than 40 years ago, before there were body scanners of any type other than anatomical X-rays. He envisioned the future and inspired generations of scientists and clinicians. Today we have blade-free surgery with gamma knives and many, many types of noninvasive imaging such as ultrasound, CT scans, PET scans, and MRI to detect tissues with abnormal concentrations of blood vessels and faster metabolic rates.

Although it is impossible to predict with certainty, it is quite possible to dream, vision, and create a future that will probably be more like the starship *Enterprise* sick bay than not. As we have seen in Section V, the future holds many more exciting developments, ranging from embedded nanosystems and robotic limbs to conservation medicine and proteomics. The Future Health Timeline in Chapter 13 highlighted the intersection of medical advances and computing/communications technology. But the views we have shared about the potential futures have been an attempt to stimulate the imagination and right-brain conceptual/creative thinking.

The research, development, and diffusion of electronic and emerging technology (eTechnology) must be grounded in solving human problems, such as health, environment, and energy. As discussed earlier, this includes supporting the whole person and valuing the complex multidimensional interrelationships of mind, body, spirit, and the environment. In Section V, we have attempted to look well beyond current boundaries and deliver insight on driving forces and the role of the next-generation Medical Informatics 20/20 to empower and enable better medical care and support optimum health, contributing to improved quality of care through 2020 and beyond.

Today, medicine is moving beyond the reactive, curative medicine of the past to a preventive, health-optimization model of the future. Tomorrow, the focus will be "preemptive medicine." The nature of the advances in medical science, technology, "-omics," EHRs, and genetics is laying the foundation for this era of "preemptive medicine." Intel Corporation's research and innovation effort in this area is called "Proactive Health," and GE calls it "Early Health." Regardless of the label applied, it means that going forward, the focus will be on curing and pre-empting disease to achieve the goal of health optimization.

The foundation for pre-emptive medicine is the field of preventive medicine. At a public health level it focuses on population health, and at the individual health level it's delivered by providers and health plans. The first stage of pre-emptive medicine is personalized medicine, which incorporates the use of detailed diagnostic information to guide medical therapy. Personalized medicine uses knowledge such as a patient's genotype or level of gene expression to select a treatments or therapy that specifically aligns with the genetic characteristics. Since different patients have different genotypes and gene expression levels, each patient can receive a therapy that is *personalized* rather than all patients receiving the same generic therapy. Using the foundations of prevention and personalized medicine, combined with the next generation of medical advances in the areas of omics, regenerative medicine, and nanotechnology, the field of pre-emptive medicine has already begun to arrive.

Collaboration, Open Solutions, and Innovation (COSI) in Action . . . in Space

The National Aeronautics and Space Administration (NASA) is a great example of the leadership, deployment, and synergy of the COSI Strategies. ***As a leader in Collaboration*** through a vast public–private endeavor, NASA has enabled humans to land on the moon, rovers to explore Mars, and launch telescopes such as Hubble into space to explore the universe. In 2005, NASA announced a collaborative project with Google that includes large-scale data management, massively distributed computing, bio-info-nano convergence, and encouragement of the entrepreneurial space industry.

NASA is a leader in open source software and Open Solutions. On Mars, the operations of the Mars rovers require the extensive use of Linux, the leading open source software operating system. In addition, NASA is both a user of open source software and a leader in development of software packages released to the open source community through its NASA Open Source Agreement (NOSA), an open source license. One of the primary objectives of this license is to ensure that the software is available to the community and that any improvements made to the software are contributed back to the community, including the NASA project team that manages the software. There are several benefits of open source software for NASA including: increasing NASA software quality via community peer review, accelerating software development via community contributions, maximizing the awareness and impact of NASA research, and increasing dissemination of NASA software in support of NASA's education mission. For more information about NASA open solutions work, visit http://opensource.arc.nasa.gov/.

There are significant numbers of successful open source projects at NASA that have received widespread publicity and generate the following benefits: improved software development and faster evolution of the software;

Goal: Off to Mars

Picture a solar-powered, wearable, health intelligent information system used by astronauts on the planned mission to Mars in 2020. The wearable systems are connected wirelessly to the onboard eHealth Advisor Live^{TM}, which includes many self-care and supported self-care procedures and treatments along with an electronic health record (EHR) system, which in turn is interfaced to the master medical advisor and EHR system back on Earth. The master system is a state-of-the-art virtual doctor that includes a robust real-time health data repository, as well as a genomic bioreposi-tory. The system is continuously being fed data by nanotechnology biosensors that are embedded in the wearable systems used by the international crew of NASA astronauts. Nanotechnology will also be implanted inside the team. A micro–chemical laboratory on a chip will also control the creation and rate of delivery of drugs or the repairing of tissues as needed. Other nanoparticle, molecule-sized sensors inside a person's cells would warn of the health impacts from space radiation.

These types of systems, based on current research directions, could be used by NASA in 2020 and beyond on its future Lunar and Mars missions. Spin-offs of these emerging medical informatics solutions will also improve the quality of medical care on Earth.

http://science.nasa.gov/headlines/y2004/28oct_nanosensors.htm?
    list687582

http://www.nasa.gov/centers/marshall/news/news/releases/2004/
    04-129.html

enhanced collaboration that supports NASA's mission to work with public and private sectors; and more efficient and effective diffusion by which open solutions, coupled with the Internet, help NASA meet its directive to provide the widest practical spread of knowledge. Several examples include:

- *Livingston2*—An artificial intelligence software system designed to support life support systems during space travel.
- *Mission Simulation ToolKit*—supports the development of technology for vehicles that explore other planets.
- *BigView* is a linux-based image viewer for very large images.

<u>***NASA is a leader in Innovation.***</u> In addition to the innovations needed for space missions, there have been many, many spin-offs from NASA in the areas of computer technology, consumer products, environment, health and medicine, industry, public safety, and transportation. Some of the health and medical innovations are:

- *Digital Imaging Breast Biopsy System*—This stereotactic, large-core, needle biopsy, nonsurgical system was developed with Space Telescope Technology and is less costly than traditional biopsies. It also greatly reduces the side effects associated with surgical biopsies.
- *Breast Cancer Detection*—Solar cell sensor technology helps reduce mammography X-ray exposure, reduces radiation hazard, and expands the productivity of each machine.
- *Laser Angioplasty*—Using an excimer laser, this procedure does not damage blood vessel walls and offers precise, nonsurgical cleanings of clogged arteries with extraordinary precision and fewer complications than balloon angioplasty.
- *Ultrasound Skin Damage Assessment*—This advanced instrument uses NASA's ultrasound technology to enable immediate assessment of burn damage depth, and can save the lives of serious burn victims.
- *Human Tissue Stimulator*—Employing NASA satellite technology, this device is implanted in the body to help patients control chronic pain and involuntary motion disorders through electrical stimulation of targeted nerve centers or particular areas of the brain.
- *Programmable Pacemaker*—Incorporating multiple NASA technologies, this system consists of an implant and a physician's computer console, which communicates information to the physician through wireless telemetry signals.

Let us examine one medical product that was only made possible as a result of NASA research in the miniaturization of components for satellites and the spread of that technology from the public to private sector has resulted in significant benefits to diabetics. NASA technology has provided diabetics with very small computerized pumps that serve as an electronic artificial pancreas. These pumps deliver insulin at a pre-programmed rate, allowing for accurate control of blood sugar levels, without complications such as kidney disease or blindness. The pump improves the quality of life by freeing diabetics from the burden of daily insulin injections. This consumer technology is based on the Programmable Implantable Medication System (PIMS), developed by NASA's Goddard Space Flight Center as part of a dedicated technology transfer program focused on moving aerospace technology to the medical field. The PIMS was created by the Applied Physics Laboratory of Johns Hopkins University in cooperation with Goddard and MiniMed Technologies, a California-based manufacturer of medical equipment. The PIMS is surgically implanted in a small titanium case that is only three inches in diameter with a thickness of less than an inch. This case has a refillable drug reservoir, a pumping mechanism, a catheter leading from the pump to the diabetic's intestines, a microcomputer, and a lithium battery.

NASA's continued exploration of the solar system will stimulate better health and medical technologies through Collaboration, Open Solutions, and Innovations. NASA's use of the COSI strategies has demonstrated their ability to move from research and theory to products and action that can achieve set goals.

Better Thinking + Better Execution = Better Quality

Medical Informatics 20/20, by the year 2020, delivers a vital methodology focused on people and processes for the deployment of health and medical technologies within a medical informatics framework and in the context of radically transforming health care quality. Many of the challenges, such as the large number of uninsured and the rising cost of care, must be met with policy initiatives, more information transparency and consumer empowerment, reimbursement changes, and fundamental healthcare reform. Many aspects of clinical performance, such as the

Resources of the Future

- **Institute for Alternative Futures:** A futures think tank that offers a wealth of knowledge and insights: www.altfutures.com. The following report is a must-read: *The 2029 Project: Achieving an Ethical Future for Biomedical R&D* (http://www.altfutures.com/2029/The%202029%20 Report.pdf).
- **EPIC 2014:** A creative glimpse at a future, this eight-minute Webisode is thought provoking (www.eipc2014.com).
- **Institute for the Future:** An organization dedicated to foresight to insight to action (http://www.iftf.org/index.html).
- **Health Technology Center:** the leading not-for-profit health and medical technology research and knowledge transfer organization (http://www.healthtech.org).
- **MIT Media Lab:** A worldwide researcher, developer, and incubator of new media and products (http://www.media.mit.edu/).
- **Foresight:** A UK-based center that scans three or four industries simultaneously to develop visions of and effective strategies for the future using science-based methods (http://www.foresight.gov.uk/).
- **Medical Informatics 20/20:** A nexus of knowledge to help achieve quality in health care through the appropriate use of technology (www.medicalinformatics2020.com).
- **World Future Society:** An independent membership organization that serves as a clearinghouse for ideas about the future including forecasts, recommendations, and alternative scenarios (http://www.wfs.org).

major components of IHI's effort to save 100,000 lives being lost to medical errors are vastly easier to manage and measure through the use of advanced clinical informatics systems. But once the low-hanging fruit issues have been addressed through process improvement, collaboratives, and knowledge transfer as embodied in the IHI campaign, all parties will recognize that significant improvement in quality will require clinical and medical informatics systems to support performance excellence. Much of today's inefficiency, fragmentation, and errors that exist are a result of insufficient deployment of health and medical information technologies. Without the ability to manage and measure quality powered by Medical Informatics systems, significant improvements and gains cannot be made and sustained.

The Medical Informatics 20/20 strategies of:

> ### *Collaboration*
> ### *Open Solutions*
> ### *Innovation*

must be applied to the research, planning, selection, deployment, ongoing management, and continuous improvement of our health and medical sciences and informatics ecosystems for people and clinicians throughout the continuum of care.

As the Medical Informatics 20/20 model dimensions were examined throughout the book across each of the strategies of Collaboration, Open Solutions and Innovation, there were tactics that were described. Within the tactics, there are technologies and tools to support smarter, better execution.

Collaboration, Open Solutions, and Innovation is a universal set of strategies and tactics that can be applied to nearly any endeavor. Our focus has been to shed light on trends and development in other industries and in health care, and to share examples, stories, information, knowledge, and insight on how the lessons being learned and applied in other industries that can help health care transform. Our goals are to share knowledge and to stimulate innovation and collaborative action so executives, managers and clinicians can have a better understanding of the possibilities and can use the most appropriate technology as they go forward to improve quality and create the future.

"Just do it" doesn't really cut it anymore. Success today and tomorrow in transforming health care for the better demands better knowledge, better thinking, and better execution. The Medical Informatics 20/20 model with its strategies and tactics is the way to more intelligently deploy technologies that can accelerate the adoption of EHRs and other health informatics solutions to achieve the realization of quality care.

The health care of 2020 is not science fiction, it is fact. It can and is being created through our vision and action. Digital technology, biotechnology, and nanotechnology are converging to create new ways of curing disease and caring for people. The Medical Informatics 20/20 model delivers the strategies, and most importantly, a methodology, for effective and efficient deployment of intelligent information technology systems that empower professionals to deliver excellence in care and enable people to seek optimum health.

Healthcare professionals must transform through leadership, technology, and innovation. At the beginning and throughout the entire process of realizing quality care, success rests on stimulating and supporting clinicians and managers to radically improve processes and achieve excellence.

Index

Italicized page locators indicate a figure; tables are noted with a t (italicized t).